This Abominable Slavery

This Abominable Slavery

Race, Religion, and the Battle over Human Bondage in Antebellum Utah

W. PAUL REEVE, CHRISTOPHER B. RICH JR., AND
LAJEAN PURCELL CARRUTH

OXFORD
UNIVERSITY PRESS

Oxford University Press is a department of the University of Oxford. It furthers
the University's objective of excellence in research, scholarship, and education
by publishing worldwide. Oxford is a registered trade mark of Oxford University
Press in the UK and certain other countries.

Published in the United States of America by Oxford University Press
198 Madison Avenue, New York, NY 10016, United States of America.

© Oxford University Press 2024

All rights reserved. No part of this publication may be reproduced, stored in
a retrieval system, or transmitted, in any form or by any means, without the
prior permission in writing of Oxford University Press, or as expressly permitted
by law, by license, or under terms agreed with the appropriate reproduction
rights organization. Inquiries concerning reproduction outside the scope of the
above should be sent to the Rights Department, Oxford University Press, at the
address above.

You must not circulate this work in any other form
and you must impose this same condition on any acquirer.

CIP data is on file at the Library of Congress

ISBN 978-0-19-776502-9

DOI: 10.1093/oso/9780197765029.001.0001

Printed by Marquis Book Printing, Canada

Contents

Acknowledgments vii
List of Abbreviations ix

Introduction: The 1852 Utah Territorial Legislative Session 1

1. Servitude and Slavery in Antebellum America 21
2. Slavery among the Latter-day Saints, 1830–1847 43
3. Slavery among the Latter-day Saints, 1847–1852 58
4. The Trial of Don Pedro León Luján 82
5. An Act for the Relief of Indian Slaves and Prisoners 102
6. An Act in Relation to Service 120
7. Race and Election Law 157
8. Implications 173
9. Slavery, Priesthood Denial, and Brigham Young versus Orson Pratt 198
10. Utah's Juneteenth 224

Appendices 231
   1. Legislative Chronology, 1852 231
   2. Preamble and An Act for the Further Relief of Indian Slaves and Prisoners 237
   3. An Act in Relation to Service 239
Notes 243
Index 289

Acknowledgments

This manuscript brought the three of us together in a collaboration that none of us expected but that has forged a friendship along the way. We have become indebted to a variety of people who supported the project and strengthened the final results. Steven E. Snow, first and foremost, made this study possible, and we owe him a debt of gratitude for his unflinching commitment to transparency and an open assessment of the past. Richard E. Turley Jr. was also influential in supporting the project and ensuring its viability. Matthew J. Grow has been a key proponent of this study and has provided support and feedback at all stages of the work. He has demonstrated a collaborative spirit and a willingness to work with us to ensure access to sources. We are grateful for his assistance.

Ardis E. Parshall first introduced Christopher Rich and Paul Reeve and offered her own encouragement, sources, and expertise. This study would not be what it is without her. She is a key scholar of Brigham Young, and we are grateful to her for her encouragement and wisdom. Sylvia Ghosh verified all transcriptions from Pitman shorthand in this volume. She is also an expert in Thomas Bullock's unique mixture of shorthand and longhand. She transcribed the Bullock manuscripts used in this study, and we are thankful for it. Darius Gray also encouraged us and shaped our thinking, and we are the beneficiaries of his insight and wisdom.

A variety of friends read various chapters or iterations of the manuscript or simply allowed us to bounce ideas off of them and shared their wisdom and perspectives with us. Nathan Oman, Jordan Watkins, and Eric Herschthal read versions of the manuscript and shared helpful feedback. Christopher Jones, Matthew Mason, Brendan Rensink, Grace Soelberg, and the BYU Slavery Project engaged with our ideas and collaborated along the way. Sarah Barringer Gordon, Brian Cannon, Sondra Jones, Matthew Harris, and Newell Bringhurst also offered feedback, guidance, and suggestions for improvement. Kevin Waite deserves special mention. He read various drafts of the manuscript and offered key advice that shaped the final product in significant ways. We are indebted to him for the time and wisdom he graciously shared. Paul Reeve benefited from a Faculty Fellowship at the University of

Utah that allowed him a semester leave to complete an initial draft of the book. The History Department and College of Humanities at the University of Utah both supported this research project, and we are grateful for such institutional backing. Anna Neatrour, Jeff Turner, and Rachel Jane Wittman deserve credit for the digital documentary collection that offers open access to all the speeches quoted here and can be found at www.ThisAbominableSlavery.org. The Marriott Library at the University of Utah continues to be a welcoming place for such digital projects as is Rebekah Cummings and the Digital Matters Lab at the University of Utah. The Church History Department and Library aided with manuscripts and images and were professional and gracious with their time and resources. The staff at the Utah State Historical Society and Utah State Archives were friendly and always helpful in locating sources. We are grateful for their assistance.

Family and friends, of course, also deserve credit for the sounding boards that they became and the support networks they created. Peter Bennion, Jonathan Stapley, Tarik D. LaCour, Thomas Griffith, Margaret Blair Young, Cris and Janae Baird, Mauli Bonner, and Robert and Alice Burch have long supported scholarship on this topic and our work is the beneficiary. Our families also deserve credit for their encouragement and long suffering. Thank you to Beth, Porter, Eliza, Josh, Rebecca, Emma, Hunter, Ruth, and James Reeve. Thank you also to Abigail, Eleanor, and C. B. Rich.

Abbreviations

CHL	Church History Library, Church of Jesus Christ of Latter-day Saints, Salt Lake City, Utah
FHL	Family History Library, Church of Jesus Christ of Latter-day Saints, Salt Lake City, Utah
HBLL	Harold B. Lee Library, Brigham Young University, Provo, Utah
JWML	J. Willard Marriott Library, University of Utah, Salt Lake City, Utah
UDARS	Utah Division of Archives and Record Services, Salt Lake City, Utah

Introduction

The 1852 Utah Territorial Legislative Session

On July 22, 1847, a group of about forty religious refugees entered the Salt Lake Valley, a remote portion of Mexico's northern frontier and the predetermined location for their new settlement. That night they formed an encampment at roughly the future intersection of 1700 South and 500 East in what would become Salt Lake City. They camped on land that belonged to Mexico but was more directly used as a buffer zone between Ute and Shoshone peoples. Its utter remoteness from Euro-American settlements had prompted other overland migrants to press on to Oregon or California, but seclusion is precisely what attracted these new arrivals. They comprised an advance party of settlers, members of the Church of Jesus Christ of Latter-day Saints, who had fled the United States the previous year in search of isolation and religious freedom.[1]

Three of the men who entered the valley that day were in search of not only religious freedom but freedom from human bondage as well. Hark Wales, Oscar Smith, and Green Flake were enslaved men who arrived in the valley two days ahead of Brigham Young, a pioneer prophet and leader of his faith. Green Flake and Oscar Smith were baptized members of the same faith.[2] The frontier settlements that would take shape over the coming years were built in part by enslaved as well as free labor.

The question of whether the Latter-day Saints would legally accept or reject slavery in their new Zion thus arrived with them on the first day they camped in the Salt Lake Valley. It would take five years before the Saints would answer that question with a law of their own making, an answer that bore the weight of a fraught American racial, religious, and legal culture, as well as the fact that enslaved men and women like Flake, Wales, and Smith were pioneer settlers of the Great Basin in their own right but not necessarily of their own choice.

Slavery of another sort also existed in the Great Basin and predated the Latter-day Saint arrival. Trading relationships between Ute peoples and

Spanish colonizers in New Mexico had been ongoing for over 200 years by the time Latter-day Saints arrived and for over sixty years among the western Ute in what would become Utah Territory. Those trade relationships sometimes involved Ute enslavers bartering captive Goshute and Paiute women and children to the Spanish in exchange for weapons and manufactured goods.[3] For Ute traders the Latter-day Saint arrival represented an influx of prospective new markets. No longer would they have to travel to New Mexico or California to trade; they now had Euro-American settlers living nearby.[4]

It did not take long for one Ute to recognize that potential. According to Brigham Young, within months of the Latter-day Saint arrival, a Ute trader named Baptiste came into the Latter-day Saint camp with two teenage captives for sale, one boy about sixteen years old and one girl about eighteen or nineteen. When the Latter-day Saints refused to purchase the teens, Baptiste killed the young man, and the horrified Saints then traded a gun for the young woman. Latter-day Saints changed her name to Sally, and Young took her into his household and claimed to raise her with his own children even though she lived among the servants in his household.[5]

As Young later recalled, Baptiste had traded Indian children for as long as the Saints had lived in the territory. "When he cannot trade for them, he steals them, and takes them to New Mexico and sells them to the Navaho's or Spaniards," Young claimed.[6] Indian slavery thus existed in the Great Basin alongside the enslavement of African Americans from the moment of the Latter-day Saint arrival.

The Latter-day Saints selected the northern Mexican frontier as their Zion in retreat because it was outside the bounds of firm governmental control. In March 1845, leaders of the main body of Saints in Nauvoo, Illinois, considered potential locations outside the United States to build their religious kingdom anew. Erastus Snow, a member of the Council of 50 at Nauvoo, a governing body in charge of temporal and political affairs, set his sights on northern Mexico. He described the Mexican government as "weak" with "a mere form of government but not much power." He predicted that if Mormons were to settle there, they would not encounter the same type of obstacles that they had faced in the United States. At the same meeting, John Taylor, another leader, anticipated that the Saints would "soon be independent of this nation, and we will be the head and not the tail."[7]

By the summer of 1846, however, the United States had declared war against Mexico. From the beginning of the conflict, Brigham Young anticipated that a vast region stretching from the Rocky Mountains to the

Pacific coast would ultimately fall into American hands.[8] Within seven months of their arrival in the Salt Lake Valley, the United States and Mexico formalized the expected land transfer by treaty. The Latter-day Saints thus found themselves back within the boundaries of the United States. After the U.S. Congress granted them territorial status in 1850, as "the head and not the tail" it would be up to Latter-day Saint leaders to decide what to do about Indigenous and African American enslavement in the territory, decisions that would reverberate into the twentieth century and beyond.

The question of human bondage itself was an outgrowth of the great American paradox: a country founded on principles of liberty and equality also countenanced chattel slavery.[9] It was a conundrum that the nation's founders were unable to resolve, even though some of them refused to relent on one key point, that human beings could be reduced to property.[10] In fact, some enslavers across the North and some in the South responded to the ideals of the American Revolution to free their slaves. They took Thomas Jefferson at his word when he declared that "all men are created equal" and are "endowed by their creator with certain unalienable rights" including "life, liberty, and the pursuit of happiness."

Even so, other enslavers looked to the Constitution for protection of their slaves, especially as the cotton gin in 1794 touched off slavery's revival. Cotton provided an economic incentive for slavery's spread across the Deep South and its entrenchment as a way of life. Rather than diffusing and gradually dying out as some American founders had hoped, it increased and hardened behind various defenses. The Constitution protected property, enslavers argued, and it would be unconstitutional for any government to take away the property of individuals. The nexus of the impasse between the two sides thus centered on the question of whether enslaved human beings were property. Antislavery reformers insisted that freedom, as an inalienable right, was superior to property claims. Enslavers countered that emancipation was theft and "wholly illegitimate."[11] Others tried to find a middle ground; they recognized the property rights of enslavers as a matter of law even as they decried slavery as a moral travesty. It was a deadlock that ultimately ended in war. It proved beyond the capacity of the nation's best minds to resolve, and the debate in Utah Territory was no different.

* * *

It was not only lawmakers in Utah who had to grapple with such questions. Politicians in the two other political entities carved from the Mexican

Cession following the U.S. war with Mexico did so as well. Political leaders in New Mexico and California wrestled over the question of whether human beings could be held as property and crafted policies concerning slavery and unfree labor. New Mexico, in fact, explicitly legalized African American slavery in 1859, while legislators there chose to ignore the pervasive practice of Indian slavery in the territory.[12] Even California, an ostensibly "free state," was not unambiguously "free." The new California state legislature included a contingent of Southern-born politicians, some of whom owned slaves in their home states, and many of whom had aspirations to make the southern half of California open to slavery. In fact, anywhere from 400–600 African American slaves labored in California during the gold rush period. One scholar places the number as high as 1,500 by the year 1852.[13] As a result, in the decade prior to the Civil War pro-slavery factions in the California legislature and judiciary implemented a number of measures meant to protect human bondage there.[14]

The West was thus riddled with legal and political exceptions that muddied the distinctions between freedom and slavery. Recent scholarship has offered complex views of various labor categories in operation in both California and New Mexico.[15] Utah, however, has not received the same level of inquiry; it has primarily been viewed within the context of Later-day Saint history, somehow divorced from the broader forces then fracturing the nation.[16] The bill that legislators passed to regulate white enslavers has been poorly understood, incorrectly labeled a "slave code," and Utah branded an anomaly in the American West. Indeed, Utah is sometimes erroneously described as the only territory created from the Mexican Cession to legalize African American slavery.[17] A trove of newly discovered documents, scrutinized here for the first time, allow us to integrate Utah into the national story and fill in this missing piece of the Mexican Cession puzzle.

It is uncommon in historical research to uncover new sources, especially sources previously unknown to prior scholars. This volume represents just that. In 2013 while doing research for his book *Religion of a Different Color*, Paul Reeve inquired at the Church History Department of the Church of Jesus Christ of Latter-day Saints if Pitman shorthand versions of Utah territorial governor and Latter-day Saint prophet Brigham Young's speeches to the 1852 territorial legislature existed, either for a speech on January 5 or a speech on February 5.[18]

Young's discourses were important because they contained the first known public articulation of a racial priesthood restriction in the Latter-day Saint faith by a prophet/president of the Church. Young's pronouncement would grow in accumulating precedent over time to bar men of Black African descent from ordination to the lay priesthood and Black men and women from missionary service and temple rituals (except for proxy baptisms for deceased relatives and friends).[19] Prior scholarship had only offered a vague chronology of events for the legislative session and sometimes suggested that Young's most forceful articulation of a priesthood restriction came on January 5 and sometimes on February 5. Reeve hoped to resolve the discrepancies as well as to get as close as possible to what Young said. The written response to his request at the Church History Department only indicated that there was no Pitman shorthand for a speech delivered on January 5 but did not include a response regarding February 5.

In the meantime, Reeve drafted a version of events at the legislature for a chapter in his book and then asked Christopher Rich to review that chapter. Rich was a legal scholar who had published an article in the *Utah Historical Quarterly* on the bill passed that legislative session designed to govern Black enslaved people brought to Utah Territory by their white enslavers.[20] Many of those enslavers were converts to Mormonism from the South, and some of the Black enslaved people were converts too.[21] Rich was convinced that Young's most forceful speech to the legislature was delivered on February 5, not January 5.

Rich's response prompted Reeve to submit a new request to the Church History Department, this time only inquiring about a February 5 speech. This new appeal led to not only the uncovering of a Pitman version of Young's February 5 speech but also to previously unknown speeches by Latter-day Saint apostle and legislator Orson Pratt; legislator and University of Deseret Chancellor Orson Spencer; legislator and first counselor in the Latter-day Saint First Presidency Heber C. Kimball; and a protracted debate over a Native American indenture bill—all of which have never before been transcribed. George D. Watt, the official legislative reporter, captured those speeches in Pitman shorthand but did not transcribe them into longhand during his lifetime, and so they sat in his collection at the Church of Jesus Christ of Latter-day Saint's Church History Department in their original format for more than 150 years.

In 2013, LaJean Purcell Carruth, a scholar of Pitman shorthand at the Church History Department, transcribed all of the known speeches from the January through March 1852 legislative session. These new speeches now form the backbone to the story told here and offer new insights into the verbal battles over human bondage that played out in Utah. The speeches themselves, along with the rest of the primary source documents on which this study is based, are now publicly available at www.ThisAbominableSlavery.org, a website hosted by the J. Willard Marriott Library at the University of Utah.

* * *

The number of enslaved African Americans in Utah Territory was never large. The federal census listed twenty-six slaves in Utah in 1850 and twenty-nine in 1860. Those census counts, however, were merely snapshots of two moments in time and underrepresented slavery there. A separate 1851 census, which was never sent to Washington D.C., recorded forty-six enslaved people spread between Davis, Utah, and Salt Lake counties—the actual number was closer to fifty-six.[22] Recent scholarship further suggests that there were likely around one hundred slaves who at one moment or another, but not simultaneously, lived in or passed through Utah between 1847 and 1862 when Congress outlawed slavery in the territories. After the spring of 1851, however, the number of enslaved people living in the territory typically hovered somewhere between thirty and forty.[23]

Young and his colleagues were thus forced to address the question of slavery during a period of intensifying national debate concerning the practice. Political advisors, such as Thomas L. Kane, strongly urged Young to take no official position in regard to the institution lest he provoke the ire of pro- or antislavery ideologues in Congress.[24] Starting in 1849, leaders of the Church of Jesus Christ of Latter-day Saints publicly espoused a neutral position regarding slavery. In addition to avoiding repercussions on the national stage, this policy was also meant to forestall an internal rift within the Church. The issue had already caused divisions in several major American denominations, including Baptists, Methodists, and Presbyterians. Even so, Brigham Young and other leading Latter-day Saints were largely sympathetic to a free-soil ethic. In fact, they argued that since there were no laws in Utah to recognize slavery, the region was legally free soil. In 1850, Young maintained that "the idea of property in men would not be entertained a moment by any court in this State."[25] Young thus seemed comfortable with a free-soil regime without explicit legislation one way or the other. Had events unfolded differently, he might have continued this policy indefinitely. Yet even a prophet cannot escape facts on the ground.

Like it or not, slavery was a reality that the Saints had to grapple with, a lesson that became all too clear when Utah marshals arrested Don Pedro León Luján in late 1851 on charges of trading without a license. Luján was a Spanish trader from New Mexico who was caught in central Utah with captured Native American children in his possession. The Mormons suspected that Luján intended to take these children back to New Mexico and sell them. The case ultimately convinced Young and the territorial legislature to take action in regard to slavery. At the end of two consecutive trials, federal judge Zerubbabel Snow concluded that without positive laws designed to legalize slavery in the territory, the Indian captives who had been confiscated from Luján were free.[26] The decision held far-reaching implications for the Black and Indian slaves who already lived in Utah. Snow concluded that the act which created Utah Territory included "a clause giving to the people here the right to introduce slavery, or reject it."[27] It was up to the legislature, not the court, to determine the answer to that question.

Snow's decision merely reiterated what Brigham Young and other leading Mormons already believed; without specific legislation to the contrary, Utah was legally free soil. Young still had no plans to legalize chattel slavery. Yet the Luján case convinced Young that the legislature must take steps to define and regulate various labor relationships that were being practiced in the territory as a matter of custom. This included the informal relationships that existed between Latter-day Saint enslavers and their African American slaves, as well as the relationship between Latter-day Saints and Native American captives. Prodded by Young, the legislature acted to formalize these relationships without recognizing property in man.

In frontier Utah lawmakers attempted to chart a moderate course, somewhere between the harsh brutality of chattel slavery as practiced in the South and immediate abolitionism advocated by a radical minority in the North. Their answer was a middle path that Brigham Young and his supporters described as "servitude." This included a conservative form of gradual emancipation that legally transformed African American slaves into "servants" and implied that the condition of servitude did not pass on to the children of enslaved parents who were born in Utah. The legislature also authorized twenty-year indentures for Native American slaves. These strategies were codified in two statutes: An Act in Relation to Service, and An Act for the Relief of Indian Slaves and Prisoners. Even so, at least one legislator strongly objected to these proposed laws on the grounds that they legalized slavery in

Utah. To complicate matters even more, some Southern enslavers did not believe that the legislature went far enough in defending their property rights. They asserted power over their enslaved people and their children "for life."

Protracted debates animated the decision-making process and highlight the complex legal and moral issues at stake. Lawmakers agonized over the conundrums that they faced. They argued over the status of Black people within Utah Territory and within the Latter-day Saint faith. At the same time, they saw no easy way to end the human trafficking that had become a vital part of the Ute trading-and-raiding economy.[28] By 1853, Brigham Young's determination to prevent slave traders from New Mexico from plying their trade in Utah Territory led to armed conflict between the Ute and Latter-day Saints, a clash known as the Walker War. In part, the two groups fought over competing economic visions grounded in rival ideas about Native American labor.[29]

While lawmakers who supported the two proposed laws believed that "servitude" offered an acceptable solution to the challenges posed by slavery, legislator and Latter-day Saint apostle Orson Pratt wanted both bills rejected. "Shall we hedge up the way before us by introducing this abominable slavery," he asked. "No! My voice shall be against it from this time until the bill shall pass if you are determined to pass it," he told fellow lawmakers.[30] He also equated the Native American indenture bill to slavery: "Though it may not continue down through other generations," he said, "yet it is binding them to slavery [for] at least 20 years."[31] The legislative debates ultimately hinged on the perceived differences between a servant and a slave.

In addition to debates over slavery, lawmakers also sparred over the status of Black people within Latter-day Saint theology. Historians have long understood that discussions about An Act in Relation to Service produced Brigham Young's most pointed commentary on racial priesthood restrictions within the Church he led. But until now, they have failed to recognize that a debate over An Act Regulating Elections also informed Young's strident position and accounted for some of his most racist claims. In that regard, we offer new evidence and an important corrective that includes the fact that apostle and legislator Orson Pratt advocated Black male voting rights in 1852, a position for which he faced the ire of Young. Pratt lost that debate but nonetheless persisted, even after weathering Young's stinging rebuke. He cast two "no" votes on municipal incorporation bills because they failed to allow Black men to vote.[32]

To complicate matters even more, white enslavers in the territory were not satisfied with the law passed in 1852 because of the legal restrictions it placed on them. The proceedings of a constitutional convention for Deseret that met in 1856 reveal another heated debate in which Utah enslavers attempted to shore up their right to human bondage. Southern Latter-day Saints and their supporters tried to adopt slavery in a new constitution written to apply for statehood. They were soundly defeated, yet the episode demonstrates the intense disagreements about slavery that continued to exist in the Latter-day Saint community during the 1850s.[33] Although Southerners represented a small minority of Utah's population and a minority of legislators and delegates in 1852 and 1856, that they were nonetheless able to exert such influence is testament to their tenacity in clinging to enslavement as a divinely sanctioned way of life.

In the 1850s, frontier Utah thus became one more site of conflict in the nation's seemingly intractable debate over slavery. Ultimately this debate dragged the country into bloodshed and war. The major cleavages took place between the North and the South. Even so, the American West experienced various fractures as well. A pro-slavery contingent of voters in Southern California, for example, repeatedly petitioned for a separate territory, in part to institutionalize slavery there.[34] When Oregon passed a state constitution in 1857, a significant minority voted to enter the Union as a slave state. Although this proposal failed, over three-fourths of the electorate voted for Oregon to prohibit free African Americans from residing within its boundaries.[35] Kansas deteriorated into pro-slavery and antislavery factions that ultimately turned violent.[36] After the Civil War broke out, a group of Southern sympathizers in New Mexico Territory organized the Confederate Territory of Arizona and swore loyalty to the South.[37] The fraught question of slavery thus proved beyond the ability of lawmakers to contain both nationally and throughout the West.

In the end, despite the deep divisions that threatened to rupture religious and political unity throughout the nation in the 1850s, lawmakers in Utah managed to escape the breakaway territories or serious fractures experienced elsewhere in the West to forge an untidy center that held.

* * *

What follows, then, is a history of the 1852 Utah Territorial legislative session and its aftermath up through the 1862 congressional law that outlawed slavery and involuntary servitude in all U.S. territories. We provide readers with a sense of the unfolding nature of events in relationship to three key bills (An Act in Relation to Service, An Act for the Relief of Indian Slaves and Prisoners, and An Act Regulating Elections) that spawned the debates and various speeches considered here.

Legislators drafted and debated An Act in Relation to Service and An Act for the Relief of Indian Slaves and Prisoners simultaneously, making it impossible to follow a strict chronology without causing more confusion. We therefore present the debate surrounding the Native American bill first and follow it through to its passage. We then backtrack chronologically to cover the events and speeches concerning An Act in Relation to Service. We then explore the context for the debate that unfolded on February 4 and 5 over An Act Regulating Elections. Finally, we consider what the passage of these bills meant in the lives of those who these laws were designed to regulate, Black enslaved people and captive Native Americans.

George D. Watt (see figure I.1) the official reporter for the territorial legislature, captured in Pitman shorthand much of the proceedings of the January through March 1852 session, including debates and speeches on race and slavery.[38] Watt transcribed a small portion of those debates into longhand, including both of Young's speeches on race and priesthood, one delivered on January 23 and the other delivered over one week later on February 5. Yet, Watt did not always transcribe all of a given speech and sometimes modified language as he transcribed. We therefore have relied on newly transcribed versions of both speeches.[39] Locating the shorthand of Young's speeches in the Watt collection led to another important discovery: Watt captured speeches by other legislators that session, most notably those by Orson Pratt and Orson Spencer as well as a protracted debate over the Native American indenture bill.

Our analysis is thus based on new primary source evidence previously unavailable to scholars. Watt did not transcribe into longhand the Pratt and Spencer speeches or the debate over the Native American indenture bill. LaJean Purcell Carruth, a scholar of Pitman shorthand at the Latter-day Saint Church History Library, transcribed those speeches in 2013, and we now bring them to light.

Pitman is a system of shorthand developed by Sir Isaac Pitman in 1837. It was a tremendous improvement over previously published shorthands. A skilled writer using Pitman could make a verbatim report of a speaker, an achievement not possible with earlier English language shorthands. Pitman

Figure I.1 George D. Watt (1812–1881) served as reporter for the 1852 Utah territorial legislative session. As such he captured in Pitman shorthand many of the debates and speeches regarding An Act in Relation to Service and An Act for the Relief of Indian Slaves and Prisoners. Courtesy Ronald G. Watt.

shorthand is written phonetically, without reference to conventional orthography. Basic consonants are represented by light and dark lines and curves. Additional consonants are represented by hooks and loops and by lengthening or shortening the line or curve that represents the consonants. Vowels are written as diacritics, are considered optional, and usually omitted, though they may be implied by the placement of the shorthand symbol above, on, or below the line of the paper.

In 1852 Watt was still developing his Pitman skills, and speakers often spoke too fast for him to capture every word (see figure I.2). As a result, Watt frequently recorded incomplete sentences. His shorthand improved over time, making his later recordings more thorough. Even still, his 1852 legislative work offers scholars significant insight into the thoughts of some legislators on pressing issues of their day. In this case, it also provides important new glimpses into the unfolding theology of race in Mormonism.

Watt's newly transcribed speeches also help clarify the confusion that has dominated prior histories, especially the timeline of events at the legislative session in relation to Brigham Young's speeches.[40] At least a part of that confusion likely stems from the fact that Young gave three speeches that mention race and slavery, but only one of those speeches was published. Young opened the 1852 legislative session on January 5 with a prepared speech that his secretary Thomas Bullock delivered to a joint session of the legislature. It was subsequently printed in the legislative journal as well as in the Latter-day Saint–owned *Deseret News*.[41]

Young gave two additional speeches about race and slavery that legislative session (one on January 23 and the second on February 5), neither of which was published. Young delivered both speeches extemporaneously and in his typically forceful style. Both speeches offer Young's rationale for a racial priesthood curse within the faith he led as well as his views on slavery, servitude, and race more broadly. The newly transcribed speeches thus establish a clear legislative timeline as well as offer new insights into Utah's place within antebellum political, religious, and racial landscapes.

* * *

A study of the proposed bills under consideration during the 1852 session makes it clear that legislators were trying to codify the entire gamut of "unfree labor" relationships for all races not only Black "servants." This included apprenticeships for minors, forced servitude for vagrancy or other crimes, indentured servitude for European immigrants, and forms of servitude for Native Americans and African Americans. By the time the legislature met, the nation, at least in the industrial North, was largely on its way to a free labor ethic. Instead of pushing that trend forward, the Utah legislature looked backward. The unfree labor relationships that Utah legislators codified in the 1852 session were quite normal in the early decades of the nineteenth

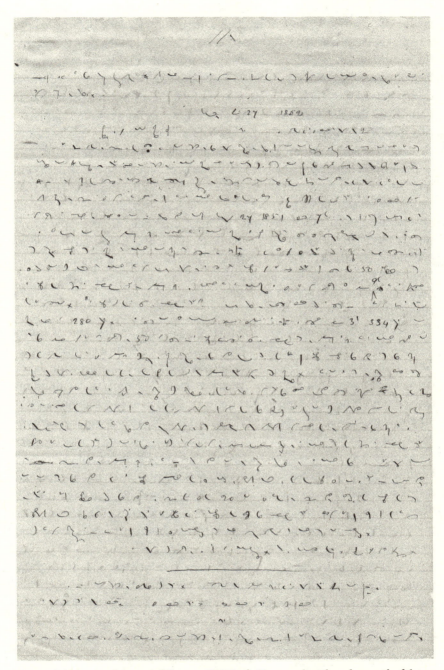

Figure I.2 A sample page of George D. Watt's Pitman shorthand record of the Utah territorial legislature. This page contains speeches made on January 27, 1852. Courtesy Church History Library.

century when Young and other Latter-day Saint leaders became adults. Lawmakers had long used such laws as ways to fit the rising generation into the economic and social order or to control "disorderly" people. Moreover, it made sense in a cash poor territory like Utah to use labor as a medium of exchange and a method to repay debt. In fact, the ability to discharge debt obligations through work was essential to Brigham Young's ambitious plan to subsidize the immigration of thousands of European converts. In the Latter-day Saint frontier economy, labor was a uniquely valuable asset.

Because a complexity of labor categories operated in the nineteenth century, and because those categories came to so heavily impinge upon the 1852 legislative session, a clear understanding of how legislators across the nation legally defined labor relations and how those definitions changed over time is crucial to understanding as precisely as possible what Utah legislators debated and created in 1852. The legal labor classifications familiar to Utah legislators have largely disappeared from common knowledge in the twenty-first century to be replaced by a false binary between "slavery" and "free labor."

Placing Utah's legal codes within their nineteenth-century context allows us to situate the decisions that 1852 legislators made within a broader framework of what historian Andrés Reséndez refers to as "kaleidoscopic labor categories" in operation in the Americas from the time that Columbus arrived to the end of the nineteenth century. Debt peonage, indentured servitude, convict leasing, apprenticeships, and the Spanish systems of *encomienda* and *repartimiento* were all labor distinctions, which in practice were sometimes designed to skirt laws against slavery while extracting labor and holding human beings against their will. This study seeks to understand and define such distinctions from the perspective of those who enacted them.[42] For the Utah territorial legislature that meant a spectrum of legal categories to choose from, far more complicated than a choice between slavery and freedom.

We also seek to understand what the new laws in Utah meant from the vantage point of the Black and Indigenous people who were enslaved. Our purpose is thus twofold: First, to offer a legal analysis of legislative intent in chapters 5 through 7. Then, in chapters 8 through 10 we analyze the same laws, but this time from the perspective of those who they were intended to regulate—the Native American and African American enslaved.

Choosing accurate terminology to describe both the legal and practical effects of these laws is challenging. Nineteenth-century language about slavery, especially as it intersected with other categories of unfree labor, was not always precise. This was a particular problem in Utah. For example, Brigham Young insisted that the name of the originally drafted service bill be changed from "An Act in Relation to African Slavery" to "An Act in Relation to Manual Service." He did this for several important reasons. First, Young sincerely believed that the statute did not legalize chattel slavery. Second, the law applied to European immigrants and African American enslaved people. On a number of occasions, Young went to great lengths to draw a bright-line distinction between "servitude" and "slavery." He nonetheless conflated these words in many of his extemporaneous comments. To further complicate matters, Southern enslavers consistently used "slave" and "slavery" to refer to Black enslaved people even after An Act in Relation to Service legally defined them as "servants." Certainly, the finer distinctions of the law and the particularities between "servant" and "slave" made little difference to those who did not enjoy their freedom no matter what label white people chose to apply.

Throughout this book, our objective is to understand the laws that legislators passed within the context of nineteenth-century labor practices, as well as acknowledge the realities on the ground for those who were enslaved. Consequently, we will use the terms "servant" and "servitude" when referring to An Act in Relation to Service and its legal ramifications. Not only does this reflect the kind of labor relationships that the legislature wished to codify, but it also recognizes that the law applied to European immigrants as well as Black enslaved people. The statute itself will alternately be referred to as the "Service Act" or "servant code." At the same time, we will use the terms "slave," "slavery," and various forms of "enslavement" when attempting to understand life in territorial Utah between 1847 and 1862 from the vantage point of African American bondservants.

We have further chosen to use the term "gradual emancipation" to describe the ultimate legal effects of the Utah servant code. We use this expression advisedly and with the understanding that it may imply a more defined and comprehensive schema than actually existed. Yet we believe that broadly construed, it reflects an accurate interpretation of the law. For years, Governor Brigham Young and other senior Latter-day Saints argued that slavery could not legally exist in Utah without explicit statutory authorization. Federal judge Zerubbabel Snow agreed in a legal opinion issued just days after the Service Act was signed into law. The original draft of An Act in Relation to Service provided that lifetime servitude was a heritable condition for the children of enslaved parents. But after Orson Pratt's significant criticism, the legislature removed this clause from the final version of the statute. We argue that without that vital clause, lifetime servitude was not a heritable condition in Utah Territory. In other words, the children of enslaved parents were born free, much like the "free womb" laws passed in more than half of Mexico's states between 1824 and 1827. Such laws were designed to end slavery within a generation by stipulating that the children born to enslaved people would be free.[43]

We likewise wish to provide an accurate depiction of the purposes behind An Act for the Relief of Indian Slaves and Prisoners as well as its practical realities. The law defined Native American children who were indentured under its provisions as "apprentices." There is strong evidence that Utah legislators believed that this status was similar to involuntary apprenticeships for Euro-American children. The ideal for many Latter-day Saints was to take Indigenous children into their homes in a type of guardian-and-ward relationship with religious and ethnic acculturation as the goal. In practice, however, these indentured children likely experienced a spectrum of circumstances from fictive kinship adoption to cheap domestic labor to "exploited Indian servants" to "the other slavery."[44] Indeed, we acknowledge that these children were typically "captives" or "slaves" when Latter-day Saints purchased or traded for them and then sought to raise them in their homes. We therefore use all of this terminology to describe the status of these children depending on context. Generally, we will refer to the law as the Indian Indenture Act.

The statutes enacted by the Utah legislature legally defined Black slaves and Indian captives as "servants" and "apprentices." These categories were not merely semantic. If the laws were followed, they entailed a number of practical changes in a servant's life. Indian children in particular were no longer subject to casual murder by their Ute enslavers. Servants could move about the territory without a pass and without fear of roving slave patrols as in the South. A servant could not be sold or transferred to a new master without consent. A servant could even testify against her master during court proceedings. Both laws required that servants be sent to school as conditions of servitude, something expressly prohibited in chattel slave codes in the South. Yet Black and Indian servants were still not free. Even if they were aware of their legal status, such distinctions may have appeared hollow as they continued to work for their masters on a day-to-day basis.

The servant code required that white masters register their Black enslaved people with a probate judge. We have found several such registrations, although many more were likely lost. When servants entered the judicial system through probate or criminal cases, it also offers glimpses into their status. We attempt to tease meaning from such sources, as well as from letters and other documents.

As historians it is our obligation to understand what type of laws Utah legislators believed that they were passing in order to accurately situate Utah within a charged national political contest over slavery. Doing so, however, should not ignore the impact that those laws had on the lives of the people they most directly concerned: African American and Indigenous slaves. Any version of unfree labor was precisely that, "unfree." If territorial laws did not grant them freedom then, from their perspective, those laws amounted to nothing more than "the other slavery."[45]

Thus, it is our hope to understand both the perspective of the legislators and the perspective of those who were enslaved. In doing so we seek to grasp the legal, racial, religious, and social implications of the speeches, debates, and laws that animated the territorial legislature in 1852. It is difficult enough to analyze the meaning of laws and speeches for those who left a written record behind. It is infinitely more difficult to endeavor to understand what those laws and speeches meant in the lives of those who were given no voice in the legislative process, the African American and Indigenous captives. It is our hope to honor—always imperfectly—their humanity along the way.

* * *

Beginning on January 5, 1852, lawmakers met on the southwest corner of South Temple and Main Streets in the Council House, a square two-story structure completed in December 1850, under the direction of Daniel H. Wells, superintendent of Public Works (see figure I.3). Built of red sandstone, the walls measured forty-five feet on each side and were capped with a sloping roof and a cupola at top. Besides legislative sessions, the building was also used for City Council meetings, to host visiting dignitaries, and other public events. Most notably, it would become the site where federal officials would negotiate a peaceful end to the Utah War in 1858. The Council House later housed the University of Deseret until it was destroyed by a fire in 1883.[46] In January, February, and March of 1852, however, it was the site of sometimes heated debates as territorial lawmakers grappled with the weighty matters of human bondage.

Figure I.3 The Council House on the southwest corner of South Temple and Main Streets in Salt Lake City served as the site of the 1852 legislative session. This image was taken c. 1850. Courtesy Church History Library.

White Euro-American men delivered all the speeches and enacted all the laws under consideration here. Utah Territory was second in the nation, behind Wyoming, to grant female suffrage, but that was still eighteen years in the future. It was longer still before women were elected legislators. Martha Hughes Cannon, a medical doctor and Latter-day Saint plural wife, holds the distinction of being the first female state senator in the nation, but she was not elected in Utah until 1896 (twenty-four years ahead of national female suffrage).[47] White men created the documents cataloged here, delivered the speeches, and made the decisions that governed the lives of Black women and men and Native American men and women, an important perspective to keep in mind.[48]

Thirty-nine white men comprised the legislative body in 1852, thirteen in the Council, or upper chamber, and twenty-six in the House of Representatives. They were deeply committed Latter-day Saints who were among the founding generation of the faith; all legislators joined the Church of Jesus Christ of Latter-day Saints prior to the exodus of its members from Illinois, with ten of them converting within the first four years of the Church's founding. Almost half had previously served proselytizing missions, and all but three practiced polygamy at one time or another.[49]

Mormon ecclesiastical leadership was also well represented among legislators. Brigham Young's two counselors in the governing Latter-day Saint First Presidency, Heber C. Kimball and Willard Richards, were both legislators and three Latter-day Saint apostles were among the lawmakers: Orson Pratt and George A. Smith served in the Council, and Wilford Woodruff in the House of Representatives. Presiding Bishop Edward Hunter was a member of the legislative Council, and three presidents of the Seventy (missionary quorums in the nineteenth century) were also lawmakers.[50] At least four men served as bishops or ecclesiastical leaders of their congregations at the time of their legislative work, and another four served in stake presidencies, regional leaders roughly equivalent to bishops in Catholic dioceses.[51]

Only House member John Brown from Tennessee owned one slave. In fact, the vast majority of legislators, a total of thirty (77 percent), hailed from Northern states, and of those, fifteen came from states (New York, Pennsylvania, Connecticut, and New Jersey) that had enacted gradual emancipation laws. Only seven legislators came from states where slaveholding was legal (North Carolina, Tennessee, Maryland, Kentucky, and Georgia), while the remaining two lawmakers were foreign born.[52]

The 1852 territorial legislature was thus completely white, male, Mormon, and heavily Northern in its composition. Yet, the small contingent of legislators from the South wielded influence well beyond their numbers in asserting control over the enslaved people who Southern enslavers brought with them to the territory, even "for life."

Obviously, there were no enslaved African Americans or indentured Native Americans elected as legislators, but neither were they called on to testify regarding the bills that were passed to govern their lives. In fact, it is not clear if Black or Indian servants became aware of their new legal status or how they might have learned about the laws enacted in 1852, if they did at all. The same is true for their white enslavers. There is no indication how they might have learned of passage of the servant code and the Indian Indenture Act or how they may have interpreted the provisions of the new laws. Still, there is clear evidence that after the legislative session was complete, at least some Utahns were aware of these statutes and attempted to comply with their provisions.

The *Deseret News* did publish notice in 1862 that the U.S. Congress had passed a law outlawing slavery in the territories; and John M. Bernhisel, Utah's delegate to Congress, notified Brigham Young of this fact.[53] It is not evident how or when news of this congressional law reached enslavers or those whom they enslaved. Thus, the impact of the 1852 territorial legislative session on the people who mattered most remains elusive.

In the end, the debates over slavery chronicled here for the first time reveal a group of lawmakers who grappled with questions of national importance, but who did so with ideas filtered through a religious lens. Like their counterparts in the North, most Latter-day Saints did not favor chattel slavery, but that did not automatically mean they favored racial equality either. Unlike legislators in some Northern states and territories, political leaders in Utah did not pass a law to prevent Black people from migrating there. Men and women of African descent were welcome in the territory, and those who were baptized Latter-day Saints worshipped in integrated congregations. Even so, leaders of the faith implemented racial priesthood and temple restrictions that limited full participation for Black adherents.[54]

In fact, the 1852 legislative session seems to have opened the door for public discussion of the racial restrictions that predated the lawmaking term but found their fullest articulation at the session. Whatever hesitancy Latter-day Saint leaders felt over publicly addressing the racial restrictions before the session, it disappeared quickly thereafter. Five Latter-day Saint publications openly discussed the racial bans in the 1850s, beginning with a column published in the *Deseret News* within a month of the lawmakers' final gavel. Utah's Act in Relation to Service only survived for a decade before Congress outlawed slavery and involuntary servitude in all U.S. territories, but racial restrictions in the Church of Jesus Christ of Latter-day Saints dragged on for nearly 130 years.

1
Servitude and Slavery in Antebellum America

In July 1818, Thomas Eddy, a New York philanthropist and political activist, wrote a letter to a friend in England about a subject that was dear to his heart: penal reform. Eddy supported a number of liberal causes, and he sincerely hoped that British humanitarians would succeed at improving conditions in local prisons. But despite his high ideals, Eddy was a pragmatist who believed that any great endeavor could be frustrated by men "who, actuated by an overstrained zeal, do not know how to take hold of things at the right time; like many religious zealots, they press on the people more than they are able to bear." He reminded his friend that the "light with which Providence has been pleased to enlighten the minds of men, as it regards moral or religious truths, is gradual—as was the commencement of the abolition of slavery."[1] Eddy knew whereof he spoke. In 1785, Eddy had been a charter member of the New York Manumission Society along with other "first movement abolitionists" such as Alexander Hamilton and John Jay.[2] After fourteen years of intense lobbying from reformers like Eddy, the New York legislature passed a gradual emancipation statute in 1799. Finally, on July 4, 1827, the state abolished slavery forever. Eddy died the following September at the age of sixty-nine.[3]

Over the course of his lifetime, Thomas Eddy participated in a momentous shift in the way that Americans viewed acceptable forms of work. His colleague John Jay, a man who had personally owned slaves, once recalled, "Prior to the [American] revolution, the great majority or rather the great body of our people had been so long accustomed to the practice and convenience of having slaves, that very few among them even doubted the propriety and rectitude of it."[4] But for over a century, Western political theorists had been constructing a new ideology of liberty and universal rights that fundamentally challenged the practice of slavery. Liberal objections to human bondage were bolstered by a powerful antislavery critique among various Christian denominations such as the Quakers. Thomas Eddy's parents were, in fact, Irish Quakers. By the 1770s, these converging strains of thought initiated what historian David Brion Davis called a "revolutionary shift in moral perception" about slavery.[5] People "long accustomed" to the practice began to question the justice of holding men, women, and children in a state of bondage. During the following decades, politicians in the United States, France, and Great Britain slowly put these new ideals into action.[6]

Men like Thomas Eddy and John Jay were convinced that slavery was a moral evil. Nevertheless, they relied on gradual shifts in public opinion to drive long-term institutional change.[7] In 1788, Jay claimed to have "good reason to hope and to believe that if the natural operations of truth are constantly watched and assisted, but not forced and precipitated," slavery would ultimately be abolished throughout the United States.[8] Jay was overly optimistic. During the early nineteenth century, slavery firmly re-entrenched itself in the American South. There, liberalism was never able to overcome a noxious mixture of fear and economic self-interest. Even so, by the time that Jay and Eddy died in the late 1820s, every Northern state had either abolished slavery or enacted a gradual emancipation law. Moreover, the United States and Great Britain had both banned the international slave trade. These men experienced firsthand how a society could steadily evolve toward greater freedom.

As important as the abolition of slavery was, it was only part of a more general transition away from all labor relationships that were considered "unfree." In America, this trend was grounded in the liberal values of the Revolution and fueled by the expansion of market capitalism. Although the Mormon prophet Brigham Young and his contemporaries were some forty years younger than Thomas Eddy, they too experienced these broad developments. The decisions that these men made in Utah during the 1850s concerning various forms of unfree labor must be understood in the context of this ongoing cultural, economic, and legal transformation.[9]

* * *

Unfree labor encompasses a wide spectrum of employment relationships with varying degrees of personal freedom, compensation, and length of service. Historical examples of unfree labor in the United States include apprenticeship; indentured servitude; peonage, or debt servitude; and of course, slavery. At its most general level, unfree labor signifies a formal association between an employer, or master, and an employee, or servant, in which the servant is legally obligated to serve his or her master for a certain period of time or until certain conditions are fulfilled. The servant is not free to leave his master's service until he has done so. If a servant attempts to leave his master, a court may jail the offender or resort to the remedy of specific performance.[10] That is, a court could return the servant to his or her master to serve out the obligated term of service. Masters or their agents could likewise recapture a runaway servant and force them to return to work without resorting to state action. In the first half of the nineteenth century, unfree relationships were characterized by a collection of reciprocal and mutually enforceable duties between master and servant. Yet the labor of a servant, and sometimes the body of a servant, was regarded as a species of property that belonged to the master.[11]

Today, the idea that an individual might hold any form of enforceable property right in another person's labor is shocking. As legal historian Robert Steinfeld has written, "In modern law and culture, it is not even imaginable that persons may be the subject of property. Or if it is imaginable, our imaginations are limited to thinking that such property must make one the outright chattel of the other."[12] Stated differently, contemporary Americans tend to divide labor relationships into two stark and easily distinguishable alternatives: free labor and slavery.[13] This is, however, a false dichotomy. Anglo-American law long recognized a variety of unfree statuses that existed somewhere between the extremes of chattel slavery and absolute freedom. Yet because we as a society have (rightly) come to see slavery and any condition resembling slavery as wholly illegitimate, we often lack the conceptual tools and even the vocabulary to describe the fine distinctions between different "types of coercion" that earlier generations took for granted.[14]

Some contemporary scholars have chosen to ignore these historical distinctions and consciously lump assorted forms of unfree labor into the single category of slavery.[15] This approach appears to make sense in the light of recent and entirely laudable efforts to recover the experiences of those people who were held in unfree conditions. Surely the individuals who were obligated to participate in these relationships must have *felt* as if they were enslaved even if they were technically held in some lesser form of bondage. Our current aversion to virtually any form of hierarchy, dependency, or coercion in the realm of employment likewise predisposes modern observers to conflate many discrete categories of unfree labor with slavery. Nevertheless, such a methodology is problematic. It ignores the practical and legal distinctions between various unfree conditions and thereby tends to obscure the past rather than to elucidate it.[16]

Unfree labor can be divided into two basic varieties: voluntary servitude and involuntary servitude. In early America, voluntary servitude included relationships such as apprenticeship and indentured servitude in which a prospective servant ostensibly chose to enter an employment contract with his or her master. Although the agreement was voluntary *ab initio* (from the beginning), it could still be specifically enforced once it had been consummated. On the other hand, involuntary servitude is a form of unfree labor that is nonconsensual from its inception. Both apprenticeship and indentured servitude had involuntary analogs, such as the state indenturing criminals or the poor. Yet the clearest and most disturbing example of this genre of labor was of course chattel slavery.[17]

After the Revolutionary War, the distinctions between voluntary servitude and involuntary servitude slowly began to blur in the United States. By the early nineteenth century, some modes of labor that were long considered to be voluntary, such as indentured servitude, were coming to be described as involuntary.[18] At the same time, involuntary servitude evolved into a discrete legal category that encompassed those varieties of unfree labor that fell short of *de jure* (legal) slavery but that still appeared nonconsensual in some manner. The category was ill-defined, however, and the precise boundary between voluntary and involuntary servitude remained contentious for decades.[19] But like slavery itself, involuntary servitude was stigmatized and finally proscribed except as a punishment for crime.[20]

In contrast to these specifically enforceable kinds of work, free labor represents a condition in which a worker has the ability to quit his employment at any time.[21] In this kind of relationship, an employer might appeal to certain financial sanctions, such as wage forfeiture, in order to enforce a labor contract.[22] However, he cannot legally force an employee to return to work. Today, free labor is virtually synonymous with popular understandings of liberty and personal dignity. During the early decades of the twentieth century, the U.S. Supreme Court went so far to declare that the Thirteenth Amendment to the Constitution was meant "to render impossible any state of bondage; to make labor free, by prohibiting that control by which the personal service of one man is disposed of or coerced for another's benefit."[23] But the shift to a free labor model of employment took place in stages over an extended period of time.[24] When Brigham Young and other early Mormon leaders were learning their trades in the 1810s and 1820s, unfree labor of all sorts was still a common feature of their society.[25]

The first generation of Latter-day Saints generally experienced unfree labor as a kind of quasi-familial relationship. During the early nineteenth century, the household remained the primary site of economic production. In this context, husbands, wives, children, and servants often lived and worked together as a discrete economic unit that was conceived of in terms of family. Within this unit, only the male head of household was truly "free." All other members of the household existed in some "legally defined position of submission" to the patriarch. Servitude and slavery were only the most extreme forms of subordination that generally characterized American society. The development of free labor ideology during the nineteenth century was in part based on the emergence of the firm as the locus of production and the attendant belief that labor relationships should be defined by contract rather than family law.[26]

Of the various forms of unfree labor that persisted in the early nineteenth century, apprenticeship was the most familiar to the Latter-day Saints.[27] In 1817, Brigham Young apprenticed himself to a furniture maker at the age of sixteen. His father, John Young, was apprenticed by his widowed mother at the age of four and was "brought up in the kitchen" of his master along with several other servants, both white and Black. Like many apprentices during the American Revolution, John finally escaped his master by joining the Continental Army after thirteen years of servitude.[28] Brigham's friend and counselor Heber C. Kimball was apprenticed to his father as a blacksmith and later to his brother as a potter.[29] Bishop Edward Partridge was apprenticed for four years as a hatter.[30] Apostle John Taylor, a native of England, was bound as an apprentice twice.[31] Although apprenticeship began a steep decline after the War of 1812, it remained a common practice well into these men's adulthood.[32] In 1835, the LDS Church's printing office in Kirtland, Ohio, employed "three apprentices and four journeymen."[33] Eight years later, the leaders of the Nauvoo Legion (the city militia for the Saints while in Nauvoo, Illinois) determined that masters would pay any fines adjudged against members of the militia who were apprentices, further evidence of the practice in use among Latter-day Saints through the 1840s.[34]

During the early nineteenth century apprenticeship functioned as a vital form of education, discipline, and moral socialization for the young. It was also an acknowledged pathway to the middle class. American parents regularly negotiated apprenticeships on behalf of their children that could bind them until the age of twenty-one for boys and eighteen for girls.[35] At the same time, local municipalities were empowered to involuntarily indenture poor or idle children in order to subject them to "proper family government."[36] Apprenticeship thus served important economic and pedagogical needs while reenforcing community values and social order. At its best, apprenticeship was characterized by a kind of benevolent paternalism administered within a surrogate family. Yet it could also be a vehicle for domination and abuse.

Indenture contracts created a relationship of mutual obligation between a master and an apprentice. The apprentice promised fidelity and obedience to his master. In turn, the master promised to educate the apprentice in the "art and mystery" of his craft, as well as supply food, shelter, and clothing. In a traditional arrangement, the apprentice lived with his master and became a part of the family; literally, the apprentice became his master's legal dependent. Consequently, if an apprentice fell ill or was unable to work, the master was still bound to care for his apprentice. In some cases, masters were actually prosecuted for attempting to abandon their apprentices in violation of their indenture agreement.[37] Yet the contract also kept the apprentice within a strict hierarchal structure dominated by the master.

As head of the household, a master exercised a kind of jurisdiction over his apprentice just like any other dependent.[38] The master also held a property right in his apprentice's labor.[39] This innate power disparity meant that apprentices could be subject to exploitation and brutal violence at the hands of unscrupulous masters.[40] Joseph Smith's grandfather Solomon Mack wrote concerning his apprenticeship to a Connecticut farmer in the mid-eighteenth century that "I was treated by my Master as his property and not as his fellow mortal."[41] Brigham Young's father, John, was regularly threatened with floggings by his master's wife.[42] Writing in the late 1820s, Chancellor James Kent observed in his *Commentaries on American Law* that the "temptations to imposition and abuse to which [apprenticeship] is liable, have rendered legislative regulations particularly necessary."[43] Unsurprisingly, it was not unusual for dissatisfied apprentices to run away.[44] Contemporary laws provided for the capture and return of runaway apprentices as fugitives from labor, just like runaway slaves. Indeed, the fugitive clause of the U.S. Constitution ensured that such relationships could be enforced across state lines.[45]

Despite the long-standing importance of apprenticeship, the practice began a long, slow decline in the decades after the Revolutionary War.[46] In major cities like Philadelphia, apprenticeships were already becoming rare by the early 1840s. Thirty years later, conventional middle-class apprenticeships had all but disappeared in the United States.[47] Nevertheless, poor children continued to enter voluntary and involuntary apprenticeships as late as the twentieth century.[48]

The collapse of traditional apprenticeship was based on a combination of social, legal, and economic transformations that challenged the fundamental relationship between master and apprentice.[49] But for men of Brigham Young's generation, apprenticeship was both commonplace and respectable. Working in a condition of unfreedom was considered a normal stage of one's professional experience that might last for a decade or even longer. Moreover, it was entirely unremarkable for families to raise an unrelated child in their homes as an apprentice. During the first half of the nineteenth century, many Americans celebrated apprenticeship as a way to uphold social order and inculcate virtue in children.[50] Brigham Young wholly agreed with these sentiments. By the end of Young's lifetime, however, the structured paternalism that characterized apprenticeship for three centuries had given way to the chaotic independence of free labor.[51]

* * *

In addition to apprenticeship, many early Latter-day Saint leaders were familiar with the practice of indentured servitude. For example, Bishop Edwin D. Woolley (1807–1888) grew up not far from Philadelphia and must have been aware of the trade in European indentured servants that continued in the region during his childhood and teenage years.[52] Furthermore, during the early decades of the nineteenth century, indentured servitude was still widely utilized by local communities as a method to settle debt, punish criminals, and assert control over the poor and other "disorderly" members of society.

Apprenticeship and indentured servitude were closely related in English law.[53] Yet indentured servitude was primarily designed to create a cheap and dependable labor supply in North America. It is estimated that between one-half to two-thirds of all European immigrants who came to America in the colonial period did so as indentured servants.[54] During the last decades of the eighteenth century, the ports of Baltimore, Annapolis, and Philadelphia remained major centers of the servant trade.[55] The last mass shipments of indentured servants arrived in Philadelphia as late as 1820, and servants continued to trickle into the United States from Europe for another decade or so thereafter.[56]

Migrant servitude was largely consistent over two centuries of practice. In exchange for the cost of a voyage across the Atlantic, basic subsistence during the term of service, and some form of freedom dues at the end of service, a prospective servant would sign a contract promising four to seven years of unfree labor in America. Upon disembarkation, the shipper typically sold the servant's contract to a new master who might personally employ the servant or transport the servant to another location for resale.[57] One servant who arrived in Virginia during the 1770s under a four-year indenture described how so-called soul drivers would purchase large numbers of indentured servants in the ports and then "drive them through the Country like a parcel of Sheep untill they can sell them to advantage."[58] This system typically involved young, unmarried British men, roughly 10 percent of whom were criminals or prisoners of war.[59]

During the eighteenth century, the conventional form of migrant servitude was supplemented by the redemptioner system. Under this model, entire families, usually of German extraction, entered a contract with a shipper in which they promised to either repay the cost of travel within a certain period of time after arriving in port or to indenture themselves to satisfy the debt. When they arrived in America and found it impossible to repay their debt, it was not unusual for these families to be split up and sold to different masters.[60] Moreover, if a redemptioner died aboard ship after a voyage was half finished, the decedent's debt was repaid by extending the terms of service of a surviving spouse or child.[61] In 1818, the legislatures of Pennsylvania and Maryland finally responded to such "cruel and oppressive impositions" by providing that redemptioners could no longer be held liable for the debts of their dead family members.[62]

An indenture contract can be conceived of as a kind of debt instrument secured by the promise of future labor. In other words, indentured servitude served as a method of extending credit to poor people who had no collateral other than their own capacity to work. Between 1688 and 1821, transatlantic passage rates could equal 50 percent of average per capita income or more. Considering the high costs of travel, servitude was a necessary condition for many Europeans who wished to go to America.[63] In return, lenders received a guaranteed labor supply for a specified period of time.[64] Securing debt through the promise of future labor made eminent sense before the emergence of a cash economy. In seventeenth-century Virginia, for example, debts were payable either in tobacco, which constituted the principal form of exchange, or in labor.[65] Similar economic conditions would prevail in Utah Territory two centuries later.

Indentured servitude was not simply a form of immigrant labor, however. Adult, native-born Americans were also indentured voluntarily and involuntarily. Domestic indentured servitude was often utilized as a method for individuals to pay off debts or as a criminal punishment for property crimes such as theft. Many townships also resorted to the practice of "public indenture" to assert control over paupers, transients, and other undesirables. In some cases, these individuals were sold at public auction for a term of service that could run from days to years. Evidence indicates that municipalities disproportionally indentured people of color who fell into debt or traveled without having a proper legal settlement. Nevertheless, white, native-born adults were also subject to involuntary indenture by the community or could choose to indenture themselves.[66]

Once an indenture contract was properly executed, masters exercised immense power over their servants. A runaway servant could be hunted down and returned to his master with time added to his or her term of service. Servants could likewise have time added to their terms for other infractions such as becoming pregnant or marrying without permission.[67] They were also subject to "moderate" correction by their masters as well as more severe punishments by a local magistrate.[68] Nevertheless, masters routinely abused their servants.[69]

The labor of an indentured servant was always viewed to be a form of alienable property.[70] In fact, servants traveling to America were often regulated as articles of commerce rather than passengers.[71] A servant's labor could be passed by will upon the death of her master or attached by a court in order to satisfy her master's debts.[72] Most importantly, a servant's labor could be sold from one master to another.[73] In the 1620s, one Virginia servant lamented that he had been sold by his master "like a damned slave."[74] Yet many jurisdictions ultimately passed laws to protect indentured servants from involuntary transactions. As early as 1700, Pennsylvania prohibited the sale of an indentured servant outside of the colony without the consent of the servant and two local magistrates.[75] In 1792, Virginia required that a servant provide written consent before the "benefit of [his] contract of service" could be assigned to another person.[76]

Despite the fact that a master held a property interest in his indentured servant, this interest was limited to the servant's labor, not his body.[77]

A servant always retained the character of a legal person and could own property in his own name, sue his master, and appear as a witness in court.[78] For all of these reasons, Americans traditionally considered indentured servitude to be in a separate category than chattel slavery. However, attitudes toward servitude began to shift in the decades after the Revolutionary War. As Americans began to reject long-established hierarchies and place greater emphasis on personal autonomy, especially the autonomy of white men, the distinction between indentured servitude and slavery began to break down in popular culture.[79]

After 1820, the market for indentured servants collapsed due to a significant decrease in the cost of transatlantic travel as well as greater access to cash and banking services.[80] In the meantime, state legislatures had already begun to enact statutory limitations on the institution of servitude. During the 1790s, a number of states formally prohibited indentured servitude for adult white Americans, although the practice continued for minors, immigrants, debtors, and in some cases, former slaves.[81] This trend continued over the next forty years. By 1828, New York had restricted bound servitude to minors and former slaves only.[82]

* * *

Although many early Latter-day Saints came from the Northern United States, they had more experience with slavery than is generally appreciated. In fact, a significant proportion grew up in states that implemented gradual emancipation programs during the late eighteenth or early nineteenth centuries. Consider the first two prophets of the faith. Both Joseph Smith and Brigham Young were born in Vermont, which in 1777 became the first jurisdiction in the Western Hemisphere to abolish slavery. Yet in childhood, they moved to New York, which was then in the midst of a thirty-year gradual emancipation process. As late as 1820, when both men were teenagers, there were still over 10,000 enslaved people spread throughout the state, although most were located close to New York City and the Hudson River Valley.[83] That year no slaves were reported in Joseph Smith's home county of Ontario, although there were approximately fifty free people of color living near the Smith farm in the township of Palmyra, and over 750 free people of color in the county as a whole.[84] Two counties to the east in Cayuga, where Brigham Young served as a carpenter's apprentice, almost fifty enslaved people were reported in the 1820 census along with over 190 free people of color. The majority of these men and women lived in the vicinity of Young's residence in Auburn.[85] Young must have had opportunities to interact with people of color in a variety of legal conditions, as well as to soak up local opinions concerning emancipation. Decades later, he recalled a time when "slavery was tolerated in the northern and eastern States, if you touched that question it would fire a man quicker than anything else in the world; there was something very peculiar about it, and it is so now."[86]

Young was twenty-six-years old and Smith was almost twenty-two when the New York legislature formally abolished slavery. But even then, the children of emancipated slaves remained in a form of servitude until they reached their early to mid-twenties. This process left a profound impression on the Mormon leaders. In 1844, Joseph Smith ran for president on a platform that included gradual, compensated emancipation.[87] As late as 1856, Brigham Young could more or less accurately recount the provisions of New York's gradual emancipation law to an audience in Utah Territory.[88]

The institution of slavery had developed slowly in the Anglo-American colonies. At the beginning of the seventeenth century, English settlers lacked a strong historical or legal basis for chattel slavery.[89] As late as 1660, there were still relatively few enslaved people in the region. Moreover, colonial laws did not clearly spell out who could be held in slavery, whether slavery was a lifetime status, or whether the condition could pass on to one's children. At first, slavery was premised on religion rather than ethnicity, and serious debates arose concerning whether baptism would free an enslaved person.[90] A number of early statutes even permitted European colonists to sell themselves into slavery or to be enslaved as a criminal punishment.[91] But over the next several decades, colonial officials enacted laws to differentiate slavery from the contemporaneous practice of indentured servitude. By the turn of the eighteenth century, Anglo-American slavery had coalesced into a form of lifetime hereditary servitude that was expressly based on race rather than religious affiliation. The condition applied predominantly to people of African descent, although it could also apply to Native Americans.[92]

At its most basic level, Anglo-American slavery was characterized by the classification of a human being as alienable property.[93] In 1849, James W. C. Pennington, a former American slave and graduate of Yale, conveyed this idea in stark terms. "The being of slavery," he wrote, "its soul and its body, lives and moves in the chattel principle, the property principle, the bill of sale principle; the cart-whip, starvation, and nakedness, are its inevitable consequences to a greater or lesser extent."[94] Slaves were sometimes held to be real property like land, while in other circumstances they were treated as chattels, or personal property. Yet legislators and judges occasionally found it necessary to recognize the humanity of enslaved people, as when a slave was tried for criminal activity.[95] Slaves were therefore said to have a "a double character of person and property."[96] Yet this grudging recognition that a slave was actually a human being only highlighted the fact that under the law, a slave could be bought, sold, inherited, and mortgaged just like any other piece of property. Although the labor of an indentured servant was also alienable, servants retained a legal personality and basic civil rights. In contrast, an enslaved person had no legal personality. A slave could not sue or be sued, own property in his own name, contract a binding marriage, or appear in court as a witness.[97]

Although slavery was typically considered to be a lifetime condition, slavery and lifetime servitude were not entirely synonymous. It was not unusual for enslavers to place temporal limits on the service of their enslaved workers, sometimes in their wills or other legal documents.[98] Furthermore, Anglo-American jurists long believed that an individual might be held in indentured servitude for life and that this did not constitute slavery.[99] While courts in England steadfastly refused to condone chattel slavery, they nonetheless permitted slave owners to bring their human property onto the island, at which point the enslaved person was considered a lifetime servant with a legal personality and individual civil rights.[100] In the mid-eighteenth century, Sir William Blackstone described this legal metamorphosis in his *Commentaries on the Laws of England*, a work that was enormously influential in the early United States.[101] In America, a distinction between lifetime servitude and slavery was recognized in some jurisdictions until the end of the Civil War. During Utah's first legislative session in 1852, Brigham Young and his colleagues would likewise apply this principle to enslaved African Americans.

After the American Revolution, states in the northern portion of New England abolished slavery relatively quickly. Yet many Northern legislators were leery of immediate emancipation, particularly in states with large enslaved populations. The census of 1800 recorded over 20,000 enslaved people in New York and another 12,000 in New Jersey.[102] In these states, lawmakers worried incessantly about curtailing the property rights of enslavers. Moreover, they feared that emancipated slaves without education or any apparent means of support would prove disruptive to society and ultimately become wards of the state.[103] Consequently, a number of jurisdictions enacted statutes meant to abolish slavery over a much longer period of time.

Pennsylvania passed the nation's first gradual emancipation law in 1780. Connecticut and Rhode Island followed in 1784, New York in 1799, and New Jersey in 1804. In every case except New York, these statutes commenced a process that lasted for forty years or longer. New Jersey, Pennsylvania, and Connecticut did not finally abolish slavery until 1846, 1847, and 1848 respectively.[104]

Gradual emancipation statutes attempted to balance the growing moral discomfort with slavery against deep-seated concerns over property rights and the economic and social impacts of abolition.[105] During the early nineteenth century, this moderate approach was adopted in many areas throughout the Western Hemisphere. For instance, a number of Latin American nations initiated gradual emancipation after their own liberal revolutions. This included so-called free womb laws that provided that all children born to enslaved women after a certain date were born free.[106] In 1834, Great Britain likewise freed all of its colonial slaves through a program of gradual, compensated emancipation. Even some Southern states such as Kentucky and Virginia considered gradual emancipation statutes at various times.[107] By the 1830s, however, a less compromising abolitionist movement was coalescing around men such as William Lloyd Garrison. These new abolitionists were not interested in Thomas Eddy's brand of slow, steady change. Instead, they demanded the immediate and uncompensated emancipation of all slaves throughout the United States.[108] Yet gradual emancipation remained a quixotic goal for some antislavery moderates. As late as 1863, West Virginia became the last state to enact gradual emancipation as the price of admission to the Union.[109]

Northern gradual emancipation laws all followed a similar pattern. The statutes provided that those people who were enslaved at the time of a given law's adoption would remain enslaved for life. But their children who were born after a particular date were considered "free." Even though these children were not legally slaves, gradual emancipation laws bound them to their parents' master as a kind of apprentice or indentured servant until their mid- to late twenties. Joanne Pope Melish has described this noncontractual, uncompensated service by the children of slaves as "statutory servitude."[110] Eventually, these laws were amended by appointing a date upon which all persons in a state of slavery would be freed. There were exceptions, however. After slavery was abolished in New Jersey in 1846, the small number of slaves who remained in the state were legally transformed into "apprentices for life" rather than being freed outright. This policy endorsed the distinction between slavery and lifetime servitude outlined by Blackstone. As a result, enslaved people in New Jersey remained in a state of involuntary servitude until the end of the Civil War.[111]

New York's gradual emancipation statute of 1799, An Act for the Gradual Abolition of Slavery, was typical.[112] During the preceding four years, the state legislature engaged in fierce debates about the costs of abolition, including the possibility that freed slaves would ultimately become paupers.[113] The final statute provided that any slave born before July 4, 1799, would remain a slave for life. In contrast, any child born after that date was "deemed and adjudged to be born free." But the act provided that such a child "shall be the servant of the legal proprietor of his or her mother" until the age of twenty-eight for a male and twenty-five for a female.[114]

Jurists opined that a child born into statutory servitude "never was a slave" and that such a child was instead "on the footing of an apprentice."[115] But the labor of these children was still considered alienable property that could be leased, sold, and inherited during their terms of service. In legal documents, these children were sometimes listed with monetary values appended next to their names.[116] Indeed, many contemporary observers used the terms "servant" and "slave" interchangeably regardless of the actual legal status of a particular person.[117] As one scholar has noted, gradual emancipation created a complex legal environment in which "the apparently enslaved may or may not have been actual slaves."[118]

In 1817, when Brigham Young was a teenager, Governor Daniel D. Tompkins threw his weight behind a new measure that would free all individuals in New York who remained in slavery. The resultant Act Relative to Slaves and Servants would free the vast majority of slaves on Independence Day 1827, a further ten years in the future. It also reinforced controls over both masters and slaves. For example, the law prohibited masters from selling their slaves into another state before the ten-year period was up. The statute also made slight alterations to the condition of children held in statutory servitude. Those children who were born after March 31, 1817, would now be subject to servitude only until the age of twenty-one. Masters were also required to teach statutory servants to read or send them to school for "four quarters" when the child was between the ages of ten and eighteen.[119]

Despite some significant abuses of the system, gradual emancipation was largely successful in freeing the North's remaining slaves.[120] Indeed, many enslavers began to voluntarily manumit their bondservants in anticipation of the final abolition of slavery. Between 1800 and 1820, the free Black population in New York almost tripled from approximately 10,000 to 29,279.[121]

Early Latter-day Saints like Joseph Smith and Brigham Young were raised in areas with small but visible minorities of free African Americans, many of whom were likely emancipated only a short time before. Yet these demographic trends were correlated with intensifying racism throughout the North.

Even as white Northerners increasingly scorned the institution of chattel slavery, they came to perceive Black people as undisciplined, ignorant, and totally lacking the virtues necessary to participate in a republican government. During the late eighteenth and early nineteenth centuries, antislavery advocates blamed the alleged shortcomings of African Americans on the lingering effects of slavery rather than some innate disability. The problem, they argued, was one of environment rather than race. Since these negative traits were not intrinsic to people of color, but were merely incidents of slavery, they were subject to improvement through education and social programs.[122] But as ever larger numbers of free African Americans began to gather in urban neighborhoods or move about the countryside, they came to be viewed as a dangerous and even criminal element who were inherently dependent and incapable of responsibly exercising the rights of citizenship. Environmental explanations for these alleged infirmities gave way to explanations based on race. Rather than being subject to improvement, they were fixed and immutable.[123]

Northern officials took a variety of actions to assert control over "disorderly" Black people, including the imposition of public indentures and involuntary apprenticeships. Moreover, as state legislatures began to enfranchise ever larger numbers of white men, there was a concomitant push to limit the civil rights of African Americans. During the first two decades of the nineteenth century, a number of states that had permitted people of color to vote after the Revolution revoked the franchise.[124]

New York pursued a similar course during its Constitutional Convention of 1821. As some delegates pushed for expanded voting rights, others made dire predictions of democracy run amok. One conservative delegate argued that "there is and must be, in every great community, a class of citizens, who, destitute alike of property, of character, and of intelligence, neither contribute to the support of its institutions, nor can be safely trusted with the choice of its rulers."[125]

As a result, proposals to expand suffrage for white males were joined with proposals to eliminate suffrage for African Americans.[126] Delegate Peter Jay (former president of the New York Manumission Society and son of John Jay) was aghast at these plans. "This state," he declared, "has taken

[the] high ground against slavery, and all its degrading consequences and accompaniments. . . . Adopt the amendment now proposed, and you will hear a shout of triumph and a hiss of scorn from the southern part of the union." Yet when pressed, even Jay haltingly admitted that, as a result of slavery, "in general the people of colour are inferior to the whites in knowledge and industry."[127]

Delegate Samuel Young (no relation to Brigham) took these opinions even further. Young argued that "the minds of the blacks are not competent to vote. They are too much degraded to estimate the value, or exercise with fidelity and discretion that important right. It would be unsafe in their hands. Their vote would be at the call of the richest purchaser." Young allowed that if "this class of people should hereafter arrive at such a degree of intelligence and virtue, as to inspire confidence, then it will be proper to confer this privilege upon them." For the present, however, his advice was to "emancipate and protect them; but withhold that privilege which they will inevitably abuse."[128] Young expressed an opinion that was common throughout the North. Black people should be freed from slavery, but they should not be made equal members of the community. They were essentially a dependent population, much like women and children.

In the end, the New York Convention did not categorically deny African Americans the right to vote, but the franchise was limited. Property requirements were dropped for white males who were now permitted to vote as long as they had resided in the state for at least a year and provided some service to the community such as paying taxes or performing militia duty. All in all, the new Constitution increased the pool of eligible voters by over 50 percent. But "no man of colour" was permitted to vote unless he had resided in the state for at least three years and owned a freehold estate valued at $250 on which he paid taxes.[129]

These debates occurred while Brigham Young was a twenty-year-old apprentice or young journeyman in Auburn, New York. He could hardly have failed to take notice. In fact, the Constitution of 1821 provided Young and men like him with several paths to the franchise that had not been enjoyed by earlier generations, even as it effectively disfranchised most African Americans. Many of the same arguments made during the 1821 Convention concerning Black suffrage would appear with a theological gloss during the first session of the Utah legislature some thirty years later.

* * *

As Northern states pursued gradual emancipation, it was not unusual for enslavers to utilize indenture contracts in order to temporarily maintain the labor of slaves whom they transported into "free" jurisdictions. Pennsylvania's gradual emancipation act of 1780 specifically authorized slave owners who wished to become permanent residents of the state to enter indenture contracts with their slaves; otherwise, enslaved persons migrating to Pennsylvania with their masters would become free after six months. These contracts were limited to seven years of service for adults or until the age of twenty-eight for children. The practice of indenturing slaves continued in Pennsylvania at least into the 1830s. As historian Paul Finkelman concluded, this indenture system had the "important side effect" of achieving "gradual emancipation of slaves from other states," in addition to those already held in Pennsylvania.[130]

A similar program was instituted in Indiana and Illinois during the early nineteenth century. The Northwest Ordinance of 1787 stipulated that "neither slavery nor involuntary servitude" could be introduced into the Northwest Territory, encompassing the modern states of Ohio, Indiana, Illinois, Michigan, and Wisconsin. Nevertheless, many early settlers in the southern portions of this region were "Butternuts" from Kentucky and Virginia who brought enslaved people to the Northwest Territory with them. Some of the original French settlers also kept slaves. Starting in the 1790s, a coalition of enslavers therefore petitioned Congress to either repeal the antislavery provisions of the Northwest Ordinance or modify them to allow slaves to enter the region as part of a gradual emancipation program. However, Congress took no action.[131]

Between 1803 and 1807, legislators in the Territory of Indiana resolved to create their own statutory scheme that would allow masters immigrating to the region to lawfully maintain the labor of their enslaved workers without transgressing the federal ban on chattel slavery. Like contemporary gradual emancipation regimes in New York or Connecticut, this system hinged on legally transforming slaves into indentured servants prior to granting them complete freedom. It is likely that this policy exerted significant influence over Brigham Young and other Latter-day Saint leaders during the 1850s.

As approved on September 17, 1807, An Act Concerning the Introduction of Negroes and Mulattoes into This territory permitted slave owners to bring enslaved people into Indiana and retain their service as long as their legal status was changed to one of two categories: "indentured" servant or "registered" servant. The first category was for enslaved persons who were over fifteen years old when they came into the territory. The second category was for enslaved persons who were under fifteen years old when they entered Indiana, as well as for the children of indentured servants who were born in the territory thereafter.[132]

The law required masters to enter formal indenture contracts with their slaves specifying a term of service.[133] As one scholar notes, the appearance of consent that was manifest in such a contract was "the glue" that held this system together.[134] But the law provided no upper limit for these terms. Following the reasoning of jurists such as Blackstone, the Indiana legislature determined that lifetime servitude was not synonymous with slavery.[135] A few of the subsequent indenture agreements stipulated terms of ninety-nine years. Most contracts were for shorter periods of time, but even so, they often lasted for several decades.[136] Evidence indicates that in some cases, enslaved people were able to successfully bargain with their masters for shorter terms of service and even for compensation. But if an enslaved person absolutely refused to enter such an indenture, it was lawful for the master to remove him from Indiana to a jurisdiction where slavery was legal.[137]

The statute was more specific concerning the service of enslaved children who were under fifteen years old when they entered the territory. These children could only be held as registered servants until the age of thirty-five for males and thirty-two for females. Their service, like that of a statutory servant in New York, did not require any formal agreement between master and slave. Rather, an enslaver simply had to register these children before a clerk of court. Any child who was subsequently born in Indiana to a "parent of colour, owing service or labor by indenture" could likewise be forced to serve his parent's master until the age of thirty for males and twenty-eight for females.[138]

The indenture law did create at least one notable protection for former slaves and their children. Once a servant had been properly indentured or registered before a local court, she could not be removed from the territory without her express consent as provided to a judge. Anyone convicted of attempting to remove a servant from the territory without his or her consent could be fined $1,000, two-thirds of which was to go to the servant.[139] This provision was designed to preclude the sale of an African American servant back into slavery in some other jurisdiction. A second statute called An Act Concerning Servants required masters to provide sufficient food, clothing, and lodging to a servant during his or her period of service, as well as freedom dues when the term was complete.[140] The statute did permit masters to sell a servant's labor to a third party who was a citizen of the territory, but only if the servant would "freely consent" to the sale in front of a justice of the peace.[141]

Slave owners could only register their slaves in Indiana for a short time. In 1810, the indenture law was repealed by the legislature. Six years after that, a new state constitution declared that there "shall be neither slavery nor involuntary servitude in this state, otherwise than for the punishment of crimes, whereof the party shall have been duly convicted. Nor shall any indenture of any negro or mulatto hereafter made, and executed out of the bounds of this state be of any validity within the state."[142] But in 1809, Congress carved Illinois Territory out of a large portion of western Indiana. There, the territorial legislature quickly adopted the indenture law. Over the next nine years, hundreds of enslaved people were brought into Illinois and transformed into indentured servants.[143]

When Illinois became a state in 1818, it followed the example of Indiana and banned the further introduction of slavery or involuntary servitude into the state. However, Article VI of the new constitution protected any such relationships that existed prior to that time, including the service of indentured servants. The Constitution did significantly lower the terms of service for the children of indentured slaves who were born in Illinois, yet they also remained bound until their terms expired.[144] Although judges gradually liberalized these constitutional provisions, this was still the legal status quo when Mormon refugees began to filter into western Illinois in 1839 and founded the city of Nauvoo.[145] Finally, in 1848, two years after the Latter-day Saints struck out for the Rocky Mountains, Illinois adopted a new constitution that invalidated those service relationships still in existence.[146] However, it went on to require that "The general assembly shall, at its first session under the amended constitution, pass such laws as will effectually prohibit free persons of color from immigrating to and settling in this state."[147] The end of servitude did not mean the end of racism.

The system of indentured and registered servitude in the Old Northwest allowed slave owners to enjoy the labor of their enslaved workers while promising eventual freedom to the enslaved or their children. How this system should be described was a matter of great controversy in the nineteenth century, just as it is today. As the national debate over slavery grew ever more contentious, politicians sparred with one another about how to label the now-defunct law as they sought to secure their legacy or gain rhetorical advantage over rivals. In his memoirs, Governor John Reynolds of Illinois (1830–1834) described the practice as a "species of slavery." Nevertheless, Reynolds emphasized that the law "operated as a kind of gradual emancipation." He added, "I knew many slaves and their families who were manumitted by the operation [of the law], and are now free."[148] During debates over the Compromise of 1850, Senator Stephen Douglas argued that Illinois Territory had created laws "the object and effect of which was to introduce slavery under what was called a system of indentures."[149] Four years later, during the same speech in which he declared that "there can be no moral right in connection with one man's making a slave of another," Abraham Lincoln insisted that African servants in Illinois were really "indentured" and therefore not slaves. However, he went on to label the Illinois system as "quasi slavery."[150]

Modern scholars are similarly divided. In his study of slavery in Illinois, M. Scott Heerman contends that the territorial legislature did not enact true gradual emancipation and that the "servitude system kept slavery alive."[151] While recognizing the slave-like provisions of the law, other scholars have concluded that this system did not legalize slavery and that registered and indentured servants occupied a separate legal category than chattel slaves. Paul Finkelman has written that the laws of Indiana and Illinois "did not establish *de jure* slavery. That would have directly violated the Northwest Ordinance, and perhaps led to congressional intervention." However, Finkelman concludes that the system "sanctioned and supported bondage and involuntary servitude."[152] Allison Gorsuch likewise argues that although the Illinois system would almost certainly fall under a modern description of slavery, it was "decidedly *not* chattel slavery under nineteenth-century definitions. It was precisely and ably constructed to be not-slavery."[153]

Antebellum courts universally held that the Illinois system did not constitute chattel slavery. Yet there was significant disagreement as to whether these forms of servitude were voluntary or involuntary.[154] This was a vital point because, like slavery, involuntary servitude had been forbidden in the Northwest Ordinance and would be further prohibited by the Illinois Constitutions of 1818 and 1848, and finally by the Thirteenth Amendment to the U.S. Constitution. It was not always clear what involuntary servitude might mean in an era that countenanced many forms of unfree labor. Yet by 1830, the states of Ohio, Indiana, and Illinois had all concluded that placing enslaved people in long-term indenture contracts amounted to involuntary servitude.[155]

In a pivotal 1828 case, the Supreme Court of Illinois made this position plain. In tones of moral indignity, the court declared: "Nothing can be conceived farther from the truth, than the idea that there could be a voluntary contract between the negro and his master. The law authorizes the master to bring his slave here, and take him before the clerk, and if the negro will not agree to the terms proposed by the master, he is authorized to remove him to his original place of servitude." The court then struck at the heart of the matter when it declared that "it would be an insult to common sense to contend that the negro, under the circumstances in which he was placed, had free agency. The only choice given him was a choice of evils. On either hand, servitude was to be his lot." Despite this, the court held that such relationships were legal in Illinois because the Constitution of 1818 had voided the provision of the Northwest Ordinance that barred involuntary servitude. The services of former slaves could therefore be "considered as property," just like the services of white indentured servants and apprentices.[156]

The court's reasoning was upheld for the next thirty years and would eventually become the common view throughout the United States. But this did not occur without significant dissent along the way, both in Illinois and elsewhere. In separate concurring opinions in an 1843 case, two justices of the Illinois Supreme Court argued that the state's indenture statute did not create involuntary servitude per se. They argued that when a slave entered a service contract with his master that was not based upon "fraud or collusion," such an arrangement was voluntary, just like other forms of indentured servitude.[157] In short, these justices believed that even a slave was a moral agent capable of making a genuine choice between remaining in a state of chattel slavery or entering indentured servitude. Similar arguments would endure for decades, including in Utah Territory.

* * *

Following the Revolutionary War, men like Thomas Eddy helped initiate a fundamental transformation in American labor practices. They did so amidst a proliferation of liberal ideals as well as the expansion of a cash-based market economy. A generation later, the early Latter-day Saints also took part in this prolonged transition to a free labor system. When Brigham Young was born in 1801, various forms of unfree labor were still common for people of all races. Apprenticeship was a standard experience for lower and middle-class children; indentured servitude remained customary for immigrants, "disorderly" persons, and former slaves; and New York and other neighboring states were in the initial stages of gradual emancipation. These conditions lasted into Young's early adulthood. By the time that Young and his followers fled Nauvoo in 1846, traditional apprenticeship was dying, indentured servitude was dead (at least for white adults), and gradual emancipation had largely run its course.

Despite the growing discomfort with unfree labor in the North, there was still significant disagreement about what kinds of work might be acceptable within the United States. After all, slavery remained vital to the Southern economy. These disputes only intensified after the U.S.-Mexican War. In Alta California and New Mexico, unfree relationships were common among the local Hispanic population as well as Native Americans. Although many of these practices were not expressly sanctioned by law, they were based on centuries of custom that could not easily be suppressed. As historian Howard Lamar noted almost forty years ago, the American West, far from being a bastion of free labor, was suffused with numerous forms of compelled work.[158] At the same time, Southerners saw an opportunity to expand African American slavery into these new territories; a proposition that was vociferously opposed by advocates of free labor.[159]

After Congress organized the Mexican Cession in 1850, legislators and judges from the Pacific coast to Santa Fe sought to incorporate two centuries of Anglo-American law and tradition into that vast region. In so doing, these officials were forced to determine which of these traditional labor practices were voluntary, which were involuntary, and whether any of them would be recognized under the administration of new state and territorial governments.[160] Latter-day Saint leaders in Utah were no exception. By 1852, they had concluded that they must encourage long-term vocational training for children by formalizing apprenticeships, create rules to govern the enforcement of debt obligations that were secured by the promise of future labor, and, perhaps most importantly, draft comprehensive legislation in regard to African American and Native American slavery.

2
Slavery among the Latter-day Saints, 1830–1847

In the waning months of 1844, Latter-day Saint missionary John Brown baptized an enslaved woman named Charlotte in Franklin County, Alabama, a rural area in the northwest corner of the state. He also baptized a white man named Reuben Copeland who was likely Charlotte's enslaver, although Brown failed to specify.[1] Charlotte was one of at least four enslaved people baptized that year into the upstart faith, and one of at least twelve enslaved women and men baptized since the faith's founding in 1830. Latter-day Saint missionaries continued to baptize enslaved people up through the outbreak of the Civil War. In fact, at least twenty-six enslaved people (likely more but record-keeping was spotty at best) joined the Church of Jesus Christ of Latter-day Saints before the nation outlawed slavery in 1865.[2]

Baptizing enslaved people did not make the Latter-day Saints unique. Christian churches in the United States viewed mission outreach to enslaved people as part of their divine mandate to take the gospel message to all people. However, there was considerable disagreement among denominational adherents in the nineteenth century over the morality of slavery.[3] More specifically Methodist Church members questioned whether white enslavers should be given leadership roles in the Church, while Baptists debated if white enslavers should be allowed to serve as missionaries.[4]

In fact, in 1844, the year that Charlotte was baptized in Alabama, the Methodist Church split along a North/South divide over whether one of its bishops, James O. Andrew of Georgia, would be allowed to retain his episcopal office after he inherited two slaves from his deceased wife and his second wife also brought slaves into their marriage. The laws of Georgia prevented enslavers from manumitting their slaves, and therefore Andrew was in a bind. He offered to resign as bishop, but fellow Southerners refused to allow it. Northern antislavery Methodists in turn demanded it. Andrew thus became a test case in the Methodist Church over slavery and leadership—one it did not survive intact.[5]

This Abominable Slavery. W. Paul Reeve, Christopher B. Rich Jr., and LaJean Purcell Carruth, Oxford University Press.
© Oxford University Press 2024. DOI: 10.1093/oso/9780197765029.003.0003

Following an almost two-week long debate, Methodist delegates voted 110 to 68, primarily along sectional lines, that they would not tolerate a bishop who held slaves. The Northern majority concluded that Andrew's connection to slavery "will greatly embarrass the exercise of his office if not in some places entirely prevent it" and therefore instructed him to "desist from the exercise of his office" so long as he remained an enslaver. Southern Methodists in turn could not abide such a decision. They split the Church in two and formed the Methodist Episcopal Church, South with a half-million adherents.[6]

As these events played out nationally, Methodists in Alabama registered their disapproval of the decision that they claimed their "brethren of the North" foisted on the Church. One Alabama conference, for example, called the national decision a product of "misguided zeal and false philanthropy" and suggested it was "an unnecessary interference with our rights." Alabamans deemed the decision to be "at war with the true interests of the Church, and in violation of that spirit and temper that should govern the conduct of Christ's people." In consequence, they resolved that it was "for the glory of God and the salvation of souls, that the Church peaceably divide; for we feel assured that we shall never be able to reconcile our brethren of the North to the institutions of the South."[7]

This Alabama conference thus articulated the real conundrum facing the three largest Protestant denominations in the United States in the 1830s and 1840s—how to reconcile congregants of the North to the institution of slavery in the South. The Presbyterians, Methodists, and Baptists were unable to solve that puzzle. Slavery tore all three Churches in two along a North/South divide and signaled the deepening sectional political rift that would follow in the 1850s, which would then devolve into a bloody Civil War by 1861. The Presbyterians split first in 1837, followed by the Methodists in 1844, and the Baptists in 1845. As one historian of American religion put it, "the divided churches painfully exposed the deep moral chasm between North and South, furthering the alienation between sections and contributing to the eventual disruption of the Union."[8]

The Church of Jesus Christ of Latter-day Saints, in contrast, was numerically smaller and structurally different than the three largest Protestant denominations. It struggled to gain a foothold in an American religious culture that in theory honored religious freedom but in practice denigrated new religious sects that did not conform to prevailing notions of what proper religion looked like as defined by the Protestant majority.[9] Latter-day

Saints initially attempted to navigate America's fraught racial culture with a welcoming attitude toward all believers, including free Black people, enslaved Black people, abolitionists, white enslavers, anti-abolitionists, and Native Americans alike. Joseph Smith claimed five revelations in which he declared that the Latter-day Saint gospel message was to be preached "unto every creature," an unambiguous pronouncement that left no one out (Doctrine and Covenants 58:64, 68:8, 84:62, 112:28). His new book of scripture, the Book of Mormon, also described the universal reach of Jesus Christ's grace, "Hath he commanded any that they should not partake of his salvation? Behold I say unto you, Nay" (2 Nephi 26:27).

Even if their approach to conversion was expansive, Latter-day Saint leaders still had to contend with questions regarding slavery and abolitionism, both prominent national issues at the time. In doing so they adopted an approach grounded in political expediency more than in a theology of moral compunction against slavery. Their responses were firmly grounded in time and place, depending on whether the Saints were in a slave or free state. Smith nonetheless evolved over time to advocate government-funded emancipation by the time of his murder in June 1844. Circumstances, however, changed dramatically after the Latter-day Saints arrived in the Great Basin with slaves in tow. It would now be up to them to decide whether to accept or reject the "peculiar institution." No longer were they beholden to preexisting laws, but an all Latter-day Saint legislature and a prophet-governor could decide for themselves what to do about the slavery that already existed among them.

* * *

A formerly enslaved Black man named Peter who was commonly referred to as "Black Pete" is the first know Black person to join the Church of Christ, as it was initially called. He did so in 1830, at Kirtland, Ohio, and there have been Black Latter-day Saints ever since.[10] By 1835 three enslaved women and two enslaved men had joined the faith in Tennessee, and John Burton, also enslaved, received baptism in Missouri.[11] Free Black men and women also embraced the Latter-day Saint message. In fact, in the fall of 1842, Jane Manning James led at least six other family members into the waters of baptism in Connecticut, and her family group then migrated to join the main body of Saints at Nauvoo, Illinois, by the end of 1843.[12]

Missionary John Brown baptized several enslaved people in Alabama and Mississippi in the 1840s, just like he did Charlotte in 1844.[13] At the same time,

Latter-day Saints did not attempt to withhold priesthood ordination or ecclesiastical positions from white enslavers like some of their counterparts in the Methodist and Baptist Churches. Instead, after Brown baptized Reuben Copeland, Charlotte's likely enslaver, he ordained Copeland, an elder in the lay priesthood. Copeland and Charlotte then became members of the Little Bear Creek congregation, a small "branch" of the Church led by Joseph L. Griffin who served as "presiding elder." Griffin enslaved four people of his own in 1830 and continued to hold slaves up through 1850.[14]

Unlike the Northern Baptists and Methodists, then, the Latter-day Saints ordained slaveholders to the priesthood and gave them ecclesiastical positions within local congregations. It was a move that may have prevented the same type of split that ruptured the Methodists, Presbyterians, and Baptists, and it kept Southern converts in the fold. It was a system that worked in a fledgling faith that was more preoccupied with sheer survival than with imposing a unified policy against slavery on its converts scattered in small congregations across the South. Even still, this approach merely delayed the issue until 1852 when the Saints gathered in Utah Territory, a political entity without prior laws on slavery.

The Latter-day Saint system of authority that relied on a lay priesthood and a lay leadership structure meant that as missionaries formed congregations in the antebellum South those congregations depended on Southern white men to lead. Some of those lay leaders enslaved other human beings, in some cases their fellow congregants. The same lay system of leadership prevailed in the North, with local leaders of various political leanings appointed to preside over given congregations. In Ohio and Massachusetts, leaders there even ordained free Black men to the lay priesthood; in contrast, no Black enslaved men were ordained to the priesthood in the South.[15] This Latter-day Saint system grounded in local control thus avoided an organized effort to force a uniform antislavery standard churchwide like that among Presbyterians, Methodists, and Baptists, at least in the 1830s and 1840s. As long as local leaders in each congregation, North or South, presided in their respective congregations according to regional laws and customs, Latter-day Saint universalism worked.

The morality of slavery, however, was a different matter than decentralized congregations. It was a question that Joseph Smith and other Latter-day Saint leaders could not avoid, especially as Smith declared the slave state of Missouri to be the center of his American Zion. It was in Jackson County, Missouri, in 1833, when one Saint, William Wines Phelps, first weighed in on the matter of slavery. He did so with an antislavery stance that brought swift retaliation from Missouri settlers. It was a negative lesson for Latter-day Saint leaders that prompted a more cautious approach to slavery and a more sympathetic attitude toward slaveholders, at least for as long as the Saints attempted to establish a religious kingdom in a slave state. Phelps was the editor of the Latter-day Saint newspaper in Jackson County, *The Evening and the Mormon Star*. Because Joseph Smith had articulated Jackson County as the gathering place for his envisioned holy community, Phelps published an article titled "Free People of Color" in the *Star* that quickly earned not just Phelps but also the entire Latter-day Saint community condemnation and public scorn.[16]

Phelps's article was aimed at Black Latter-day Saints who might consider migrating to Jackson County. He wanted them to be aware that Missouri was a slave state and as such specific laws governed the ability of Black people to move freely in the state. Free Black people were required to carry papers to substantiate their legal status as freed. If they were caught without such papers they were subject to ten lashes on a bare back followed by expulsion from the state. Phelps quoted two sections of the Missouri state code as evidence of the laws that would govern Black Saints if they moved to Zion. "So long as we have no special rule in this church, as to people of color, let prudence guide," he wrote. Latter-day Saints, in other words, did not discriminate; they had no "special rule" regarding people of color, but the state of Missouri did. Phelps did not want his fellow congregants who were Black to run afoul of the law, so he encouraged "prudence" if they migrated.[17]

In the same edition of the *Star* Phelps wrote a second article, one that made it clear that he advocated a conservative form of emancipation, one that included sending former slaves to Africa once freed. Phelps thus indicated that he was aware of the way that the majority of nineteenth-century antislavery Americans understood the slavery problem as twofold. Slavery was wrong because it violated America's founding principles—all men are created equal and that "life, liberty, and the pursuit of happiness" are inalienable rights. But the second part of the slavery problem was racial. The majority of Americans who opposed slavery in the nineteenth century did not do so because they believed Black people to be equal to white people, but because they believed slavery to be wrong. Once the slaves were freed, it thus presented a racial problem: what to do with 4 million Black people who white Northerners did not want living and intermarrying among them. The solution was to form colonization societies and send the freed slaves to

Africa. "As to slaves," Phelps wrote in his second column, "we have nothing to say. In connection with the wonderful events of this age, much is doing towards abolishing slavery, and colonizing the blacks, in Africa." It was a clear indication of his moderate brand of antislavery sentiment, but such nuance was lost on the Missouri majority.[18]

Missouri settlers focused their attention on Phelps's article, "Free People of Color." Some read it as an invitation from the Mormons for free Black people to migrate to the state in order to incite a slave rebellion and steal their white wives and daughters. Especially in the wake of Nat Turner's 1831 slave revolt in Virginia, Southerners remained on edge, and Phelps's article touched a raw nerve in Jackson County. Fear of slave rebellion and race mixing were thus projected onto the Latter-day Saints. Phelps quickly backpedaled, but to no avail. He issued an "extra" edition of the *Star* in which he claimed his original column had been "misunderstood." He disingenuously suggested that the real intent of his article "was not only to stop free people of color from emigrating to this state, but to prevent them from being admitted as members of the church." It was a poor attempt at managing public perception, and it was simply not true.[19]

Missourians saw through Phelps's denial. They demonstrated their ire when they formed a vigilance committee and complained that Phelps's original article was an open invitation to "free negroes and mulattoes from other States to become mormons and remove and settle among us." Such an influx of free Black people, the vigilance committee suggested, would inevitably promote a slave rebellion as well as facilitate race mixing. In response they stormed Phelps's printing office, destroyed copies of the newspaper and his "extra" broadsheet, scattered his type and the press itself, and demolished his office and home. It marked the beginning of the Latter-day Saint expulsion from Jackson County, Missouri. It also shaped a more cautious attitude toward slavery for the remainder of the 1830s as Latter-day Saint missionaries continued to seek converts in the South, both Black and white, as well as struggled to reclaim their property in Jackson County and build settlements in other Missouri counties.[20]

In the wake of the Latter-day Saint expulsion from Jackson County, Missouri, the *Star's* new editor, Oliver Cowdery, pushed back against the claim that the Saints were complicit in a scheme to incite a slave rebellion. To find common ground with white Missourians, Cowdery argued that Mormon settlers would be just as much a target of violence during a slave revolt as would Missourians. "The life of every white inhabitant in the country" would be subject to attack Cowdery reasoned. "For the moment an insurrection should break out," Cowdery said, "no respect would be paid to age, sex, or religion; by an enraged, jealous, and ignorant black banditti."[21] Cowdery thereby attempted to put white Mormons on par with their Missouri neighbors and simultaneously distance white Latter-day Saints from their Black coreligionists. It was a pattern Latter-day Saints followed for the rest of the century. When push came to shove, they chose to protect the white majority within the faith at the expense of the Black minority. Political expediency, such as that which prompted Phelps's "extra" broadsheet, thus characterized the Latter-day Saint approach to slavery until the 1840s when they settled in Illinois and again adopted a more potent antislavery stance.[22]

The Jackson County episode also colored the Saints' view of broader national concerns over the immediate abolitionist movement then gaining ground in some locations. Rather than denounce slavery, the Latter-day Saints instead joined other denominations to distance themselves from immediate abolitionism. William Lloyd Garrison, a prominent leader among radical abolitionists, founded a newspaper, *The Liberator*, just nine months after the organization of Joseph Smith's new church. Rather than gradual emancipation stretching over decades, Garrison advocated immediate freedom for all slaves. Rather than sending freed slaves to Africa as the colonizationists advocated, Garrison argued for full Black equality in America. As Garrison's brand of abolitionism gained ground, he and his followers were quickly branded amalgamationists in disguise.[23] "Amalgamation" was the pre–Civil War term borrowed from metallurgy (meaning the mixing of metals) used to signify the mixing of races. Those who rejected the immediate abolition of slavery argued that those who favored such a position really favored race mixing. Turning 4 million freed slaves loose, without jobs and without means of support, they feared, would create lawless mobs who would invade the North, steal white jobs, and intermarry among white people.[24]

In response to such fears, Methodists, Baptists, Catholics, Presbyterians, and even Quakers issued formal statements or spoke out against immediate abolitionism.[25] In 1835, Latter-day Saint leaders followed suit. They issued a conservative statement that honored the master-slave relationship and was designed to squelch fears that Latter-day Saints promoted slave revolts. "We do not believe it right to interfere with bondservants neither preach the gospel to, nor baptize them, contrary to the will and wish of their masters," they declared. It was not right, the statement continued, "to meddle with or influence [enslaved people] in the least, to cause them to be dissatisfied with their situations in this life, thereby jeopardizing the lives of men." The statement was calculated to officially reject any notion that Latter-day Saints were intent on fomenting slave rebellions. At the same time it favored the status quo for enslaved people and implied that they were somehow not "dissatisfied with their situations in this life," something that Latter-day Saint meddling might somehow encourage but the harsh realities of slavery itself would not. Latter-day Saint leaders did not claim the decree was a revelation; rather, they called it a "Declaration of Belief Regarding Governments and Laws in General." They nonetheless included it in the Doctrine and Covenants, a collection of Smith's writings and revelations accepted as scriptural canon.[26] That collection already included an 1833 revelation that declared it was "not right that any man should be in bondage one to another," a passage that the Saints seemed to overlook as they struggled to establish Zion in a slave state.[27]

The appeasement to enslavers continued in 1836 when Smith again spoke out on the issue. This time he did so in an effort to distance the Church from the immediate abolitionist movement and the corresponding accusation that Latter-day Saints favored amalgamation. John W. Alvord, an activist in the abolitionist movement, had recently visited Kirtland, Ohio, one of the Church's headquarters. In the wake of his visit, residents of Kirtland and the surrounding area organized a chapter of the American Anti-Slavery Society with eighty-six members, some of whom were Latter-day Saints. In other locations, Alvord's speaking tour was sometimes met with resistance as anti-abolitionists pelted him with snowballs and apples or drowned out his voice with ringing bells and blowing horns. The state of Ohio, in fact, was home to more anti-abolitionist violence in the 1830s than any other state in the nation. One report of Alvord's visit to Kirtland, in contrast, suggested that he was "well received."[28]

In response, Smith sought to clarify his position on immediate abolitionism in a way that again placated Southern slaveholders and even drew on long-standing biblical rhetoric to justify slavery. Smith's response appeared in the *Messenger and Advocate*, a Latter-day Saint newspaper published in Kirtland with Smith's friend and former scribe Oliver Cowdery as editor. Smith wanted it known that even though Alvord preached abolitionism at Kirtland and was not met with "mobs or disturbances," it did not automatically follow that "all he said was concurred in, and received as gospel and the word of salvation." In fact, Smith suggested that Alvord's reception at

Kirtland was tepid at best, and he was left "to hold forth his own arguments to nearly naked walls."[29]

Smith then acknowledged that an antislavery sentiment seemed to dominate among his followers in the North. Latter-day Saints from the North "complain against their brethren of the same faith, who reside in the south," Smith noted. Similar to the movements that would develop in the Methodist and Baptist faiths, Smith worried that some Latter-day Saints "are ready to withdraw the hand of fellowship [from slaveholders in the South] because they will not renounce the principle of slavery and raise their voice against every thing of the kind." Smith urged "candid reflection" among his followers instead. He encouraged them to consider the consequences of immediate abolitionism, especially its potential to "lay waste the fair States of the South and set loose upon the world a community of people who might peradventure, overrun our country and violate the most sacred principles of human society—chastity and virtue."[30] It was a clear indication of Smith's understanding of the closely related accusation among anti-abolitionists, that if people favored freeing millions of enslaved people, what they really favored was race mixing.

In a particularly convoluted argument, Smith suggested that if slavery really were evil "who could we expect would first learn it," those who participated in it or those who opposed it? He suggested Southern slaveholders would be the first to recognize it as evil, and once they did so, "who would be more capable than they of prescribing a remedy?" In Smith's illogic, those who held slaves were "persons of ability, discernment and candor" and were thus capable of regulating themselves and recognizing the abuses bound up in slavery if it were truly abusive. He reasoned that slaveholders would eventually "give an account at the bar of God for their conduct," and if they "live without the fear of God before their eyes" then others should withhold judgment. It was a live and let live philosophy that ignored life, liberty, and the pursuit of happiness as inalienable and God-given rights. "I do not believe that the people of the North have any more right to say that the South shall not hold slaves," Smith suggested, "than the South have to say the North shall."[31]

He recognized that his stance would not sit well among some of his followers, especially those "who have been forward in raising their voices against the South." He predicted his message would be met with opposition and the antislavery crowd would label him "uncharitable, unfeeling, unkind, and wholly unacquainted with the Gospel of Christ." In that regard, he then drew on the Bible to articulate a standard Christian defense of slavery, that God cursed Canaan, "a servant of servants shall he be unto his brethren" (Genesis 9:25). From that fraught interpretation of scripture Christian leaders of various denominations had long defended white people who enslaved Black people, and Smith now joined them. Smith admitted that he did not know "what could have been the design of the Almighty in this singular occurrence," but he was sure that "the curse is not yet taken off from the sons of Canaan." As a result, he cautioned that those who "interfere the least with the purposes of God in this matter, will come under the least condemnation before Him."[32] More succinctly, two years later in response to the question "are the Mormons abolitionists," another Latter-day Saint publication, the *Elders' Journal*, flatly declared "we do not believe in setting the Negroes free."[33]

These were politically expedient stances designed to temper the growing chorus of voices among Smith's Northern followers who advocated withdrawing fellowship from Southern slaveholders. Smith's position on slavery was also calculated to suppress opposition to Latter-day Saint missionaries then preaching in the South as well as to appease slaveholding Latter-day Saints and keep them in the fold.

Smith's views evolved, however, as the Saints abandoned Ohio and were driven from Missouri under a state-sanctioned extermination order. Antiabolitionist violence diminished nationally at the same time that the 1840s saw an increase in antislavery sentiments in Illinois, the Saints' new gathering place.[34] Smith was thus freed from the earlier need to be overly sympathetic toward slavery but was nonetheless constrained by a desire to keep Southern converts in the fold. Even still he was now ready to "interfere" with slavery and propose a national plan for emancipation.[35]

In 1843, in a discussion at Springfield, Illinois, Smith expressed his most open ideas regarding racial equality. Black people were not biologically inferior but were impeded by a lack of educational opportunities and other environmental circumstances common to enslavement. "They come into the world slaves mentally & phy[s]ically. change their situation with the white & they would be like them," he argued.[36]

A year later Smith moved from a mere belief in equality toward an actual plan for national emancipation. In 1844, out of mounting frustration over the failure of national politicians to address the Saints' ongoing grievances over their expulsion from Missouri and their corresponding loss of land, life, and property, Smith decided to run for president of the United States. His unlikely bid for the White House prompted him to put his ideas regarding slavery into a political plan grounded in compensated gradual emancipation. Smith proposed to free the slaves throughout the South, a process that he predicted could be complete by 1850. It was not immediate emancipation, in other words, but he did advocate emancipation over the coming six years, a significantly accelerated pace of freedom in contrast to the existing gradual emancipation laws then in operation in some states.[37]

His plan called on the federal government to compensate white enslavers for the loss of property such an emancipation would represent. It was an idea similar to the emancipation scheme which the British Empire enacted in 1833, with compensation for white enslavers coming out of government coffers. The British system was also gradual in that it required former slaves to enter an apprenticeship phase before they were set free.[38] In the United States, Smith proposed to pay for the freedom of the enslaved through the sale of public lands and from a pay reduction leveled against members of Congress. "Break off the shackles from the poor black man, and hire him to labor like other human beings," Smith insisted.[39]

Although Smith forcefully denounced slavery, his tone toward Southerners remained conciliatory. Rather than condemning slaveholders, his platform referred to the "goodly inhabitants of the slave states" and called enslavers "southern gentlemen."[40] Moreover, in a speech he delivered in March 1844 he maintained sympathy for colonizationist ideals when he suggested sending freed slaves to Mexico "where all colors are alike."[41] Smith yet again wanted to make it clear that because he advocated the eradication of slavery, it did not automatically mean he favored race mixing.

By the spring of 1844, Smith's prior biblical justification for slavery disappeared and was replaced by an expansive understanding of the interrelated nature of the entire human family. He now drew on the Bible as well as the founding documents of the United States to argue for universal human rights. He pointed to the great American paradox as a problem that needed resolution: a nation founded on the principles that "all men are created equal" simultaneously held "some two or three millions of people ... as slaves for life, because the spirit in them is covered with a darker skin than ours." At least a part of the solution to that paradox came through an understanding of the broad commonality of the human family. Rather than the book of Genesis and its curse of Canaan, this time Smith drew inspiration from the book of Acts to assert that "God has made of one blood all nations of men for to dwell on the face of the earth" (Acts 17:26).[42]

Smith thus came to view all people as members of the same human family. As a brother in that family who had experienced the violation of his rights, he asserted a platform grounded in racial equality. In his view, political officials were "nothing more nor less than the servants of the people" and as such "ought to be directed to ameliorate the condition of all, black or white, bond or free." He similarly called on the promises of the U.S. Constitution to "establish justice, ensure the domestic tranquility, provide for the common defense, promote the general welfare, and secure the blessings of liberty to ourselves and our posterity." He left no doubt that in his view that document "meant just what it said without reference to color or condition."[43]

Even as Smith laid out his racial ideals and attempted to grapple with slavery, his followers continued to struggle with its more practical implications. In early 1844, Lyman Wight, one of Smith's apostles, and George Miller, a bishop, both proposed their own solutions to what to do with Southern converts who enslaved other human beings. Miller had served a mission to Kentucky in 1842 and Wight to Tennessee the same year.[44] Both men were thus familiar with the conversions taking place in the South and desirous to appease slaveholders who had converted there. They proposed to establish a Latter-day Saint colony in Texas, "and let it be a place of gathering for all the South," as Miller put it, since Southerners were "incumbered with that unfortunate race of beings the negroes."[45]

Wight was perhaps overly optimistic in his plan. He envisioned "thousands of the rich planters" of the South who would embrace the gospel if only "they had a place to plant their slaves." He imagined them living a consecrated life wherein they would "give all the proceeds of their yearly labor ... for building up the Kingdom." In Wight's view the "Southerner with his Slaves and abundance of wealth" would do better to take them to some slaveholding point where the enslaver could donate his yearly proceeds to the Church than if the Church were to force a slaveholder to abolish slavery and move north to settle "in a climate uncongenial to his nature and entirely derogatory to his former occupations in life."[46]

Miller's and Wight's plans for slave-based gathering places in Texas were in many respects more realistic propositions than Smith's government funded emancipation. However, Wight's vision of Southern enslavers living a communal economic system grounded in the inherent inequality of Black people ignored the very capitalistic commodification of human bodies in which slavery was based and assumed an altruistic willingness among Southern planters to live a utopian ideal that Saints in Missouri failed to achieve without the complicating factor of slavery.[47] In simple theological and moral terms, Smith's vision of racial equality was far superior to Miller's and Wight's proposals that were based in perpetuating inequality.

Smith was murdered before he had to confront the challenge of translating his ideals into action, even among his followers. Miller's and Wight's plans were reviewed by the Council of Fifty, the temporal and political arm of Smith's religious kingdom, but they did not receive significant consideration, although Council members did pursue Texas as a possible site for relocation as they looked for a place to practice their religion free of outside detractors. Those efforts did not bear fruit for the majority of Saints who migrated to northern Mexico under Brigham Young in 1847, but Wight did lead his own group of roughly 150 followers to Texas in 1845. Wight's colony never did serve as a base for Southern enslavers but instead developed into an independent church with Wight at its head. The Church of Jesus Christ of Latter-day Saints excommunicated Wight in 1848, and his death ten years later spelled the end of his movement.[48]

In the meantime, Smith's vision grounded in racial equality seemed to resonate with other leaders who expressed their own antislavery sentiments and desires for racial equality. Smith's counselor in the First Presidency, Sidney Rigdon, for example, believed that the nation's founders established a "government where every man should be free; the slave liberated from bondage, and the colored African enjoy the rights of citizenship." In Rigdon's view the country was founded on principles designed to ensure that all people enjoyed "equal rights to speak, to act, to worship, [with] peculiar privileges to none."[49] David D. Yearsley, a member of the Council of Fifty at Nauvoo, was more concerned about the nation's failure to live up to such lofty ideals. He noted the progress of the "sectarian world" that he perceived to be grounded in "bloodshed and oppression," including "the principle of slavery being cherished in the United States."[50]

The fact that many Council of Fifty members, including Joseph Smith, came to believe that the U.S. Constitution failed to protect minority rights seemed to move them in a more empathetic direction toward those who were enslaved. Smith in fact appointed a committee to draft a new constitution that would guarantee the preservation of minority rights. That constitution never came to fruition, but an early draft of it decried "cruelty, oppression, bondage, slavery, rapine, bloodshed, murder, carnage, desolation, and all the evils that blast the peace, exaltation, and glory of the universe." It declared that "God hath created all men free and equal" and repeated Smith's earlier claim that "one blood" united humankind.[51]

It was a resounding endorsement of the equality and brotherhood of the entire human family. At least one member of the Council, Erastus Snow, argued that such lofty ideals needed to be practiced and not merely espoused. "We do not want to inculcate principles which we will not carry into effect," he urged. How could they claim that "all men are born free and equal," when "millions of our fellow men are born in bondage" and "never enjoyed a breath of liberty" he wondered. Joseph Smith concurred and noted that the draft constitution should be modified to read all men "ought to be" free and equal rather than state it as fact when slavery demonstrated that it clearly was not fact. In his view, "all men were in the designs of God created equal, and inasmuch as some had greater capacities than others, it was required of them to possess the greater philanthropy." Greater capacity, in other words, did not bestow superiority and the right to enslave other human beings, instead it carried greater altruistic obligations.[52]

It was not only Council of Fifty members who expressed antislavery sentiment but at least some international Saints also advocated against enslavement. The *Latter-day Saints Millennial Star*, an English Church publication, registered its disapproval of slavery in 1843 when it noted that English Saints "look with abhorrence upon the slave-holder who deprives his fellow-beings of liberty" but nonetheless said that the English were more indignant toward religious leaders who fettered the mind and obscured the truth.[53] Dan Jones, a convert from Wales and later a missionary in his country of origin, also registered his dislike of slavery. Jones edited a Welsh Latter-day Saint newspaper called the *Prophet of the Jubilee* in which he decried the Methodists, Baptists, and Presbyterians in the United States for holding hundreds of thousands of slaves in "a bloody trade." In contrast, he incorrectly claimed that "the Latter-day Saints are completely innocent of making merchandise of the souls and the bodies of black or white men." He called on his Protestant counterparts to "set their enslaved brothers free by the hundreds."[54]

While it is impossible to know how many Latter-day Saints shared such views, there were likely many among the thousands of converts from Great Britain who had gathered in the Great Basin. In fact, over half of those in Utah Territory by 1850 were British born, and they, along with those from Scandinavia and the American North, far outnumbered converts from the South.[55] Such a majority may account for Brigham Young's statement in 1852 that when Southerners arrived in Utah Territory with their slaves in tow, "a strong abolitionist feeling [prevails]" and "the devil [is] raised" with people "saying 'do you think it's right, I am afraid it is not right.'"[56] Young's own assessment was that abolitionism dominated in Utah Territory and was a source of tension among the Saints.

The Latter-day Saint gathering from the various regions of the United States and internationally thus forced the young Church to finally grapple with the very issue that had split the Presbyterians, Methodists, and Baptists less than a decade earlier. No longer would it work for Southern Saints to preside over congregations in the South, slavery included, and Northern Saints to ordain Black men to the priesthood and complain about slavery in the South. Saints from the North and the South, free Black people and enslaved Black people, abolitionists, and enslavers were no longer strangers and foreigners separated by distance and ideologies but were now fellow citizens in a very mortal and ethically messy household of God.[57]

Had sentiments from the 1844 Council of Fifty discussion prevailed, or Joseph Smith's presidential platform been used as a guide, it is difficult to imagine the Saints opting for slavery. Putting those ideals into practice was an entirely different matter. Prior to his death, Smith had adopted a theology roughly grounded in the ideals of racial equality that allowed Black men priesthood authority and envisioned people of "every color" worshipping in Latter-day Saint temples.[58] In politics, he espoused an antislavery position. Even so, Smith had still attempted to conciliate Southerners to avoid a sectional rift within the Church. Indeed, he fully recognized that enslavers had a property interest in their enslaved workers that would have to be addressed in some fashion.[59]

As the Saints began to gather to the Great Basin, it was up to Brigham Young to determine how to carry this legacy forward. In 1845, Young had yearned for a place outside the bounds of the United States where the Saints could "exalt the standard of liberty and make our own laws."[60] Young's wish did not entirely come true, but by 1850, the U.S. Congress created Utah Territory with no preexisting regulations to govern or prohibit slavery. The Latter-day Saints, at least in terms of slavery, were free to establish their own laws.

3

Slavery among the Latter-day Saints, 1847–1852

When the first company of Latter-day Saints arrived in the Salt Lake Valley, their new home was just inside the Mexican province of Alta California. Technically, Mexican law applied throughout the entire region, including prohibitions on slavery found in the 1829 Constitution. But Mexican officials on the Pacific coast had never effectively extended their jurisdiction to this remote area. Since the 1820s, merchant caravans had regularly traveled through the southern portion of the Great Basin along the Old Spanish Trail. Trading expeditions from New Mexico had maintained contact with the local Utes for even longer. But outside of a few forts built by American fur trappers, there were no non-Indigenous settlements in the vicinity of the Great Salt Lake, and no government presence. Moreover, by the summer of 1847, the populated areas of Alta California and New Mexico were under military occupation by the United States, and temporary governments had been established there. Brigham Young knew that in time, the federal government would also extend its laws over the new Mormon settlements. A year before, Young had even notified President James K. Polk that the Saints intended to petition Congress for a territorial government "as soon as we are settled in the Great Basin."[1] He hoped that such an organization would allow the Saints sufficient independence to govern themselves. Until this happened, however, the Saints appeared to have a free hand to create laws and regulations to suit their preferences.

This apparent discretion could not change realities on the ground. Whatever the legal conditions of the Great Basin may have been in the summer of 1847, slavery was a fact of life. Ute and New Mexican traders were then engaged in a vast human trafficking enterprise that transported enslaved Southern Paiute and Goshute south toward Santa Fe or west to California along the Old Spanish Trail. The Indian slave trade was so pervasive that within a few months of entering the Salt Lake Valley, the Saints were compelled to buy a teenaged girl or watch her be murdered by her Ute enslavers. In addition to the moral implications of this practice, it was clearly a driver of violence and instability throughout the region.[2]

At the same time, a number of Southern Mormons brought enslaved Black people with them to the Great Basin.[3] For the first time in the Latter-day Saint experience, a small slave-owning minority had to be integrated into a community that was dominated by Yankees and European immigrants who were fundamentally opposed to African servitude.

The Saints also faced significant external pressures concerning slavery. The United States had been in an uproar concerning the potential expansion of the institution ever since the introduction of the Wilmot Proviso the previous year. In August 1846, Congressman David Wilmot of Pennsylvania proposed legislation which stipulated that slavery and involuntary servitude would be prohibited in any territory that might be acquired from Mexico as a result of the ongoing conflict. The Wilmot Proviso immediately created a political firestorm that only grew with time. Adherents of the emerging Free-Soil movement demanded the immediate adoption of the Proviso. In contrast, radical Southerners like John C. Calhoun wanted the entire Mexican Cession opened to slavery and threatened secession if the Wilmot Proviso was enacted.[4]

Some moderates advocated simply extending the old Missouri Compromise line all the way to the Pacific. Senators Lewis Cass and Stephen Douglas instead argued that the settlers of these new acquisitions should be able to decide for themselves whether to allow slavery through the mechanism of popular sovereignty, or "Congressional non-intervention."[5] Under these fraught conditions, it was apparent that any position the Mormon leadership took in regard to slavery might jeopardize their principal goal of self-government. The lessons of Jackson County were never far from their minds.

In the years after the Saints were expelled from Nauvoo, Brigham Young gradually moved away from the rough racial equality that Joseph Smith had established in the Church of Jesus Christ. It is likely that this transformation was rooted in fears of amalgamation, or race mixing. As late as March 1847, Young argued that Q. Walker Lewis, a Black Latter-day Saint living in Lowell, Massachusetts, was "one of the best Elders" in the Church.[6] It does not appear that Young had any objections to the fact that Lewis had been ordained to the priesthood. But Young did not know that Lewis's son, Enoch, had recently married a white Latter-day Saint woman. Mormon elder William I. Appleby traveled to Lowell the following summer and was troubled upon learning of Lewis's ordination and Enoch's interracial marriage. Appleby subsequently sought guidance from Young by letter and in person. In early December, Young responded to Appleby that "the law is their seed shall not be amalgamated," although he did not mention the priesthood.[7] Even so, these events triggered a fundamental change in Young's thinking about the place of Black people within the Church he led.[8]

By 1849, Young had adopted pervasive social attitudes concerning people of African descent that maintained they were incapable of fully participating in a free society. Young ultimately came to view Black people much like women and children, dependent members of the community who should be cared for and protected but who could not and should not legitimately exercise the rights of citizenship. In much the same way, Young came to believe that people of African descent could be baptized into the LDS Church, but they could not exercise the priesthood. Theologically, Young based his position on an idiosyncratic interpretation of the biblical curses of Canaan, Cain, and Ham. Joseph Smith had occasionally discussed these curses without any firm direction about their practical application. Such ideas were a product of their upbringing in early nineteenth-century New York as much as any connection with Mormonism. Young remained committed to Joseph Smith's teachings that all humans were "of one blood" and children of the same beneficent God. Like Smith, Young believed that African Americans were capable of moral and intellectual improvement. Moreover, Young showed genuine affection and sympathy for African Americans on an individual basis. But Young's increasing emphasis on an ambiguous collection of ancient curses would form the basis for all his future policies concerning people of Black-African descent.[9]

Despite this ongoing shift in Young's thinking about race, he did not completely abandon the antislavery position that Joseph Smith had staked out during his presidential campaign. Yet during the initial stages of the westward migration, the topic of slavery receded into the background as Young and his colleagues focused on the task at hand: gathering all the Saints to Zion, be they white, Black, enslaver, or enslaved. Soon after arriving in the Salt Lake Valley, Young allegedly told the three enslaved members of the company, Green Flake, Hark Wales, and Oscar Smith, "Brothers, you are now free as I am."[10] If so, this was an isolated act. There is no indication that the three men's enslavers considered them free, and no official pronouncements or policies concerning slavery were forthcoming from Church leaders. By December 1847, the ecclesiastical High Council of Great Salt Lake City had begun to enact a number of municipal ordinances to govern the settlement "in the absence of any organized jurisdiction of any Territory."[11] Although dozens of enslaved African Americans and free Black people came to the Salt Lake Valley over the next two years, the Council made no provision for or against the practice of slavery.

While the High Council pointedly ignored the topic of slavery, it quickly instituted a form of involuntary labor for people who did not properly contribute to the community. The very first ordinance enacted by the Council prohibited an individual from "idling away his or her time, or neglecting in any manner to use the necessary exertions," to provide adequate sustenance for his or her family. Upon conviction, a so-called vagrant could be taken into custody and forced "to be industriously employed."[12] Under the leadership of the Council, compelled labor on public infrastructure projects quickly became a standard punishment for crimes, such as theft, or a method to pay off fines.[13] In early 1849, the Council took this one step further. On March 4, the Council convicted a man named Ira West for some kind of fraud and fined him $100. Hosea Stout alleged that West also attempted to flee Great Salt Lake City without making restitution. Although there was loose talk about killing the man, upon Brigham Young's suggestion, West was instead placed in chains and offered for public sale to whomever would pay off his obligations. Similar action was taken against another man named Thomas Burns.[14] This was essentially a revival of the concept of public indenture with which the Saints were familiar in the east. It plainly demonstrated the willingness of the Mormons to employ unfree labor to maintain order in their settlements and serve as a method to defray debt. As in colonial Virginia, this made immanent sense in a community where labor was desperately short and hard currency was difficult to come by. Only two months before, the Mormon leadership had decided to issue paper money backed by gold dust due to the lack of minted specie in the valley.[15] It turned out that when West was placed on auction, no one was willing to buy his labor, and he was taken away by his brother. Still, the Saints' willingness to utilize unfree labor as a tool to repay debt would have important implications after the Perpetual Emigrating Fund was established later that year.[16]

In the meantime, Congress had entered serious debates concerning the organization of the Mexican Cession. The extension of slavery into this vast area, what apostle Wilford Woodruff called the "great bone of contention," was at the very heart of these discussions.[17] On December 5, 1848, President Polk declared in his last annual message to Congress that it was a "solemn duty to provide with the least practicable delay for New Mexico and California regularly organized Territorial governments." Nevertheless, Polk came out strongly against the Wilmot Proviso. Although he preferred a congressional policy of "noninterference" in regard to slavery, he suggested continuing the Missouri Compromise line all the way to the Pacific, or even submitting the question to the Supreme Court.[18]

Just eight days later, Senator Thomas Hart Benton introduced a petition from the people of New Mexico asking for a territorial government that was free of slavery. This memorial was immediately opposed by pro-slavery Senator John C. Calhoun.[19] If the Saints wanted a government of their own in the Great Basin, it was clear that they needed to take proactive steps soon. However, this likewise meant that they would need to determine how to address the fraught issue of slavery. As the debate continued in Congress, the Mormon leadership vacillated between publicly supporting free soil in the Great Basin or adopting an outward neutrality toward slavery reminiscent of Joseph Smith's policy in Missouri after the expulsion from Jackson County.

Brigham Young had considered a territorial government to be essential for the welfare of the Latter-day Saints since the summer of 1846. For two years, the Mormon leadership had made tentative moves in that direction, aided by the counsel and political influence of Thomas L. Kane, a well-connected philanthropist from Philadelphia.[20] Some top Mormons, such as Willard Richards, advocated the creation of a state government instead.[21] But on December 9, 1848, three months after Young permanently settled in Great Salt Lake City, the reconstituted Council of Fifty voted to petition Congress to create a territory called "Deseret." In early July 1849, the Council suddenly determined that a state government would indeed be preferable. This change in tack was almost certainly precipitated by a letter from Kane who had personally met with President Polk the previous November. In this letter (now lost) Kane likely advised the Mormons that under a territorial organization, Polk would appoint unsympathetic carpetbag officials to govern them rather than men from their own community.[22] Although a member of the Free-Soil Party and a professed opponent of slavery, Kane advised the Saints to take no position on the slavery question.[23] Over the next several weeks, the Council of Fifty hastily drafted a constitution for the State of Deseret, a second memorial to Congress, and produced fictitious minutes for a constitutional convention that had never taken place. Almon W. Babbitt was selected as delegate to Congress and left with the documents before the end of the month.[24]

Neither the original petition for a territorial government nor the subsequent Constitution of Deseret mentioned slavery in the least. Whether or not the Mormon leadership had received a prior warning from Thomas Kane, they clearly understood that taking an affirmative stance on slavery could damage their prospects for local rule. In November 1849, Woodruff explained to Kane that the Saints did not "wish to have anything to do with the 'vexed question of Slavery'. . . and therefore we deemed it expedient not to introduce a clause into our Constitution prohibiting the introduction of Slaves into the State of Deseret."[25] Given the furor over slavery in the United States, such obfuscation was neither surprising nor unique. When California presented a state constitution to Congress that prohibited slavery that same year, the accompanying petition meekly explained that this provision resulted "not so much from the prejudices against the system . . . as from a universal conviction that in no portion of California is the climate and soil of a character adapted to slave labor."[26] Kane heartily agreed with the Mormons' course of action, telling Woodruff and John Bernhisel that it "will not do for you to take the slavery question or Antislavery or any other side but the nutral [sic]. . . . We may have to favor the South some though they are your Enemies and I hate to do it."[27] Still, Woodruff assured Kane that slavery would "never be tolerated" in Deseret.[28]

The problem was that over the previous two years, Southern Latter-day Saints had brought approximately fifty-five enslaved African Americans to the vicinity of the Salt Lake Valley. The vast majority arrived in the fall of 1848 with two companies of Saints from Mississippi. By this time, the High Council had still not enacted any regulations governing slavery, and it does not appear that Brigham Young and his counselors had even considered a comprehensive policy on the subject.[29]

Problems began to arise in the spring of 1849. In late March, just as the Saints were putting the last signatures on their memorial for a territorial government, Brigham Young was notified that two people of color had escaped from an outlying settlement. One young man "belonging" to Robert Smith, probably Rande, made his way to Great Salt Lake City and hid in the community with the aid of sympathetic Latter-day Saints. A man named Benjamin Matthews was sent to track this individual down. Suspicious that he was being hidden by a company that was preparing to leave for California, Matthews wrote to Young asking for instructions. Unfortunately, Young's reply, if any, has not survived, although Rande likely succeeded in freeing himself.[30]

Simultaneously, an unnamed young woman escaped from her enslaver, Francis McKown, and eventually came to Brigham Young's house. Rather than attempting to leave the Salt Lake Valley, this woman was frightened that her master was going to take her away, possibly back to Mississippi. Young wrote to McKown informing him of the situation. McKown responded that the girl was "Borne mine and I raised hur and it seems as though there was one out of the family ever since she has bin away." He promised that he would not "correct" the girl if she returned and asked that Young send her back under the care of William Hooper. Once again it is uncertain how the case was resolved, although it is likely that she returned to McKown and eventually accompanied him back to Mississippi. Still, these incidents must have weighed on Young's mind a few months later as he contemplated his position on slavery in Deseret.[31]

The available evidence indicates that despite cultivating a facade of neutrality toward slavery in their petitions to Congress, Young and his closest advisors were firmly opposed to legalizing the practice in the Mormon settlements. Nevertheless, they did not wish to be connected to the Wilmot Proviso or any other national antislavery schemes. When Almon Babbitt left Great Salt Lake City with the Deseret Constitution at the end of July 1849, the members of the Mormon First Presidency sent several letters that outlined their opinion concerning slavery. On July 19, Young wrote privately to John Bernhisel: "In regard to slavery, free soil, &c ... I can only say that to the latter principle we are favorably disposed, and adverse to the former, nevertheless we do not wish a prohibitory clause [such as the Wilmot Proviso] to attach itself to our Territory in relation to that subject."[32]

The same day, Young wrote a letter to apostle Orson Hyde. Hyde presided at Kanesville, Iowa where he published the *Frontier Guardian*, a Mormon newspaper. Young's statements to Hyde were meant for publication and represented the official policy of the Church. He wrote, "In regard to the Wilmot Proviso, Slavery, &c, we wish you distinctly to understand, that our desire is to leave that subject to the operations of time, circumstances and common law, you might safely say [crossed out] that as a people we are averse to slavery, but that we wish not to meddle with this subject, but leave things to take their natural course."[33]

Young's allusion to common law was repeated in a letter from Willard Richards to Thomas Kane a few days later, and in an issue of the *Frontier Guardian* that Hyde published in September.[34] That same month, Young and his two counselors once again made the point in a letter to apostle Amasa Lyman, writing that "the Wilmot proviso and such like things properly belong to common law, and not to constitutions."[35] These references to common law in the context of slavery were highly meaningful and far from neutral in their implications.[36]

Since the famous *Somerset* case of 1772, it had been widely believed in both England and America that common law did not recognize the institution of chattel slavery. Rather, slavery required the sanction of positive law, that is, some kind of legislative act. Without a statute, slavery could not legally exist within a given jurisdiction. No such regulations existed in Deseret, and Young had made it clear that none would be forthcoming. In other words, the highest-ranking members of the Mormon hierarchy were communicating their belief that Deseret was legally free soil and would remain so without the need for any statutory or constitutional provision to that effect.[37]

This position was reiterated in a number of circumstances over the next several years. For instance, in September 1850, a traveler named Asa Call who had spent time in Great Salt Lake City wrote a letter to the editor of the *National Era*, an abolitionist newspaper in Washington, D.C. He explained that Deseret had "no legislation on the subject of slavery . . . and [the Mormons] very sensibly conclude that slavery can have no legal existence where it has never been legalized." According to Call, no less a figure than Brigham Young had personally assured him that "the idea of property in men would not be entertained a moment by any court in this State."[38]

Be that as it may, at the end of August 1849, a new opportunity arose to secure local rule that required a firmer declaration concerning slavery. The previous March, General Zachary Taylor had succeeded James Polk as president. Taylor was eager to remove the poisonous question of slavery in the Mexican Cession from Congress. He therefore formulated a plan to bring all of California, including the Mormon settlements, immediately into the Union as a state and bypass the territorial phase. This would theoretically leave the question of slavery to the inhabitants of the region. To further this plan, Taylor dispatched General John Wilson to Great Salt Lake City as his personal representative. Wilson explained to Brigham Young and his counselors that although Taylor personally owned slaves, he was willing that California should enter the Union as a free state to further "the public good." However, in order to accomplish that goal, Taylor believed that the Latter-day Saints in the Great Basin needed to "counterbalance" the influence of pro-slavery men on the West Coast.[39]

The Mormon leadership quickly agreed to Wilson's proposal insofar as they received a guarantee that Deseret would be divided from the remainder of California to form an independent state within two years. Based on these terms, they appointed Wilson and Amasa Lyman, already in California, as delegates for Deseret. The First Presidency wrote to Lyman that they preferred the question of slavery to be settled by the common law rather than a constitutional prohibition. Nevertheless, Lyman was free to accept such a provision. Indeed, Young and his counselors were convinced that "should the Wilmot Proviso, or slave question, by any means, become settled before our admission into the Union, politicians might feel themselves more independent, and our interest might not lay so near their hearts."[40]

The plan was doomed to failure, however. By the time Wilson left Great Salt Lake City in early September, a convention to establish a state government for California was already in progress. In October, the Monterrey convention finalized a constitution that prohibited slavery in the land between the Sierra Nevadas and the Pacific coast. Wilson was caught by a winter storm in the mountains and did not finally arrive in San Francisco until December. Nevertheless, in January 1850, Lyman and Wilson presented the so-called Deseret Petition to the governor of California. In it, they requested a new convention to form a state that included the entire province of Alta California. In regard to slavery, the petition explained that while "there is a respectable minority of the people of the [Salt Lake] Valley in favor of Slavery, still a very large majority are opposed to it; and therefore the delegates feel themselves instructed to vote for a provision in the Constitution prohibiting Slavery for ever." But having just organized a government, the California legislature was not about to do it again in order to accommodate a community situated over 400 miles away. Consequently, the legislature rejected the Deseret Petition the following month.[41]

On the other side of the continent, Almon Babbitt and John Bernhisel were busy lobbying Congress on behalf of Deseret, while Orson Hyde continued to write occasional articles in the *Frontier Guardian* describing the Mormons' position on slavery. Both Bernhisel and Hyde dutifully followed the strategy outlined by Thomas Kane and the First Presidency: official neutrality toward slavery with adherence to the free-soil principle as the practical result. In January 1850, Hyde editorialized that the Deseret Constitution had made no mention of slavery because the Saints "view these questions as a prolific source of bitterness and strife, the agitation of which would tend to sour and alienate the feelings of our own people one against another."[42] Two months later, Bernhisel informed Brigham Young that he had "made it a *point*, not only during my travels last Summer and fall, but since my arrival in Washington, *not* to make *slavery* nor politics a *point*; and I am happy to be able to inform you that this course has met the approbation and sanction of our best friends both in and out of Congress."[43] When pressed by various congressmen to provide a more explicit answer in regard to slavery, Bernhisel retreated to the widely accepted "natural limits" argument, which held that Deseret was geographically unsuited for slave labor, and thus, slavery could not exist in the state. The Monterrey convention had used the same argument to explain the prohibition of slavery found in the California constitution. Furthermore, Bernhisel reported to Young that "a large majority of the members of both branches of Congress, and a vast majority of the jurists in the United States, entertain the conviction that slavery does not, and cannot exist in the Territory of Deseret, without the sanction of positive law, yet to be enacted."[44] This was essentially the same position that the Mormon leadership had adopted in the summer of 1849, although it was based on a separate legal theory. While Brigham Young and his associates had relied upon antislavery interpretations of the common law, it was widely believed in Washington that Mexican prohibitions on slavery were still operative in the Cession lands and would remain in force until replaced. Unsurprisingly, this notion was vociferously opposed by pro-slavery Southerners, and it became the subject of heated debates in Congress.[45]

In all his conversations, Bernhisel carefully avoided acknowledging the fact that dozens of enslaved African Americans were then living and working in the Salt Lake Valley. Almon Babbitt, however, went in quite the opposite direction. To the disgust of Thomas Kane, Babbitt attempted to ingratiate himself with Southern congressmen by declaring that Deseret was "ultra pro-slavery" and up to 400 slaves were held in the Mormon settlements.[46] These flagrant exaggerations were dismissed by Congress and badly hurt Babbitt's credibility. Representative James Brooks of New York argued that the Mormons "as a mass, abhor slavery almost with a religious fanaticism—and ... are emigrants, not from the slave States, but from Old England, Ohio, New York, Pennsylvania, and the Northwest, all non-slaveholding regions." Following the logic of "natural limits," Brooks believed that the "negro can no more work for his master, and prosper in Utah, than in Canada or in Maine. It is a soil that demands irrigation; the farms are, and are intended to be, small." According to Brooks, there "may be a few officers of the army with their servants [in Utah], perhaps a few others. There are, no doubt, in my own city [of New York] just now, from eight hundred to one thousand slaves this traveling season."[47] As to Babbitt's claims, Brooks thought that perhaps the representative from Deseret was "riding a little on both sides. . . . Some four hundred slaves will be good for the South, and the soil and the climate, and the character of the people, will do for the North."[48]

Such perceptions were ultimately beneficial for the Latter-day Saints. As part of the Compromise of 1850, Congress finally organized Utah as a territory under the principle of popular sovereignty. New Mexico was likewise organized as a territory under popular sovereignty, while California was admitted to the Union as a free state. Popular sovereignty was a deceptively simple concept. It held that the residents of a territory should have the authority to decide for themselves whether slavery would be legal. As Lewis Cass wrote in December 1847, congressional power "should be limited to the creation of proper governments for new countries, acquired or settled, and to the necessary provision for their eventual admission into the Union; leaving, in the meantime, to the people inhabiting them, to regulate their internal concerns in their own way." Cass further indicated that he was "opposed to the exercise of any jurisdiction by Congress over [slavery]; and I am in favor of leaving to the people of any territory, which may be hereafter acquired, the right to regulate it for themselves, under the general principles of the Constitution."[49]

Popular sovereignty had ample precedent in various American territories over the previous sixty years.[50] The model had nevertheless grown objectionable to both pro- and antislavery partisans. As a result, the contours of popular sovereignty were purposely left vague in the final legislation.

The organic acts that created Utah and New Mexico Territories stated that each would be admitted to the Union "with or without slavery, as their constitution may prescribe at the time of their admission." Their territorial legislatures were granted authority to pass laws "regarding all rightful subjects of legislation, consistent with the Constitution of the United States and the provisions of this act." Still, Congress retained the power to nullify territorial statutes. Finally, any court case in the territories "involving title to slaves" was appealable to the U.S. Supreme Court, as were appeals based upon "any writ of habeas corpus involving the question of personal freedom."[51]

Although the acts specified that the citizens of Utah and New Mexico would eventually be able to decide whether slavery was legal within their boundaries, they did not specify at what moment that such a decision was to be made. Some contemporaries argued that the territorial legislatures could immediately exclude slavery by statute, while others contended that slavery could not be excluded from the territories until they drafted constitutions and were admitted to the Union as states. Still others believed that since slavery had been abolished in the region under Mexican law, the institution could not be legalized in the Mexican Cession without affirmative action on the part of Congress or the territorial legislatures.[52] Rather than providing clear answers, Congress deferred to the Supreme Court to make a final determination on the status of slavery in Utah and New Mexico.[53] This did not finally occur until 1857 when the Supreme Court handed down the infamous *Dred Scott* decision. In it, Chief Justice Roger Taney declared that neither Congress nor a territorial government had the authority to prohibit slavery in a territory prior to its admission to the Union as a state.[54]

In 1850, however, many congressmen accepted popular sovereignty largely because they did not believe that settlers in New Mexico or Utah would ever adopt slavery. John Bernhisel later wrote to Brigham Young that

> the members of Congress from the non-slaveholding States were so fully determined not "to bow the knee to the dark spirit of slavery," that if they had believed that there were even half a dozen slaves in Utah, or that slavery would ever be tolerated in it, they would not have granted us a Territorial organization, nor can our Territory ever be admitted as a State into the Union, unless our constitution contain[s] a clause prohibiting the introduction of slavery.[55]

Bernhisel was so thoroughly convinced that any hint of slavery would scuttle the Saints' chances for self-government that he had previously written Young to urge that "no person of African descent be reported as a slave" during the upcoming federal census. Bernhisel no doubt wished to disguise the fact that there were indeed enslaved or formerly enslaved people in Utah and certainly more than half a dozen. However, his stated motive for this request was legal rather than political. As he had done on previous occasions, Bernhisel reminded Young that a large number of legislators and jurists believed that slavery could not exist in any portion of the Mexican Cession "without the sanction of positive law, yet to be enacted."[56] In other words, no one in Utah could lawfully be held as a slave.

Many Latter-day Saints fully agreed with this proposition, including Brigham Young. Bernhisel not unreasonably concluded that if no one could be held as a slave, it followed that no one should be counted as a slave on the census. But to the chagrin of Bernhisel, the Utah census ultimately reported some twenty-six slaves and twenty-four free Black people in the territory. It further stated that all the slaves were "on their way to California."[57] This was both true and misleading. Most of the twenty-six individuals enumerated on the census were in fact members of an expedition that left Utah in March 1851 to build a Mormon colony at San Bernardino, California. But this was an undercount of the actual enslaved population of the territory. In fairness, Utah was not unique in this regard. California did not report a single slave on its 1850 census return, although hundreds of enslaved people were then laboring in the gold fields.[58]

In January 1851, there were fifty-four to fifty-seven enslaved African Americans and approximately thirty free Black people living in and around the Salt Lake Valley.[59] Brigham Young himself counted two free people of color as members of his household. When the San Bernardino company departed for California two months later, it included almost half of the total enslaved population. By the summer of 1851, roughly thirty enslaved people remained in the Mormon settlements distributed in pockets across four counties. This number would remain relatively stable for the next decade. The total number of enslaved people in Utah was quite small, both in absolute and relative terms. The free state of California boasted anywhere between 400–1,500 enslaved African Americans. New Jersey still held over 200 apprentices for life. Up until this point, the Latter-day Saints had still made no effort to enact legislation in regard to slavery. Instead, they continued to function under a laissez-faire arrangement that had emerged over the last four years. This policy reflected an overriding desire to avoid external scrutiny as well as internal dissension.

Since the summer of 1849, Brigham Young, Willard Richards, Wilford Woodruff, and other Mormon leaders had indicated their belief that chattel slavery was illegal in the Great Basin and would not be recognized by any local court. Still, they were apparently willing to allow the small minority of slave owners to exercise some form of de facto authority over their enslaved workers. This state of affairs was noted by outside observers. After returning from his sojourn with the Mormons over the winter of 1849–1850, John W. Gunnison of the Topographical Engineers wrote that in Utah, "Involuntary labor by negroes is recognised by custom; those holding slaves, keep them as part of their family, as they would wives, without any law on the subject."[60] Based on his conversations with Brigham Young in the fall of 1850, Asa Call likewise reported that the Latter-day Saints had refused to codify slavery through positive law. As a result he believed that the "few black persons ... in the valley, who have been sent in by, and who still live with, their former masters ... are not considered as *slaves*."[61]

Soon after Utah was officially organized as a territory, Orson Hyde provided a detailed description of this policy. On December 11, 1850, Hyde wrote in the *Frontier Guardian*: "There are several men in the Valley of the Salt Lake from the Southern States, who have their slaves with them. There is no law in Utah to authorize Slavery, neither any to prohibit it. If the slave is disposed to leave his master," Hyde explained, "no power exists there, either legal or moral that will prevent him. But if the slave choose to remain with his master; none are allowed to interfere between the master and the slave."[62]

Hyde then outlined a policy for Southern enslavers who converted to the Latter-day Saint faith and desired to gather in the Great Basin. "When a man in the Southern States embraces our faith and is the owner of slaves, the church says to him, if your slaves wish to remain with you, and to go with you, put them not away; but if they choose to leave you, or are not satisfied to remain with you, it is for you to sell them, or to let them go free, as your own conscience may direct you." It was a matter of individual choice as Hyde described it. But in doing so, he failed to account for the lack of freedom enslaved people had to actually make such choices. He also failed to account for the financial investment enslaved people represented to their enslavers, a built-in deterrent against enslavers giving their enslaved the type of choices Hyde described. In any case his explanation was also designed to shift accountability for the practice of slavery in Utah Territory away from Latter-day Saint leaders and toward Southern enslavers. "The church on this point, assumes not the responsibility to direct. The laws of the land recognize slavery,—we do not wish to oppose the laws of the country. If there is sin in selling a slave, let the individual who sells him, bear that sin, and not the church."[63]

In his editorial, Hyde publicly disclosed a compromise that the leaders of the Church had fashioned in regard to slavery since their arrival in the Salt Lake Valley. After a year of embarrassing questions from Congress that were alternately met with obfuscation from John Bernhisel or pro-slavery bluster from Almon Babbitt, it was time to set the record straight and provide much needed guidance to the Mormon faithful. In many ways, however, the compromise that Hyde outlined was merely a reformulation of policies that dated to the Jackson County persecutions.[64]

After the murder of Joseph Smith, Brigham Young and his associates were convinced that self-government was absolutely essential to ensure the long-term safety of the Latter-day Saints. With this goal firmly in mind, they believed that there was nothing to be gained by taking a public stand against slavery as Smith had done during his presidential campaign. The Deseret Petition was, of course, a conspicuous exception. Thomas Kane and other Mormon allies had consistently advised the Saints to pursue a neutral approach while petitioning Congress for a state government. At the same time that Mormon leaders were attempting to deflect the attention of external critics, they refused to court an internal rift between Latter-day Saints by demanding that Mormon enslavers free their slaves in order to remain in good fellowship. Smith had never gone so far even after he espoused a national gradual emancipation plan.

Consequently, Hyde's article took an essentially neutral posture toward the "peculiar institution" and emphasized that the Latter-day Saints would obey all relevant laws, presumably including the Fugitive Slave Act. Hyde wrote that Mormon enslavers who lived in slave states could continue to hold their slaves and even sell them if the slaves were "not satisfied to remain" with their masters, and if the enslavers could harmonize such action with their own conscience. Furthermore, he admitted that enslavers who migrated to Utah were permitted to keep their enslaved workers as dependent laborers as long as the workers consented to the arrangement. But Hyde also affirmed that Brigham Young and the central leadership of the Church were fundamentally opposed to chattel slavery. Where Latter-day Saints held political power, as in Utah, they would not recognize either a legal or moral right to hold property in man, except as required by federal law.[65]

Hyde's editorial at once acknowledged the presence of enslaved people in the Mormon settlements while denying that they were actually held as slaves. His central argument was that an enslaver had no cognizable property interest in his enslaved workers once they settled in Utah Territory. Hyde maintained that as a matter of law, such relationships were entirely based on the consent of the slave. Under Hyde's theory, if an enslaved person came to Utah and did not openly complain about her situation, a master could continue to yield significant authority over her like any other dependent member of a household. But if a person of color initiated some kind of freedom suit against her master or attempted to leave, Hyde strongly implied that she would be granted liberty by a local court.[66]

For Hyde, as for Young, it was no contradiction to permit masters to continue to exercise authority over their enslaved workers while insisting that those workers were not, in fact, slaves. In their minds, the exercise of authority over a person of color was not synonymous with slavery. Indeed, the exercise of authority was a necessary and valid function within a well-ordered society. Parents exercised authority over their children, masters exercised authority over their servants, priesthood leaders exercised authority over the body of the church, and God exercised authority over all. Hyde and Young still clung to traditional social norms that held that some members of the community were suited to exercise authority while others were not. In their view, the head of a household could legitimately exercise considerable authority over a servant or a dependent without that person sinking to the level of a slave. Slavery was instead defined by two conditions: the reduction of a person to alienable property, and a lack of consent to the relationship.

In this context, however, the nature of consent was itself a fraught question. Contemporary courts frequently wrestled over the capacity of enslaved or formerly enslaved people to make decisions that could affect their legal status. As early as the 1820s, the Supreme Court of Illinois held that to offer an enslaved person a choice between remaining in a state of slavery or entering a long-term indenture contract was not an authentic choice and therefore constituted involuntary servitude. Yet this contradicted long-standing practice in jurisdictions such as Pennsylvania, where enslaved persons who migrated to the state were permitted to enter indenture contracts with their masters precisely because it offered them a chance for freedom. Courts in free jurisdictions often permitted enslaved people who were otherwise entitled to liberty to voluntarily return to a slave jurisdiction with their masters if they demonstrated a genuine desire to do so. There were many reasons that a slave might make such a seemingly inexplicable decision. In some instances, these individuals stated a preference to remain with their masters or to return to enslaved spouses or other relatives. As late as 1855, a court in Ohio permitted two slaves who would have been freed under local law to travel with their enslaver back to Kentucky after determining that their "request was perfectly sincere and made with a full knowledge of its consequences."[67] The next year, a California court recognized that a formerly enslaved woman could choose to accompany her former master to Texas and risk re-enslavement as long as she fully understood the nature of her decision.[68] At other times, especially in the case of children, courts in free jurisdictions would overrule the stated preferences of an enslaved person and forcibly separate him or her from an enslaver.[69]

Orson Hyde presumed that an enslaved person had the moral capacity to choose to accompany her master to Utah. She had the ability to consent.

Hyde did not discuss how an enslaved person should indicate that consent, nor the manner in which an enslaver should present his enslaved workers with such a choice. He did not deliberate on the pressures or threats that an enslaved person might endure while making such a decision. Nor did he consider the extreme difficulty of legally emancipating slaves in the South even if an enslaver had been so inclined. He spoke instead in broad concepts and ideals that may have had little to do with the day-to-day realities faced by enslaved people. Hyde was crystal clear in one respect, however. Once an enslaver had come to Utah, Hyde affirmed that he could no longer use the law to retain possession of his slaves as property.

Putting such a policy into practice was predictably messy and full of contradictions. It required enslaved African Americans to effectively assert their own rights or for white allies to intervene on their behalf. Although Young and Hyde communicated their views regarding slavery to other white Latter-day Saint leaders and to influential political allies, there is no indication that they described their philosophy to Utah's Black enslaved people. Moreover, they made no attempt to organize an antislavery society to coordinate freedom suits such as those that successfully freed enslaved people in the East.[70]

At present, there are only a handful of known cases in which a Utah court had to consider the status of an enslaved or formerly enslaved person. The most important, the Luján case, occurred over the winter of 1851–1852 and will be discussed in detail below. Moreover, after 1849, there are very few documented cases in which an enslaved person in Utah either attempted to escape servitude or sought outside intervention. What little evidence is available suggests that this policy was usually administered informally rather than through the courts, and with an eye toward maintaining social harmony. To this end, it was not unusual for Brigham Young to become personally involved in mediating disputes that arose between enslaver and enslaved. Moreover, while some Latter-day Saint enslavers may have sought the consent of their enslaved workers to remain with them, others still spoke in the language of ownership and property rights. In fact, in the few surviving probate registrations, Latter-day Saint enslavers often used words such as "owner" "slave" and "for life" to assert control over those whom they enslaved.[71]

In March 1851, Young was called upon to address some of these knotty problems. A party of Latter-day Saints was then preparing to leave the Salt Lake Valley to build a colony in San Bernardino, California. This party included a large number of Southern Mormons and a significant proportion of the territory's enslaved population. Included in this company were Green Flake and Hark Wales (often referred to as Hark Lay). Both men were members of the original pioneer company of 1847. Although Brigham Young had allegedly declared them free, they still remained in the service of their enslavers. Prior to the departure of the San Bernardino expedition, Green and Hark personally visited Brigham Young to ask for his help. It is likely that during this meeting, Green and Hark outlined a series of concerns stemming from the pending expedition to California. These were later documented in an exchange of letters between Young and William Crosby, a leading member of the company.[72]

On March 12, Crosby wrote to Young asking for his advice. Crosby acknowledged the meeting that had occurred between Green, Hark, and Young and stated he was writing on behalf of Hark's enslaver (and Crosby's brother-in-law), William Lay. According to Crosby, Hark had expressed a willingness to accompany his master to California. But Hark was married to a woman named Nancy who was then pregnant and enslaved to George W. Bankhead. Bankhead was then in California, and Nancy was left under the supervision of Bankhead's brother, John. Hark naturally wished Nancy to come with them. However, John refused to allow Nancy to leave unless Lay purchased her for cash, something Lay was unable to do. In truth, Hark's family was not the only family that would potentially be broken up by the move. Under the circumstances, Lay wished Young to tell him whether he should take Hark to California. Concurrently, Crosby reported that Green had grown disobedient toward his enslaver Agnes Flake, a widow suffering from tuberculosis. He therefore suggested that Green should be conveyed to another master if Young could make the appropriate arrangements.[73]

Young was faced with a dilemma. He fundamentally objected to treating Nancy or any other person of color as alienable property to be bought and sold. Yet he also wished to maintain harmony within the fragile Mormon community and keep enslaved families together. He therefore tried to chart a middle course. The same day, Young wrote Crosby plainly that "we do not wish to encourage the sale of Blacks in these vallies." Moreover, he strongly objected to forcibly separating "Man and wife." Even William Lay apparently had doubts about this course of action. At this point, Young might have reminded Crosby that under Utah law, neither Lay, Bankhead, or Flake could assert legal title to any of these individuals. But Young was not looking for a fight and was highly averse to litigation in any case. Instead, in Solomonic fashion, he suggested several possible solutions to keep Hark and his wife together: Lay might take Green and leave Hark in Utah; or Green might stay in Utah with John Bankhead while Bankhead would release Hark's wife to go to California and provide the widow Agnes Flake with some kind of "consideration" for her loss. Finally, Young tried to defuse the situation by pointing out that all the affected parties would be free once they arrived in California, so there was no cause to be "very strenuous to take many of them to that country."[74]

Young's letter initiated a series of exchanges between enslavers in an effort to keep several enslaved families together. For unknown reasons, Hark ultimately went to California while Nancy remained in Utah. However, in another agreement, an unnamed enslaved man belonging to John Bankhead joined the San Bernardino company to stay with his wife, Mary, who was also enslaved. Bankhead later expressed deep dissatisfaction with this arrangement. On the other hand, Green Flake remained in Utah although Bankhead refused to accept responsibility for him. Instead, hoping to provide some needed financial support to the widow Agnes, and perhaps to make good on his earlier promises to Green, Brigham Young purchased or rented Green's labor for a year. After this time, Young freed Green from all future obligations. Two other enslaved women belonging to William Crosby, Rose (possibly Green's wife) and her mother, Violet, also remained in Utah and were freed due to Young's intervention. In 1854, Rose gave birth to a child she named Daniel Freeman to celebrate their emancipation.[75]

This episode illustrates all of the complexities and paradoxes of the Mormon compromise. While slavery, in the absence of positive law establishing the practice, was presumably illegal in Utah, most Mormon masters continued to treat Black people as slaves. At the same time, Brigham Young rejected the concept of property in man. He was aghast that families might be forcibly separated from one another and personally freed Green Flake, Rose, and Violet. But he felt compelled to compensate the widow Agnes for the loss of Green's labor. Latter-day Saint leaders taught that enslaved people must consent to continued service. But to avoid conflict, Young did not demand that the Bankheads immediately free Hark's wife to join her husband in California. The Mormon policy, much like the national Compromise of 1850, was a desperate attempt to hold together people of different social backgrounds raised with different values. Although Young and his colleagues genuinely cared about the plight of enslaved African Americans, these concerns were sometimes subordinated to the interests of stability and in ways that favored white enslavers over Black enslaved.

In February 1851, roughly a month before the San Bernardino company left for California, Thomas Kane wrote to Young and urged him to keep up a pretense of neutrality toward slavery and continue to handle any cases that arose informally. "I am good authority, here," Kane wrote, "for my feelings are strongly Anti-Slavery, and my impulse unstaid by my judgment, would be strong to have you declare yourselves, especially when I hear you misrepresented on this question." As Kane well knew, the recent organization of Utah Territory under popular sovereignty ostensibly provided the Saints with the opportunity to immediately enact legislation prohibiting slavery. But Kane believed that the political stakes were simply too high if the Saints wished Utah to be admitted to the Union as an independent state. He therefore advised Young "not only to avoid passing Legislative Resolutions in reference to Slavery; but to manage all your affairs affecting it, *without unnecessary legislation.*" If it was necessary to prevent "some one calling himself an owner, depriving a negro or other person of his liberty under color of law, there is no necessity of such action being governmental, so as to declare your sentiments as an organized Society. Other and quiet arrangements are just as efficient as those which can become political manifestoes in the hands of strangers."[76] Kane would probably have wished Young to take stronger action in the case of Hark Wales and his wife. But his letter reinforced Young's instinct to handle these questions internally and without recourse to the courts.

* * *

After the San Bernardino party left for California, the slavery question momentarily receded into the background as Governor Brigham Young began to organize a territorial government. He probably received Kane's letter sometime in late spring. Around the same time, he received another letter from James Monroe, a former schoolteacher in Nauvoo, informing him that there was currently "considerable prejudice existing against [the Latter-day Saints] under the supposition of Indian Slavery at the Valley which has been forwarded by the Abolitionists and others. Mr. Cooper [the Indian Agent for Utah] received instructions from the Department at Washington to inquire into the matter and use all his authority for its suppression if he found it existed." Monroe further reported that Cooper "has conversed with several individuals from the Valley in relation to it, and has written to the Dept that he has ascertained that there are some Indian women there, who have been received and protected by the Mormons, who labor for their board but not as slaves, putting the thing in a very favorable light."77

Notwithstanding this seemingly positive resolution, Young was angry. On several occasions over the past two years, he had stipulated that he was in favor of free soil and an opponent of chattel slavery. But Young did not have much use for abolitionists, especially those of the Garrisonian persuasion. An alleged connection with abolitionism had precipitated the Jackson County persecutions almost twenty years before. Now, it appeared that the abolitionists were actively stirring up trouble for the Latter-day Saints. As Young often did, he vented his feelings during his Sunday sermon. On June 1 he told an audience in the Bowery, "there is a great Excitement in the world about slavery & the Abolitionest are vary fearful that we shall have the Negro or Indian as Slaves Here. We have a few [Indians] that were prisioners [sic] that we have bought to save their lives," Young admitted. "But what will the Abolitionest do? If you owe them a dollar they will Jog you up. Neither will they liberate the slave by buying them & setting them free. The Master of Slaves will be damned if they Abuse their slaves," he insisted. "Yet the Seed of Ham will be servants untill God takes the Curse off from them. But they are not all the Slaves their is in the world. The whole world are Slaves to sin & wickedness & passion.... I Have two Blacks. They are as free as I am," he declared. "Shall we lay a foundation for Negro Slavery? No God forbid. And I forbid. I say let us be free."78

Young's sermon touched on many of the themes that would characterize his teachings on slavery for the next decade. It also presented the contradictions in his own thinking that have befuddled and frustrated modern readers. In his oration, Young roundly condemned abolitionists, not because they were opposed to slavery, but because they demanded immediate, uncompensated emancipation. Whatever Young's personal feelings concerning property in man, he believed that this uncompromising attitude was a source of division and conflict.79 In contrast, Young claimed that Latter-day Saints bought Indian slaves to "save their lives." Young bought Green Flake's labor and then he freed him. In the future, he would attempt to do the same thing with other enslaved Black people. Joseph Smith's gradual emancipation plan had likewise been premised on providing compensation to enslavers, and antislavery moderates such as Abraham Lincoln would advocate similar policies even in the midst of a civil war. Young had no patience for the Garrisonians because he believed that they would not put their money where their mouth was. He more closely emulated the eighteenth-century Quakers who made emancipation a personal responsibility. At the same time, Young strongly opposed the legalization of chattel slavery in Utah. His position since the summer of 1849 was that the Great Basin was free soil, and he was not about to "lay a foundation for Negro Slavery."[80]

Despite his antislavery instincts, Young's sermon demonstrates that he fully believed in the curse of Canaan dogma, here conflated with the curse of Ham. Moreover, Young expressly connected the curse with servitude for people of African descent. This was entirely unexceptional. For centuries, Muslims, Christians, and Jews had all used the curse of Canaan as a justification for African slavery.[81] In the 1850s, the curse was still commonly referenced in American polemics defending the practice. It is difficult to reconcile Young's commitment to freedom on the one hand with an overriding belief in the servility of Black people on the other. From time to time, Young's comments regarding the curse of Canaan even made it appear that he theoretically supported slavery. Young never attempted to resolve these incongruities, nor did he articulate his position with any sort of precision or completeness. But upon inspection, a rough consistency can be discerned within his jumbled philosophy.

When Young spoke of Black people as servants, he was not voicing support for chattel slavery; that is, the ownership of one human being by another. Young fundamentally opposed the idea of property in man and said so repeatedly. Instead, Young had a conception of African servitude that is perhaps best described as subordination or dependence. In essence, Young imagined that the curse of Canaan subjected Black people to a kind of public guardianship. This guardianship could be exercised within a household or by society at large. In either case, Black people assumed a quasi-dependent status in relationship to white people. Young believed that in certain circumstances, this status could be expressed as a legally enforceable relationship such as apprenticeship or indentured servitude. Indeed, Young, a former apprentice, had no inherent objection to the practice of unfree labor in a variety of circumstances. Still, Young was most comfortable with a kind of informal guardianship or dependency that existed within the context of a Latter-day Saint family.

Benevolent paternalism was always Young's preferred method of social control. This did not require explicit codes or restraints. It was freedom in a legal sense. Young was perfectly serious when he stated that he had two Black people in his household, Jane Manning James and Isaac James, who were free. Green Flake, Rose, and Violet were likewise free, or soon would be at Young's instigation. The prophet insisted that these individuals were people and not property. But they were still to some degree dependents, much like women and children. For Young, the service mandated by the curse of Canaan did not imply ownership. Rather, it entailed a fully integrated yet subordinate position within a social and religious hierarchy. Young firmly believed that one day God would lift the curse and Black people would receive the same privileges as other races. But until that time came, they would remain dependent members of society.

Young's attitudes concerning slavery and race placed him within the mainstream of Northern public opinion, especially for the generation that came of age during the 1810s and 1820s. Young objected to chattel slavery, yet his instincts favored gradual emancipation rather than the immediatism of the Garrisonians. Like many of his contemporaries, Young also concluded that African Americans were not prepared to fully participate in civic life. He attributed this disability to a biblical curse rather than to biology or some kind of environmental explanation. Even so, Young subscribed to the notion espoused by the first generation of abolitionists that people of color were susceptible to moral and intellectual improvement. As a result, he believed that sympathetic white people should educate Black people and prepare them for a time when God would lift the curse. In place of slavery, Young substituted paternalism.

Young's idiosyncratic version of the curse of Canaan was consistent with the policies outlined by Orson Hyde the previous December. In Utah, the Saints would not legally recognize property in man. Nevertheless, enslavers could continue to hold their slaves informally as dependents or servants. Young's sermon also signaled his approval of purchasing Indian slaves for humanitarian purposes. However, Young's denunciation of any attempt to "lay a foundation" for chattel slavery was powerful. His words may have merely been a heated response to accusations by the abolitionists. Yet they may also have been directed toward a domestic audience. Even after the departure of the San Bernardino company, there were still approximately thirty enslaved African Americans in the vicinity of the Salt Lake Valley. As of yet, enslavers had no legal mechanism to reclaim these individuals if they should escape or publicly demand their liberty. In fact, Young's intervention in the spring had resulted in the freeing of at least three enslaved people and the transfer of others. Enslavers such as John Bankhead had already voiced displeasure with the results. It is therefore possible that Young was responding to pressure from Mormon enslavers to legally secure their slave property. If so, he responded to them with a resounding "no."

Over the next several months, new territorial officials began to arrive in the Salt Lake Valley in order to form a government. In September, after a series of public and private disputes with Brigham Young, several of these officers left the territory, triggering a crisis. As this crisis slowly unfolded in Washington over the subsequent months, Young encountered a situation that finally convinced him to take positive legislative action in regard to slavery in Utah.

4
The Trial of Don Pedro León Luján

In the late fall of 1851, a Latter-day Saint posse in central Utah arrested a group of New Mexican traders led by Don Pedro León Luján.[1] The Mormons accused Luján and his companions of illegally engaging in the slave trade with members of the Ute tribe. In the aftermath of the U.S. war with Mexico, Luján attempted to reinvigorate a long-standing commercial relationship between New Mexican merchants and the western Ute; it was a relationship that often involved the human trafficking of Southern Paiute women and children. After two trials before a federal judge in Great Salt Lake City, the court found Luján and his company guilty of trading without a license, confiscated their goods, and freed the captive Paiutes.

These events formed the most immediate context for the passage of An Act for the Relief of Indian Slaves and Prisoners (originally titled An Act for the Protection of the Rights of Indians). In fact, many of the issues raised in the Luján trial spilled over into the debate over the Indian indenture bill as legislators grappled with a series of complex legal questions as well as difficult moral dilemmas. Yet the results of the trial were not limited to Indian servitude alone. The case ultimately convinced Brigham Young and other Latter-day Saint leaders that the legislature must legally define all unfree labor relationships in Utah Territory.

In North America, enslaving prisoners was a normal incident of Native American warfare, and sometimes its primary objective. Indians acquired war captives for a variety of reasons including social prestige, physical labor, kin replacement, marriage, and in some cases, human sacrifice. Slavery also functioned as an essential tool of Native diplomacy. The exchange of captives was often employed to cement a prospective alliance between two nations, and captives were vital for facilitating trade between disparate groups. In some cases, Indigenous people turned to slavery as a form of social welfare. It was not uncommon for impoverished Indians to sell themselves or family members into bondage to obtain food or access to beneficial kinship networks. The available evidence hints at an extensive pre-Columbian slave trade.[2]

Native Americans generally enslaved women and children while male captives were executed.[3] Unlike adult men, children were relatively easy to assimilate into a new culture, while female captives were an important source of both "productive and reproductive labor."[4] In many cases, Indian slaves were eventually integrated into their captors' societies through a structure of real or fictive kinship relationships. While not biologically related or officially adopted, for example, they may have been integrated into a family and been viewed as a son or daughter or as a sister or brother even though they were at once servants in the same household.[5] As historian James Brooks noted, it is extraordinarily difficult to draw a precise line between servitude and kinship within many Indigenous cultures. Captives could simultaneously be considered both kin and chattel.[6] Yet some captives, particularly older boys, remained slaves for life; permanently removed from the protective status of kin.[7]

Historian Brett Rushforth has emphasized that European colonists did not find "a benign form of captivity that they would transform into slavery."[8] Indigenous captivity practices were already violent and dehumanizing. Nevertheless, it is apparent that European settlement and the introduction of global market forces altered Native incentive structures and greatly increased the demand for slaves. The colonists were in constant need of cheap manual labor, which was necessary for everything from agriculture to domestic service. At the same time, Indians were eager to obtain a variety of manufactured products from the colonists. Consequently, many Indigenous peoples enriched themselves and enhanced their relative power by kidnapping a steady supply of captives and selling them to European buyers in exchange for guns and other trade goods.[9] American Indians also became involved in a number of lucrative commercial enterprises, such as the fur trade, that necessitated their own pool of captive labor for maximum profit.[10]

After the Spanish established the province of New Mexico in 1598, they practiced several forms of unfree labor that involved Native Americans. Many of these originated in Europe during the Reconquista, an 800-year holy war between Muslims and Spanish Christians that was marked by extensive slave taking on both sides.[11] As early as 1500, King Ferdinand and Queen Isabella of Spain expressly prohibited the enslavement of Indians.[12] This was followed by more comprehensive laws in 1542 and 1681.[13] But in frontier provinces like New Mexico, the Spanish frequently conducted punitive raids against nomadic tribes such as the Navajos, Comanches, and

Apache, which included taking captives. *Esclavos de guerra*, or war slaves, were held under the provisions of just war theory and bound to serve their new Spanish masters for up to twenty years.[14]

The Spanish also justified the purchase of Indigenous slaves from other Indians on humanitarian grounds. They argued that Native Americans often tortured or killed their captives.[15] In fact, this proved to be a highly effective sales technique.[16] In 1694, King Carlos II of Spain authorized New Mexican officials to use royal funds to buy Pawnee children who had been captured by Navajo raiders because the Navajos routinely killed those captives who were not purchased.[17] The Comanche used similar tactics in their interactions with Spanish colonizers. From the Spanish perspective, this violence served to rationalize the purchase of captive children, a custom they called *rescate*, or ransom.[18]

In New Mexico, the Spanish purchased Indian children to save their lives as well as to educate and Christianize them. In 1751, one Spanish official in Mexico City called the practice "laudable work" and defended it. "By means of this exchange these captive children can be educated and brought into the fold of this church, and if the traffic should discontinue, the Cumanches would kill them," the officer wrote.[19] As historian Pekka Hämäläinen explained, Comanche brutality "helped legitimize slave markets in Spanish eyes."[20] Yet by custom, Spanish benefactors insisted that *Indios de rescate* owed a debt to them that must be repaid by ten to twenty years of unfree labor.[21]

Because Indian servitude was not positively sanctioned by law, its practice in New Mexico was informal and varied according to time, place, and individual preference. Indian captives were conceived of as property that could be bought, sold, and inherited. Some were probably treated little better than slaves and were vulnerable to abuse. Indian captives were nevertheless legal persons who could hold property and testify in court.[22] Moreover, they were ultimately assimilated into the Hispanic community through baptism and fictive kinship relationships with their masters. During his 1852 trial in Great Salt Lake City, Don Pedro León Luján claimed that Indian captives were "adopted into the family of those who get them," and "as soon as they are baptized they cannot be sold anymore."[23] In New Mexico, as in local Indigenous societies, "kinship and ownership could overlap without contradiction."[24] After an extended period of unfree labor, Indian captives were typically freed although some kind of dependent relationship may have endured.[25]

By the early nineteenth century, Indian captivity in New Mexico was becoming increasingly difficult to disentangle from the contemporaneous practice of debt peonage that extended over poor Indians and poor Hispanics alike.[26] Peonage was a form of debt bondage in which an employer advanced an employee cash or goods in exchange for which the employee was bound to work for the employer until he or she could repay the debt.[27] Although peons could ostensibly repay their debt at any time, in practice, this was extraordinarily difficult. As a result, some peons were probably held for life. Moreover, a peon's debts could be inherited by his or her children, creating a kind of generational servitude.[28]

Yet peonage was also mediated by a social background of honor, paternalism, and fictive kinship between masters and servants. In both Hispanic and Native American society, the dividing line between kinship and slavery was ambiguous and highly permeable. Whatever the legal, cultural, or customary relationships may have been, by 1850 one estimate suggested that over 2,000 Native Americans were held in some form of bondage in New Mexico.[29] Many of these people originated in Utah and the Great Basin.

* * *

Concern over Indian slavery had percolated among Latter-day Saints ever since their arrival in the Salt Lake Valley in 1847. Within months, an Indian named Baptiste approached a Mormon camp with two teenaged captives for sale. When the Mormons refused to purchase the hostages, Baptiste resorted to an old technique used against the Spanish and threatened to kill them. Not willing to believe such a threat, the Mormons again resisted; Baptiste in turn made good on his promise and killed one of the teenagers. To save the other captive's life, Charles Decker, Brigham Young's son-in-law, purchased her. She was subsequently raised in Brigham Young's home as Sally where she worked as a servant until 1877 when she married the Pahvant chief Kanosh.[30] Similar exchanges for Indian children continued to play out in various forms over the ensuing years as Mormon settlers established communities throughout the Great Basin.[31]

Following the creation of Utah Territory as a part of the Compromise of 1850 and the subsequent appointment of Brigham Young as territorial governor and ex-officio superintendent of Indian affairs, Young prepared to move against the long-standing slave trade. Commerce between the Ute and Spanish colonizers dated back over 200 years by the time the Mormons arrived in northern Mexico in July 1847. Although the western Ute whom the Mormons encountered were not engaged in trade with the Spanish for the same length of time as other Ute bands to the south and east, trade relations still predated the Mormon arrival by at least sixty years. The Old Spanish Trail, which wound its way through Utah Territory, grew to accommodate this trade and frequently included human trafficking. Ute chief Wákara built a vast and powerful trading and raiding economy based in part on Indian captives. He presided over an extensive network of sometimes violent relationships that stretched from the Great Plains to California.[32] According to Brigham Young, Wákara was "in the habit for years of trafficking in Indians. He has never been here with his Band, without having a quantity of Indian children, as slaves. He offers them for sale, and when he has an offer that satisfies him in the price," Young explained, "he sells them, and when he cannot get what he thinks they are worth, he says he will take them to the Navaho Indians or Spaniards, and sell them, or kill them."[33]

Thus when Brigham Young (see figure 4.1) encountered "a company of Spanish traders" on November 3, 1851, in remote Sanpete County, Utah, he had to decide what to do. The leader of the trading company, Don Pedro León Luján, presented Young with a license signed by James S. Calhoun, now promoted to territorial governor and superintendent of Indian affairs for New Mexico. Luján then applied to Young for a license to trade with the Indians in Utah Territory, a request Young denied. Young believed that Luján's trading company had come to Utah Territory "with the express purpose to trade for Indian children to take to New Mexico." Young informed Luján that his trading party was welcome to trade with white settlers in the territory but that he "must not trade with the Indians." Young testified that Luján agreed to return to New Mexico and to deliver a letter to Governor Calhoun explaining Young's stance.[34]

It was what happened next that became fodder for the subsequent trial. The Luján defendants reported that as they began their journey back to New Mexico, they were approached by Indians who desired to trade with them. When the New Mexicans refused the trade, the Indians stole six of their animals and another five or six in subsequent raids. Over the next several weeks, as the New Mexicans attempted to recover their stolen livestock, the Indians forced a captive woman and eight children upon them as compensation for the lost property.[35] By early December local Indians in Sanpete Valley alerted authorities at Manti that Luján and his party were still in Utah Territory at Salt Creek, about half a day's journey from Manti, and that they had captive

Figure 4.1 Brigham Young (1801–1877) was a key witness in the trial of Don Pedro León Luján and governor of Utah Territory in 1852. He was also president of the Church of Jesus Christ of Latter-day Saints and considered to be a prophet by the Latter-day Saint faithful. This photograph was likely taken by Marsena Cannon around 1850. Courtesy Church History Library.

Indians in their possession. A posse from Manti then arrested Luján and his men on charges of trading without a license in Utah Territory.[36]

The trial thus revolved around the willfulness of the trade. If the jury believed the traders' story, that the captives were forced on them, then it was no different than the circumstances Mormon settlers faced when similarly confronted with Indian captives. If the jury did not believe Luján's story and believed instead that he and his party had willfully exchanged horses for Indian captives, then the New Mexicans were guilty of illegal trade. The jury swiftly rejected Luján's story and found him and his men guilty. Their property and horses were confiscated in order to meet the $500 fine established by the Trade and Intercourse Act (1834) and because they were deemed illegal trade goods.[37] Luján and his companions were sent back to New Mexico on foot. Even though Young supplied the traders with provisions for the return trip, it was an arduous trek through the mountains in midwinter; they sometimes waded through snow to their armpits.[38]

Three people who played a role in Luján's trial also took part in the lawmaking session that began as trial events continued to play out. Brigham Young testified at the trial as a key witness for the prosecution and delivered several speeches to the legislature. Apostle and legislator George A. Smith served as Luján's lead defense attorney. He then went on to introduce the Indian indenture bill to the legislature on January 23, less than a month after the initial trial. Isaac Morley, a leader in the Mormon colonization of Sanpete County, served as bailiff at the trial and testified as a witness for the prosecution and then represented his county as a member of the legislature.[39]

* * *

The first full session of the Utah Territorial legislature convened during the early months of 1852. Up until this time, Brigham Young and the Mormon leadership had consciously avoided creating any laws in regard to Native American or African American slavery. The extension of popular sovereignty into the region under the Compromise of 1850 did not immediately change their minds. Young and his counselors remained convinced that slavery was illegal in the Great Basin without local legislation to protect it. As late as June 1851, Young had publicly declared that he would not permit the creation of a "foundation for Negro slavery" in Utah.[40] Yet the issues raised by the Luján case forced Young to re-evaluate his strategy. He thus began the legislative session on January 5, with a prepared speech that would lay out his ideas regarding African American and Native American slavery in the territory. In it he urged lawmakers to take up the challenges that those two systems of bondage represented.[41]

It is unclear if Young ever understood the true extent of African American slavery in Utah Territory. He seems to have genuinely believed that virtually the entire enslaved population left the region between 1851 and 1852. But as the legislature was about to convene, he knew that there were at least some enslaved African Americans still in Utah. The actual number was around thirty. In comparison, New Jersey reported some 236 slaves on the 1850 census, although most were quite aged and had been legally transformed into apprentices for life.[42]

As Young contemplated the upcoming legislative session, he might have urged lawmakers to continue his policy of quietly permitting masters to maintain some kind of informal relationship with their enslaved workers without granting these relationships any form of legal recognition. This would have conformed with Thomas Kane's political advice, in addition to matching Young's own demonstrated preferences. But Young must have been aware that Mormon enslavers like John Bankhead were deeply upset by their inability to assert any sort of legal claim over the enslaved people whom they brought to Utah. The legislature included seven delegates from the South, one of whom owned a slave, and they may have pressed the issue.[43] Furthermore, maintaining the status quo would provide no statutory guidance concerning how the enslaved people already in Utah should be treated or their legal status.

The same was true of Indigenous servitude. Had Young opted to pass no legislation, the terms of the Trade and Intercourse Act would have continued to govern transactions with local Indians. From a legal perspective, this would have allowed Young to permanently keep New Mexicans like Luján out of the Ute slave trade by refusing to grant them trade licenses. If New Mexicans continued to trade with the Utes, they could be prosecuted. Nevertheless, without some kind of statutory framework, Latter-day Saints had no legal basis to purchase enslaved Southern Paiutes and keep them in their households. Young and other Latter-day Saint leaders believed that these captives were in mortal danger if they were not rescued. Moreover, they concluded that if the Mormons did not buy the captives, the Utes would simply sell them in New Mexico to Catholic colonizers and thus prevent Latter-day Saints from raising them according to their version of Christianity.[44]

Although there is no direct evidence conclusively showing why Young changed his mind, by early 1852 he had sketched out a new policy concerning servitude in Utah. The Luján trial offers the most immediate context for the new direction he articulated; in fact he referred to it in his speech when he mentioned "traders of late" from New Mexico who had "been arrested and are now on trial in this city."[45]

On January 5, Brigham Young's secretary, Thomas Bullock, stood in the Council House in Great Salt Lake City to deliver Young's prepared remarks. In the accent of the English West Midlands, Bullock began to read Governor Young's first annual message to a joint session of Utah's Legislative Council and the House of Representatives. Among other important subjects, the address broadly laid out Young's vision for acceptable labor practices in the new territory. He first proposed a law governing apprenticeship for minors.

Apprenticeship was slowly dying in the rest of the country because of changing economics and changing values. In California, no apprenticeship law was passed until the Panic of 1857 threw many young men onto the street.[46] But the almost fifty-one-year-old Young was firmly rooted in the small-town labor practices of his youth, where he himself had labored as an apprentice, as had his father.[47] He understood that apprenticeship and other forms of indentured labor had the potential for great abuse. Indeed, the elder Young's master had treated all of his servants, both Black and white, "cruelly."[48] But Young still saw apprenticeship as an important method for passing on valuable skills to the next generation within a paternalistic web of quasi-familial relationships. He had no qualms about the fact that apprenticeship was unfree, insofar as it was not abusive. "Deplorable indeed must be the situation of that people whose sons are not trained in the practice of every useful avocation, and whose daughters mingle not in the hum of industry," Bullock declared on behalf of Young. He therefore urged passage of a law concerning masters and apprentices that would "equally secure the rights, and protect the interests of both."[49] The legislature responded with a statute that allowed parents to bind out their children as apprentices. It also permitted local officials to involuntarily bind out "idle, vicious, or vagrant" children if their parents failed to properly control their "actions and education."[50] Young and his legislative colleagues were perfectly willing to employ unfree labor as a method of welfare and social control, just as it had been when they were growing up.

After discussing state funding for public schools and recommending that the territorial capital be moved to Fillmore, a town several hundred miles to the south, the governor then addressed the burning questions of African American and Native America slavery. Young's comments on this "nefarious traffic" comprised the largest portion of his message by far. But his treatment was not comprehensive or particularly profound. It haphazardly combined Christian benevolence with Jacksonian racism, and frontier theology with hard-nosed Yankee pragmatism. He did not define key terms, and he overlooked potential contradictions. Still, Young forcefully stated his position: "It is unnecessary perhaps for me to indicate the true policy for Utah in regard to slavery. Restrictions of law and government make all servants," he wrote, "but human flesh to be dealt in as property, is not consistent or compatible with the true principles of government. My own feelings are, that no property can or should be recognized as existing in slaves, either Indian or

African. No person can purchase them, without their becoming as free, so far as natural rights are concerned, as persons of any other color."[51]

Whatever his beliefs may have been in regard to race or biblical curses, Brigham Young firmly believed that Native Americans and African Americans were human beings, and it was not right for one human being to own another as a piece of property. Young and other members of the Mormon leadership had made this point with greater or lesser clarity since at least 1849. Here, Young unequivocally declared that chattel slavery was both legally and morally wrong. An early draft of Young's speech was even more explicit, stating that "it would seem to be our true policy to utterly discard the system of African slavery as it exists in the United States."[52] Although this phrase was ultimately deleted, the final draft follows the same basic logic. Young urged the assembled legislators to rescue God's children from "servile bondage" and place them "upon a platform upon which they can build; and extend forth as far as their capability and natural rights will permit."[53]

Young believed that slavery had never been recognized as a legal status within the Territory of Utah. Judge Snow's subsequent decision in the Luján libel case would confirm this interpretation of the law. From a purely legal standpoint, it was not necessary for the legislature to take any action at all to free enslaved people. But the fact was that the local Ute continued to enslave other Indigenous people, and they would not part with their captives without payment. At the same time, Latter-day Saint enslavers still held some thirty enslaved African Americans in the territory. Whatever theory Young had worked out in his mind about Utah Territory as free soil, men like John Bankhead continued to treat these people as alienable property.

Brigham Young genuinely believed that it was wrong for one person to own another as property. But like many of his colleagues, Young had grown-up in the midst of gradual emancipation. Like Joseph Smith, he recognized that slaves represented a substantial monetary value for their owners. Only months before, he had purchased the labor of Green Flake prior to freeing him and then publicly castigated abolitionists because they would not "liberate the slave by buying them & setting them free."[54] Young also had to consider the very real possibility that his actions might stir up irreconcilable divisions within the Mormon community or scuttle their chances of obtaining statehood for Deseret. Finally, Young fully accepted the argument that freed slaves might pose a danger to social order if they were emancipated immediately without proper education or financial resources.

Young therefore faced a dilemma. His primary goal was to ensure that Native Americans and African Americans could not be reduced to a state of slavery; in other words, he did not wish these people to be legally categorized as chattels who could be bought and sold like any other commodity. However, he needed to account for the substantial outlays of cash or goods that would be necessary to ransom Indian captives. He likewise needed to account for the value of enslaved Black people who lived in the territory with their enslavers.

Faced with similar challenges, Joseph Smith had proposed a national system of compensated emancipation in 1844.[55] The British had used this method in the 1830s, while Abraham Lincoln continued to advocate compensated emancipation as late as 1862.[56] These models relied on the state expending huge sums of money to compensate enslavers for the emancipation of their slaves. If the Latter-day Saints attempted such a plan on their own, outside of government channels, it would have been prohibitively expensive in cash-poor Utah even to purchase and free the thirty to forty enslaved people in the territory. If attempted through government channels, it would have had to win congressional approval, something that the nation proved unwilling to do in the antebellum period. Consequently, Young suggested an approach which had been used in the North for over fifty years as part of various gradual emancipation programs.[57]

"Servitude," Young believed, was a morally acceptable alternative to chattel slavery.[58] "Service is necessary," Young wrote, "it is honorable; it exists in all countries, and has existed in all ages. It probably will exist in some form in all time to come." Young was not very clear about what "servitude" would actually entail. But he argued that permitting Mormon families to keep enslaved or formerly enslaved people as household servants was justified as repayment for the cost of their purchase and upkeep and would provide a means of control and acculturation. In effect, the legalization of "servitude" as an intermediate stage between slavery and freedom would privatize the costs of emancipation while maintaining public order.[59]

Young emphasized without a hint of irony that this program was in the servants' own best interest, especially when compared to the absolute slavery to which they would otherwise be doomed in the American South or among the "Mexicans." "So shall the benevolence of the human heart be called into action," Young wrote, "to promote the improvement of the downtrodden race, whose fathers long swayed the destiny of empires, so shall the condition of the poor, forlorn, destitute, ignorant savage, or African, as the case may be, become ameliorated, and a foundation laid for their advancement in the scale of useful, exalting existence, useful to themselves, to their nation, and all who shall come within the purview of their influence."[60]

To Young, this highly paternalistic concept of servitude could be roughly compared to the practices of ancient Israel. Moreover, it was consistent with his understanding of the curse of Canaan. Indeed, Young argued that servitude was a status for which Indians and particularly Africans were uniquely suited. "Thus, while servitude may and should exist," Young wrote, "and that too upon those who are naturally designed to occupy the position of 'servant of servants,' yet we should not fall into the other extreme, and make them as beasts of the field, regarding not the humanity which attaches to the colored race; nor yet elevate them, as some seem disposed, to an equality with those whom Nature and Nature's God has indicated to be their masters, their superiors."[61]

Young's proposals incorporated many contemporary assumptions about race including white superiority. But they were also infused with idealistic notions of Christian charity. Young would elevate enslaved people from the status of property and place them in good homes where they could be educated and taught the Latter-day Saint gospel. He seemed to view servitude as a long-term apprenticeship or perhaps a form of guardianship. In Young's mind, servitude would create a web of mutual obligations between master and servant that tended toward the familial rather than the economic. Yet it also institutionalized a master's legal authority over his servant. In the end, Young's notion of servitude was rooted in a long-standing Anglo-American tradition of unfree labor wherein master and servant were enmeshed in a relationship that could not be dissolved unilaterally.[62]

Young's ideas were conditioned by his own experience as an apprentice and tradesman in the rural North, as well as the prevailing economic conditions of the Great Basin. In Utah Territory, hard currency was virtually nonexistent.[63] Labor was one of the few commodities that any person had to exchange, and courts would be left with few remedies if they could not force individuals to preform labor contracts. In fact, the economic situation in mid-nineteenth-century Utah was not dissimilar from mid-seventeenth-century Virginia where debts could be paid with either physical labor or tobacco.[64] In Utah, the Saints often had to trade physical labor or wheat for desired goods.[65]

Despite all of this, Young remained uncomfortable with the idea of labor without consent. Young clearly believed that people of African descent had been cursed to be "servant of servants." His commitment to this biblical gloss was unyielding. But in his own idiosyncratic way, the Mormon prophet interpreted the curse of Canaan as a badge of subordination or dependence rather than involuntary labor. To Young, this suggested paternalism, not slavery. In certain circumstances, Young was willing to use bound labor as a mechanism to repay debt or to maintain social order. But he believed that the ideal relationship between master and servant should be voluntary, and he viewed their association largely in terms of contract. In 1859, he would tell journalist Horace Greeley that slavery is "generally... a curse to the masters. I myself hire many laborers, and pay them fair wages; I could not afford to own them. I can do better than subject myself to an obligation to feed and clothe their families, to provide and care for them in sickness and health."[66] During the course of debates over An Act in Relation to Service, Young would take an active role in shaping the legislation and strongly supported provisions that favored a contractual view of servitude.

Young's opening speech to the legislature outlined "servitude" only in the most general terms. He did not address how long this condition might last once it had been entered. He did not address whether it was meant to pass on to a servant's children. He did not raise the issue of free people of color at all. Young did mention the idea that service was a method to defray a debt that a servant owed his or her master "in return for favors and expense which may have been incurred on their account." While this seemed to imply that any "debt" could eventually be discharged, it was not clear whether this applied equally to enslaved Indians who were ransomed in Utah and to enslaved African Americans who were brought into Utah from other parts of the United States.

Over the next few days, Young's proposals and others coming from the body of the legislature were divided among both houses and then assigned to various committees. His suggestions regarding slavery were taken up by the Legislative Council and entrusted to a committee that probably consisted of apostle George A. Smith and Orson Spencer with Spencer serving as chairman.[67]

* * *

The overlap between the Luján trials and the legislative session continued after Young's opening speech. Even though the jury found Luján guilty of trading without a license on January 1, U.S. Attorney Seth M. Blair subsequently filed actions for libel and indebtedness against Luján designed to confiscate his property and defray the $500 fine authorized for violations of the Trade and Intercourse Act. Unlike many of his coreligionists, Blair was a Southerner through and through. He was born in Missouri and had fought in the Texas Revolution. His case against Luján and his associates was based solely on their failure to obtain a valid trade license. He was not at all concerned with the practice of slavery. In fact, Blair argued to Judge Snow that slavery was legal in Utah Territory because it existed according to established custom between Indigenous and Spanish peoples. This perspective was out of synch with most members of the Mormon leadership. It provides some notion of the debates that would take place within the community in the succeeding years.

Brigham Young and Isaac Morley testified in the libel case on January 15. In his testimony, Young described the long-standing human trafficking that quickly entangled the Mormons in its web shortly after their arrival in the Salt Lake Valley. He included the story of Baptiste bringing the teenagers to the Mormon camp and explained how Sally became a part of his household. "She has lived in my family ever since," Young remarked. She "has fared as my children and is as free," he claimed.[68] Sally did live in the Young household but among his servants, not with his children.[69]

Morley testified next regarding his knowledge of Luján's activities in Sanpete County and how Luján came to be arrested there. George A. Smith (see figure 4.2), as Luján's defense attorney, cross-examined Morley and in doing so turned the spotlight on Mormon settlers. He questioned Morley about the nature of Mormon interactions with Indians in Sanpete County. Morley admitted that "the whites at San Pete trade with the Indians, have been counselled so to do by the Governor, before the Territorial organization, to purchase Indian children to save them from misery, starvation, cruelty, and death." He did not know how many Indian children Mormon settlers had purchased but claimed that when Mormons did so, it was done in order to "make them free."[70] Young had made a similar argument just six months earlier when he publicly admitted, "We have a few [Indians] that were prisoners that we have bought to save their lives."[71]

It was a particularly ironic exchange given the fact that Smith was personally aware of the type of events that sometimes led Mormons to purchase Indian children. In December 1850, Smith recorded one such incident in his journal. As he traveled south from Salt Lake City at the head of a company of Mormon colonizers, Ute men stole two of his oxen and other cattle somewhere south of present-day Nephi, Utah. Smith and his men subsequently

Figure 4.2 George A. Smith (1817–1875) served as Don Pedro León Luján's defense attorney at the trial. He was also an apostle in the Church of Jesus Christ of Latter-day Saints and a member of the territorial legislature in 1852. Courtesy Church History Library.

captured a Ute man and a young boy who they accused of shooting Smith's oxen with arrows; after clinging to life, one of the oxen died from its wounds. In exchange for the dead ox Smith suggested a trade. He told the older Ute, "if he would let me have the Boy, he might have the ox." It was a bargain to which the Ute "readily agreed." Smith promised that "the Boy should be well fed, comfortably clothed, and made a man of if he would be a good boy." According to Smith, "the Indian said he wanted to see [the boy] dressed like a white man, on his return." Clearly Smith was familiar with the type of exchanges for human beings that took place in Utah Territory because he had participated in one himself. In Smith's case he initiated the trade; the Ute boy was not forced on him under threat of death as Latter-day Saints sometimes characterized the exchanges.[72]

At least a part of Smith's cross-examination of Morley was designed to demonstrate to the court that the Mormons were engaged in many of the same type of trade activities for which only Luján and his men were being held accountable. The Luján trial thus highlighted for the Mormons the need to legally define the nature of the trade in Indian captives in which they already participated. At the same time, Mormons hoped to cut off the demand for Indian slaves that they believed was created in part by the influx of traders from New Mexico. Cut off the demand and the supply should dry up. Latter-day Saints thus hoped to squeeze the exchange in Indian captives out of existence.

The day after Young and Morley testified, the court deposed one member of Luján's trading company, Phillipe Santiago Archuleta. He described the Indian children that were found in the Mexicans' possession as being forced on them by Ute traders in exchange for the stolen horses the Utes had taken. When asked if Luján and his men came to Utah Territory with the express intent to trade for Indian children, Archuleta responded that it was impossible for him to know what the objectives of his companions were "but he supposed they came to trade for anything they could trade for." He then admitted that he heard one member of the company say that he "came here to trade for Indian children or anything else he could trade." It was a damning admission in the libel case.[73]

As Luján's defense attorney, George A. Smith filed a variety of procedural motions as well as a countersuit against the state claiming it had illegally confiscated the Mexicans' property. The court brushed aside all of Smith's filings and Associate Justice Zerubbabel Snow found Luján liable; he issued his decision on January 24. In doing so, he concluded that even though the enslavement of Indigenous people in the region took place according to long-standing custom, without laws to sanction such custom, the Native Americans confiscated from Luján could not be held by the court and were judged "to be free."[74]

* * *

Despite the chronological overlap between the Luján case and the legislative debates, how much Judge Zerubbabel Snow (see figure 4.3) communicated to lawmakers about his reasoning and at what point he did so is difficult to tease from surviving sources. Snow appeared before lawmakers, perhaps on January 23, the day before he issued his ruling in the Luján libel case and the day that An Act for the Protection of the Rights of Indians was first introduced to legislators.[75] The debate over that bill likely began that day, although George Watt failed to record the date. At the top of Watt's undated minutes he recorded in shorthand the words, "Judge Snow," followed by a half sentence—"I have no particular feelings relating to particular acts from"—and then his record of Snow's remarks abruptly ends. It is impossible to know what Snow might have said to lawmakers or when he said it.

Figure 4.3 Associate Justice Zerubbabel Snow (1809–1888) presided over Don Pedro León Luján's two trials in Salt Lake City. He was a federally appointed judge and a Latter-day Saint. Courtesy Church History Library.

Nonetheless, circumstantial evidence suggests that Snow spoke to the legislature, likely on January 23, and his remarks framed the debate over the Indian indenture bill that ensued. Snow likely shared his conclusions from the Luján trials with lawmakers and may have forecasted the decision he would issue the following day.[76]

Because of the complex legal questions at play in the case, including the question over what constituted "Indian country," Snow felt compelled to make details of the case public, including the rationale behind his decision. Snow wrote a lengthy account of the key arguments in the case on February 10 and addressed it to Willard Richards, president of the Legislative Council. He subsequently submitted a copy of the document to the *Deseret News* that published it on March 6, the last day of the legislative session and the day the Indian indenture bill became law. In essence, Snow's remarks offered the lawmakers justification and even prodded them to enact laws to govern Indian and Black servitude in the territory. If Willard Richards received Snow's fully articulated decision sometime around February 10, it likely influenced lawmakers as they continued to revise the Indian indenture bill. Whatever ideas Snow expressed to legislators as early as January 23 also probably shaped their ongoing debates over the bill.[77]

Snow devoted considerable space in his published decision to explaining his argument regarding the legal nature of Indian country. The Trade and Intercourse Act of 1834 regulated trade on land deemed "Indian country," an area defined in the law as "all that part of the United States west of the Mississippi" River excluding the states of Missouri, Louisiana, and the territory of Arkansas, and any land east of the Mississippi River in which Indian title had not yet been extinguished.[78] Among other things, the act required that all individuals who wished to trade with the Indians in Indian country must obtain a license by an authorized Indian agent. It further provided that "any person other than an Indian who shall attempt to reside in the Indian country as a trader, or to introduce goods, or to trade without such license, shall forfeit all merchandise offered for sale to the Indians, or found in his possession," as well as pay $500.[79]

At the time that the Trade and Intercourse Act was passed, however, Utah Territory did not exist nor was the land even part of the United States. Were Mormons therefore living in Indian country and did the Trade and Intercourse Act apply to them and to Luján? If it applied to Luján, then it must also apply to Mormons who regularly traded with Indians and who purchased Indian captives. As historian Sondra Jones explained, "if Utah Territory were deemed Indian country and trading therefore illegal, then all white settlements, trading, and travel through it was illegal (including that done by the Mormons)."[80] It was a significant legal conundrum only made worse in Latter-day Saint eyes because it threatened to prevent them from their version of *rescate,* or ransom of Indian children when they purchased them from traders.

If the entire Mexican Cession was Indian country under the Trade and Intercourse Act, then a significant number of white settler activities might have been deemed illegal, including trade between white people. Judge Snow determined that this could not have been Congress' intent, especially considering the fact the Congress had recently organized the region and created civil governments for its inhabitants. In his more detailed analysis, Snow opined that Utah Territory was not Indian country for the purposes of the act. Nevertheless, he believed that Congress still had clear authority to regulate trade with Native Americans. Snow argued that Congress had done so through an 1851 statute that extended "all the laws now in force, regulating trade and intercourse with the Indian tribes, or such provisions of the same as may be applicable ... over the Indian tribes" in New Mexico and Utah.[81] Snow interpreted the word "tribe" to refer to the people themselves and the word "country" to refer to the land. He determined that the provisions of the Trade and Intercourse Act still applied to the Indian tribes in Utah, even if they did not apply to the entire Territory of Utah. In this context, Snow reinterpreted the phrase "Indian country" to mean "the country occupied by the Indians for their usual hunting camps or ranges, including their towns or villages, &c., from which the White settlements are separate, or in which the white[s] are not included."[82]

This was a rather ingenious solution to the conundrum. In essence, Snow's decision required individuals such as Luján who wished to trade with the Indians outside of Mormon settlements (Indian country) to obtain a proper license under the terms of the Trade and Intercourse Act. On the other hand, it permitted Mormons to trade with the Indians in the vicinity of Latter-day Saint settlements (not Indian country) without obtaining such a license. In this way, Snow upheld the right of the Latter-day Saints to trade with local tribes while delivering a judicial coup de grâce to the New Mexican captive trade.

As for the captive woman and seven Indian children, Snow ordered them released. He concluded that there was not then in force any laws that recognized "Indian slavery" in the territory. He noted that the act that created Utah Territory included "a clause giving to the people here the right to introduce slavery, or reject it." That right, he said, was "in the Governor and Legislative Assembly, not in the court." He acknowledged that "the Indians for a long series of years have been in the habit of selling their children, and stealing others to sell," but that precedent was not "sufficient to justify any other decree or order" other than the release of the captives.[83] The Luján case and Judge Snow's decision thus created an immediate and pressing need in the minds of Latter-day Saint leaders for a law to allow Mormon settlers to legally absorb captive Indians into their society.

Snow's decision vindicated the long-standing position of Brigham Young concerning slavery in the Great Basin. Since at least 1849, Young and other Mormon leaders had insisted that slavery could not legally exist within the jurisdiction without the sanction of positive law and that no court would recognize the practice. Snow had fully upheld their arguments. His decision applied not only to Indian slavery but also to any form of enforceable service relationship that was not specifically authorized by statute. This only highlighted the fact that there were several categories of labor relationships that existed in the territory by custom without any governing legislation.

In the Luján case, what this meant in practice was that the court subsequently freed the captive woman and children, but they were then placed into Mormon homes under the provisions of the new indenture law, a move Luján found to be the height of hypocrisy. After his return to New Mexico, he registered a complaint with Governor Calhoun about his treatment in Utah Territory. Acting superintendent of Indian affairs for New Mexico, John Greiner, then forwarded a report of that complaint to Luke Lea, U.S. commissioner of Indian affairs in Washington D.C., but nothing came of it.[84]

It is not clear what the realistic options were for the court in regard to the captive woman and children. Assuming that the parents of the captives were alive, locating them and returning the children would have been difficult without knowing what band or tribe they belonged to, how long they had been held captive by their Ute traffickers, or if the children were able to communicate answers to any such questions. It is impossible to know, too, how traumatized the children were by a series of profound disruptions in their lives and impossible to guess at their wishes when their voices do not enter the written record. The adult woman was likely aware of her band and kinship relations and would have been better able to help locate them than the children. Even still, there is no indication that legal, civic, or religious authorities considered reunification with parents and family as a possibility. Reuniting the captives with their families was the most humane option but was not entertained so far as the written record indicates. Setting the captives free with no resources and no one to provide for them might have led to starvation and possible death.

In the end, authorities were likely motivated by humanitarian impulses blended with a Mormon theological vision of Native Americans as fallen descendants of ancient Israel in need of economic and religious redemption. Paternalism and Euro-American settler colonialism were tightly intertwined with the Saints' religious views and provided an overarching approach to the captives. The confiscated woman and children thus became an opportunity for Mormons to fulfill their perceived mission to "redeem" fallen Israel, and so they were placed in Latter-day Saint homes.[85]

5

An Act for the Relief of Indian Slaves and Prisoners

During the winter of 1851–1852, the trial and conviction of Don Pedro León Luján finally prompted Brigham Young and the Utah legislature to regulate the purchase of Indian captives in the territory. It likewise convinced Young to legally define the de facto relationships that existed between Mormon enslavers and their Black slaves. Judge Zerubbabel Snow's opinion confirmed that chattel slavery was illegal in the Great Basin without positive legislation to the contrary. This had been the stated position of the LDS First Presidency since the summer of 1849. In his address to the legislature on January 5, 1852, Young made it clear once again that he was unwilling to legalize chattel slavery in Utah. However, he urged the legislature to create some lesser form of "servitude" as a temporary condition for enslaved Indians and African Americans.

The newly transcribed debates concerning An Act for the Relief of Indian Slaves and Prisoners (what we refer to as the Indian indenture bill) reveal a group of deeply conflicted lawmakers, some of whom were not convinced that they had the authority to legislate for what they deemed to be "Indian country." All the legislators were anxious to solve the problem of Indian slavery in a humane manner, yet they strongly disagreed about how to do so. At least one legislator, Orson Pratt, charged that the body was instituting a form of slavery for Native Americans. Others emphasized that they were rescuing Indian captives from slavery and quite possibly death.

The legislative process ultimately lasted for two months. In fact, the main text of the Indian indenture bill was not approved by the legislature until March 6, the last day of the session. The final statute created a form of involuntary apprenticeship for Native Americans who Latter-day Saint settlers ransomed from Ute traffickers. Although the Utah legislators thought of this as a uniquely benevolent solution to the problem, it shared similarities with practices that existed in other parts of the Mexican Cession.

During the 1850s, legislators in California and New Mexico were also forced to address the question of Indian slavery. Various forms of servitude had existed among the local Hispanic and Indigenous populations for centuries. Since the opening of the Old Spanish Trail, the Great Basin had served as a convenient slaving ground between Santa Fe and the Pacific coast. The California legislature quickly took steps to regulate and ameliorate Indian servitude, although it ultimately authorized long-term apprenticeships for Native Americans. In New Mexico, the legislature enacted statutes to govern debt peonage but ignored the trade in Indian captives.[1]

In April 1850, the California legislature passed An Act for the Government and Protection of Indians. This statute was aimed at softening the traditional rancho system in which large numbers of Native people were held on private estates in a status that combined debt servitude with quasi-feudal obligations.[2] The law provided a stiff fine if "any person forcibly conveys any Indian from his home, or compels him to work, or perform any service against his will."[3] Still, the law authorized several less objectionable forms of unfree labor. For instance, the law permitted Euro-Americans to enter binding labor contracts with Indians if a written agreement was approved by a justice of the peace. An individual could also be granted a kind of guardianship or apprenticeship over an Indian child as long as a justice of the peace determined that "no compulsory means were used to obtain the child from its parents or friends." The statute further provided that a court could sentence Indians to labor for private individuals to pay off fines or if they were determined to be vagrants.[4]

During the same session, the legislature also passed a general guardianship statute that allowed courts to take orphans or the children of "unsuitable" parents and place them in the care of another family.[5] While this statute could apply to any child regardless of race, it was often used to place Native American and African American children into white households where they were sometimes used as domestic servants.[6] Despite the legislature's efforts, the customary practice of kidnapping Native women and children and using them for household labor also continued illegally.[7]

The second half of the 1850s was marked by major violence between Native Americans and Euro-American settlers in northwestern California. As a result, the legislature amended California's Indian labor law in April 1860 in an attempt to acculturate local Indians.[8] The new statute authorized county and district judges to involuntarily apprentice Indigenous people if they were held as "prisoners of war" or were determined to be vagrants. A judge could likewise apprentice Indigenous minors under the age of fifteen with the consent of a parent or guardian. Depending on the age and sex of the individual, Indian children could lawfully be bound until the age of thirty, while adults could be bound for up to ten years.[9]

California Republicans immediately condemned Indian apprenticeship as "slavery." Indeed, it appears that the law's most immediate result was to exacerbate the illicit trade in captives who could now be legally held as apprentices. Over the next three years, Indian apprentices made up close to 40 percent of the population in some areas in northwest California.[10] Consequently, in 1863, a coalition of Republicans and Free-Soil Democrats rescinded those portions of the law allowing the apprenticeship of Indian children and prisoners of war.[11] However, no provision was made for freeing Native Americans who had already been apprenticed. Further, the law still permitted the binding out of Indians considered to be vagrants or those convicted of petty crimes.[12]

In New Mexico, Indian servitude was ubiquitous. During the 1850s, it is estimated that more than 2,000 Native Americans were held in some form of bondage in the territory. For over a decade, the legislature ignored the trade in Indian captives that operated as a matter of custom.[13] After the American conquest, New Mexicans continued to purchase captives from Indigenous slavers through the mechanism of *rescate*, or ransom, while other captives entered the community as prisoners of war. As late as 1864, the New Mexico superintendent of Indian affairs reported that ransomed Indian captives were "usually adopted into the family, baptized, and brought up in the Catholic faith, and given the name of the owner's family, generally become faithful and trustworthy servants, and sometimes are married to the native New Mexicans."[14] However, the first session of the territorial legislature immediately moved to address the related question of peonage, or debt servitude.

In July 1851, the legislature passed a "Law regulating contracts between masters and servants." The statute authorized civil courts to specifically enforce labor contracts that were based on debt and provided masters with legal means to recapture escaped servants. As drafted, the law did attempt to defend the most vulnerable members of society from the abuses traditionally associated with peonage. For example, it forbade fathers from "bind[ing] out their children to serve, contracting excessive debts until they are driven into a state of slavery." An individual's debt could likewise not pass on to other family members if the debtor died. Finally, the act limited debt servitude to "free white men and women," thereby permitting Hispanos to be held as peons but not Indians.[15]

Despite the protections outlined by the legislature, customary forms of peonage endured. In practice, this could involve a lifetime of debt servitude.[16] Furthermore, peonage and Indian captivity were linked for all practical purposes.[17] One report made to the commissioner of Indian Affairs in the mid-1860s claimed that peonage "either in the ordinary Mexican form, that of a state of continual imprisonment or service for debt, or in that of practical enslavement of captive Indians, 'is the universally recognized mode of securing labor and assistance.' No less than four hundred Indians are thus held in Santa Fé alone. Their treatment varies with the whims and feelings of their holders."[18]

Many observers argued that peonage was a voluntary form of servitude distinct from slavery and authorized by federal law. In September 1865, an army colonel ordered his subordinates to aid in the return of escaped peons to their masters. He explained to a reluctant officer that "[p]eonage is voluntary and not involuntary servitude. . . . It is an apprenticeship, or an agreement between the master and servant."[19] Congress was not convinced, however. On March 2, 1867, Congress passed the Peonage Abolition Act to suppress this "system of slavery" in New Mexico.[20] Nevertheless, legislators recognized that there was still significant disagreement concerning the boundaries of involuntary servitude. As a result, Congress went beyond the express provisions of the Thirteenth Amendment to criminalize the "service or labor of any persons as peons," whether that service was involuntary or *voluntary*.[21]

By the summer of 1868, over 360 New Mexican citizens were brought before a federal grand jury for illegally keeping peons and/or Indian slaves. Most of the servants were granted liberty by the court, although some chose to remain with their former masters with whom they shared bonds of dependency as well as real or fictive kinship. The members of the grand jury, many of whom were probably involved in these practices to one degree or another, refused to return a single indictment.[22]

* * *

The trial of Don Pedro Luján convinced Brigham Young that New Mexican traders viewed the Great Basin as an important source of Indian captives. Regardless of the ways that the *rescate* functioned in New Mexico, Young and other members of the Utah legislature viewed it as a particularly onerous form of slavery. They were determined to cut off the demand for captives that they believed New Mexican traders like Luján represented. They hoped to stem the flow of captives into New Mexico as well as to protect from torture and murder the captives who Ute traffickers offered them. For Young, the best way to do so was to eliminate traders from outside of Utah Territory and then regulate Latter-day Saint purchase of the captives from their Ute enslavers and place them in some form of temporary servitude.

On Friday, January 23, 1852, George A. Smith reported the first draft of "An Act for the Protection of the Rights of Indians" to the Legislative Council. Unfortunately, none of the working drafts of the bill have survived. Smith was almost certainly the author of the law, perhaps with the aid of Daniel H. Wells or Orson Spencer.[23] Smith was keenly aware of the proceedings in the Luján case, having served as Luján's attorney. Moreover, he had significant personal experience with the captive trade in Native peoples, and it horrified him. "I have seen half a dozen of [them] gambled for, sold for a bed quilt," he told the Council. "[If the Indians] could not have sold [the captive] the result would have [been] its brains knocked out and nothing said about it."[24]

Smith failed to mention, however, other ways that Latter-day Saints acquired Native American children. He had instigated one such trade himself. In 1850, he took a Ute boy in compensation for two oxen that Ute men had killed on his trip to settle southern Utah. The boy was not forced on him, and he was not enslaved to Ute traffickers.[25] Like Luján had done at his trial, Smith and other Latter-day Saints emphasized stories that involved Ute traffickers who induced the purchases through violence or the threat of violence but failed to mention examples in which Latter-day Saints directly acquired Indigenous children with no Ute traffickers involved.[26]

As drafted, the Indian indenture bill was open as to how a white person might acquire a Native American "whether by purchase or otherwise." One study of sixty-six documentable cases found that Latter-day Saints traded with Indian traffickers for almost 60 percent of the children. Latter-day Saints traded with Indian relatives for an additional 18 percent of Indigenous children, while they acquired 14 percent as prisoners of war. Of the remaining 8 percent, Latter-day Saints sold or traded the children between themselves, married them, or acquired the indentured children after they ran away from their tribe.[27]

After Smith introduced the draft bill on January 23, it was ultimately returned to a committee for a preamble and resolutions.[28] It is possible that a debate on Indian servitude began that day, but it is not clear from George

Watt's transcription. The following Monday, January 26, Smith reported a preamble to the Indian Apprentice Act, now called "An Act for the Relief of Indians." At this point, debate over the bill began in earnest and continued until the afternoon of January 27.[29]

The first recorded speaker was Judge Zerubbabel Snow. If debate began on January 23, then Snow appeared before lawmakers the day before he handed down his decision in the Luján libel case, a decision in which he declared the Native American prisoners confiscated by the court in that case to be free. If debate began on January 26, then Snow appeared two days after he issued his ruling. Snow was not a member of the legislature, but he was apparently called on to provide legal insight. It is possible that he shared his thinking behind his short opinion in the Luján case even though his extended written legal analysis concerning a number of important questions would not come until later. In that longer opinion Snow weighed in on whether Utah Territory was "Indian Country" for the purposes of federal law and other important questions before legislators. Such questions could significantly affect the ability of the Latter-day Saints to enact laws in relation to Native Americans and to trade with them. Frustratingly, George Watt failed to record anything more than Snow's first half sentence, making it impossible to know what he said or how his comments may have shaped the debate that ensued. Watt merely recorded Snow as stating that he had "no particular feelings relating to particular acts," a tantalizing initial sentiment left unfinished.[30]

No matter when Snow spoke, even his short decision in the Luján case provided lawmakers with motivation to act. The preamble and draft bill that Smith introduced on January 26 no doubt structured the ensuing debate. Assuming that this draft was similar to the final statute, the preamble described the captive trade in Utah and provided legal and moral justifications for its regulation. It portrayed a grotesque state of affairs in which local Utes routinely obtained Indian captives "by war, or theft" and sold them to New Mexican traders as slaves. According to the document, the Indians even "gamble away their own children and women." These captives "are frequently bound with thongs made of raw hide, until their hands and feet become swollen, mutilated, inflamed with pain, and wounded; and when with suffering, cold, hunger, and abuse, they fall sick, so as to become troublesome, are frequently slain by their masters to get rid of them." The preamble further claimed that Ute traffickers "frequently kill their women and children taken prisoners, either in revenge, or for amusement, or through the influence of tradition, unless they are tempted to exchange them for trade."[31]

In order to rescue these victims, the proposed bill stipulated that if "any white person within any organized county of this Territory, shall have any Indian prisoner, child or woman, in his possession, whether by purchase or otherwise," he could take the captive to a probate judge or the county selectmen to execute a written indenture "for the term of not exceeding twenty years, at the discretion of the Judge or Select men." A copy of the indenture along with identifying information was to be filed in the probate clerk's office. However, the official executing the indenture first had to determine that the prospective master was "qualified to raise or retain and educate" an Indian apprentice. County selectmen were further "authorized to obtain such Indian prisoners, children, or women, and bind them to some useful avocation." The master of an indentured Indian was required to send a child between the ages of seven and sixteen to school for at least three months every year. Early drafts of the bill may have said four months. A master was likewise required to "clothe his apprentice in a comfortable and becoming manner, according to his, said master's, condition in life."[32]

In many ways, Utah's bill was comparable to the California acts of 1850 and 1860 that authorized various forms of servitude for Native Americans. Whether Utah legislators knew it or not, it also bore similarities to the practice of *rescate* in New Mexico. Still, the bill was clearly based on traditional American institutions with which the Latter-day Saints were familiar: involuntary apprenticeship and public indenture. These were mechanisms whereby local municipalities bound-out children or adults to work for private individuals for a defined term of service. These conditions historically served as a paternalistic form of control and social welfare for poor or "disorderly" persons within a given community. During this same term, the Utah legislature also authorized involuntary apprenticeships for white children, although these could only last until the age of majority. The legislature further authorized public indenture as a punishment for vagrants or to pay off fines.[33]

The twenty-year maximum term of service proposed in the bill was long but not unheard of. California's Indian apprenticeship act of 1860 permitted a maximum term of twenty-five years. The New Mexican *rescate* normally entailed ten to twenty years of unfree labor. In Utah, these service requirements were intended to repay masters for the costs associated with ransom efforts. On January 5, Brigham Young had urged the legislature to enact regulations that would serve this very purpose.[34] It was a nod to fiscal realities in the cash-poor territory. In this way, the bill largely privatized the costs of ransoming Indian captives while permitting those who paid the ransom to recoup their losses over time through the captives' labor. The lengthy term of service also provided sufficient time for indentured Indians to be acculturated into Latter-day Saint society, an unstated but implied goal of the law. Although the Indian indenture bill largely fulfilled Young's requirements, it would prove to be controversial within the legislature.[35]

Following the rest of Judge Snow's unrecorded remarks, the next documented speaker was Orson Pratt. During several addresses over the next day and a half, Pratt's unvarnished objections to the bill set the tone for the debate. In fact, Pratt attempted to either table the bill or to remove key sections of the law, both times losing 6-4.[36] He focused on two main points. Pratt first argued that because the bill authorized Latter-day Saints to purchase Indian captives and place them in servitude, it amounted to a form of slavery. "It is buy[ing] and selling," Pratt insisted. "Though it may not continue down through other generations, yet it is binding [the Indians] to slavery [for] at least 20 years." Pratt told the Council forthrightly that when "we touch the principle of enslaving the aborigines of this country, binding them by certain laws to be bought and sold, [it] is preposterous and [I] wonder [why] any gentleman present [would bring] such a bill."[37]

While Indian apprenticeship was not heritable and had a definite endpoint, in Pratt's mind it still constituted slavery because it was based upon "buying and selling" a person, or at least that person's labor.[38] Pratt's comments were an implicit rejection of the traditional categories that existed within unfree labor. Others strongly disagreed with him. One legislator, probably George A. Smith, responded, "The object of the bill is to abolish slavery; this is the object set [*sic*] which was set forth. . . . In my opinion, if you can place an Indian child in [a] position by his serving 20 [years], [to] receive school, learn some trade, instead of being shot for sport, [then we should do so]."[39] For Smith, the law created a form of gradual emancipation that placed Indian captives in a temporary form of servitude that resembled apprenticeship for whites. Daniel H. Wells likewise argued, "[To] buy [Indian captives] from the most loathsome slavery is their freedom." He compared the indenturing of Indians to a kind of guardianship. "Shall we permit [Indian captives] to be purchased and held as slaves or shall we make a law which [allows] the purchase of them, which takes them from the purchaser and places them under protection of our court?" Lorin Farr, legislator from Weber County and LDS stake president over the Weber Stake, emphasized that "I [do] not consider [Indian apprenticeship] to be servitude any more than it is with the white [child]. I therefore, I differ with the one gentleman [Pratt]. Take up a boy in [the] street [who is] bound out until he is of age—[but] not to exceed 20 years—[and who is] educated four months in [a] year and if that master does not take care of [his] children then he is liable to be dealt with. They are under the same law and regulation as our own children would be if we take care of them ourselves."[40]

The debates in Utah concerning the legal boundaries of slavery were not unique. Two years earlier, members of the U.S. Senate had engaged in similar arguments in relation to peonage in New Mexico. In June 1850, Senator Isaac Walker of Wisconsin proposed banning peonage, or what he called "peon slavery," in the Mexican Cession. Senator Thomas Hart Benton of Missouri agreed with Walker in principle but insisted rather than calling it slavery, "the word 'servitude' would be more technically correct." Walker quickly accepted Benton's suggestion. Thomas Pratt of Maryland then emphasized that peonage was "servitude existing by virtue of the contract of the individuals." Senator Dayton of New Jersey voiced concern about the propriety of meddling with existing contracts, and Senator Hunter of Virginia agreed. Hunter argued, "The Indian who can pay his debt is entitled to be released from servitude by the Mexican law.... I believe in this case the master may require a specific performance of the contract; that is, he may require it to be performed in service or labor, and there may be a punishment if he does not so perform it; in other words, it is a relation subsisting between the Indian and the master similar to that which subsists between the master and the apprentice."[41]

But to Senator William H. Seward, a man who grew up in a slave-owning family in New York and then transformed into an ardent abolitionist, Congress had every right to legislate on the subject. "Now, we know this in regard to peon servitude," he said, "that it is SLAVERY, and that it is slavery that is created there either by law or by contract. If it is created by law, and without the consent and will of the slave, then it is void, or ought to be, and ought to be abolished. If it be created there by contract, then, sir, I have no difficulty in regard to the proposition [of abolishing the practice]." Ironically, Senator Stephen Douglas, the prophet of popular sovereignty, also argued that Congress should take action to ban peonage. Yet this was because it might allow "white men, our own kindred," to be "reduced to a system of slavery, provided they should happen to be so unfortunate as to be unable to pay a debt of five dollars."[42]

The debate in Congress demonstrated the ongoing shift in American attitudes toward unfree labor. For men like Benton and Hunter, where some form of debt or contract formed the basis of a labor relationship, it was servitude and not slavery. This represented the traditional view of unfree labor in the United States. Seward represented an emerging perspective that was aggressively committed to a free labor ethic. His understanding of slavery was more capacious. For him, the degree of coercion and abuse associated with peonage could transform a contractual labor relationship into slavery. Douglas represented yet another perspective. He referred to peonage as slavery largely because it could apply to white men.[43]

The indenturing of Indians in Utah was not entirely analogous to debt peonage in New Mexico. Still, Latter-day Saint legislators divided on this issue in much the same way that the senators had. George A. Smith, Daniel H. Wells, and Lorin Farr all viewed Indian indenture as a conventional form of servitude that was used to provide care and education to poor members of the community. Farr did not believe that it was any different than involuntary apprenticeships for white children. In fact, eight years later, the California legislature authorized a similar institution for Native Americans despite a state constitution that expressly prohibited slavery and involuntary servitude. From this perspective, the indenturing of Indians was unfree, yet it did not constitute slavery. For Smith and his supporters, this conclusion was obvious when they compared their version of apprenticeship to captivity among the Ute. Based on contemporary law and practice, it was a reasonable position to take and won support from fellow lawmakers. For Orson Pratt, however, the purchase of human beings and their classification as servants was nothing more or less than slavery. The fact that he personally supported purchasing Native American children from their captors for humanitarian purposes did not change his opinion.[44]

Lawmakers were clearly vexed with difficult questions and wrestled to find reasonable solutions. Perhaps Charles R. Dana from Weber County captured the sentiment of his fellow legislators best as the debate over the Indian indenture bill began: "I believe in legislating in wisdom," he said; "it is wisdom I want." What the debate over An Act for the Relief of Indian Slaves and Prisoners makes clear is that lawmakers actually desired to bring relief to Indian slaves and prisoners, even if they could not agree on how to do so.[45]

Whether or not the indenturing of Indians was a form of slavery, Pratt firmly believed that the Utah legislature did not have the authority to create laws in relation thereto. He argued that this was solely a prerogative of the federal government. Partly, the question revolved around whether Utah Territory could be considered "Indian country" under the Indian Trade and Intercourse Act. Judge Snow's initial decision in the Luján trial did not settle this question, nor did it specify whether Mormon settlers had the right to trade with Indians. Once again, a number of legislators rejected Pratt's reasoning. "The very moment [when the] territory of Utah [was] organized by law, this ceased to be Indian country, providing it ever was Indian country," George A. Smith retorted. "You might as well [argue that] the state of Illinois has not the privilege of legislating in relation to vagrants as [to] say we [do not have] the liberty to legislate." Smith had made similar arguments to the court while acting as Don Pedro Luján's attorney. Daniel H. Wells likewise claimed to "have no fears of legislating upon this matter. I consider we have a perfect right." Lorin Farr concurred: "If this territory which has been organized, if [it] is deemed for a moment as Indian territory we then are, all of us, subject to heavy fine and [to] having all of our property confiscated every day of [our] lives.... I am persuaded [that] this is not Indian country, but United States territory," Farr said. "We are legislating for and having a right to make such laws as we think proper for the benefit of this territory."[46]

Many legislators believed that even if their legal authority was questionable, they still had to take immediate action to save the victims of the captive trade. One man, probably George A. Smith, insisted that "the case is a clear one and calls for humanity to save bleeding Israel." Smith still had bitter recollections of the federal government's failure to protect Latter-day Saints in Missouri and felt that the situation would be similar for Indian captives. "Now to suffer this order of things to go on another month or year, to give no sanction or color of law to stop it [is unconscionable]," he declared. "If we was to memorialize them [Congress] [for] three years, what [would] be the result of it? 'God bless you, we can do nothing for you.'"[47]

The legislators were fully aware that under the Utah Organic Act, Congress had the ability to nullify territorial statutes. Lorin Farr therefore suggested that they simply play a shell game. "I believe this territory have a right to make laws for [the] protection of Indians as much as they have for the whites," he said. "I would make a law and let it go and [if] Congress reject[s] it, just by the time it gets back [we could] make another [law] with slight variation [and keep] it going." Although Orson Pratt did not believe that the territorial legislature had the ability to regulate Indian captivity by law, he still wanted Latter-day Saints to respond with compassion to the plight of captives who were brought into their communities and offered for sale.

He therefore advocated that his fellow Saints continue to purchase captive Indians on their own without legally defining them as servants.[48]

Lawmakers discussed other potential objections. Lorin Farr was most concerned about the separation of children from parents that the traffic in Indian captives entailed. He described the Indian slave trade as drawing away "the child from the breast" and said it consisted of "taking children from parents that would like to have them themselves." At one point, he suggested passing a law aimed at wholly prohibiting the sale of Native Americans and punishing the slave traders: "Cannot we make our laws to punish those men who do such things?," he demanded. "[We should pass] something whereby we can protect those Indians in their rights. [We should enact] laws that if any buy or sell [Indian captives, they] shall be subject to severe penalty." George A. Smith thought this was a waste of time and would do little to stop the practice. "[The gentleman] from Weber [said that we should] pass a law that Indians not be sold in the territory," he said. "All that is necessary [is for them to] pass the [boundary] line." By this, Smith meant that Ute traffickers would simply take their captives into New Mexico for sale. Smith believed that the license that Don Pedro Luján received from Governor Calhoun proved that "the authorities of New Mexico encourage the buying and selling of Indian children."[49]

Despite Farr's objections to the separation of families, legislators did not propose to reunite Indian captives with their relatives. As a practical matter, this would have been difficult. The Ute obtained captives from a variety of nomadic or semi-nomadic peoples spread from California to the Great Plains, although Southern Paiute and Goshute women and children were among them. Depending on age and experience, the captives may not have been able to adequately communicate their place of origin. In some cases, Latter-day Saints traded or purchased children from their families. Moreover, as the final bill was crafted, returning Indian captives would have undermined the incentive structure on which the law was based. The bill authorized county selectmen to "obtain" Indian captives, possibly using public funds to do so. The law in essence viewed the Indian slave trade as an issue of social regulation, much as vagrancy or someone who could not care for themselves and became a public charge. Nevertheless, it largely pushed the costs of ransom onto private individuals who had few resources with which to purchase and care for captives. On the one hand, instituting a period of servitude for ransomed captives was a method to reimburse these costs and to promote such efforts. On the other hand, a policy of repatriation would have been very expensive for private citizens and the territorial government with little hope of remuneration. It also may have required substantial federal involvement. The Latter-day Saints were not eager for greater federal oversight, nor did they believe that the government would provide sufficient funds or personnel to do the job. Religious paternalism also played a significant role in the bill.[50]

The final statute did require probate judges who registered captive children to record their names, ages, places where they were born, the names of their parents "if known," and the tribe to which they belonged. The collection of this information, however, was not to facilitate reunification. The bill, in fact, did not specify a purpose for the collection of this basic biographical information other than to require it. Instead of a bill designed to reunite children with their parents, legislators drafted a law to deter the Indian slave trade, especially with traders from New Mexico, while they legalized the indenturing of Indians in Utah Territory.[51]

In doing so, lawmakers implied that white Latter-day Saint parents were a superior substitute for Native American parents. Latter-day Saints were generally appalled by the material condition of Indigenous people in Utah. This was especially true of the non-equestrian Southern Paiute and Goshute who lived in the most difficult environments of the Great Basin and often subsisted on roots, seeds, and small animals. Mounted Ute slave raiders regularly targeted the small family bands of Goshute and Southern Paiute. George A. Smith believed that the pressures on these people were so great that "if we will not extend the hand of friendship, the race must come to an end."[52]

Utah legislators suggested that in purchasing Indigenous children from their captors, Latter-day Saints would in fact "redeem" them from racial decline and possible extinction. Even Farr eventually conceded that he "would be in favor of making a law to purchase these Indians from their low degraded filthy state" and then include "such laws and regulations as for their happiness after we obtain them." Daniel H. Wells, concurred. He claimed, "Every man in [this] territory may with a gun or any other thing purchase them[selves Indian children] and take them into the bosom of their own families." In his estimation, Latter-day Saint homes were "the most suitable place you can find for them. [There is no] better place for them," he insisted.[53] It was an assertion that indicated that at least some legislators believed Latter-day Saint families were superior to New Mexican Catholic families. Latter-day Saints, thus joined with their Catholic counterparts to view the purchase of Indian captives as a form of religious and racial uplift. Both groups believed their families were superior to Native American families and that the reunification of captives with their biological kin was less desirable than their respective versions of white paternalism.

The question of what to do when presented with Indian captives, then, was a driving force behind the legislative debates over An Act for the Relief of Indian Slaves and Prisoners. It was a difficult moral dilemma as one legislator articulated it, when children were offered to Latter-day Saint settlers for sale and then summarily killed if the settler did not purchase them. In what seems a clear reference to the Luján trial, one lawmaker, perhaps George A. Smith, told his fellow legislators that it was "proven here before the court the other day that there are Indians here that follow the business of stealing children, offering them for sale, and if not sell them, kill them. [T]hese things [or] facts are fairly before the United States court." As a result, this lawmaker believed that the Mormons had a moral obligation to act for the preservation of the Indians.[54]

As this lawmaker viewed it, when Latter-day Saints purchased Indigenous children they provided them with food, clothing, and "a way to obtain an honest living." What exactly were Mormons to do when Ute slave traders brought women and children to them and insisted that the Mormons buy them? "[I have] seen droves of them lariated out," he declared in a reference to the practice of Ute captors who used leather cords or a lariat to bind their captives and then anchor them to the ground via a rope much like a dog on a leash. If Mormons did not intervene, this lawmaker feared that the loss of life among Indian captives would continue unabated. If Mormons did not purchase the children, he also feared that Ute traders would simply continue the practice outside Utah Territory and sell the captive women and children to Mexican settlers whom he believed had less enlightened intent. "If we do not lay the plan to come completely out [to redeem] these Indian children, [then] the trade will be [had] by crossing the line. This trade is going on all the time in Indian country; just cross the line and the trade continues," he worried.[55] While the facets of the story which this lawmaker emphasized were true, his focus on the compulsory nature of the slave trade was at least in part a politically motivated excuse for curtailing the relationship between Ute traders and the New Mexicans while justifying Latter-day Saints interactions with the Indians.

What the newly transcribed debate makes clear is that none of the legislators approved of the Indian trade in which they found themselves entwined.

Even though a form of Indian indenture servitude emerged from the legislative session as the method of regulating the trade, the debate highlights the fact that not all lawmakers found it to be the most desirable solution. At least some of the legislators advocated outlawing the trade altogether rather than legalizing it as a form of servitude in which Latter-day Saints would be allowed to participate. Lorin Farr argued that any law produced by the legislature should "prevent any Indian or white man from selling an Indian in this territory." To enforce such a measure, he advocated "severe punishment." Those who "brought an Indian here in our territory to sell . . . [should] lose their heads or perhaps get a severe flogging," he demanded. Orson Spencer also opposed the bill; instead, he called for sending missionaries among the Indians as a means of uplift. Edward Hunter, a legislator from Salt Lake County and LDS presiding bishop, also believed that there had to be a better way of curtailing the trade: "We must devise such plans [to] save ourselves [from] this thing of purchasing and keeping them for 20 years and give them four years schooling." He recognized that the ideals advocated in the bill would likely not play out so idealistically in practice. "Who will [be] doing it," he wondered? "I would not take one of those Indian women; it would be [the] worst punishment [that] could be placed upon me. We must introduce a plan to hinder this barbarous treatment," he insisted. "No person is going to take an Indian child and school it and bring it up," he claimed.[56]

The debates concerning the Indian indenture bill continued until the afternoon of January 27. After that, the bill was referred to the Committee on Indian Affairs chaired by Daniel H. Wells. George Watt did not record any more debates about the bill during the rest of the legislative session. However, Pratt's objections to the bill were still on some legislators' minds. On January 29, Willard Richards, president of the Legislative Council, wrote a letter to Thomas Kane in which he wondered if the Latter-day Saints had "become so sordid and devilish in their feelings as to suffer the brains of a fine promising child to be dashed out in their presence, rather than give a quart of wheat for said child, because the laws of the U.S. would make it slavery." Under a strict interpretation of the Trade and Intercourse Act, Richards believed that all the property of those who purchased Indian children "must be confiscated because they have been trafficking with the Indians contrary to laws made and provided." In his estimation such an interpretation preferred "martyrdom, and [the Latter-day Saints] not lend the helping hand." "The U.S. laws are against salvation of life in these things," he complained, "and Utah has no authority from mother to make laws to the contrary."[57] Richards and other legislators clearly believed that passing some applicable law was worth the risk. However, Pratt's concerns about the scope of the legislature's authority merited close attention.

On January 31, the full legislature approved a preamble to the Act for the Relief of Indian Slaves and Prisoners. It is likely that portions of the preamble were added in the days after the debate in the Legislative Council. The document began by acknowledging that the Territory of Utah was organized "within and upon what would otherwise be considered Indian Territory, and which really is Indian Territory so far as the right of soil is involved." Although Judge Snow had yet to issue his final opinion in the Luján libel case, the Committee on Indian Affairs had apparently come to the conclusion that federal laws pertaining to "Indian country" applied to Utah. The preamble argued that this state of affairs presented "the novel feature of a white legalized Government on Indian lands." The document went on to describe the outrages of the captive trade in lurid detail. Yet because of the legislature's questionable authority, the preamble meekly requested federal lawmakers to concur with the provisions of the act. For some reason, the legislature did not approve the main text of the bill at this time, nor is it mentioned in the legislative record for several weeks.[58]

On or about February 10, Judge Snow provided a more detailed legal opinion to Willard Richards. It had been over two weeks since Orson Pratt made his objections to the Legislative Council. Snow's opinion was clear that slavery was illegal in Utah without positive legislation to the contrary. This refuted the arguments made by U.S. Attorney Seth M. Blair during the Luján trial and confirmed Brigham Young's long-standing position. Although the preamble to the Act in Relation to Indian Slaves and Prisoners affirmed that Utah was in "Indian territory," Snow's opinion held that Utah was not "Indian country" within the meaning of the Trade and Intercourse Act. The decision strengthened the position of men like George A. Smith who had always claimed that Utah was not Indian country and that the legislature had the authority to enact a statute designed to indenture Native Americans. Nevertheless, Snow maintained that Congress had a right to govern trade with Native Americans and had already extended applicable laws to Utah. Moreover, Congress clearly had the authority to nullify territorial statutes. Consequently, no attempt was made to alter the deferential tone of the preamble. The legislative record indicates that the main text of the act was passed on February 28, although Representative Hosea Stout claimed that the vote was rescinded for some reason. The final statute was approved on March 6, the last day of the legislative session. The existing record does not indicate what happened to the bill after January 27 or why the legislative process took so long.

An Act for the Relief of Indian Slaves and Prisoners was an effort by the territorial legislature to establish a legal framework within which Mormon settlers could confront a long-established slave trade, attempt to regulate it as indenture and apprenticeship within Utah Territory, and to eradicate it at the hands of New Mexican traders from without. The effort was inspired and informed by the contemporaneous trial of Don Pedro Luján. As the majority of legislators saw it, the new statute was the most reasonable remedy—a solution designed to be "the most conducive to ameliorate" the condition of Indian captives.[59]

The form of servitude that the law instituted for Indian captives was involuntary. The bill stipulated that any white person in possession of "any Indian prisoner, child or woman" was required to register the prisoner with a probate judge. The prisoner would then become in essence a ward of the territory, bound out as an apprentice to a white master for a term not to exceed twenty years. The Native Americans being indentured did not have a say in the agreement. Their labor for up to twenty years would pay off the indenture. Orson Pratt thought of this as a form of slavery. Yet for most Latter-day Saints who had been raised among many forms of unfree labor, it was a moderate form of servitude. This was especially true when compared to captivity among the Ute. As some legislators pointed out, Indian apprenticeship was analogous to the traditional practice of involuntary apprenticeship. This had long been used as a paternalistic form of social welfare.

The indenture law shared similarities with the California apprenticeship acts of 1850 and 1860, as well as the practice of *rescate* in New Mexico. It stipulated that the master "bind them to some useful avocation," and it legally defined them as "apprentices," similar to New Jersey's gradual emancipation law that freed its enslaved Black people and then bound them as "apprentices" back to their masters. In Utah, the master was required to send the "apprentice" to school for three months each year for as long as the Indian child was between the ages of seven and sixteen years. Masters were also required to clothe their Indian apprentices "in a comfortable and becoming manner" according to the "master's condition in life."[60] The hope was that the apprentices would learn a marketable trade during their term of indenture and be prepared to fend for themselves once the period of servitude ended. In practice, however, there was no regulatory oversight or any enforcement mechanism put in place to ensure that Indian captives learned a trade or were treated according to the provisions of the bill. In the absence of such oversight, the system was ripe for potential abuse.

After the Utah legislature transmitted the new territorial laws to Congress, there is no evidence of any debate concerning the Indian indenture act. Although Congress had the authority to nullify territorial statutes, it chose not to interfere with affairs in Utah. But the law quickly proved a significant disruption to the Ute economy, a substantial portion of which was based on raiding and trading. In the fall of 1852, Wákara's brother Arapeen attempted to trade captive children to the Latter-day Saints but was rebuffed. Latter-day Saint sources then describe Arapeen becoming "enraged saying that the Mormons had stopped the Mexicans from buying these children; that they had no right to do so, unless they bought them themselves." Arapeen then "took one of these children by the heels and dashed its brains out on the hard ground," underscoring from the Latter-day Saint perspective a key reason why the legislature had enacted the indenture law in the first place.[61] When combined with the continued encroachment of Mormon settlers on Ute lands, these disputes erupted into what Mormons called the Walker War the following summer. The conflict lasted less than a year, but it signaled a dramatic diminishment of Ute economic and political power in the Great Basin.[62]

6

An Act in Relation to Service

An Act in Relation to Service (i.e., Service Act) has long been a kind of embarrassing curiosity in Mormon historiography, while it has been virtually ignored in antebellum historiography more broadly. There is no question that the law was an attempt by the Latter-day Saints in Utah Territory to exercise their prerogatives under the Compromise of 1850 to address the fraught question of African American slavery. Like the Indian indenture bill, it received no congressional debate and was largely unknown outside Utah.[1] Even within the territory, it is not clear how many people were aware of the Service Act, let alone understood it.

The consensus among the few historians who have studied the Service Act has been that the statute legalized chattel slavery in Utah with perhaps a nod toward Christian humanitarianism.[2] Yet this conclusion has only rarely been accompanied by significant analysis of the law itself. Moreover, up until now, historians have been unable to review the substantial legislative record concerning the statute. This has been a major shortcoming of any discussion of the Service Act. Indeed, An Act in Relation to Service is probably the most ambiguous law concerning slavery to be enacted in any of the three polities originally carved from the Mexican Cession.[3]

Even with the aid of the legislative debates, some of the most important provisions of the act remain difficult to decipher. It is unclear whether this was merely the result of poor draftsmanship by novice legislators or a purposeful attempt at obfuscation. What is clear is that the act did not include an outright prohibition of slavery as the California Constitution did in 1849.[4] Yet, neither did the act include any express protection of slavery as the New Mexico slave code did a decade later.[5]

Recent scholarship focused on a close reading of the statute has made the case that the Service Act actually created a system of quasi-indentured servitude for enslaved African Americans that closely approximated laws drafted in Indiana and Illinois after the passage of the Northwest Ordinance. Under the law, enslaved workers were required to consent to this arrangement. Even so, the statute unquestionably recognized that Latter-day Saint enslavers held a property interest in the labor of their slaves. Courts in some Northern states had already begun to describe similar relationships as "involuntary servitude." But the Service Act was ultimately designed to elevate enslaved Black people from the status of property to contract servants while phasing out compulsory servitude, thus implying a form of gradual emancipation.[6]

The recently transcribed legislative debates concerning the Service Act lend support to this interpretation with a few needed refinements. For instance, the debates and the associated legislative journals reveal a hotly contested bill that was greatly modified in form and effect before it was signed into law by Governor Brigham Young on February 4, 1852. Moreover, they record in detail a series of fundamental disagreements between members of the Latter-day Saint leadership regarding theology, race, and the nature of slavery. The debates also confirm that the law had a broader purpose than has been previously reported. It is now clear, as noted, that the act authorized two related systems of indentured servitude: one for enslaved African Americans, and one for Mormon immigrants traveling from Europe and other locations.

Despite this new wealth of knowledge, the terms of the Service Act remain ambiguous either by design or by accident. There are no contemporary court decisions specifically interpreting the act or explicit statements by the drafters about how the law was supposed to function. The legislative debates indicate fundamental disagreements among the legislators about what they had created. If this was not enough, the legal context in which the statute operated shifted significantly over the next decade.

Five years after the Service Act was signed into law, the U.S. Supreme Court handed down the *Dred Scott* decision. This ruling ostensibly forced all territorial governments to legally recognize chattel slavery within their borders. In essence, it rejected Congress's power to prohibit slavery in the territories and stipulated that the territories had to recognize an enslaver's right to her or his enslaved people in a given territory. That same year, President James Buchanan dispatched a federal army to Utah to put down a supposed insurrection.[7] By the fall of 1858, Mormon political and judicial autonomy had been severely circumscribed. As this unfolded, Stephen Douglas began to advocate his controversial Freeport Doctrine, which he argued permitted territorial governments to prohibit slavery in spite of *Dred Scott*. Southern Democrats responded with demands for a federal slave code.[8] Finally, in 1862, Congress forbade slavery and involuntary servitude in Utah, New Mexico, and all other federal territories.[9]

The Luján trials in late 1851 and early 1852 prompted Young to finally support legislation in regard to slavery. This included providing legal recognition to the informal service relationships that already existed in the territory. At the time, Latter-day Saints held between thirty and forty enslaved African Americans in and around the Salt Lake Valley. Still, Young did not alter his fundamental opposition to chattel slavery. In his January 5 speech to the legislature, he explicitly denounced property in man. Instead, Young urged the legislature to codify a transitional form of "servitude" for enslaved African Americans and Native Americans. This would hopefully satisfy Mormon enslavers while providing clear guidance about what they could or could not do with their "servants."[10]

In making this proposal, Young was likely influenced by the status of enslaved Black people in Illinois or, perhaps, during gradual emancipation in New York, a process he had personally observed. He may have also considered New Jersey's recent transformation of its remaining slaves into "perpetual apprentices."[11] Young's proposal was clearly grounded in his own paternalistic interpretation of the curses of Cain and Canaan. Even still, Young's ideal conception of servitude was ill-defined. He likely thought of it as a form of apprenticeship. In this way Mormon enslavers could lawfully assert some kind of limited control over their former slaves without reducing them to property. Such a plan was unlikely to threaten Young's ultimate goal of statehood for Deseret.[12]

During the 1850s, legislators in California and New Mexico faced similar challenges concerning the regulation of African American slavery. On the surface, these jurisdictions took opposite paths. California's Constitution of 1849 explicitly barred slavery and involuntary servitude. Ten years later, New Mexico enacted a slave code. But the truth is that their paths were not quite so divergent as it might at first appear and provide necessary context for the Service Act.[13]

After the discovery of gold at Sutter's Mill in 1848, hundreds of thousands of migrants poured into California from the United States, Latin American, and the Pacific Rim. As in Utah, the vast majority of American settlers came from the Northern states and strongly advocated free-soil policies.[14] By 1850, however, some 36 percent of American-born Californians were Southerners, and they formed a powerful pro-slavery bloc in the state government.[15]

After the American conquest, local courts tended to free enslaved Black people as a result of Mexican prohibitions on slavery.[16] By the fall of 1849, a proposed constitution provided that neither "slavery, nor involuntary servitude, unless for the punishment of crimes, shall ever be tolerated in this State."[17] Congress later approved this constitution as part of the Compromise of 1850. But despite these early free-soil victories, American slave owners experimented with a number of legal strategies to maintain the labor of their enslaved workers.

Many enslavers followed long-standing American precedent by entering labor contracts with their slaves. These contracts stipulated that a slave would work for a certain period of time or raise a certain amount of money for his master, in consideration for which the slave would be emancipated. Unlike the indenture contracts that had been executed between masters and slaves in the Old Northwest, the terms of these agreements were typically much shorter, lasting for only a few months or, at most, a few years rather than decades. Although enslavers sometimes refused to honor their bargains, California courts consistently upheld the legality of these contracts.[18] As a result, enslaved African Americans continued to be held in California as indentured servants well into the 1860s.[19]

Enslavers also used their influence in the state government to legalize African slavery for a limited duration. In April 1852, the California legislature passed An Act Respecting Fugitives from Labor, and Slaves Brought to this State Prior to Her Admission into the Union, sometimes called the California Fugitive Slave Act. Among other things, the act stipulated that until April 1853, a master could lawfully remove any enslaved person from the state as long as he or she had been brought to California before the state's admission into the Union. In effect, the law retroactively legalized slavery for individuals who had arrived in California prior to September 1850, as long as their enslavers ultimately removed them from the state.[20] Future legislation extended the grace period for removal from the state until April 1855.[21]

Even after that, the status of enslaved people remained contested in California. In 1858, one enslaver attempted to take his slave with him back to Mississippi, and the state supreme court sided with the enslaver before a federal court declared the slave free. Even as those events played out, the California legislature debated a bill that would have prevented the immigration of "free negroes and other obnoxious persons" into the state. The bill passed the California House before dying in the Senate. In the wake of such events, a group of Black people left California for Canada where their freedom would not be under threat from the state's strong pro-Southern faction.[22]

New Mexico did not see the massive population boom that occurred in California. By 1860, only about 6 percent of the New Mexican population was Anglo-American. Still, government officials, army officers, and some settlers did move to the region from the United States bringing African American slaves with them.[23] While their numbers were always small compared to those in California, anywhere from ten to sixty-four enslaved Black people were brought into the territory by 1860.[24] This was roughly comparable to the number of enslaved African Americans in Utah.

At first, New Mexican elites showed little interest in legalizing African American slavery. The practice had already been prohibited for nearly two decades under Mexican law, and other forms of unfree labor, such as peonage, were readily available. With the encouragement of men like Senator Thomas Hart Benton and President Zachary Taylor, New Mexicans applied to enter the Union as a free state in the summer of 1850. Unlike the Constitution of Deseret, which did not mention slavery, the proposed Constitution of New Mexico prohibited slavery and involuntary servitude for adults. However, "voluntary" forms of servitude, such as peonage, were protected.[25] But in 1850, New Mexico was organized as a federal territory under the hazy conditions of popular sovereignty.

For most of the ensuing decade, the territorial legislature entirely ignored the question of African American slavery, just as it ignored the trade in Indian captives. As a result, slavery was practiced on a small scale as a matter of custom. However, in January 1857, the legislature enacted a discriminatory Black Code;[26] it prohibited free Black people from entering the territory for more than thirty days, criminalized miscegenation, and decreed that any enslaver who emancipated his slaves in New Mexico was required to transport them outside the territory's boundaries.[27]

Then, in February 1859, the New Mexican legislature passed an explicit slave code. Two years before, the *Dred Scott* decision had compelled all territorial governments to legally recognize the institution of slavery. However, Stephen Douglas responded with his controversial Freeport Doctrine. As articulated during his debate with Abraham Lincoln at Freeport, Illinois, Douglas argued that territories could prevent slavery by simply not passing legislation favorable to it. As a result, Southern congressmen agitated for a national slave code that would apply to all federal territories. The fact is that African American slavery remained economically inconsequential in New Mexico, just as it was in Utah. Nevertheless, Hispanic legislators who were originally opposed to slavery now changed their opinion to protect their own interests in unfree labor. New Mexico's Territorial Secretary Alexander Jackson, a Mississippian, later wrote that these legislators had been assured that passage of a slave code would "protect their own system of peonage."[28] There is also substantial evidence that the law was conceived as a "temporary expedient" to appease Southern interests in Washington.[29]

An Act to Provide for the Protection of Property in Slaves in this Territory was originally drafted by Secretary Jackson. There were sections of the law similar to the Mississippi slave code of 1857, but it was likely based on a combination of statutes and case law from various jurisdictions that were known to Jackson. The law gave some protection to enslaved persons, criminalizing the unlawful killing of a slave, as well as cruel and unusual treatment, and requiring masters to provide proper "food, lodging and raiment." Any person who wrongfully held as a slave "any negro or mulatto who is entitled to freedom" could be imprisoned for between five and ten years and be fined up to $2,000. Nevertheless, penalties against inducing a slave to leave his master were steep. Escapees could be lawfully apprehended by any person who might "use or employ such force as may be necessary" during the capture. Enslaved persons were not permitted to leave their owner's home after dark without a pass, and any slave who gave "insolent language, or signs, to any free white person" could be whipped up to thirty-nine times "upon his bare back." A slave convicted of a crime normally resulting in a fine could instead be whipped or even branded.[30]

Unlike the Black Code of 1857, the new statute absolutely prohibited the emancipation of a slave in New Mexico. Lawmakers also included a stronger anti-miscegenation provision. Finally, the new slave code banned any "slave, free negro or mulatto" from giving evidence in court against "a free white person." The only change to the law that was made by the predominately Hispanic legislature was a section providing that it would not apply to "contracted servants," or peons, and that the word "slave" would only apply to "the African race" and not to Indians.[31]

The New Mexico slave code lasted for less than three years. In 1860, the legislature amended the law in an attempt to codify slavery for Native Americans as well as African Americans. The territorial governor refused to sign the bill, however, arguing that Indians could not be held as slaves under U.S. law. Instead, they must be held as "captives or *peons.*" Yet beginning that same year, there were several efforts to repeal the law both in New Mexico and in Congress. Finally, in December 1861, with a Confederate army occupying the lower Rio Grande Valley, the legislature fully repealed the slave code.[32]

* * *

Brigham Young's proposed solution to the slavery problem shared similarities with the contractual servitude utilized in California. But unlike lawmakers in other portions of the Mexican Cession, Young was not prepared to legalize chattel slavery to appease enslavers. He instead urged legislators in Utah to take a more moderate path.

In the days after Young's January 5 speech, his proposals and others coming from the body of the legislature were divided among both houses and then assigned to various committees. His suggestions regarding servitude were taken up by the Legislative Council and entrusted to a committee that probably consisted of apostle George A. Smith and Orson Spencer. There is no evidence of discussions between Smith and Spencer over the next two weeks, although they almost certainly occurred. On January 23, Smith reported the first draft of An Act in Relation to African Slavery to the full Council. Later that same day, he also introduced the first draft of An Act for the Protection of the Rights of Indians. On the motion of Orson Pratt, Smith's report was accepted by the Council, the bill was read for the first time, and it passed. This was a notable start to the legislative process as Pratt would soon become the bill's most vocal critic. However, after a second reading, the bill was referred back to committee, and Orson Spencer was instructed to write a preamble for it.[33] This suggests that Spencer may have been the bill's principal author.

The name that Spencer and Smith selected for their bill was somewhat misleading. Although the proposed legislation was clearly meant to address the problem of African slavery, it was not the bill's sole focus. Section 1 stated its general purpose: "That any person or persons coming to this Territory and bringing with them servants justly bound to them, arising from special contract or otherwise, said person or persons shall be entitled to such service or labor by the laws of this Territory: Provided, That he shall file in the office of the Probate Court written and satisfactory evidence that such service or labor is due." On its face, then, the bill was designed to recognize service relationships that existed between individuals who migrated to the territory. Still, the legislative debates make it clear that Spencer and Smith had two specific forms of labor in mind. Section 3 of the act was meant to authorize some form of servitude for enslaved African Americans. However, Section 2 of the act was meant to authorize a related form of servitude for European immigrants.[34]

In almost every way, European immigrants and Black slaves were to be treated identically under the proposed law. Both were referred to as "servants" within the text and the labor agreements between master and servant were referred to as "contracts." These contracts were intended to be voluntary. The reality of this for enslaved African Americans is of course open to question, as we will discuss below. Still, the proposed law guaranteed that no servant could be "transferred" from one master to another unless the servant provided explicit consent to a judge in the "absence of his Master or Mistress." Furthermore, no servant could be removed from the territory without his or her consent. Violation of these provisions was punishable by up to five years in prison as well as a $5,000 fine.[35] Similar protections had been codified for indentured servants going back at least 150 years.

Although these requirements implicitly recognized that a servant could be conveyed from one person to another, it was also clear that a servant could not be treated as property. The law would not permit a master to sell an enslaved worker without his or her consent or break up an enslaved family. Brigham Young had strongly objected to such activities prior to the departure of the San Bernardino company a year before.[36] The bill unambiguously recognized servants as human beings with personal agency. It is also significant that these provisions essentially mirrored those in the old Indiana and Illinois laws permitting African slaves to enter those states as registered or indentured servants.[37] The Saints had encountered these laws during their sojourn in Nauvoo from 1839 to 1846.

Just as the bill protected all servants from involuntary sale, it also assured them sufficient food, shelter, and recreation; and excessive corporal punishment could nullify the contract. If this occurred, courts were obliged to indenture a freed servant to another master. This provision would prove to be controversial in the coming weeks, and at Brigham Young's insistence lawmakers revised it before it became law.[38]

In contrast, the education requirement in the proposed law produced no discussion at all. As drafted the law required masters to send their servants between the ages of six and twenty to school for at least eighteen months. It was a requirement that stood in stark contrast to slave codes in many Southern states, which made it a crime to teach a slave to read and write. In the late 1820s, for example, when Hugh Auld learned that his wife Sophia was teaching the couple's enslaved boy, the future abolitionist Frederick

Douglass, to read, Auld forbade it. Auld told his wife that "it was unlawful, as well as unsafe, to teach a slave to read." As Douglass later recalled, Auld warned his wife that "a nigger should know nothing but to obey his master—to do as he is told to do. Learning would *spoil* the best nigger in the world." Sophia Auld complied with her husband's demands and eventually concurred that "education and slavery were incompatible with each other." Lawmakers in the South agreed. Virginia and Alabama prohibited white people from teaching both enslaved and free Black people to read and write. It was just one of the features of Utah's Service Act that distinguished it from slave codes elsewhere.[39]

The bill proposed no restrictions on property ownership or the ability to testify in court, did not require travel with a pass, or contain any of the other countless disadvantages with which American legislatures had traditionally shackled slaves, unfree laborers, and even free Black people. Nevertheless, these service relationships were legally binding as long as the parties filed evidence of their agreement with local officials. Any servant, white or Black, could be compelled to labor for his or her master even if that servant wished to leave.[40]

Despite these similarities, the servitude created under Section 2 of the bill differed in several important respects from the servitude created under Section 3. Section 2 ensured the enforceability of agreements made between Mormon converts emigrating from Europe and lenders who financed their journey to the United States. These lenders included private citizens as well as the Perpetual Emigrating Company. During the legislative debates, George A. Smith explained that similar arrangements had existed, "since [the] settlement of America. [P]ersons in Europe would say to some individual if you will take me and my family and move me in such a place in America we will serve you until you are paid." Smith then linked such practice to Utah Territory. "[P]ersons in Wales and in [England] have made such promises [to our citizens in Utah]; bring us here [and] we will serve you until you are paid. [S]ome persons have [expended] their fortunes in helping persons [come to Utah]. [I]t is the design of that section that until the debt due [is paid] we will serve you."[41]

Many members of the Utah legislature had already enacted a similar form of unfree labor when they sat as lawmakers for the provisional State of Deseret. In September 1850, the Deseret legislature incorporated the Perpetual Emigrating Company in order to manage the assets of the Perpetual Emigrating Fund, or PEF. This fund was created to help defray travel costs for poor Mormons going to Utah. There was little hope that these immigrants would be able to repay the donations in cash, and consequently the law provided that they might "reimburse the same in labor or otherwise, as soon as their circumstances will admit."[42] Participants were expected to sign contracts to that effect, further stipulating that they would obey PEF agents during transport. In practice, this created a form of indentured servitude.[43] Immigrants who received funds from the PEF after voluntarily entering a contract could be compelled to labor until their debt was paid off. Whether formal legal action was ever taken to force such debtors to satisfy their debts through labor is an open question. But on at least one occasion, Brigham Young urged bishops not to allow people who were still indebted to the PEF to leave Utah Territory without repayment, presumably through cash or work.[44] This may help explain the experience of at least some individuals who later claimed that they were forced to remain in Utah against their will.[45]

While Section 2 of the service bill conformed to the basic ideas outlined by Smith in his speech, it was sparse on detail. In fact, it seems likely that Spencer and Smith purposely drafted Section 2 loosely to provide maximum flexibility to lenders and debtors. According to the draft, satisfactory evidence of these agreements might include anything from a written indenture to testimony of an oral contract. Unlike traditional forms of indentured servitude, there was no set form for this kind of agreement, nor did the bill establish any maximum term of service. The only legal restriction was that a servant must have received "reasonable compensation" for his or her service. PEF contracts were vague and specified that once an immigrant arrived in Utah, he must hold his time and labor "subject to the appropriation of the PEF company," until the "full cost" of the journey was paid. Moreover, the PEF Company could charge an unspecified amount of interest if it so chose.[46] Apparently, the details of repayment had to be worked out once an immigrant arrived in Utah. Contracts with private lenders may have been similar.

Section 2 indentures could last for any period of time and take virtually any form as long as a probate judge determined that the individual arrangement was "reasonable" in comparison to the debt. Consider the PEF. Although ostensibly a private organization, debts owed to the fund were sometimes paid off through periodic labor on the public works (but sometimes not paid off at all). Under this practice, a portion of the laborer's daily salary was held back and used to satisfy the debt.[47] This procedure more closely resembled "contract labor" than indentured servitude, and individual lenders may have relied on similar arrangements.[48] Yet based on the provisions of the law, it is possible that some debtors labored in a true indentured status for a specified time. In any event, a judge had the power to order an insolvent and otherwise recalcitrant debtor to labor for his or her benefactor until the debt was fully discharged. In the absence of specific language in the text of the bill, it was entirely up to the parties and a judge to determine what was fair.[49]

What is more, the bill actually made these contracts heritable. If a debtor died still owing money, his heirs could be compelled to labor until the debt was repaid. This provision proved highly controversial in the legislature.[50] Pennsylvania and Maryland had abolished such practices over three decades before.[51] Even New Mexico ostensibly banned heritable debt servitude in 1851, although it continued in practice.[52] Hosea Stout, a Kentucky-born lawyer, believed it was inconceivable that a parent could bind his child to labor beyond the age of majority. "At the age [of] 21 I shall be clear of all contracts my father made," he argued. "I cannot see how to make a law to bind a child to pay the debts of [a] father after he is 21."[53] In fact, the law the Utah legislature passed concerning apprenticeship stipulated that these relationships could only last until the "age of legal majority," that is, twenty-one for males and eighteen for females.[54] George A. Smith answered Stout's concerns with a hypothetical. "I suppose myself to be in England with half dozen boys big and small. I pledge myself to Mr. Stout that I [will] pay [if he takes me to America]. [If] I die on the road shall my children kick up their heels and say my daddy [is] dead [and] I shall not pay?"[55]

For Smith, once a debt was contracted it must be paid, even by those who were not actual parties to the agreement. His position made sense as a way to incentivize cash-poor Mormons to continue to finance the immigration of European converts. Lenders were guaranteed repayment in labor even if the contracting party happened to die. It was a concept far closer to debt peonage than to contemporary American practices. Nevertheless, this hereditary servitude could not last forever. The bill specified that no contract could "bind the heirs of the servant or servants to service for a longer period than will satisfy the debt due his, her, or their master or mistress."[56] Once the debt was paid, the indenture was at an end.[57]

In contrast, Section 3 indentures were designed to recognize the established interest that Southern Mormons held in the labor of their enslaved workers. Spencer and Smith's bill made the evidentiary requirements for this mode of servitude both more and less exacting than those for European immigrants. It first required a sealed court certificate attesting that the master was entitled to the labor of his servant. But no further proof of consideration or contract was necessary as long as it "appeared" that the servant came to Utah voluntarily.[58] This prerequisite was not merely cosmetic. The principle of consent was at the heart of the law. However, the bill did not specify how consent was to be proven. Instead, the law gave probate judges the exclusive responsibility to determine whether an enslaved person had come to Utah voluntarily or not.[59]

The greatest difference between Section 2 and 3 indentures involved the term of service. While labor contracts for European immigrants were limited to the repayment of an established debt, Spencer and Smith proposed that enslaved African Americans and their children could lawfully be held in servitude until "the curse of servitude is taken from the descendants of Canaan." It is not entirely clear from the text of the bill if this applied to the children of slaves who were born in Utah. A reasonable case could be made either way, and the legislative debates shed no light on the matter. But it is clear that an enslaved person who "voluntarily" entered the territory with his or her master could be held in servitude for life.[60]

Lifetime service contracts were not unknown in Anglo-American law, particularly in the case of former slaves. Sir William Blackstone, considered one of the most important legal authorities in early America, argued in his *Commentaries* that a slave who was freed by operation of law might still be held as a servant for life.[61] The laws in Indiana and Illinois that permitted enslavers to enter indenture contracts with their enslaved workers had no prescribed maximum term, effectively allowing for lifetime servitude.[62] In New Jersey, the abolition of slavery in 1846 transformed former slaves into "apprentices for life."[63]

In extending perpetual servitude to the children of enslaved Black people, however, Smith and Spencer's bill went further. As it was originally drafted, the law provided a number of rights and protections for African American servants that raised them above the status of alienable property. But at the very least, lifetime hereditary servitude would likely qualify as a form of serfdom or villeinage even if it did not amount to de jure slavery. Certainly, it was involuntary servitude as the term was then understood. But whatever Smith and Spencer hoped to accomplish, it turned out that hereditary servitude for African Americans was even more controversial than hereditary servitude for European immigrants. After significant debate, this and several related provisions were removed from the final version of the Service Act.

***

On the same day that Smith and Spencer reported their draft bill, Brigham Young made a speech to the Council supporting it but also suggested revisions. This would prove to be one of the most consequential speeches in Young's long career and, in conjunction with his February 5 address, perhaps the most infamous. Unlike his remarks to the legislature earlier in the month, it was not prepared beforehand or even written down except in George Watt's contemporaneous shorthand account and his later longhand transcription. Young essentially restated the positions that he had espoused during his prepared statement of January 5, although with some significant additions. For instance, he now voiced strong support for placing European immigrants in a condition of servitude until they could pay off their debts.[64]

Financing immigration was a top priority for Young and one of his greatest challenges in a region with a limited supply of hard currency. Young saw this as a pious effort to gather the "Lord's poor" to Zion as well as a means to obtain workers for new settlements. When Latter-day Saint immigrants refused to pay their debts, it was not only a sin, but it also jeopardized the entire system. Consequently, Young pushed for stronger regulations to protect private lenders. "Suppose I am in England and bring over [to America] 100 persons, males and females, and they pledge themselves to work so long to [be able to] get with those they love and [then what] if they come here and abuse their benefactors?," he asked lawmakers. Young had a particular example in mind. "See [the] abuse [heaped] on Dan Jones who prevailed on Sister Lewis to spend every dime [she had]? They curse her and him. I say they ought to be her servants. This they [will] continue [to do] until they go [to] hell!" Young thundered.[65]

Young here referred to Dan Jones, a Welch convert and missionary, and his wife Elizabeth Lewis. Lewis was a wealthy benefactor who aided many of her fellow converts to immigrate to the United States. In 1849 Lewis sailed from Liverpool as one of 249 Saints who emigrated on board the *Buena Vista*. Lewis married Jones as a plural wife after arriving in Utah. On her death in 1895, she was honored for using her wealth "with great liberality in enabling the Welsh Saints to come to Utah." Her obituary noted that she "fitted out an entire company across the plains."[66]

Migrant servitude had already disappeared from the eastern United States. Yet Brigham Young believed that it was a reasonable policy to ensure that Mormon immigrants paid their debts. Still, he concluded that some degree of formality was necessary and advocated that the parties enter written contracts. "In [the] future let them perform their labors according to writing, or I hope it will be in writing," he said.[67] Like the other legislators, he understood that Section 2 of the Service Act applied specifically to immigrants from Europe.

Young also provided a fuller explanation for his support of African servitude. In his January 5 remarks, he had already explained that servitude was a natural consequence of the curse of Canaan. Young now reiterated this dogma. However, he also publicly declared for the first time that men of African descent could not hold the lay priesthood within the LDS Church. He explained to the Legislative Council, "They [people of Black African descent] enjoy the rights of receiving the first principles of [the] gospel which is liberty to all. These servants enjoy the privilege of being baptized [and having] hands laid on [their heads] for the Holy Ghost. They enjoy [the privilege] of so living before the Lord, [before their] masters, [and before their] friends [so] as to enjoy the spirit of [the] Lord continually." Young then explained, "As far as [the] comforts [of] salvation, light, truth, enjoyment, [and] understand[ing] [are concerned] the blacks have the same privilege [as] white [men except] they cannot hold the priesthood. Inasmuch as they cannot bear any share in [the] priesthood, I ask whether they can bear rule in any place until that curse is removed? Consequently, they are 'servant of servants.'"[68]

Young's comments would have a profound effect on Mormon theology and practice for over a century. Although he confirmed the essential universality of the gospel, Young clearly laid out a scriptural basis for denying ordination to men of Black African descent and for a system of African servitude. "Inasmuch as I believe in [the] Bible, [inasmuch as I] believe in [the] ordinances of [God and in the] priesthood order of God, I believe in slavery," Young declared.[69] Here Young echoed an argument that even Northern Protestant theologians sometimes made—the Bible was the word of God, and it sanctioned slavery. As some clergy articulated it, an attack on slavery amounted to an attack on the Bible itself. For example, Charles Hodge, an old-school Presbyterian and the dominant figure at Princeton Theological Seminary for fifty years, believed that "the Scriptures do sanction slaveholding." Hodge argued that to call slavery "a heinous crime" was tantamount to "a direct impeachment of the word of God."[70]

Young's position was also similar to an argument Joseph Smith made in 1836 when he claimed that "the curse is not yet taken off the sons of Canaan, neither will be until it is affected by as great power as caused it to come." Smith continued that "the people who interfere the least with the decrees and purposes of God in this matter, will come under the least condemnation before him."[71] By 1844, however, Smith's views had evolved to the point that he was willing to "interfere" with slavery. He advocated a government-funded gradual emancipation process.[72] Eight years later, however, Young argued that "[Black Africans] have brought curses upon themselves and until the curse is removed by Him who has put the curse on this class, I am not authorized to [re]move it."[73]

Young further drew on an earlier biblical curse, the so-called curse of Cain, to justify a racial priesthood restriction, something that Smith never did. In his speech on January 23, Young conflated the curse of Cain (Genesis 4:11–16) with the curse of Ham or Canaan (Genesis 9:25). In other speeches he was more precise. He argued in 1859 that the "mark" that God put on Cain after he murdered his brother Abel was "the flat nose and black skin."[74] Like many people in the broader Christian tradition, Young believed that Cain's murder of Abel and the resulting curse and mark explained the origins of black skin and meant that Black Africans were descendants of Cain. It was an idea in circulation centuries before Mormonism began; Young brought it with him into his chosen faith and gave it unique theological meaning.[75]

In Young's mind, Cain's murder of Abel resulted in a curse in which God blocked Cain's descendants from receiving the Latter-day Saint lay priesthood. Young believed that this specifically meant people of Black African descent. They would have to wait until all of Abel's descendants received it first. "The Lord God said that cursed [be] old Cain and [God] said that [only after] the last drop of [the] blood of Abel receives the priesthood and enjoys the blessings [of it], then Cain is calculated to have his share [but] not until then," Young told the legislature.[76] The second curse, the curse of Ham or Canaan, suggested that because of Ham's supposed indiscretion toward his father Noah, Ham's son Canaan would be cursed as a "servant of servants" (Genesis 9:25). This curse was used among Christians, Jews, and Muslims as "the single greatest justification for Black slavery for more than a thousand years."[77]

On January 23, Young invoked the cumulative effects of the curse of Cain and the curse of Canaan to argue against Black priesthood ordination, against Black civil rights, and in favor of Black "servitude." It was a subject that he had been mulling over since the winter of 1847 when he learned that Enoch Lewis had entered an interracial marriage with a white Latter-day Saint woman. Young began with the premise that people of African descent were the lineal descendants of both Cain and Canaan. In his interpretation, the curse of Cain denied males of Cain's line the ability to receive the priesthood and to rule in God's church. Young argued that the inability to rule in the church rendered African Americans unfit to participate in civil government or to vote. Finally, Young concluded that the inability to rule in either the church or the political community rendered these individuals "servant of servants," in fulfillment of the curse of Canaan. Young essentially argued that those who cannot rule must serve. In this way, he conveyed divine sanction upon the social and political conventions of the era and emphasized that it was both natural and pious for white people to rule over Black people.[78]

Young's racist dogma was tempered by a conviction that such inequalities were temporary and that someday God would lift these twin curses. Until that time came, he taught that white people must fully recognize the humanity of African Americans, baptize them, educate them, and improve their situation in life. For Young, these were preparatory activities. Just as he must prepare the Latter-day Saints for the coming millennium, the Latter-day Saints must prepare Black Africans for a time when they would be granted the right to officiate in the priesthood. It was a paternalistic argument that portrayed white people as parents and Black people as children in need of oversight.

This was not simply an abstract interpretation of scripture, however. Young had been influenced by years of public debates stretching back to his youth in New York concerning the ability of formerly enslaved African Americans to live orderly and productive lives in a democratic society. Gradual emancipation itself was partially based on the idea that the enslaved must be carefully prepared for freedom over time. Intermediate forms of servitude functioned as a method to exercise control over formerly enslaved Black people as they made the slow transition to liberty. But even when free, African Americans were often not permitted to vote or participate in government.[79]

Young's position reflected these traditional republican concerns, but he couched his arguments to the legislature in theological terms. His interpretations of various biblical curses both influenced and justified his own preconceptions of African Americans. Still, Young did not support labor relationships based on brute force. Instead, he advocated voluntary associations that respected individual agency. Young was perfectly comfortable with employing free African Americans as wage workers and maintaining them as members of his household. He employed Isaac James, a Black convert from New Jersey, as a coachman and servant for years, and at one point also counted Isaac's wife Jane Manning James as a servant in his household as well.[80] This kind of relationship was Young's ideal. In his paternalistic vision, the curse of Canaan subjected people of color to a condition of social dependency rather than property or forced labor.

Young's January 23 speech marked an important change in his public rhetoric, particularly in regard to a priesthood ban for African American men. But his comments were not meant to break new theological ground nor to fully describe his views. Instead, his immediate goal was to demonstrate support for the service bill and alleviate the growing friction within the Latter-day Saint community concerning slavery. He argued, "[Many] brethren in the south [have means vested in slaves]. Those of their servants want to come here, [but] when they come here, the devil [is] raised. This one talking, that one talking, [and a] strong abolitionist feeling [prevails with some people] whispering etc., [saying "do you think it's right, I am afraid it is not right."] I know it is right. There should be a law made to have the slaves serve their masters because they are not capable of ruling [themselves]."[81]

Here, Young stressed his belief that many enslaved African Americans were simply not prepared for independence. He also acknowledged a significant rift among his followers. There were a number of Southern Mormons who wished to legally secure the labor of their enslaved workers. Yet many Latter-day Saints strongly objected to this practice. Bubbling just beneath the surface of an outwardly united Latter-day Saint community was a division over slavery that had the potential to be just as toxic and bitter as anywhere else in the country. If given expression, this division could split the Church he led as it had other denominations. It was something that weighed on Young's mind even after the Civil War had ended. In 1866, he publicly recalled that "Baptists of the south was so opposed to events of the north in regard to their abolition proclivities" that the "Baptist Church in the north arose to that degree against slave holders that they withdrew fellowship from each other and about [a] year after that the Methodists did likewise." Young lamented that those denominations had "severed that Christian accord of benevolence and brotherly love and kindness," so much so that they split into "two nations of Christians." He blamed such divisions on "the spirit of abolition and slavery" that became so intense that it "severed their religion and they sacrificed the whole of it."[82]

In response to the extremism he perceived among enslavers and abolitionists alike, Young adopted a moderate approach to slavery similar to some of his Protestant contemporaries. Leonard Bacon, "one of New England's most prominent religious leaders," was a graduate of Yale and the pastor of New Haven Connecticut's prestigious First Church. As such, Bacon hoped for "a peaceful, orderly end to slavery," one that attempted to "carve out a space between increasingly virulent abolitionism and increasingly hostile defenses of slavery." As moderate Protestants viewed it, the Bible sanctioned slavery, which was an unavoidable fact. In contrast, radical abolitionists argued that slavery was a sin that needed to be eradicated immediately. In the minds of the moderates, the abolitionist position amounted to an attack on the Bible. Even still, moderates acknowledged that slavery contradicted fundamental Christian principles and should not be perpetuated. As one historian put it, "the moderates occupied a rhetorical no-man's-land between a morally absolute abolitionism that lacked biblical support and biblically forceful defenses of slavery."[83]

Young attempted to thread the same needle. The Protestant moderates, however, occupied a moral middle ground that did not garner significant support in the nineteenth century because of their failure to fully commit to one side or the other. Young fundamentally objected to property in man, stating that "human flesh to be dealt in as property, is not consistent or compatible with the true principles of government."[84] Even so, Young firmly defended biblical justifications for servitude and condemned what he considered to be the excesses of the abolitionists. While he generally supported free-soil policies, and personally emancipated several enslaved people, he also attempted to conciliate Mormon enslavers. Young and the Protestant moderates occupied a moral middle ground that some historians have judged harshly. "Moderates stand condemned as both moral and intellectual failures," one historian notes, but "in their own minds, the antislavery moderates were peacemakers, people who stood in the middle of two extremes and charted the reasonable and tolerant path forward."[85]

Like his moderate Protestant contemporaries, Young positioned himself in the middle of two extremes in the 1850s. His effort to navigate between those in his flock who expressed "strong abolitionist feeling[s]" on the one hand, and Southern enslavers such as John Bankhead on the other hand, highlight his effort to strike a balance. "They came in good faith," Young said, implying that Southerners who arrived in the Great Basin did so with an expectation that their property in slaves would be protected.[86] His effort to carve out a position between those competing groups made Young a peacemaker in his own mind, a leader who was charting a tolerant path forward. Young's stance was not fully satisfying to either side in the nineteenth century, and like that of the Protestant moderates, it has not held up well over time either.[87]

Young's ad-libbed remarks on January 23 also muddled important legal issues. In his January 5 address, Young had carefully differentiated between the concepts of chattel slavery and servitude, condemning the former while supporting the latter. But in this later speech, he often used the words "slavery" and "servitude" interchangeably and in a variety of different contexts. In one passage, Young declared that he was "a firm believer in slavery." Later, he stated that he was "firm in belief of servitude." At various points, Young referred to African Americans, the English working class, and even the Latter-day Saints as either "slaves" or "servants" without any attempt at consistency. This imprecise use of language was not unusual in antebellum America, nor for Young in particular. Slavery was not simply a defined legal status; it was also a powerful metaphor. But Young's poor word choice clouded the issues and presents difficulties in interpretating his views.[88]

Despite the numerous ambiguities, Young made it clear that he supported enforceable labor contracts for both European immigrants and Black slaves as long as the working conditions were humane. "Good wholesome servitude," he said, "I know nothing better than that."[89] He likewise suggested that the name of the bill should be changed from "An Act in Relation to African Slavery" to "An Act in Relation to Manual Service." Although Young was often inconsistent with his word choice, he evidently believed that this change in terminology better conveyed the bill's purpose. Finally, Young indicated his willingness that the bill be "thrown back" for further revisions, including greater protections for African American servants.[90] Afterward, the bill was returned to committee so that Orson Spencer could draft a preamble to the legislation.[91]

The next day, January 24, Orson Spencer reported a preamble to the service bill. Unfortunately, the text of that preamble has not survived. On motion from George A. Smith, the report was accepted, and Spencer was instructed to continue his labors. Two days later, Smith reported a bill that was now entitled An Act in Relation to Service to the Council, apparently without the preamble. This was laid on the table for further consideration the next day. Throughout the afternoon of January 26 and the morning of January 27, debate raged in the Legislative Council concerning An Act for the Relief of Indian Slaves and Prisoners. Orson Pratt raised a number of forceful objections, including that the bill instituted "slavery" for Native Americans. But these sharp disagreements were only a prelude to the debate that would follow regarding African American slavery.[92]

In the early afternoon of January 27, 1852, An Act in Relation to Service was read to the assembled Council. Orson Pratt (see figure 6.1) immediately motioned that the entire bill be rejected. Instead, the bill was read by sections. The first section concerning the enforceability of labor relationships was read without objection, as was the second dealing with servitude for European immigrants. But when Section 3 was read, Pratt stood once again. "I am opposed to that section and wish to make a motion in relation to it," he said. But

Figure 6.1 Orson Pratt (1811–1881) was an apostle in the Church of Jesus Christ of Latter-day Saints in 1852 and a member of the Utah territorial legislature. Courtesy Church History Library.

before he made his motion, Pratt begged the Council to hear his views on the subject of African American slavery. He then bluntly attacked slavery and any attempt to introduce it into Utah on ethical, theological, and political grounds.[93]

Pratt first described the institution of slavery as a "great evil." In fact, he claimed that even "the slave holders in [the] south look upon it as an evil." "Slavery doesn't exist here," he observed, anticipating Judge Snow's legal opinion in the Luján case. "We are not under the necessity of legislating and devising plans to get rid of evil, but we stand in [the] same relation to [our] fore fathers that introduced slavery into the southern states," Pratt argued. "They [were] pirates that went to Africa, purchased Negros and made them slaves in [the] United States. They introduced the evil and who is the most under condemnation? The children that have this evil riveted upon them and know nothing of the manner to get rid of it? Or the individuals that introduced [it[94]] into the country?" "Shall we introduce this evil in our midst?" Pratt asked the Council. "No!"[95]

Pratt then directly challenged Brigham Young's interpretation of the curses that had supposedly been placed on Black Africans. Interestingly, he did not deny that such curses existed. Rather, he argued that the "Curse of Cain" had nothing to do with servitude. God "did not curse [Cain] to slavery," Pratt declared, "but cursed him with a mark." Even if servitude was a condition of the curse of Ham or Canaan, Pratt argued that no people were justified in executing a divine curse unless they had specific authorization from God to do so. Curses, in Pratt's mind, were specific to a given time and place. Moreover, no people were authorized to execute a divine curse unless they received direction from God to do so. The Children of Israel offered a prime example. According to Pratt, their "transgressions" brought God's judgments upon them and "exposed them to some [of the most severe] curses ever upon the human family." They suffered not only "disease, sicknesses, and death, [but also] dispersion [and] disasters [that] tongue cannot name. They were to be cursed by all the nations of [the] earth and [the nations of the earth would] buy them and sell them as bond men and bond women." Even though such consequences were pronounced "by the authority of [the] Almighty," Pratt argued, it did not justify anyone in that day "to lay their hands upon Israel." More importantly, Pratt said, "Neither does [it justify others] to lay their hands upon [the] descendants of Canaan." He explained that there "may be [a] curse upon a people, and that when that curse is pronounced by the authority of the priesthood [of the] Almighty, unless he designates the individuals to inflict it, they come into condemnation if [they] inflict it." Pratt strenuously denied that Latter-day Saints had ever received any such authorization from God. "Shall we assume the right without the voice of [the] Lord speaking to us and commanding us to [introduce] slavery into our territory?" Pratt found the idea disgraceful.[96]

Moreover, he believed that any move to legalize slavery in Utah would materially damage missionary efforts in Great Britain and other locations that were strongly antislavery in sentiment. "They consider it one of [the] worst of evils," he said. "Shall we not desire the salvation of [the] inhabitants of Great Britain and inhabitants of [the] world so much as to keep slavery out of our midst?" Pratt concluded his remarks with a powerful appeal to the Mormons' own experience with discrimination. "Shall we take then the innocent African that has committed no sin and damn him to slavery and bondage without receiving any authority from heaven to do [so]?" he asked. "The idea is preposterous in my mind and I feel almost indignant when I think that we as a new territory, after we ourselves have been damned to slavery in [the] States but came out here to enjoy the religious [liberties]— For us to bind the African because he is different from us in color [is] enough to cause the angels in heaven to blush!"[97]

Pratt apparently had no objection to unfree labor per se. He did not speak against holding European immigrants or their children in servitude until they had discharged their debts. Yet his reaction against the introduction of African American slavery into Utah was intense and visceral much like his reaction to the indenturing of Native Americans.

After Pratt concluded his remarks, Orson Spencer (see figure 6.2) stood to defend his bill. George A. Smith had just spent two days trying to disentangle the concepts of servitude and slavery in regard to Native Americans. Spencer now tried to do the same thing in regard to African Americans. He first attacked Pratt's theological premise and argued that God had "decreed servitude" on the "race of Canaan." Nevertheless, Spencer wholeheartedly agreed that slavery as it was practiced in the American South was an evil "from which humanity recoils and shutters at the observation of it." Spencer spoke from his own experience as a schoolteacher in Georgia. He argued that "[Southern slaveholders] have violated every wholesome rule that the Father of spirits of all flesh established to regulate the conduct of servants to masters.... They have denied [the] right which is due to servants. They have ground them down and riveted chains of darkness on their feet by legislative enactments and long abuses." Things were even worse in Africa, he asserted.

Figure 6.2 In 1850, Orson Spencer (1802–1855) became the first chancellor of the University of Deseret, the precursor to the University of Utah. He represented Salt Lake County in the territorial legislature in 1852. Courtesy Church History Library.

"[I]n Africa chieftains make slaves of their own people. They are the most cruel that can be named or found in [the] history of slavery. The most despotic. They will take their own women and children and take them to the shore to the masters of ships."[98]

Spencer then contrasted these ghastly forms of bondage with "servitude" as it was authorized by God in the Bible and as it was contemplated in his proposed bill. "Was it servitude?" Spencer asked. "Yes. [But] not southern slavery." According to Spencer, servitude was a humanitarian institution that edified both master and servant. He imagined a system in which African American servants, like the servants of the Patriarch Abraham, would be so loyal to their masters that they could be armed "for the chastening of [the] wicked [and] for the over throwing of despots of [the] earth. Is the slavery of [the] south like this? Could [a slaveholder] send them on [an] important ambush in foreign lands? No, [they would] never return. [Such a slave] would point his musket at his breast to him that would grind him down. [It is] not that kind of slavery I am talking about here."[99]

Moreover, Spencer worried that if the legislature did not recognize some kind of legal bond between masters and servants, then Mormon enslavers would not bring their enslaved people to Utah and thereby deny them the opportunity of receiving the gospel. This was a direct response to Pratt's concerns about missionary work in Britain. Is the gospel to be taught to every people "but the blacks?" Spencer asked. "No," he answered. It was to be taught to "every nation bond and free. They are to be instructed [and] told what duties and obligations and relation[s] [they are] placed [in]to [with] their masters. May they not come here and be taught? Throw open the door and let them come if they will come on. Shall we put up the bar and say, bond men wait, none gospel for you?" Spencer prodded. Should Latter-day Saints "extinguish the light burning in [the] slave [until it is] almost extinguished and gone out? Or shall they fashion that light and bring it forth luminous, attended by our Father in Heaven?"[100]

Spencer focused on gospel outreach as he further developed his rationale. "I have thought, how can the gospel be carried to Africa? We cannot give them the priesthood. How are they going to have it? Must we go and live there?" These were perceptive questions that Spencer asked and key conundrums that the racial priesthood restriction created. Latter-day Saints leaders would again grapple with them in the twentieth century. The newly emerging restriction crashed headlong into Joseph Smith's instructions that the Latter-day Saint gospel message was to be preached "unto every creature" (Doctrine and Covenants 58:64). Spencer recognized that the restriction automatically impeded that mandate. In response, he suggested that the Atlantic slave trade might have had a silver lining, even if based in evil. "If wicked hands go and bring [Africans] from their homes and set them down at our doors we know what is the law of the Lord touching [them]. Use their strength as did Abraham to [the] building up [of the] kingdom.... How much worse are they off if they can be brought under the pale of righteous influence [where] they can be instructed and be saved," Spencer urged.[101]

It was an argument that Puritan minister Cotton Mather had used over a century before to also justify the horrors of the slave trade by suggesting that a divine end (conversion) justified a horrible means (enslavement and forced migration to the Americas under violent and dehumanizing conditions).[102] It was an argument that ignored the fact that Christian missionaries had long traveled the globe to spread their message and were not reliant on enslavers bringing potential converts to them. The following year, in fact, Latter-day Saint missionaries would open a mission to South Africa and there baptize people of Black African descent.[103] The Atlantic slave trade was not a divinely inspired missionary tool no matter Spencer's attempt to frame it that way.

In the end Spencer said that he had "no ambiguity" about "the right to use [Africans] and to consecrate their service." He admitted that in regard to these questions, "I do not feel as I have formerly felt. I have been enlightened [by] our President [Young] upon this subject." Spencer finished with a discussion of the situation of African American servants in Latter-day Saint society. "The Negro [is] not so unhappy when placed in [the] position God would wish him," he said. More importantly, once baptized, these servants could "be happy in [the] heavens of [the] Almighty."[104]

Governor Young then rose to speak. Based on past precedent, the legislators were probably expecting a storm of criticism directed at Orson Pratt, but Young did not chastise Pratt or attempt to refute his arguments. Instead, he made his own objection to Section 4 of the bill. This section criminalized sex between a white master and her or his African American servant as well as sex between "any white person" and any person "of the African race." Both indentured servants and slaves were often victims of sexual exploitation by their masters. In fact, at least one such example already existed in Utah Territory, although there is no indication that Young was aware of it. John Hardison Redd and his wife Elizabeth Hancock Redd arrived in Utah in September 1850 after converting to the Church in Tennessee. The Redd's brought six enslaved people to Utah along with their family. According to DNA evidence, at least one of those enslaved people was Redd's son whom he fathered with an enslaved woman named Venus. Likewise, in 1867, William T. Dennis, a former Utah enslaver, fathered a child with Marinda Redd, one of the Redd family's former slaves.[105] Young had vocally opposed race mixing since the Enoch Lewis case in 1847. Although the Service Act protected the enslaved from sexual abuse, it also reflected a general opposition to miscegenation. Violation of Section 4 of the bill could result in a three-year prison sentence for the master, hefty fines, disenfranchisement, and forfeiture of the servant.[106]

Be that as it may, the bill empowered probate courts to indenture any forfeited servants, white or Black, to a new master. Brigham Young firmly opposed this. "Let [servants] live with [their masters] and serve out the time agreed on when they came here," he advised. "But when the master forfeits the rights of their servants, let them be free [the] same as white people." If a master violated provisions of the Service Act, in other words, Young insisted that the servant should go free rather than be transferred to a different master. This represented a significant policy change.

Young anticipated that some legislators might oppose the emancipation of African American servants in this manner. Ever since Young's childhood in New York, a common objection regarding manumission had been that former slaves would have no means of support, nothing to occupy their time, and would thus become at best drains on public coffers or at worst criminals. But Young pointed to laws already on the books designed to handle such problems. "If [emancipated servants] do not conduct themselves judiciously, [they shall] come under . . . laws that will correct them. If they are loitering about, [they may be] taken up and [charged as] vagrants," Young said.[107] Under territorial law, a vagrancy conviction could result in at least twenty days of forced labor on public works.[108]

Young's objections to Section 4 highlight the complexity in his thinking about race and servitude; a complexity that was not apparent in his January 23 address four days earlier. He sincerely believed that Africans were the descendants of Cain and Canaan. As such, they could not hold the priesthood and had been cursed to be "servant of servants." His faithful surrogates like Orson Spencer repeated these claims. Young had even asserted that he was a "firm believer in slavery," based on biblical precedents.[109] But Young consistently objected to holding Native Americans and African Americans as property. His suggestions to the Council on January 27 emphasized the contractual nature of the relationship between a master and servant.

Even in its original draft, Section 3 of the Service Act provided that enslaved African Americans must come to Utah voluntarily, but Young went even further. He presumed that slaves would negotiate with their masters for a specific term of service before they agreed to come to the territory, much as they did in California or, formerly, in Illinois.[110] "Let [servants] live with [their masters] and serve out the time agreed on when they came here," he said.[111] If the terms of this agreement were violated in some manner, the servants should go free. Young's attitude indicated that the natural state of all people was liberty, even if it was not absolute equality. He believed that masters and servants should be bound by a voluntary contract that both parties must honor.

In a society increasingly unsure about how to respond to relationships that involve even marginal disparities of power, it is difficult to believe that an enslaved person could effectively bargain with his or her master or enter a truly voluntary agreement. An enslaver's ability to coerce was simply too great. This was especially true where an enslaved person was given the Hobson's choice of becoming an indentured servant in Utah or remaining a slave in the South.[112] A growing number of nineteenth-century judges also had their doubts.[113] A majority of the Illinois Supreme Court had labeled such contracts as "involuntary servitude" as early as 1828. One Illinois justice pointedly argued that "it would be an insult to common sense to contend that the negro, under the circumstances in which he was placed, had free agency. The only choice given him was a choice of evils."[114] Even so, the boundaries between voluntary and involuntary servitude were still in a state of considerable flux in American thought.[115] Many contemporary Americans took seriously the idea that any rational person was capable of making a decision for him- or herself. For people like Young, an enslaved person did not, and indeed could not, lose his or her agency. Even a slave could make a choice.

In spite of manifest inequalities in bargaining power, a great many nineteenth-century slave owners entered indenture contracts with their enslaved workers in order to utilize their labor in a free jurisdiction such as Illinois or California. Often, these contracts significantly limited the worker's term of service. Some even included a wage. There is evidence that under some circumstances, enslaved people were able to successfully negotiate with their masters for better terms.[116] Brigham Young apparently believed that in Utah, the terms of labor contracts would generally be limited through negotiation between master and servant. In short, he assumed that servitude would be a temporary condition based on a contract. Young insisted that once a voluntary term of service had expired, or the agreement was otherwise violated, the servant should go free regardless of his or her race. Once freed, there were other legal means to ensure that individuals were gainfully employed, such as the vagrancy laws.[117]

* * *

After Young's comments, the service bill was once again referred back to committee on a motion by Orson Spencer himself. After listening to the objections of Pratt and Young, he apparently wished to make further revisions to his bill. It did not make another appearance in the legislative record until February 2, almost a week later. In the meantime, several important events occurred. On January 29, Brigham Young made a speech to the combined legislature urging them to reign in endless debates and to pass legislation.[118] The next day, the legislature met jointly again, and Young read a series of newspaper articles dealing with the so-called runaway judges scandal. The previous fall several federally appointed judges had abandoned the territory and publicly complained that the Latter-day Saints were un-American and disloyal.[119] After listening to these articles, the legislature voted to meet in joint session for the remainder of the term. The legislature then proceeded to sit in a secret session for the rest of the day where no minutes were taken. It is tempting to think that the service bill was discussed during this session, but there is no evidence of it.[120]

On February 2, An Act in Relation to Service was read to the legislature once again. As previously noted, Representative Hosea Stout, a Southerner and an attorney, raised objections to the heritability of debt found in Section 2. In his view, children could not be held to a contract signed by their parents beyond the age of twenty-one.[121] These objections were answered by George A. Smith. Representative Joseph Young from Salt Lake County, Brigham Young's older brother, then proposed a slight revision to Section 4.[122] Yet by this time the bill had already been significantly altered. When and where this happened is unknown. The "secret session" on January 30 seems possible, yet there is no evidence to substantiate it. Orson Spencer may have simply made the changes himself after the vocal debates on January 27.[123]

Following the suggestion of Brigham Young, the new draft stipulated that African and European servants who were released from their contracts due to abuse would no longer be indentured to another master by a probate court. Instead, all private claims to the servant would be forfeited to the commonwealth.[124] If Young's advice was followed, this meant that the servant would go free the "same as white people."[125] However, it is possible that that the servant could be hired out by the court. There is little evidence to indicate what occurred in practice. Over the next decade, there is only one highly ambiguous case in which a servant was allegedly forfeited to the territory, but there is no record of any official action.[126] The original Section 5 of the bill was also deleted. This section was an explicit guarantee of legal title to a

Table 6.1 Section 3 of An Act in Relation to Service in parallel columns

An Act in Relation to Service, Section 3, as originally drafted (changes in bold)	An Act in Relation to Service, Section 3, as passed into law (changes in bold)
SEC. 3. That any person bringing a servant or servants, and his, her, or their children from any part of the United States, and shall place in the Office of the Probate Court the certificate of any court of Record under seal, properly attested that he, she, or they **is or** are entitled lawfully to the service of such servant or servants, and his, her, or their children, the Probate Justice shall record the same, and the Master or Mistress, or his, her, or their heirs shall be entitled to the services of the said servant or servants **and his, her, or their children, until the curse of servitude is taken from the descendants of Canaan** unless forfeited as hereinafter provided, if it shall appear that such servant or servants came into the Territory of their own free will **or** choice.	SEC. 3. That any person bringing a servant or servants, and his, her, or their children from any part of the United States, **or other country**, and shall place in the office of the Probate Court the certificate of any Court of record under seal, properly attested that he, she, or they are entitled lawfully to the service of such servant or servants, and his, her, or their children, the Probate Justice shall record the same, and the master or mistress, or his, her, or their heirs shall be entitled to the services of the said servant or servants unless forfeited as hereinafter provided, if it shall appear that such servant or servants came into the Territory of their own free will **and** choice.

Note: The draft version is on the left, and the final version that became law is on the right.

servant who was transferred to a new master through sale, gift, or inheritance. However, the most extraordinary changes to the bill directly concerned African American servants.[127]

At some point after January 27, someone (probably Orson Spencer) removed any mention of the curse of Canaan from Section 3 (see table 6.1). Moreover, the new draft significantly altered the scope of African American servitude. It still permitted a master and his heirs to legally claim the labor of "a servant" who accompanied his or her master "from any part of the United States, or other country." But the words that originally followed this provision, "and his, her, or their children, until the curse of servitude is taken from the descendants of Canaan," were struck from the statute. In fact, the original draft of the bill held in the LDS Church archives clearly shows those words crossed out (see figure 6.3). The drafters did not provide any further clarification in the remaining language of the section, and there were no further debates on the substance of the law which have made it into the historical record.[128]

Even with the aid of the legislative debates, the text of the Service Act leaves many questions unanswered. The final language was still vague.

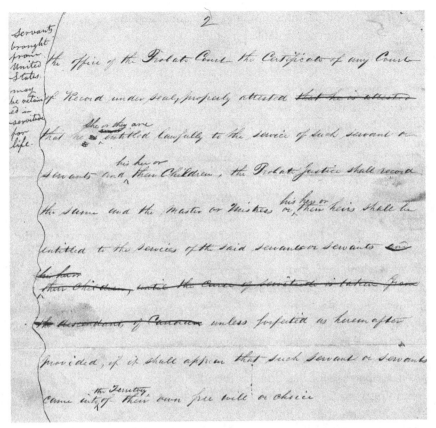

Figure 6.3 Original draft of An Act in Relation to Service, Section 3, with eighteen words (and his, her, or their children, until the curse of servitude is taken from the descendants of Canaan) crossed out. Courtesy Church History Library.

Furthermore, over the next ten years there was very little litigation that required a judge to analyze the law. An informed interpretation of the statue, nonetheless, is possible.

Here, it is important to re-emphasize the legal state of affairs in Utah during the 1852 legislative session. For years, Brigham Young and other senior Latter-day Saints had argued that slavery was illegal in Utah and could not be authorized without some kind of positive legislative act. Judge Snow agreed in his published opinion following the Luján trial. In other words, Latter-day Saint leaders understood that no one could be held in a condition of heritable servitude unless a statute *explicitly* stated that he or she could be held in a condition of heritable servitude. Whatever else it may have done, the final version of the Service Act *did not* explicitly authorize hereditary servitude for the children of enslaved parents. In fact, all available evidence indicates just the opposite.

Both extant drafts of the act refer to individuals who were held in slavery outside Utah by using a particularly long-winded euphemism that focused on the heritability of the condition. Specifically, Section 3 describes enslaved persons as "a servant or servants, and his, her, or their children" who collectively owe service to a "master or mistress, or his, her, or their heirs" in some other jurisdiction. The original draft of Section 3 used identical terminology when describing individuals who could be held in perpetual servitude after they arrived in the territory. It further added that this condition of servitude would continue until God chose to lift the curse of Canaan. It was this choice of words which indicated that perpetual servitude was a heritable condition and so incensed Orson Pratt on January 27.[129]

But in the final version of the law, the drafters purposely struck out the phrase "and his, her, or their children" when describing individuals who could be held as servants in Utah. In other words, the drafters kept this language when describing service relationships that existed *outside* the territory (i.e., permanent hereditary slavery) but removed this language when describing service relationships that could be enforced *inside* the territory. They likewise removed any reference to the curse of Canaan. As revised, a "servant or servants" who came from the United States could be held in servitude but not "his, her, or their children." The deletion of this phrase is therefore convincing evidence that the legislature did not wish the condition of servitude to pass on to the children of enslaved African Americans.[130]

According to the text and legislative history of the statute, then, the best interpretation of Section 3 seems to be this: assuming that all other requirements had been met, a slave owner who permanently settled in Utah Territory could legally retain the labor of an adult slave with whom he or she had entered a service agreement for a period up to and including life. The master was then required to register his or her slave with a probate court where the judge would determine whether the slave had entered the territory of their "own free will and choice." If the judge was satisfied that the master and slave had entered a voluntary relationship, an enslaved person was then legally transformed into a "servant." It is possible that an enslaver might also claim the labor of a child who was brought into Utah from another jurisdiction, much like a registered servant in Illinois. However, the Service Act was particularly vague on this point. The statue was clear that labor contracts between a master and his African American servants could be inherited by the master's heirs upon his or her death. They could likewise be transferred or sold to another individual, but only with the consent of the servant and the approval of a probate judge.[131]

These contracts were further limited by geography. Once an African American servant arrived in Utah, he or she could not be removed from the territory without consent. Together, these provisions ensured that a servant could not be returned to a state of slavery in some other jurisdiction.[132]

Although such a contract was specifically enforceable, it could be nullified through abuse and the servant freed. Any children subject to the act also had to be provided with an education. But perhaps most importantly, Section 3 no longer provided enslavers with a permanent hereditary claim to a slave's descendants. That language had been stripped from the final version of the statute. Without an explicit statutory authorization, lifetime servitude was not a heritable condition under Utah law. Based on his own precedent in the Luján case, a judge like Zerubbabel Snow would have to declare these children free if their status was ever challenged in court.[133]

The process outlined by the Service Act fits within a broad definition of gradual emancipation. Even so, the law differed in important respects from the gradual emancipation statutes that were enacted in the northeastern United States after the Revolutionary War. States such as New York and Pennsylvania created a system in which slavery would gradually die out through two legal mechanisms. First, the children of enslaved parents would be freed after a defined period of servitude. Second, the importation of new slaves was prohibited. In contrast, the Service Act implemented the first mechanism by implication rather than express language, and it did not implement the second mechanism at all.

The evidence demonstrates that Brigham Young and other Mormon leaders wished to discourage slave owners from bringing their human property to Utah and believed that the Service Act accomplished that purpose. In fact, Utah's enslaved population remained essentially static during the decade when the Service Act was in operation. Furthermore, Young consistently argued that Utah would be a "free state" once it was admitted to the Union. He certainly did not believe that the Service Act would incentivize the importation of more slaves. But the Service Act did not actually *prohibit* enslavers from bringing additional enslaved people to the territory. It is true that the law required enslaved people to enter the territory voluntarily and altered their legal status after their arrival. But under the terms of the law, some form of protracted servitude could have been perpetuated in the territory through the arrival of new enslaved people.[134]

In this sense, the Service Act was more analogous to statutes enacted in Indiana and Illinois during the first decade of the nineteenth century. These laws permitted slave owners to bring their slaves into a nominally "free" jurisdiction, legally transformed them into indentured servants, and provided that the children of enslaved parents would be free after a defined period of servitude. Some scholars have argued that these laws should not be considered true gradual emancipation statutes.[135] Certainly, they were not identical to the gradual emancipation laws in New York or Pennsylvania. But as written, they progressively freed immigrating slaves or their children from bondage, a fact recognized at the time.

Unfortunately, the final language of the Service Act concerning the children of slaves is extremely vague, far more so than the laws in Indiana and Illinois. The statute did not explicitly state what would happen to these children. The clause authorizing hereditary servitude was excised, an important point for interpreting the law, but no further explanation was added. It is fair to suggest that the ambiguities of the Service Act left the status of enslaved children open for future debate.

Nevertheless, the arguments that took place in the legislature and subsequent alterations to the Service Act offer substantial evidence that the law was not intended to make lifetime servitude a heritable condition. Although Utah legislators did not clearly articulate this goal within the text of the statute, by eliminating eighteen crucial words in Section 3 ("and his, her, or their children, until the curse of servitude is taken from the descendants of Canaan"), they indicated that children born to enslaved parents would be free. As written, the Service Act thus operated as a kind of free womb law like those in operation in Mexico at the time. Such laws stipulated that children born to an enslaved mother were born free. They were designed to end slavery within a generation and might broadly be described as gradual emancipation.[136]

The Service Act was so short-lived that there was no opportunity to see how this process might have functioned among children born to enslaved parents in Utah. Over the next decade, the Service Act provoked surprisingly little litigation of any sort, and there are no extant judicial opinions in which a judge directly ruled on the status of an African American servant or her children under the law.[137] Between 1847 and 1862, some fifteen children were born to enslaved parents in Utah Territory. Several left the territory with the San Bernardino company in 1851, while others died young. In 1860, there were only seven of these children still living in Utah. The oldest would have been no more than twelve or thirteen years old when the Service Act became defunct, still a minor. The available evidence suggests that all of these children remained with their parents, or at least a parent, throughout this period. In fact, all seven lived in just two households. During the years in which the Service Act was in operation, the only known sales of children that occurred under the provisions of the statute involved individuals who were born outside Utah such as Caroline and Tampian Lewis.[138] As a result, the pertinent data are extremely thin.

Despite the legislature's significant modifications of the Service Act, it is possible that some enslavers still believed that they held a kind of property interest in the children of their enslaved workers. Masters may have chosen to ignore the vague provisions of the law or to interpret them to their advantage. For example, there is some evidence that the cash value of an African American servant in Utah was roughly comparable to a slave in Southern markets. Since there was no apparent devaluation of enslaved people when they came to Utah, despite the limitations of the Service Act, it may indicate that enslavers still expected an equivalent value in labor. Historian Amy Tanner Thiriot has speculated that the expectations supporting the value of African American servants may have extended to the labor of any potential children.[139] In contrast, Indian servants, with a maximum term of service imposed by statute, were considerably cheaper than African American servants. This may have been due to their greater availability as well as their shorter terms of service.[140]

Whether or not masters believed that they could hold the children of enslaved workers as servants for life, it is also possible that they exercised a kind of guardianship over minor children who lived in their households. This would have included the ability to benefit from the labor of these children, at least until they reached the age of majority. Indeed, the children of African American servants were still subject to general apprenticeship and guardianship laws passed by the territorial legislature. In California, it was not unusual for individuals to use guardianship laws to assert control over children of color, and Mormon enslavers might have tried the same strategy in Utah.[141] But if enslavers genuinely believed that the Service Act applied to children born in Utah, they would also have been obliged to send them to school for at least eighteen months and follow the other provisions of the law.[142]

Without further information, it is impossible to know for sure why lawmakers made such significant changes to the Service Act, especially why they dropped the clause that would have passed on the condition of servitude to the next generation.[143] However, the best explanation stems from the debates on January 27. It is clear that Orson Pratt strongly objected to the original draft of Section 3. Indeed, he believed that it introduced slavery into Utah. He challenged the link between servitude and the curse of Canaan, and he angrily questioned if Africans "and their children shall be servants to us and our children?"[144] Brigham Young further objected to the fact that under Section 4 emancipated servants could be re-indentured by a probate judge. Orson Spencer did not believe that the bill introduced slavery even as originally drafted. But he appears to have taken the criticisms of Pratt and Young seriously. In the final draft, Sections 3 and 4 were both altered to reflect these concerns. In so doing, the bill more plainly authorized long-term indenture contracts rather than heritable servitude.[145]

It is evident that the final version of Section 3 still permitted a form of lifetime servitude for an enslaved adult who "voluntarily" came to Utah with his or her master. After all references to the curse of Canaan were expunged, the text of Section 3 provided that existing service relationships would be honored under Utah law and that a lawful entitlement to labor could be inherited by a master's heirs if he or she died. While it was not stated plainly in the statute, this likely meant that an enslaved person might be held in servitude for life. In fact, the marginal note included next to Section 3 in the original draft of the bill likewise states that "Servants brought from the United States may be retained in servitude for life."[146] Brigham Young may have presumed that there would be some kind of negotiation between master and servant for a shorter term of service, but that was not required by the language of the statute.

Whatever else it may have done, Section 3 of the Service Act finally recognized the interest that Mormon enslavers held in the labor of their enslaved workers; something they were desperate to secure ever since they arrived in Utah. Yet it also reflected the traditional Blackstonian position that a slave who was freed by operation of law might still be held as a servant. Brigham Young firmly believed that contractual servitude was the ideal relationship between masters and servants and interpreted the Service Act to fit this ideal. Yet some Southern enslavers asserted their own understandings of the law when they registered their servants. After passage of the Service Act, Duritha Lewis and Diannah and Williams Camp registered their enslaved people with probate judges and described them as "slaves" whom they claimed "for life." No clear record of contractual consent survives among these probate registrations.[147] The ambiguities of the Service Act allowed for such discrepancies to exist as the law was put into practice.

Be that as it may, the Service Act severely limited a master's authority over their servant. A servant was not a commodity that could be bought and sold at will. A servant was, in all legal senses, a person. Indeed, despite manifest disparities in length of service, European and Black servants had to be treated the same under the law.[148]

After the bill was read a third time, lawmakers passed it on the motion of Representative James Brown. There is no record of any objections or dissenting votes, even from Orson Pratt who had so vehemently objected to the prior version of the statute. Brigham Young then signed the bill into law on February 4, 1852. Pratt made more arguments on that day, but Watt failed to record them, so it is impossible to know for sure how he felt about the final version of the bill.[149]

* * *

Ten months later, Brigham Young praised the Service Act in his second annual message to the territorial legislature. He believed that the law created a relationship between "Master and Servant" that was based on a "righteous principle." The governor had insisted for years that no person in Utah could legitimately be considered property. In his view, the Service Act acknowledged that "Africa's sons and daughters are not goods and chattels," and granted the formerly enslaved "that humanity and moral accountability to which they are entitled." Young did not believe that the Service Act legalized slavery in Utah. For him, the distinction between slavery and servitude was quite real. Even so, he affirmed that under the new law, "'Canaan' shall be a servant of servants unto his brethren."[150] Even though all references to the curse of Canaan had been removed from the statute, it still reflected Young's paternalistic interpretation of Genesis.

Young further claimed that the Service Act had "nearly freed the Territory of the colored population," and it enabled "the people to control all who see proper to remain, and cast their lot among us." This was a curious assertion. Perhaps Young was referring to the large number of enslaved people who were taken to California in the spring of 1851 or to the deterrent effect that he hoped the law would have on slaveholders who wished to bring their slaves to the Mormon settlements. In either case, the law did not apply to the dozens of free people of color who lived in Utah except for the anti-miscegenation provision found in Section 4. But Young viewed the law as a model that could be used to relieve the worsening sectional discord over slavery. He challenged abolitionists to follow the example of Utah and "purchase [slaves] into FREEDOM, and place them in their own household, where they can partake of their kindness, wisdom, and intelligence ... thereby obviating the necessity of white servants, who should tread the theatre of life and action, in a higher sphere."[151] It was another way Young indicated a preference for freedom while asserting white superiority.

An Act in Relation to Service may rightly be seen as conservative or even backward-looking when compared to contemporaneous laws in many Northern states. But when compared to the laws in the remainder of the Mexican Cession, the Service Act takes on a far different character. After the American conquest, newly organized governments in Utah, New Mexico, and California found it necessary to regulate various forms of unfree labor that had existed during the Mexican period such as peonage and Indian servitude. They likewise had to regulate African American slavery as it was introduced by Southern migrants. Due to a combination of internal and external factors, public officials throughout the Mexican Cession accommodated these practices to one degree or another.[152]

Like legislative bodies in California and New Mexico, the Utah legislature ultimately chose to recognize a legal relationship between slave owners and their enslaved workers. Even so, An Act in Relation to Service deviated from statutes enacted in those jurisdictions. California approved a local fugitive slave act that effectively authorized slavery until 1855, while New Mexico created a slave code four years later. Both jurisdictions also authorized several lesser forms of servitude. Rather than codifying chattel slavery, Utah lawmakers created a form of servitude that encompassed European immigrants and enslaved Black people in the same law. While there were important distinctions between the two, especially in the length of service, no servant could be treated as property.

Four years after the Service Act was signed into law, there was an attempt by a few pro-slavery delegates to supersede the statute and explicitly protect slavery in a new constitution for Deseret. However, that effort failed spectacularly. Even after the *Dred Scott* decision in 1857, Utah legislators took no steps to recognize property in man. Instead, they continued to rely on the more moderate provisions of An Act in Relation to Service until 1862.

7

Race and Election Law

On February 4, 1852, the Utah territorial legislature passed a new election law; in doing so lawmakers stipulated that white men over twenty-one years of age could vote in the territory. The official legislative minutes do not record any opposition to the voting requirements in the election bill or mention any discussion on the subject. However, a few surviving sources indicate that councilman Orson Pratt firmly opposed any law denying Black men the right to vote. Pratt had already condemned An Act in Relation to Service and the Indian indenture bill, and he now expressed concerns about racial equality in Utah's election laws. As fellow legislator Hosea Stout recorded it, Pratt voted against "all acts prohibiting the right of Negroes the privileges of voting."[1]

By the mid-nineteenth century, white manhood suffrage had become the accepted practice throughout the United States. Over the previous sixty years, property requirements and other voting restrictions had crumbled along with some of the hierarchical assumptions of the early republic.[2] During the tumultuous 1830s, Jacksonian Democrats proudly championed the rise of the common man as a force in politics, while conservative Whigs warned that the republic had "degenerated into a Democracy."[3] But at the same time that suffrage was expanding for white men, African Americans and other minority groups were being disenfranchised even in locations where they had enjoyed voting rights for decades.[4] Indeed, while Jacksonians fought tenaciously for equality among white men, they also fought for the continued dominance of white men over all other groups.[5]

Suffrage requirements enacted by Utah's first territorial legislature in 1852 mirrored these national trends. During legislative debates in January and February, Brigham Young rationalized disqualifying Black men from the vote partially in terms of Jacksonian political theory. However, Young reinforced these ideas by insisting that God had placed a curse on Black Africans. Among other things, this rendered people of Black African descent incapable of holding the priesthood and presiding in the Church of Jesus Christ of Latter-day Saints. Young taught that since men of African descent could not preside in God's church, they should likewise be barred from participating in civil government. However, the disenfranchisement of African Americans was vigorously opposed by apostle and legislator Orson Pratt.

Similar debates in other states preceded Utah's decision-making process and created a national context in which lawmakers used racial justifications to prevent Black men from voting. By 1820, a number of states that permitted people of color to vote after the Revolution, including New Jersey, Maryland, and Connecticut, had revoked the franchise.[6] Nationally by 1855, only five New England states—Massachusetts, Maine, New Hampshire, Rhode Island, and Vermont—permitted African American men to vote on the same terms as white men.[7]

Early Latter-day Saints welcomed the expansion of voting rights, and at first they sided with the Democratic Party against the "aristocratic" Whigs. Nevertheless, they ultimately rejected the turmoil of Jacksonian party politics and embraced an older tradition of hierarchy and social order. Indeed, many contemporary Americans also viewed the growth of a two-party system as fundamentally at odds with republican institutions.[8] As a practical matter, this meant that social order among the Latter-day Saints was centered on priesthood leadership and that Church leaders often served in positions of civil responsibility in Mormon communities. Moreover, elections in these districts, while both free and regular, were rarely competitive in a modern sense.

Some historians have argued that the Mormons were primarily inspired by scriptural theocracies in the Bible and the Book of Mormon and that beneath a veneer of republican values their political establishments were fundamentally anti-republican.[9] Others believe that the Mormons were actually trying to recover the communal republicanism of the early American republic that had withered under expanding market forces.[10] Scholarly debate continues as to the relative importance of democratic and theocratic principles in Mormon institutions and the ideal Mormon political form—the "theodemocracy."[11] But whatever the case may be, the Latter-day Saints believed that any legitimate government, be it secular or ecclesiastical, must be founded on some version of popular sovereignty.[12] That is to say that the people are a sovereign body and must consent to the acts of their leaders.

* * *

From 1847 until 1851, the Mormon communities in the Great Basin were organized under three distinct forms of government. The first was a pure theocracy governed by a High Council, various apostles, and eventually the First Presidency of the Church. In 1849, the Saints formed a provisional civil government called Deseret under which they asked for admission to the Union as a state.[13] Finally, Congress organized the Territory of Utah in September 1850. Due to distance and poor communications, the government of Deseret retained de facto power until early the next year. The people of a territory had limited say in who would govern them and did not get to vote in national elections. President Millard Fillmore appointed the executive and judicial officers of the new territory and split them between prominent Latter-day Saints and those outside the faith. The territorial legislature, however, was elected by popular vote and was exclusively Mormon. Each of these governments from 1847 to 1851 was based on some degree of popular sovereignty although it was expressed in different ways.[14]

It is ironic that the original theocratic government was in some ways more democratic than the civil governments that followed. In December 1847, the High Council of Great Salt Lake City enacted a number of municipal ordinances to govern the fledgling community. At the time, the entire region was in a state of political limbo. Alta California, including the modern states of California, Nevada, and Utah along with large chunks of several other states, remained a vast and sparsely settled territory of Mexico. However, for over a year the U.S. military occupied its capital at Monterrey along with other population centers on the Pacific coast. The Americans had also conquered the Rio Grande settlements in New Mexico. In fact, in December 1846, the Mormon Battalion, a Latter-day Saint military unit during the U.S. war with Mexico, briefly occupied Tucson, before marching on to California and allowing Tucson to revert to Mexican rule. Yet none of these locations was closer than 600 miles from Great Salt Lake City across mountains, rivers, and deserts.[15]

As a result, the High Council determined that for the moment their community lay outside any practical jurisdiction from either the Mexican or American governments and drafted laws accordingly. The leaders of this Council had already been subjected to a vote of confidence by the Church membership in October. This gave their actions popular legitimacy. Nevertheless, they decided that the ordinances they created should likewise be "subject to approval of the people."[16] This was a form of direct democracy akin to a New England town meeting. It is likely that every Church member in the Salt Lake Valley had a vote as to whether they would approve of these laws or not. If the votes took place in the various Church congregations in the valley, then they would have included women and Black people who would have had no voice in any other political context.

Within two years, these egalitarian political structures disappeared as the Mormons created the civil government of Deseret. The provisional constitution limited the franchise to white males over twenty-one years of age.[17] This was a standard provision for the time and a movement beyond the land-holding requirements that existed when most Mormon leaders had been young. In the early decades of the republic, states dropped property requirements as a condition for voting and thereby ushered in universal white male suffrage, which simply meant that all white men over twenty-one could vote. When Congress passed an organic act for Utah Territory, its voting requirements were identical to that of Deseret. It was a well-established voting standard by that point, and it placed Utah Territory on par with the rest of the nation.[18]

While no speeches apart from Brigham Young's were recorded on February 4, the day that the election law passed, Young implied that Pratt made vocal objections to the bill. In fact, Young indicated a brewing disagreement when he claimed that Pratt's actions that day were designed to "stick his thumb into me."[19] It seems apparent that the events of February 4 directly influenced Young's speech the following day. Young spoke to the legislature on February 4 in a discourse largely aimed at rejecting the conviction among outsiders that he should not dictate in legislative matters. He likewise disregarded the notion that the religious beliefs of legislators should not influence the legislation they passed. Young wanted "senators, governors, representatives, [and] kings of [the] earth to know that we legislate[20] in [the] name of Israel's God for the benefit of Israel and we want all creation to know [it]."[21]

But Young also had a message for legislators that day. He counseled them to seek unanimity and to avoid finding fault with proposed bills without offering suggestions for improvement. "There is a spirit [of contention here that seems to suggest that] I [can] find fault with you, with your bill, and with your doing[s]," Young complained. He singled out legislators Orson Pratt, Edwin D. Woolley, and Albert P. Rockwood for censure on these grounds. "No man got up until I got up to talk," Young said. "Then Brother Pratt got up and motioned that the bill be put right through. Why [did he do this]? [It was] to stick his thumb into me," Young insisted. He then said that Rockwood was "like a hornet" and that Woolley was "smart to talk" but did not produce results.[22]

Unfortunately, any speeches from Pratt, Rockwood, or Woolley do not survive, neither does a roll call of votes. What does survive is an indication that Young's speech on February 5 came in direct opposition to Orson Pratt's views on voting rights and slavery. When Young spoke that day, he seemed to still have ideas from February 4 on his mind and was intent on swatting them down. A good portion of his February 5 speech was aimed at a rejection of Black voting rights. In doing so, he alluded to ideas already in circulation from the day before. "The abolitionists of the east have caressed" Black people, he complained on February 5, "and their whole argument is calculated to darken counsel, same as here yesterday," a likely reference to Pratt's unrecorded speech from February 4. "I may vary from others and they may think I [am] foolish and short sighted," Young added, in another likely allusion to Pratt. "[There are those] who think they know more than I do [but] I know [that] I know more than they do," Young insisted, asserting his dominance.[23]

Young's talk on February 5 is perhaps the most important speech he ever gave. It had far-reaching implications that stretched into the twenty-first century and continues to influence the Church of Jesus Christ of Latter-day Saints' efforts to grapple with its racial past. His speech is drenched in racism and built upon the notion that white people were inherently superior to Black people. Despite its long-lasting import, it was never published in the nineteenth century. It was not printed in the *Journal of Discourse* or in the *Deseret News*. George D. Watt recorded it in shorthand and then transcribed it into longhand, but it sat in Watt's collection of papers mostly ignored, even by scholars in the twentieth and twenty-first centuries.[24]

It was a speech that apostle and legislator Wilford Woodruff captured in summarized form and Watt captured in shorthand. Historians have thus primarily relied on Woodruff's truncated and highly condensed version of the February 5 speech for an understanding of Young's views on race and priesthood. Woodruff's version of the speech, however, introduced significant inaccuracies into the historical record and should no longer be trusted as a precise assessment of Young's views on race and priesthood.[25]

Moreover, Woodruff did not date his summary of Young's discourse that has been the cause of considerable misunderstanding among scholars. Lack of information regarding legislative chronology only added to the confusion especially if scholars searched for a speech dated January 5 and failed to search the files of Watt's longhand transcripts for a speech given on February 5. Finally, the "History of the Church," sometimes referred to as the "History of Brigham Young," a manuscript history prepared by a clerk in the Church Historian's Office years after the fact likely added its own layer of ambiguity. The passage in the Historian's Office History for January 5 summarized the entire legislative session in one entry and made it sound as if all the events and ideas in that entry happened on January 5. The entry was written in first person, as if Young were the author:

> The Legislative Assembly of the Territory of Utah met on the 5th, Willard Richards President of the Council and William W. Phelps, Speaker of the House.
>
> My message was read in joint session, in which was reviewed, at length, the internal policy pursued and which should be pursued to subserve the best interests of the Territory; after which I remarked to the Assembly that I was opposed to the system of slavery,—its cruelties and abuses were obnoxious to humanity. The negro, however, should serve the seed of Abraham; he should not be a ruler, nor vote for men to rule over me nor my brethren.
>
> The Constitution of Deseret is silent upon this, we meant it should be so. The seed of Canaan cannot hold any office, civil or ecclesiastical. They have not wisdom to act like white men. The decree of God that Canaan should be a servant of servants unto his brethren (i.e. Shem and Japhet [sic]) is in full force. The day will come when the seed of Canaan will be redeemed and have all the blessings their brethren enjoy. Any person that mingles his seed with the seed of Canaan forfeits the right to rule and all the blessings of the Priesthood of God; and unless his blood were spilled and that of his offspring he nor they could not be saved until the posterity of Canaan are redeemed."[26]

It was a concise summary of some of the ideas Young expressed during the legislative session, but they unfolded across the course of the session in relation to bills under consideration, not all on a single day.

In addition to the confusion over chronology that Woodruff's undated speech introduced, his report of Young's words was not exact. He managed to record about 900 words of a roughly 3,000-word speech. Woodruff's summation thus misses much of Young's argument, but more significantly it includes wording errors implying that Young said things that, in fact, are not recorded in Watt's Pitman version of the speech.[27]

The most frequently quoted sentence from Woodruff's summation, it turns out, is not a precise synopsis of Young's words: "Any man having one drop of the seed of Cain in him cannot hold the Priesthood, and if no other prophet ever spake it before, I will say it now, in the name of Jesus Christ, I know it is true, and others know it!"[28] Woodruff's summation of Young's speech is remarkably accurate in capturing the flavor of Young's sentiment, but this crucial and oft-quoted sentence inserts key ideas that are not present in Watt's Pitman shorthand version of the same speech: "If there never was a prophet or apostle of Jesus Christ [who] spoke it before, I tell you, this people that are commonly called Negroes are [the] children of Cain. I know they are; I know they cannot bear rule in [the] Priesthood, [in the] first sense of [the] word."[29] According to Watt, Young also declared that "in [the] Kingdom of God on earth, a man who has the African blood in him cannot hold one[30] jot nor tittle of Priesthood."[31] Watt's version spoke of "one jot" of priesthood, while Woodruff captured "one drop of the seed of Cain." Young's declaration was that "Negroes" were descendants of Cain and as such they could not hold "one jot nor tittle of Priesthood," an idea different in its meaning and intent than Woodruff's "one drop of the seed of Cain."[32]

Woodruff's version inserted a crucial aspect of American racial understanding into the Latter-day Saint record, the "one drop rule." It was a rule that played out especially in the South as a legal cover for white slave owners who fathered children with their Black slaves. Rather than slavery following the status of a father, some Southern states stipulated that a person's legal status followed his or her mother. In this way, children born of the unequal power dynamic between white masters and Black slaves were still legally slaves. In 1855 the Arkansas Supreme Court ruled that Abby Guy, a woman who appeared white and sued for her freedom, was nonetheless legally a slave if she had only a tiny fraction, even one drop, of African ancestry, as long as it passed through her maternal line.[33]

In general, states were more liberal than the Arkansas Supreme Court in defining "Black" and "white" rather than slave and free, but most laws still defined a person as Black who had predominantly white ancestry. In many states a person was considered Black if she or he had at least one-fourth part "negro blood," or sometimes one-eighth, meaning that a person had one Black great-grandparent. In other words, seven out of eight ancestors could be white, and a person was nonetheless considered Black. Especially after the Civil War, as Southerners attempted to shore up white racial superiority, some states tightened their standards. The "one drop" sentiment only appears in Woodruff's account of Young's remarks, not in the verbatim version. Young did not refer to a "one drop" rule in any known speech.[34]

Nevertheless, by the beginning of the twentieth century, Latter-day Saint leaders put their own "one drop" policy in place. In 1907, the First Presidency decided that "the descendants of Ham may receive baptism and confirmation but no one known to have in his veins negro blood, (it matters not how remote a degree) can either have the Priesthood in any degree or the blessings of the Temple of God; no matter how otherwise worthy he may be.[35] Eligibility for priesthood ordination and temple admission for people of Black African descent was thus to be based solely on race, not personal worthiness. Black men and women were to be excluded no matter "how remote a degree" of African ancestry, a clear expression of a one drop philosophy. There is no indication that leaders in 1907 drew on Woodruff's version of Young's speech or that it influenced their decision. Historians, however, continue to cite Woodruff's account and thus falsely imply that a one drop policy was in operation as early as 1852.[36]

* * *

Young's February 5 speech represents his most complete and forceful articulation of a priesthood restriction, but it was delivered *after* passage of An Act in Relation to Service. A joint session of the legislature, with members present from both the House and the Council, passed that act on February 2 and Brigham Young signed it into law on February 4. The legislature then passed An Act in Relation to Elections on the afternoon of February 4. When they reconvened at 10 a.m. on February 5 they asked Young to "give his views on slavery." It was a curious request considering that Young signed the servant code into law the previous day. While Young did reiterate his views on slavery in the February 5 speech, he did so in a way that suggested that he was responding to points made the previous day in the debate over the election bill as well as reaffirming his position on the servant code already signed into law.[37] Reading between the lines, it appears that Young's words were directed squarely at Orson Pratt and his support for Black suffrage. Young's discourse was wide ranging, including statements about slavery and even his emerging views on blood atonement. However, it most famously outlined a priesthood restriction for African American men as part of a larger paradigm of white male dominance over political and ecclesiastical affairs in Utah.[38]

Young made no mention of a specific revelation authorizing the priesthood restriction. Instead, he relied primarily on his interpretation of the biblical "Curse of Cain" combined with standard Jacksonian theories of race and power. In so doing, he directly attacked Pratt's contention that African Americans should be enfranchised. "I will not consent for a moment to have the children of Cain rule me, nor my brethren, when it is not right," Young explained. "If they cannot bear rule in [the] church of God, what business have they in bearing rule in [the] state and government affairs of [this] territory?"[39]

In Young's reasoning, the curse of Cain denied Africans a right to the priesthood. Since they could not officiate within God's church, they should likewise be denied the right to govern in civil government or even to choose those who would govern them. In his mind, the two subjects were inseparable. A debate over voting rights for African Americans therefore became an opportunity for Young to publicly articulate his racial theology. His racial theology in turn directly informed his politics.

Politically speaking, Young argued that African Americans were citizens of the territory. It was a position that Roger B. Taney, chief justice of the U.S. Supreme Court, would contradict just five years later in the *Dred Scott* decision. Unlike Young, Taney concluded that neither enslaved nor free Black people were citizens of the United States and reasoned that at the time that the U.S. Constitution was adopted Black people were deemed to be "beings of an inferior order" with "no rights which the white man was bound to respect."[40] In contrast, Young argued, "Every man in this [territory and every] woman [and] child in this territory is citizens of [this] territory; [to say the contrary is] all nonsense to me. The Indians are citizens, [the] Africans are citizens, and the Jews that came from Africa that are almost entirely [of] the blood of Cain [are citizens]; [it is our duty to] seek [to] take care of them." In Young's estimation citizenship should be expansive but voting rights should not. All people should "have the right of citizenship, [but] shall not have the right to dictate who shall be governor," he stipulated.[41]

More pointedly, Young did not view Black people as equal to white people. In his opinion, they were racially inferior and cursed. As such they could not hold the priesthood nor should they be allowed to vote. "Not one of [the] children of old Cain has any right to bear rule in government affairs from first to last; [they have] no business there," Young insisted. He made the connection between priesthood and voting explicit and linked the two in an effort to shore up his argument. As he viewed it, if Black men could not hold the priesthood, then they certainly could not vote. "If they cannot bear rule in [the] church of God, what business have they in bearing rule in [the] state and government affairs of [this] territory" he demanded. "No man can vote for me [or] my brethren in [this] territory [who] has not the privilege of voting [or] acting in church affairs," Young vowed.⁴²

Interestingly, Young was far more generous with the priesthood than with the franchise. Although Young taught that all men outside of Cain's progeny could hold the priesthood, voting in territorial elections was apparently a privilege for white men only. Insofar as the civil government was concerned, white men were the sovereign people, and all others were their legal dependents. This position was likely more an artifact of Young's Jacksonian background than any religious dogma. As Young put it, "When those men come here from the islands [of the sea] are they going to tell [us] who shall be governor [here]? No. It is for men who understand the knowledge [of] government affairs [to do that]. . . . If thousands come from the Pacific Island[s], ten [or] fifteen thousands [from] Japan [or] from China, not one soul of them [would] come here and know how to vote," Young claimed. "[In] Mexican territory," he said, there is "not a man there [who] know[s] how to legislate there for the benefit of [the] people. They know no more about voting [or] dictating [than] a jackass does. [We] just [as well] make [a] bill here for mules to vote as Negroes [and] Indians."⁴³

Every ethnic and racial group Young described as incapable of voting were nonetheless ordained to the priesthood, including those of African descent under Joseph Smith. Young now argued people of African descent were religiously cursed from the priesthood *and* intellectually incapable of exercising the right to vote. "You cannot find within men upon [the] earth [who are of the] seed of Cain [any] that [possess] knowledge and sensibility [enough to vote]," Young maintained.⁴⁴ In contrast, all the other groups he named—Native Americans, Japanese, Chinese, Mexicans, and Pacific Islanders—were all eligible for priesthood ordination. He was thus willing to distribute priesthood authority to people he compared to jackasses but not allow them voting rights, an inconsistency in his argument that he failed to reconcile.

Regardless, his claims about priesthood and about voting rights were both grounded in a strong conviction that white men were superior. His republican objections to broadening the franchise were no doubt sincere. But underneath it all, Young had an overpowering fear of racial equality. "What we are trying to do today [is] to make [the] Negro equal with us in all our privileges," he said. "My voice shall be against [it] all the day long."⁴⁵

Mixed in with Young's reasons against racial equality was his most forceful articulation of a priesthood restriction on record. In it he laid out a rationale for the restriction that was grounded in the biblical "mark" and corresponding "curse" that God put on Cain as punishment for killing his brother Abel. It was a racialized interpretation of a few verses in the book of Genesis that predated the founding of the Church of Jesus Christ of Latter-day Saints by several centuries.[46] Young claimed that when Cain killed Abel, God marked Cain with the same mark that was "on the face [and] the countenance of every African you ever did see."[47] Seven years later, Young was more specific when he called the mark "the flat nose and black skin."[48]

In 1829, the year before Joseph Smith founded his Church, the African American abolitionist David Walker described how deeply such racial notions permeated American society. He wrote that "some ignorant creatures hesitate not to tell us that we, (the blacks) are the seed of Cain . . . and that God put a dark stain upon us, that we might be known as their slaves!!!"[49] It was a standard interpretation of the "mark" and "curse" of Cain, one that Young likely inherited from centuries of Christian tradition through his Protestant roots. He now imported it into the Church of Jesus Christ of Latter-day Saints and gave it unique theological meaning.[50]

In Young's version of the curse, God barred Cain's descendants from priesthood ordination as a consequence of Cain killing his brother Abel. Young suggested that "the Lord told Cain [that] he should not receive the blessings of [the] priesthood until the last of [the] posterity of Abel had received the priesthood, until the redemption of [the] earth."[51] It was the only reason he ever offered for the racial restriction, and one from which he never deviated. He did not draw on sources specific to Latter-day Saints such as the Book of Mormon and its notions of skin color and curses, which he understood to apply to Native Americans not people of Black African descent. He did not draw directly from the books of Abraham and Moses either, both of which were not canonized until after his death. The Bible and the curse of Cain were his sole scriptural inspiration. Young believed that Cain's descendants were people of Black-African descent and implied that Abel's descendants were white people, but he failed to specify. Because Cain attempted to usurp Abel's position in a patriarchal order of priesthood authority, Young reasoned that Cain's descendants would have to wait for all of Abel's descendants to receive the priesthood before they would be eligible.[52]

Young did not say how he came to know of the alleged conversation between the Lord and Cain; it was not recorded in the Bible, yet he self-assuredly described the discussion. Even still, in offering context and giving life to the Bible story, Young admitted that he was ignorant of certain details. He did not know who was older, Cain or Abel, for example. He also claimed that Abel had children at the time of his death who he surmised "were in all probability young."[53] As a result, the first part of his speech reads like a free form commentary on the biblical creation narrative and the sibling rivalry between Cain and Abel. It was grounded in Young's personal assertions, nothing more.

Young further failed to specify why Cain's murder of Abel qualified for a multigenerational curse when other biblical homicidal acts did not. More importantly, Young's explanation violated the fundamental Latter-day Saint tenet of agency—that the divine plan of human existence was grounded in an individuals' right to choose good or evil with consequences that followed. Joseph Smith, in fact, rejected Calvinistic notions of original sin to argue that humankind would be held accountable for their own sins, not for Adam's transgression.[54] Yet, Young's curse of Cain held the ostensible descendants of Cain responsible for a murder in which they took no part. His explanation violated an essential doctrine of the faith and in doing so created a theological pressure point that other leaders tried to alleviate when they formulated their own explanations for the racial restrictions. To honor free will, Orson Pratt, just one year later, would indicate that Black people must have exercised their agency poorly in a pre-mortal realm and were therefore born into a cursed lineage.[55] Subsequent Latter-day Saint leaders adopted Pratt's explanation and suggested that Black people were neutral or less valiant in a pre-mortal war in heaven or made poor choices in that war and were therefore destined to be born into an accursed race.[56]

***

Interlaced within Young's rationale for priesthood exclusion were vague references to future redemption. Young admitted that someday the curse of Cain would be lifted and that Africans would enjoy the same privileges as white Latter-day Saints. At some future time, he said, "Cain's seed [will be] had in remembrance and the time come when that [curse] should be wiped off." As Young variously expressed it, the curse would last "until the residue of [the] posterity of Michael and his wife receive the blessings," "until the redemption of [the] earth," "until [the] times of [the] restitution come," "until the last of [the] posterity of Abel had received the priesthood," "until the curse be removed," and "until the time comes [that] the Lord says [he will] have it [taken away]." These were ambiguous statements that offered no clear timeline for an end to the supposed curse or a definitive indication as to what might bring about a future redemption. "That time will come," Young claimed. "They will come and have the privilege of all we have the privilege [of] and more."[57]

The idea that people of color could be socially and politically equal to white people was highly contested during the antebellum period. During the late eighteenth and early nineteenth centuries, first movement abolitionists expressed a deep faith that through education, Black people could eventually be prepared to become full citizens in a republican government. But as virulent racism began to grip the North, many people rejected this rosy outlook and asserted that Black Africans were inherently inferior and could never be trusted with the franchise. Young's February 5 speech presented a mixture of these views. With the abolitionists, he believed that every person was capable of moral progress and that one day, all people would be equal. Young's paternalism towards people of African descent and his insistence that they be educated, was meant to prepare them for this eventuality. But for the present, Black people were cursed and limited in their capacities. Young therefore pushed equality off to an indefinite future when God himself would intervene. This was the ultimate expression of gradualism and paternalism.

Even more confusing was the lack of explanation for why people of Black African descent were now cursed from the priesthood when they had not been before. Young clearly indicated that he was the first prophet or apostle to make such a declaration: "If there never was a prophet or Apostle of Jesus Christ [who] spoke it before, I tell you this people that [are] commonly called Negros are [the] children of Cain, I know they are; I know they cannot bear rule in [the] priesthood." He thus admitted that even if no other prophet said it before, he was saying it now.[58]

Young's statement also implied that doubt existed among legislators, perhaps Pratt, that Black people were in fact the "children of Cain." To try to dismiss any such uncertainty, Young forcefully declared, "I know they are" and then linked their descent from Cain to an inability to hold the priesthood. It is possible that Pratt argued on February 4 that there was "no proof that the Africans are the descendants of old Cain who was cursed" and that on February 5, Young forcefully responded to Pratt. Even if Pratt did not make such a claim on February 5, he did make that exact statement four years later, an indication at the very least that Pratt rejected Young's assertion and did not believe that Black people were descendants of Cain. People of African descent were thus not subject to Young's interpretation of a biblical curse.[59]

Young's declarative statements and his contextualizing of the priesthood curse within the Bible's genesis story made it sound as if the restriction dated to the beginning of time and had always been in place. In his retelling, the restriction had nothing to do with a fraught nineteenth-century American racial culture but rather with divine curses and skin color. It was a version of events that took responsibility out of Young's hands and placed it in the hands of God. Young even declared his position to be grounded in "the true eternal principles [that the] Lord Almighty has ordained." As Young articulated it, he was not capable of removing a curse which originated with God: "[The] angels cannot [and] all [the] powers [on earth] cannot take [it] away. The eternal I Am, what I Am, I take it off at my pleasure and not one particle of power can that posterity of Cain have, until the time comes [that] the Lord says [he will] have it [taken away]."[60] In 1836, Joseph Smith had made a similar claim about the curse of Ham or slavery, but by 1844 he offered a plan for national emancipation. Young's view of curses also differed significantly from that of Pratt who rejected any notion that Black people in the nineteenth century inherited racial curses from biblical times.[61]

The real challenge, however, to dating the restriction to the beginning of time came from Young himself. His position on priesthood in 1852 violated his own open racial attitude from five years earlier. In fact, in March 1847, Young was on record with an open racial outlook when he flatly declared that "we don't care about the color" and favorably acknowledge a Black priesthood holder. Young referred to Q. Walker Lewis, a Black man in the Lowell, Massachusetts congregation as "one of the best Elders, an African in Lowell." Now Young failed to reconcile his reversal or to explain how it was that an African priesthood holder could go from being "one of the best Elders" in 1847 to being cursed and racially disqualified from the priesthood by 1852.[62]

Fear of race mixing certainly played a significant role in the declension of Young's racial views between 1847 and 1852. Following his open perspective in 1847, he learned of two Black Latter-day Saint men who married white women (one of whom was Q. Walker Lewis's son Enoch in Lowell, Massachusetts) and he stridently spoke out against such unions, even advocating capital punishment as a penalty.[63] Race mixing clearly concerned him and he saved some of his most pointed comments for that very topic in his speech to the legislature. Young imagined a hypothetical scenario wherein the entire leadership of the church declared it right to "mingle" their seed with the seed of Cain and thereby embrace the "abolition doctrines." On "that [very] day and hour the priesthood [would be] taken from this church and kingdom [and] God leaves us [to our fate]," Young proclaimed. It was a dire prediction that Young then punctuated with force. The moment "we consent to take the seed of Cain, the church [must] go to destructions," he said. Race mixing would spell an end to the priesthood, he claimed, and to the entire church.[64]

There were moments in Young's speech when he softened his unapologetic racism with genuine concern for the welfare of African Americans, but only in a paternalistic sense. Those who enslaved Black people "should use them with all the heart [and] the feeling [as they would] use their [own] children and their compassion should reach over them [and] around them and treat them as kindly as mortal beings can be [treated]," Young specified. He also maintained an open attitude toward baptism for Black proselytes, even as he limited the scope of full participation for Black members. He said that Black people could "receive the Spirit of [the] Lord by baptism," but "that is the end of their privilege and no power on earth [can] give them any more power." Black people were welcomed into church membership and were eligible for confirmation and the gift of the Holy Ghost, but that was the end of their religious eligibility, according to Young.[65]

* * *

It was a wide-ranging sermon filled with Young's forceful opinions on a variety of racial subjects. Black voting rights clearly animated much of the speech, and despite Young's strident stance on the topic, Orson Pratt remained unconvinced. Pratt likely smarted from such an open rebuke before his fellow legislators, but he was unwilling to back down. The prophet/governor and apostle/legislator clearly disagreed over racial equality, and neither man was willing to budge. Young's speech on the morning of February 5 ended the verbal phase of the debate, at least as far as surviving evidence indicates. Legislative minutes do not specify if Pratt was allowed to respond, yet Pratt did answer Young's racism that day in a long-forgotten episode of moral conviction. Rather than a lengthy speech, Pratt's vote became his voice. After Young spoke, legislators considered An Act to Incorporate Cedar City, in Iron County, Utah Territory, and the bill passed unanimously, except for "Councilor Pratt voting in the negative." Later the same day lawmakers approved An Act to Incorporate Filmore City, in Millard County, and again the bill passed except that "Councilor Pratt opposed the bill on the ground that colored people were there prohibited from voting."[66]

Pratt voted against both the Cedar City and Fillmore municipal incorporation bills—bills typically rubberstamped by lawmakers with no controversy. Pratt, however, used his vote in both instances to stand alone for racial equality. In doing so he voted "no" on the two bills, not merely because neither municipality granted Black suffrage, but because he also wanted to make it clear that he rejected Young's ideas about the inferiority of Black people and he was willing to stand against the crowd to do so. Pratt took a stance on two innocuous incorporation bills perhaps to poke Young with his thumb again, but more so out of principle and moral conviction. It was a singular moment in Utah and Latter-day Saint history. His two votes demonstrated courage and an unwavering commitment to political equality.[67]

Pratt's position on Black suffrage would ultimately prevail in the aftermath of the Civil War even though in the long course of American history Black voting rights remained vulnerable long after. Meanwhile, Young's speeches to the legislature developed longevity of their own. They became the basis of a Latter-day Saint priesthood restriction that grew into a corresponding temple restriction and lasted for nearly 130 years.[68]

By February 19, Young and Pratt were apparently willing to put their differences aside. Legislator Hosea Stout recorded that Pratt and Young both spoke on that day, instructing legislators "to be humble & enjoy the spirit of God and act as Elders of Israel."[69] Of course, that fall when Young was ready to openly acknowledge the practice of plural marriage among the Latter-day Saints, it was to Pratt he turned to make the public announcement.[70]

8

Implications

The death of Abraham Church, a wealthy Southern planter, in Hickman County, Tennessee, in July 1851, touched off a string of events with far-reaching implications for Tom, one of the men who Church enslaved. Abraham's son, Haden Wells Church, who had converted to the Church of Jesus Christ of Latter-day Saints in 1841, was serving in Great Britain as a missionary when his father died. When his missionary service ended, Church joined a group of British Saints who migrated to Utah Territory in 1852. When the migrant company reached New Orleans, Church took a detour back to Tennessee to see family members and receive his portion of the settlement of his father's estate.[1] Abraham Church had been a wealthy planter with land and farm equipment to his name along with twenty-one men and women whom he enslaved.[2] The elder Church's wealth was thus divided between Haden and his eight siblings. Although estate documents do not survive, making it impossible to know exactly what Haden inherited, evidence does indicate that an enslaved man named Tom was included in Haden's portion of the settlement, a fact that would drastically change the course of Tom's life.

After his detour to Tennessee, Church, now with Tom in tow, rejoined the emigrant company somewhere along the Mississippi or Missouri Rivers as they made their way to Kansas under the direction of Abraham O. Smoot, the leader of the migrant company.[3] James Thomas Wilson, a member of the emigrant company, later crassly recalled that Church's father had "left him some property and a portion of it was a niger known as niger Tom."[4] Tom thus found himself taken from his Tennessee home and potentially from his family to join Church in Utah among people he did not know. There is no indication that Church was aware of the passage of An Act in Relation to Service earlier that year and its requirement that servants come "into the Territory of their own free will and choice."

At one point on the river journey, Church put Tom in a vessel with fellow migrants but did not accompany him. When the group arrived in Kansas, one Latter-day Saint recalled, "Tom lived among the Saints and he behaved himself first rate." Without Church present, however, Tom's behavior ultimately did not matter because he was Black and susceptible to accusations that he had escaped from slavery. Authorities in Kansas, in fact, concluded that Tom was a runaway slave and arrested him on that charge. According to one recollection, Tom "was asked to show his papers if he was free, but this he could not do as he had none." Tom was not free and therefore had no papers. Church retained whatever legal papers there may have been and thought that Tom would be safe with his fellow Saints until his return.[5]

Tom emphatically denied being a runaway and "refused to be taken, declaring he was Mr. Church's niger." In response, authorities "beat him very severely and thrust him into prison." A story then circulated locally that Tom "was a runaway niger and the Mormons were hiding him." The sheriff investigated the incident the following day and believed Latter-day Saint witnesses who vouched that Tom was an enslaved man who belonged to Haden Church. The sheriff returned Tom to the care of the Mormon migrant company where Church eventually caught up to the group, and they made it safely to Utah Territory without further incident.[6]

Tom and the rest of the Abraham Smoot migrant company arrived in Utah in September 1852. Tom spent the next ten years in the territory, removed from friends and family in Tennessee where he had been born. His time in Utah Territory spanned the years in which An Act in Relation to Service was in force. He arrived in the fall of the year in which the legislature passed the bill, and he died in the spring of the year that Congress outlawed slavery in all U.S. territories. His life and that of other enslaved African American and Native American women and men thus offer opportunities to assess what the law meant in the lives of those it influenced most. In the absence of primary source evidence, however, it is a difficult assessment to make.

* * *

There is no indication that Haden Church was aware of An Act in Relation to Service when he took Tom with him to Utah Territory. It is impossible to know if Church followed the law's provision that required Tom to give his consent to be taken to Utah Territory, but because Church was absent from the territory when the law passed it is unlikely that Church was aware of the law or that he followed its provisions. Even after Church arrived in the territory, there is no indication that state or county officials gave him or other enslavers a copy of the law or in some way made them aware of its stipulations. There is also no indication that Church ran afoul of the law that would have landed him in legal trouble and forced a judge to adjudicate the law in Tom's behalf. At the very least, if Church registered Tom with a probate court judge after he arrived in Utah Territory, as the law required, that registration has not been found.

The real question is what difference did the law make in Tom's life? How was his life as an enslaved man different in Utah Territory under An Act in Relation to Service than it was in Tennessee under chattel slavery laws there? Legislators clearly intended that the law they passed be legally distinct from chattel slavery and it was. But what did such distinctions mean in the lives of the enslaved? In Tom's case, it is impossible to tell. If Tom thought his life in Utah Territory was markedly different from that in Tennessee, he left no evidence behind to indicate it. What does survive is evidence that he was not free. Whether legally defined as a "servant" or as a "slave" it may not have mattered to Tom. Ultimately, he was deprived of two of what Thomas Jefferson considered inalienable rights—liberty and the pursuit of happiness.

Two years after Tom arrived in Utah Territory, he again entered the written record. In 1854, Henry A. Cheever, a member of Tom's Latter-day Saint congregation, baptized Tom a member of the Church of Jesus Christ of Latter-day Saints. The baptismal record simply read, "Tom[,] Brother Churches Black man[,] Baptized by Henry A. Cheever, June 24th 1854."[7] No indication survives regarding what prompted Tom's decision, what his new faith meant to him, or what level of devotion marked his life as a Latter-day Saint. Ecclesiastical records make no additional mention of Tom, not unusual even for white Latter-day Saints. Typically, a person only entered membership records when church rituals such as baptisms occurred.

Sometime after Tom's baptism he became enslaved to Abraham O. Smoot, Salt Lake City mayor, and Tom's Latter-day Saint bishop at the time. An Act in Relation to Service stipulated that such transfers could take place only with the oversight of a probate court judge. The law specified that "no transfer shall be made without the consent of the servant given to the Probate Judge in the absence of his master or mistress." In Tom's case that meant that the law required him to meet privately with a probate judge without Church or Smoot present. In a closed-door setting the judge would then ask him to give his consent to the proposed transfer. If Smoot and Church followed the law in this case, the probate court's record of the transfer has not been found. Smoot at least was aware of this requirement because in 1852 he and his wife Margaret Thompson McMeans Smoot sold Lucinda, an enslaved woman, to Thomas S. Williams, a Salt Lake City merchant for $400 and had the transaction sanctioned by probate judge Elias Smith. That sale was not filed in court until 1856, but it nonetheless demonstrates an awareness of the law.[8]

Beginning in August 1855, Margaret Smoot, Abraham Smoot's wife, sometimes mentioned Tom in her journal. She recorded him working on a road, building a canal, watering crops, preparing land, and working at a local sugar factory. It is clear from Smoot's entries that Tom's relationship with the Smoot family was economic even though the diary offers few clues beyond that to flesh out what Tom's experience as an enslaved man may have been like.[9] The 1860 census for Utah Territory counted Tom in the slave schedule not in the regular manuscript census, another indication of the relationship. That year Smoot claimed two forty-year-old men as slaves, Tom and a fellow enslaved man named Jerry. It is the only surviving record to indicate that Tom's approximate birth year was 1820 and to substantiate that a transfer from Church to Smoot occurred.[10]

Just two years later, Tom again entered the written record, this time under tragic circumstances. On April 29, 1862, Tom died from "inflammation of [the] chest." His death record described him as "Tom, a Negro, belong' to Bhp Smoot." He was buried in an unmarked grave in the Salt Lake City cemetery. He was forty-two years old.[11] Two months later Republicans in Congress passed a law outlawing slavery in the territories—a law that would have freed Tom had he lived long enough. Tom's hope for freedom was thus reliant on Republican congressmen in Washington D.C., not his fellow Latter-day Saints in Utah. His bishop was his enslaver. His enslaver did not free him, but congressmen in Washington D.C. would have freed him had he lived long enough.[12]

Tom's experience thus indicates that even though Utah's Act in Relation to Service legally defined him as a servant, it was a distinction without a difference. His life spanned the full duration of the law; he arrived as an enslaved man in 1852 and he died as an enslaved man ten years later. For those enslaved people who already lived in Utah Territory when the legislature passed the new law, their everyday lives did not dramatically change either. It is unlikely any of them woke up the morning after Brigham Young signed the bill into law and concluded that their lives were somehow markedly different than the day before. They were probably not informed about the passage of the law in the first place, nor were they educated regarding some of the protections it offered them.

In fact, Alex Bankhead, a formerly enslaved man, later in life recalled his experience in Utah as not much different from slavery in the South. He remembered gathering on occasion with other slaves and the conversation would turn to the possibilities of freedom. "They would discuss their condition and gaze in wonderment at the lofty mountains, which reared their snowy peaks heavenward, and completely forbade them from ascertaining how they could make their escape back to the South, or to more congenial climes." As Bankhead recalled, the life of slaves in Utah "was far from being happy and many of them were subjected to the same treatment that was accorded the plantation negroes of the South."[13]

* * *

Even though the Service Act may not have markedly changed the daily work life of Utah's enslaved population, it did provide some significant safeguards to enslaved people that could make a real difference to them. There are a few surviving examples that offer clues as to how the law played out in practice. They give us a glimpse into some of the legal protections it offered Utah's enslaved population that were distinct from chattel slavery practiced in the South. However, the evidence also indicates that the law depended on an informed and vigilant citizenry to enforce these protections.

On March 1, 1852, only a month after An Act in Relation to Service was signed into law, as mentioned, Margaret Smoot sold a "Negro Girl named Lucinda" to Thomas S. Williams for $400.[14] Margaret's husband Abraham O. Smoot was then serving a foreign mission for their church, and so she acted as the selling agent even though Abraham's name was also listed on the transaction. Williams was a successful merchant and attorney who would later serve as a delegate to the 1856 Constitutional Convention for Deseret. There, he demanded greater legal protections for slavery, and his failure to obtain them may have deepened his growing disaffection with the Latter-day Saint leadership. By the time he was killed by Native Americans in 1860, Williams had become one of the most active buyers and sellers of African American slaves in the territory. At the time of her purchase in 1852, Lucinda, or Lucy, was around sixteen years old. The available evidence indicates she had been sold to Smoot a year before when the San Bernardino company left for California, possibly so that she could remain in the vicinity of a family member.[15]

The entire transaction was documented in a bill of sale. According to the receipt, probate judge Elias Smith supervised the process as required by the new Service Act.[16] He signed the document and scrawled, "I approve of the above sale or transfer."[17] If Smith followed the requirements of the law, he must have privately interviewed Lucy to determine that she consented to the arrangement. The bill of sale does not indicate whether this interview occurred. Despite Judge Smith's certification, the receipt was not officially filed with the probate court until July 1856, over four years later.[18]

The sale of Lucy reveals that from a very early date, two prominent Latter-day Saint enslavers were aware of the terms of the Service Act and at least attempted to comply with its provisions. But over the subsequent decade, there are only a handful of documented occasions when a master registered an African American servant with a probate court or took some other action in conformity with the statute. This lack of documentation may be misleading, however. The bill of sale for Lucy and several other records preserved in the Utah State Archives indicate that at one time there was a "Probate Register of Servants."[19] This probably included a list of European, African American, and Native American servants who were registered under various territorial statutes, as well as a record of sales, transfers, and other legally significant events. Unfortunately, repeated efforts to find this register have failed.

Without this vital record, it is difficult to determine the overall level of compliance with the law. Still, there is evidence that some Latter-day Saint enslavers either remained ignorant of the Service Act or actively tried to evade it. The litigation surrounding Daniel Camp, sometimes known as "Negro Dan," illustrates such a case. At the same time, it also demonstrates how the provisions of the Service Act could be used to defend African American servants from abuse.

Daniel Camp was born into slavery in Tennessee in 1833. At the age of seventeen, he and his older sister, Charlotte, migrated to the Salt Lake Valley with their enslavers, Williams and Diannah Camp. Three years later, the Camps hired Daniel out to William H. Hooper while they journeyed to Mississippi to settle the estate of Diannah's father. Charlotte, then about twenty-three, was assigned to care for the Camps' children along with Louisa Stout, the wife of the Kentucky-born lawyer Hosea Stout. Unfortunately, Charlotte soon died of tuberculosis. Williams and Diannah returned to the territory in 1854 with two or three more enslaved people, including a young man named Shepard Greer. Based on later events, it is doubtful that any of these individuals were registered with a probate court under the provisions of the Service Act.[20]

In March 1856, Williams Camp was excommunicated from the Church of Jesus Christ of Latter-day Saints and later accused of committing fraud.

Around the same time, delegates to a constitutional convention for Deseret overwhelmingly rejected a proposal to protect slavery in a new state constitution. It is not clear to what extent this episode influenced the Camps, but by early summer, they had decided to leave the territory with their enslaved people and accompany their daughter to Texas. On June 9, Williams Camp personally informed Brigham Young of their decision. Young counseled him not to leave and advised him not to sell his property in Utah. But the next day, Diannah Camp sought Young's permission to take Daniel, Shephard, and their other servants away. The fact that Diannah felt compelled to petition Young directly suggests that the Camps understood the legally tenuous position of slavery in Utah, even if they did not observe the requirements of the Service Act. The results of this interview were not recorded, but one way or another, the Camps were determined to remove their slaves. Rather than face enslavement in Texas, however, Daniel ran away. He was then recaptured by an informal slave patrol consisting of Williams Camp and three other men. Yet Camp's actions were met with swift opposition by leading members of the community.[21]

On June 16, 1856, Bishop Edwin D. Woolley, a former Quaker, filed a complaint with Judge Elias Smith alleging that Williams Camp and his associates had kidnapped Daniel in order to transport him "beyond the boundaries of [Utah Territory], contrary to the statutes of said Territory."[22] This was clearly a reference to the Service Act. Woolley had been a member of the territorial legislature when it passed the law, and Smith certainly had a working knowledge of its provisions. If Daniel had been properly registered before Smith or another probate judge, he could not be removed from the territory without his consent. On the other hand, if Daniel had not been properly registered, the Camps had no legal claim to his labor. Over the next two days, Sheriff Robert T. Burton arrested Camp and his three accomplices in compliance with warrants issued by Smith. Burton also met with Brigham Young to discuss Camp "taking away his negro."[23] There is nothing from Young to indicate that he had given informal permission for the Camps to remove their enslaved African Americans to Texas.

Judge Smith commenced a preliminary hearing on June 17. Hosea Stout and Thomas S. Williams, both Southerners who were connected to the Camp family, defended the alleged kidnappers. Stout's wife Louisa had cared for the Camps' children when the Camps were away in Mississippi. Williams's daughter Mary Ann was one of Williams Camp's plural wives. Moreover, Williams had a significant personal stake in African American servitude.

The prosecution called several witnesses including Woolley and Daniel Camp. However, the defense objected to Daniel's testimony, likely arguing that he was enslaved and therefore precluded from appearing as a witness. Slaves were typically forbidden from providing evidence against a free person in court. Even free Black people were barred from testifying against a white man in many jurisdictions, including California. But Daniel was a legal person under Utah law, and the legislature had not provided any restrictions on the testimony of African American servants or free Black people. Consequently, Judge Smith ruled that Daniel could provide evidence against his master.[24] Testimony continued into the next morning, but Smith ultimately released the defendants for lack of evidence, perhaps an indication that although Daniel was allowed to testify, his testimony was not given significant weight. Judge Smith recorded in his journal that because "there was not sufficient proof against the accused to convict them I discharged them tho I believed truly, that they were guilty of what was alledged [sic] against them."[25]

After his release from custody, Williams Camp and his wife stayed in Utah. In early 1857, Camp was even readmitted to full fellowship in the Church by Bishop Woolley, the same man who had accused him of kidnapping.[26] Nevertheless, the Camps' daughter continued to Texas with two enslaved people.[27] It is unlikely that she sought permission from a probate judge before leaving.

Daniel and Shepard Greer stayed with the Camps. Less than a month after the hearing, the Camps finally registered Daniel and Shepard with a probate court under the provisions of the Service Act. Williams's failure to properly register Daniel had probably been an issue during his hearing before Judge Smith. By this time, Daniel had been in the territory for six years, and Shepard for two. But the Camps did not have court certificates from Tennessee or Mississippi demonstrating that Daniel and Shepard owed them service, a requirement under Section 3 of the Service Act. Consequently, Williams Camp, Diannah Camp, and another enslaver, William T. Dennis, executed affidavits before William I. Appleby, clerk of the Territorial Supreme Court, in which the Camps laid out their claims. These affidavits were then copied into the Probate Register of Servants, so it is possible that Daniel and Shepard appeared before Judge Smith before the process was complete.[28] On the same day that Camp registered Daniel, Thomas S. Williams filed Lucy's 1852 bill of sale with the probate court.[29] Like Camp, Williams wanted to ensure that his title to Lucy's labor was secure. Yet by early 1857, an increasingly embittered Williams left Utah for Missouri. It is possible that he took Lucy with him and then sold her in violation of the Service Act.[30]

Over the next three years, Daniel was sold twice within the small slaveholding community in Utah. In 1858, Williams Camp sold Daniel to Thomas S. Williams after he returned from his brief hiatus in Missouri. The following year, Williams sold Daniel to his business partner William H. Hooper for $800. Daniel disappeared from the historical record after 1860, although he may have settled in northern Utah. Williams Camp also sold Shepard to Hooper. However, Shepard was shot to death in 1859 during an argument with another enslaved African American over the affections of a young woman. Only one of these sales was officially documented, that of Daniel to William Hooper. But for some reason, Franklin Woolley, the county recorder and son of Edwin, authenticated the transaction, not a probate judge as the law required.[31] Without the Register of Servants, there is no evidence indicating whether the sale was approved by a probate judge or if Daniel or Shepard provided the requisite consent.[32]

The Camp hearing underscored the significant divisions that still existed in Latter-day Saint society concerning slavery. If anything, they had grown worse in the four years since the Service Act had passed. After the hearing, Hosea Stout recorded in his journal: "There was a great excitement on the occasion The question naturally involving more or Less the Slavery question and I was surprised to see those latent feeling[s] aroused in our midst which are making so much disturbance in the states."[33] The population of the Salt Lake Valley was largely composed of Northerners and European immigrants who had no particular attachment to African American slavery. Many thoroughly disapproved of the practice. As a result, the small number of enslavers who remained in Utah after the San Bernardino company left simply could not rely on the bulk of the community to help them enforce discipline on the enslaved as they might have in the South. These men constantly worried about their ability to retain the labor of their enslaved workers.

The fault lines running through the community had been exposed during a constitutional convention in March 1856 when a small but vocal faction had pushed the convention to adopt slavery. It is not particularly surprising that Thomas S. Williams, one of the leading supporters of slavery at the convention, later acted as Camp's defense attorney. For men like Williams, the compromise position that the legislature had adopted in 1852 did not go far enough in recognizing the property rights of enslavers, or, at least, men like

Williams hoped for clearer stipulations than what existed. At best, the Service Act had provided slave owners with an imperfect title to the labor of their African American servants that was subject to considerable judicial oversight. These "contracts" between master and servant were limited by consent, geography, and possibly duration. But Williams and his supporters wanted to maintain all the prerogatives associated with chattel slavery. During the convention, they even convinced George A. Smith, one of the authors of the Service Act, to support them. But many leading Latter-day Saints pushed back. The Camp hearing a few months later simply underlined the relatively weak position of enslavers in Utah.[34]

Despite this conflict, the litigation surrounding Daniel firmly established that the Service Act could function as Brigham Young and the Utah legislature intended it to. When men such as Edwin Woolley took an active role in enforcement, they could use the statute to protect African American servants from being removed from Utah Territory and re-enslaved in another jurisdiction. Although the daily lives of African American servants in Utah undoubtedly shared many similarities with their experience as slaves, their condition also entailed new rights and greater personal security. An Act in Relation to Service was not a slave code. The law did not institute standard methods of control such as forcing servants to travel with a pass, nor did it authorize private citizens to apprehend servants who escaped from their masters. Masters were forbidden to sell a servant or remove him from the territory without his consent and judicial approval. Furthermore, as legal persons, African American servants enjoyed basic civil rights such as the ability to testify against their masters in court.

The whole purpose of the Service Act was to elevate African American servants above the status of property in the eyes of the law and stipulate that they have a voice in their own affairs. At least in Daniel's case, the law worked. Unfortunately, there were other circumstances in which enslavers successfully circumvented the provisions of the Service Act by removing African American servants from the territory to be sold or re-enslaved somewhere else. Indeed, soon after Camp's hearing, his daughter quietly removed two enslaved people to Texas, while Thomas S. Williams likely removed his servant Lucy to Missouri.[35]

The Service Act delegated important responsibilities to probate judges when a servant was registered or if a servant was to be transferred to a new master. But enforcement of the law was largely dependent on complaints from third parties, such as Woolley, or the servants themselves. There was no requirement for judges or peace officers to regularly scrutinize the conduct of masters to ensure they were in compliance with the Service Act. This laissez-faire approach was typical of contemporary practice. If complaints were not forthcoming, enslavers were able to act as they pleased.

* * *

The last known registration of an African American servant in Utah took place in August 1858. David and Duritha Lewis were survivors of the 1838 Hawn's Mills Massacre in Caldwell County, Missouri, where Missouri militiamen killed eighteen Latter-day Saints as a part of their expulsion from the state. One of David's brothers was killed in the affair and another wounded. Later, they followed the Saints to Nauvoo, Illinois. In 1851, Duritha inherited three enslaved people from her father: Jerry (thirty), and sisters Caroline (nine) and Tampian (six), whom the couple brought with them to the Salt Lake Valley. After the Service Act was passed, they did not register Jerry, Caroline, and Tampian with a probate court. In 1855, David died intestate, and Judge Elias Smith assigned two appraisers to evaluate his assets. The appraisers listed Jerry, Caroline, and Tampian on a schedule of property and valued them at $700, $500, and $300 respectively. They also listed "2 Indian boys" on the schedule for a total value of $95.[36]

Three years later, Duritha finally registered her three enslaved people with a probate court, possibly because she intended to sell Caroline and Tampian to Thomas S. Williams. After the Camp hearing, it is likely that Williams wished to ensure that he could obtain a clear title to the girls under the Service Act. Yet Duritha had no documentation proving ownership. Instead, as Williams Camp had done in 1856, she provided an affidavit to the clerk of a U.S. district court stating that she was "entitled to the services of the said Jerry, Caroline, and Tampian during their lives."[37] Records indicate that the affidavit was later included in the Probate Register of Servants, so Duritha may have taken her servants before Judge Smith for approval. This must have satisfied Williams because he bought the girls, now sixteen and thirteen, although they later became the subject of considerable litigation. Caroline and Tampian remained in the Williams household after Native Americans killed Williams during a freighting trip to California in 1860. At some point, one of the girls was probably hired out to provide income for Thomas's widow. The sisters were finally freed in 1862 when Congress prohibited slavery and involuntary servitude in the territories. Both later married and stayed in Utah until their deaths.[38]

After the sale of Caroline and Tampian, Duritha Lewis retained possession of Jerry. Yet by early 1860, she considered selling him as well. Brigham

Young became aware of the situation, and, as he had done with Green Flake and Hark Wales nine years earlier, he decided to intervene on Jerry's behalf. On January 3, Young wrote to Duritha: "I understand that you are frequently importuned to sell your negro man Jerry, but that he is industrious and faithful, and desires to remain in this Territory," Young began. "Under these circumstances I should certainly deem it most advisable for you to keep him, but should you at any time conclude otherwise and determine to sell him, ordinary kindness would require that you should sell him to some kind, faithful member of the Church, that he may have a fair opportunity for doing all the good he desires to do or is capable of doing." Young then got to the point: "I have been told that he is about forty years old, if so, it is not presumable that you will, in case of sale, ask so high a price as you might expect for a younger person. If the price is sufficiently made, I may conclude to purchase him and set him at liberty."[39]

Young had never believed that the curse of Canaan was synonymous with permanent involuntary servitude. He was personally willing to purchase enslaved men such as Jerry "into freedom," as he had urged the abolitionists to do for a decade. He had done the same for Green Flake. Only a few months before, Young insisted to Horace Greeley that Utah would come into the Union as a free state.[40] Nevertheless, he was willing to permit enslavers to retain some form of paternalistic control over their servants as long as they were not mistreated.

Two months later, Young wrote to Duritha again after having spoken with Jerry. According to Young, Jerry claimed that he was actually free and that Duritha had "no papers or other evidence to prove that he is your slave." This was at least partially correct. Duritha had no documentation from Kentucky stating that she owned Jerry. She had merely executed an affidavit before the clerk of a district court that was then recorded in the Probate Register of Servants. Nevertheless, Young wrote that Jerry was "willing and much prefers to live with and serve you, but it is very uncertain whether he will stay long with any one else." Young therefore counseled Duritha to keep Jerry in her service, adding, "I know of no one, under these circumstances, that would deem it a safe investment to buy him."[41] Within three months, however, Jerry had either been sold or hired out to the mayor of Great Salt Lake City, Abraham Smoot. Tragically, Jerry drowned in June 1861, just a year before Congress prohibited slavery and involuntary servitude in the territories.[42]

* * *

Duritha Lewis enrolled Jerry, Caroline, and Tampian in the Probate Register of Servants nearly a year-and-a-half after the Supreme Court handed down the *Dred Scott* decision. On March 6, 1857, Chief Justice Taney overturned decades of accepted practice by ruling that neither Congress nor a local legislature were empowered to bar chattel slavery in a federal Territory. The basic contents of the opinion were publicized in Utah Territory a few months later. On June 24, the *Deseret News* reprinted a brief exposition of the ruling without further comment.[43]

If the issue had ever been taken to court, Taney's decision would have likely invalidated many requirements of the Service Act that related to African American servitude. The principles that Chief Justice Taney laid out in *Dred Scott* (Black people had "no rights" that white people were bound to respect) were simply incompatible with a statute that required masters to obtain consent from their servants prior to sale, prohibited masters from removing their servants from the territory without judicial approval, and failed to confer an absolute property right in a servant's children. These provisions had been specifically written into the Service Act to differentiate African American servitude from chattel slavery. At the very least, a judge might have ruled that enslavers could legally bring their slave property into Utah without adhering to the law's provisions. Still, there is little evidence to indicate whether *Dred Scott* actually modified the application of the Service Act in Utah. It is possible that in 1859, Thomas S. Williams executed the sale of Daniel Camp before the county recorder instead of a probate judge because he believed that the Service Act had been superseded by *Dred Scott*. But that same year, Brigham Young recommended that Horace Greeley read the Service Act before he affirmed that Utah would be a free state.[44]

Unlike the New Mexico legislature, which enacted an explicit slave code in 1859, the Utah legislature did not amend the Service Act after the *Dred Scott* decision, nor did it create any other legislation to protect slave property. In refusing to do so, Latter-day Saint legislators may have implemented a version of Stephen Douglas's Freeport Doctrine. That is, by failing to enact police regulations to protect slavery, they actually prohibited the practice.

As far back as 1849, Brigham Young and other Latter-day Saints leaders had argued that slavery could not exist in Utah without the benefit of positive law. It is also possible that they did not view the Service Act as in conflict with *Dred Scott* or simply preferred to remain silent on the matter. Whatever the case may be, the Service Act remained on the books until at least 1862 when Congress prohibited involuntary servitude in the territories. At the time, there were approximately thirty-five African American servants in Utah.[45] It is unclear if the Service Act was formally repealed by the legislature, but it does not appear in an 1866 compilation of territorial laws. In contrast, the Indian indenture bill was reprinted in the 1866 volume. The compilation also retained the old 1852 Act in Relation to Masters and Apprentices. The absence of the Service Act certainly suggests that the legislature no longer believed it was in force.[46]

* * *

As with the Service Act, it is equally difficult to determine how An Act for the Relief of Indian Slaves and Prisoners played out in practice. Religious ideals woven into racial paternalism and humanitarian impulses animated some lawmakers as they debated the act and likely motivated other Latter-day Saints who purchased Indigenous children from traffickers or otherwise acquired them. But no matter the religious or humanitarian ideals, the desire for cheap labor must have factored into the calculation as well. When Parowan settler David Lewis died in 1855, the inventory of his estate, for example, listed two unnamed "Indian boys" valued at a combined total of $95. Lewis was sent to southern Utah, in part at least, to missionize among Indigenous people. Yet whatever religious ideals he may have had in acquiring the two boys, his estate settlement still reduced them to a monetary value and placed them on a list with his other property—not on a list of family members with names.[47]

In practice the experiences of the indentured children likely varied from case to case and encompassed a blend of circumstances from fictive kinship adoption and efforts at familial and religious integration on one end of a spectrum and servitude (or "the other slavery") with its attendant proclivities for abuse and the drudgery of cheap labor on the other. The law was open as to how a white person might acquire a Native American "whether by purchase or otherwise." The majority of settlers in Utah Territory purchased Indian children from Ute traffickers, but they also traded or purchased others from family members or acquired some as prisoners of war.[48] The labor of the children for the duration of the indenture was then meant to pay back the purchase price. An economic relationship was thus bound up in the transaction from the start.

Historian Brian Q. Cannon traced 174 indigenous children who were taken into Latter-day Saint homes in various capacities in an effort to determine their different life courses. About one-fourth of his sample died before age twenty with twelve as the median age of death. Approximately 40 percent who lived to at least age twenty remained in white society but did not marry. Those who remained single "lived into middle age or beyond, often occupying a lonely, liminal state on the margins of society." Around 9 percent of Cannon's sample who lived to adulthood chose to live in Indigenous communities and reservations where they married other Native Americans. Almost half of those who lived to adulthood remained in white society and married. Some married other detribalized Native Americans, some married their former masters as plural wives, others married U.S. soldiers stationed in Utah, while the vast majority married into white Latter-day Saint society. Of those who married white Mormons only six were Native American men; the rest were women who married white men.[49] In many cases Indigenous people who were indentured as children occupied a difficult space somewhere between their Native American families and their Latter-day Saint "redeemers," not fully accepted among either group.[50]

***

In legal terms, An Act for the Relief of Indian Slaves and Prisoners approximated involuntary apprenticeship statutes that were designed to regulate poor or vagrant children. In fact, the Indian Indenture Act was much like An Act in Relation to Masters and Apprentices, which Utah legislators also passed in 1852. This general apprenticeship law stipulated that county selectmen or probate courts could bind out "any idle, vicious or vagrant minor child without his or her consent, or the consent of the parent or guardian of such minor child." If the court decided that parents or guardians neglected or refused to properly control the "actions and education" of such minors and did not train them "in some useful avocation," the court could then apprentice them.[51]

For Euro-American children, apprenticeships were generally voluntary. In most circumstances, a prospective apprentice or his parents chose to enter an indenture contract with a master craftsman to obtain vocational training. Although apprenticeship was "unfree," the relationship was grounded in consent. But local municipalities regularly indented poor or unruly children to ensure that they received proper care and socialization. Involuntary apprenticeships functioned as a kind of privatized social welfare in which communities leveraged local families to supervise worrisome children and train them in some useful avocation. Before the introduction of large, centralized bureaucracies, government paternalism was administered by citizens in their own homes. In return, the head of household was granted the right to employ the labor of an apprentice for a specified period.

The Indenture Act functioned similarly. Utah legislators struggled to know what to do with Indigenous children whom Latter-day Saints bought, traded for, or took as prisoners of war; in response they drew on involuntary apprenticeships as a model. This would ensure that Indigenous children were properly cared for and educated according to the Saints' religious values and Euro-American standards. From the vantage point of Indigenous children, however, legislative intent and religious ideals likely mattered little in the face of the loss of their families, displacement, and the erasure of their cultures.

The children taken into Latter-day Saint homes were often too young to understand the legal terms of an indenture contract, let alone to give consent. This was especially true in light of the unequal power dynamics at play. Language barriers would have exacerbated an Indigenous child's ability to comprehend any such agreement in the first place. In short, if the indenture process was supposed to be "voluntary" with some degree of contractual agency at play, it did not work that way in practice. Historian Brian Cannon, in fact, calls any notion of the "voluntary" nature of Utah's indenture system a "legal fiction," an apt description when considered from the vantage point of an indentured child.[52]

In the fall of 1852, James Henry Martineau, a Latter-day Saint settler in the small southern Utah town of Parowan, recorded one incident that offers a lens into the various complexities of such ongoing relationships and how they seemed to play out sometimes according to local custom but outside the bounds of probate oversight. Martineau recounted that the previous year fellow colonizer William Rice had "bought an Indian girl, a prisoner—from a band of Utahs," but the Ute band then "stole her away" so they could "sell her again at some other place." A dozen Latter-day Saint men attempted to recover the girl one Sunday morning when they entered a Ute camp and demanded her return. She was not present in the camp, and so the armed men took a horse as hostage and returned to Parowan with it. Because the girl was already "miles away" members of the Ute band "brought another little Indian, a boy about three years old, and gave him in place of the girl." The Ute men recovered their horse in exchange. Surprisingly, two days later the missing girl also showed up at Parowan "having escaped from her abductors." As Martineau put it, "so Rice had *two* Indians. The girl—about 13 years old—I named Cora; the boy [Rice] named Mosheim, and he kept and raised them in his family." Martineau married Cora as a plural wife over thirty years later.[53] It is not clear if Rice ever registered the children with a probate judge in southern Utah as required by the new law.

In 1859, Benjamin Franklin Johnson, a Latter-day Saint settler at Santaquin, a farming community at the south end of Utah County, counted five Indigenous children living in his household that year. His experience indicates that sometimes there was a fluid transfer of children between families with no indication of legal registrations or court oversight. Johnson's wife Sarah Jane, for example, gave Viret, "a small Pah-erd [likely Piede] girl she had bought," to another Latter-day Saint family as that family prepared to move from Santaquin in 1859. Johnson then explained that he had previously purchased "a small indian boy" who they named Kemo and that they also had "three indian children" living with them who belonged to his sister Julia Babbit. Babbit left the three children with Johnson while she traveled to Council Bluffs, Iowa, "with her own children."[54] Such transfers among families were likely disruptive for the Indigenous children who were already displaced from their biological families and then were sometimes shuffled between white families with little apparent thought for their stability or emotional well-being.[55]

* * *

To date no comprehensive survey of county probate records exists to indicate how many of the over 400 Indigenous children in Latter-day Saint homes up through the turn of the twentieth century legalized the arrangement with a probate registration as required by law, but the number was likely small.[56] Some Latter-day Saints did follow the provisions of the legal code and examples of registrations exist in scattered county archives. Two examples of Native American indentures do survive, one from Iron County in southern Utah entered on October 1, 1853, and the other from Sanpete County in central Utah entered February 1, 1859. Both probate entries make it clear that the registrations were designed to meet the requirements of the law.[57]

Richard Benson, a Latter-day Saint settler at Parowan, Utah, appeared before two Iron County selectmen in October 1853 and entered an indenture agreement with a three-year-old girl named Sarah. She was reportedly "born in Utah Territory, of the Pah Ed [Piede] tribe of Indians." The indenture agreement claimed that "the said Sarah hath voluntarily bound herself to live with and serve the said Richard Benson, until she shall have attained the age of eighteen (18) years." However, any notion that a three-year-old could "voluntarily" enter such an arrangement was an obvious fabrication. The registration also claimed that Sarah agreed "to obey all the lawful commands and counsel of the said Richard Benson, and to conduct herself at all times and in all respects as should become a child to its parent or lawful guardian." The terms of the agreement were thus couched in familial language as a pact between a parent and child.[58]

The terms were also economic. For Benson's part, he bound himself "to teach or cause the said Sarah to be taught some useful trade or avocation, and to correct and teach her to observe the principles of good order and industry, and also to send her to a good school for the term of twenty-seven (27) months, between the ages of seven and sixteen years." The "trade or avocation" clause thus conformed to the apprenticeship terminology of the Act for the Relief of Indian Slaves and Prisoners, but in this particular case it did not specify a vocation for Sarah and did not conform to standard apprenticeships where an apprentice was supposed to gain a particular set of marketable skills by the end of the apprenticeship. Benson was obligated to clothe Sarah "in a comfortable and becoming manner" according to his condition in life. He was also required to "act in all respects and at all times towards the said Sarah, as a parent or guardian should to his child or ward, except in relation to inheritance."[59]

Sarah was thus bound to Benson until she turned eighteen, at which time she would be free and in theory be able to provide for herself. Benson was required to furnish Sarah "one good suit of clothes for holidays, and one good suit for working" at the end of her apprenticeship but had no long-term obligations to her and was explicitly not required to include her in his inheritance.[60]

The 1859 indenture of "Samuel, an Indian boy aged nine or ten years" in Sanpete County followed a similar pattern with some exceptions. In the Sanpete County case, the agreement was between three selectmen of the county and John Beal, the settler to whom Samuel was to be bound. The arrangement was between the white men of the county, in other words, and did not pretend that Samuel had any agency in the agreement. The indenture made it clear that it was designed to conform to the provisions of An Act for the Relief of Indian Slaves and Prisoners.[61]

Unlike in Sarah's case, Samuel's indenture did attempt to conform to the section of the law that required the probate registration to include genealogical information about the person being apprenticed. In Samuel's case such information was sparse. The registration noted that he was born in

Utah Territory, "son of (not Known) of the Piede Tribe of Indians, obtained from Arapeen." Arapeen was Walkára's brother and known for trading captive children throughout the territory. The registration does not specify how John Beal acquired Samuel from Arapeen or what he may have paid in exchange. It does not include any other identifying information.[62] Even though the act required as much familial detail as possible to be included in the probate registration, the purpose of that information was not reunification with an indentured child's biological family. An indentured child's displacement from their own culture and family was thus inherent in the law.

The indenture bound Samuel out to Beal "as an apprentice... to be taught the trade of farming." It was a ten-year indenture that specified that Samuel would be released from the apprenticeship at age twenty, in 1869. In the meantime, Beal was given "all authority, power and right to and over the said Samuel and his service during said term." Beal was obligated "to teach and instruct the said Samuel as an apprentice or otherwise cause him to be well and sufficiently instructed and taught the trade of farming after the best way and manner that he can." He was also obligated to send him to school three months each year when Samuel was between the ages of seven and sixteen and to "train him in the habits of obedience, industry and morality." Beal was required to allow Samuel "meat, drink, washing, lodging and apparel for winter and summer and all other necessaries proper for such an apprentice." When the apprenticeship ended, Beal was required to give Samuel "a new Bible, book of Mormon, and two new suits of clothing, suitable to his condition."[63]

Samuel's and Sarah's indentures were similar on most counts but differed in important ways. Sarah's indenture suggested that she was a "voluntary" party to the agreement, while Samuel's did not. Sarah's used the language of "trade and avocation" but failed to specify a particular trade that her apprenticeship was supposed to help her acquire, while Samuel's specified an apprenticeship designed to teach him "the trade of farming." Both included paternal obligations assigned to their "masters," and both included two suits of clothing as freedom dues. Samuel's freedom dues also included a Bible and Book of Mormon, an indication of the religious colonization that permeated the objectives of the law.[64]

It is difficult to know what Samuel and Sarah experienced in practice. Sarah at least outlived her indenture. At age sixteen, two years before her indenture expired, she married a French-born convert to the Church of Jesus Christ of Latter-day Saints, a man named Henry Harrop, and the couple raised a family together. The 1870 census listed them living in Parowan with two children and specified that neither Henry nor Sarah could read or write, an indication that perhaps some aspects of the educational requirements of her apprenticeship went unfulfilled. By 1880 the couple had moved to Arizona where Henry worked for the railroad and Sarah kept house. This time the census suggested that Sarah could read but not write and that Henry could both read and write. The couple had their union "sealed" for eternity in a Latter-day Saint temple ritual in 1877, an indication that there were no religious barriers to their mixed racial marriage. Sarah gave birth to five more children between 1870 and 1880. Tragically she died in childbirth around 1881, delivering a set of twins. The twins did not survive and were buried on either side of Sarah in a cemetery in Snowflake, Arizona.[65]

* * *

Unlike Sarah and Samuel, Pidash or Kah-peputz (see figure 8.1), the woman who Latter-day Saints knew as Sally, was never indentured before a probate judge. She was likely around nineteen when Charles Decker purchased her from Baptiste, a Ute slave trader who threatened to kill her in the absence of a buyer. Sally was a Pahvant Ute from central Utah where her father had died, and she may have still been in mourning when her stepfather sold or traded her to Baptiste. When Decker bought her, Latter-day Saint accounts described her as covered with ashes, her hair cut short with cuts on her body, perhaps signs of Ute mourning rituals. The burns on her body and her starving hunger, however, were common torments suffered by many captives.[66]

Decker gave Sally to his sister, Clara (Clarissa) Caroline Decker Young, a plural wife of Brigham Young, and Sally thereafter became a servant in Young's extensive household. She was the same woman to whom Brigham Young referred to in his testimony at the Luján trial when he claimed that she "has fared as my children and is as free."[67] She was nonetheless listed in the 1850s among the "help" in Young's family and described as a "domestic servant" in the 1870 census.[68]

In the early days of Latter-day Saint settlement she lived at the fort with Clara and did laundry, childcare, sewed, darned socks, fetched water, ironed, and cooked. After moving to the Lion House, the large residence constructed for Young's multiple wives and expansive family, she mostly worked as a cook, helping prepare three meals a day for over fifty people. Later in life she transitioned to the Beehive House where she prepared food for twenty-five

Figure 8.1 Pidash or Kah-peputz (c. 1828–1878), the woman who Latter-day Saints knew as Sally Young Kanosh. Used by permission, Utah Historical Society.

people and rose in the ranks to chief cook. She received room and board as well as provisions from the family store but not wages.[69]

Sally, unlike some other captives, was old enough to know her place of origin and her mother, but over time she developed a sense of safety with Clara. She was fed and clothed and cared for at the Lion House, and any notion of escape or effort to return to her biological family was likely calculated against the risk of recapture at the hands of Baptiste and the trauma of captivity, deep hunger, and burns on her body. The fact that her stepfather had traded her to Baptiste may have only intensified her alienation from her people and could have helped develop a sense of peace and safety at Young's walled estate in Salt Lake City.[70]

When Chief Kanosh, a Pahvant Ute leader, sought to court her in the 1870s, it is thus understandable that Sally rebuffed him. Brigham Young, however, instructed her that in marrying Kanosh, she could bring the lessons of "civilization" to her people and told her to consider it her mission. She reluctantly married the chief in 1877 and then moved to central Utah with him. She died there a year-and-a-half later after falling ill. She was around fifty years old.[71]

By that point, Sally had spent the majority of her life in Salt Lake City living in the Lion and Beehive Houses, at the center of a busy household and far away from her Ute people. She had been baptized and rebaptized a Latter-day Saint and had participated in proxy baptisms for deceased family members. In many ways, she had assimilated and become "civilized" according to Latter-day Saint understandings of that term. The Latter-day Saint female Relief Society, of which she was a member, helped with her funeral arrangements, and she was buried in ritual temple clothing that Brigham Young had previously given her.[72]

Despite all the religious rituals that marked a life of belonging among the Latter-day Saints, however, there was distance as well. Her obituary, written by a white Latter-day Saint, ended with a racial note that perhaps captures the challenges she faced in creating a life for herself between two worlds: "Beneath that tawney skin," her obituary noted, "was a faith, intelligence and virtue that would do honor to millions with a paler face."[73] Despite living the bulk of her life at the center of Salt Lake City in the household of the leader of her adoptive faith, she died in central Utah, removed from the relative comfort and security that had surrounded her. More pointedly, she was still remembered in part at least for her "tawney skin."

* * *

Although there were always significant challenges to integration, some Indigenous children were fully accepted into Mormon families as fictive kin. In February 1853, a Latter-day Saint named Jacob Hamblin purchased a ten-year-old Goshute or Shoshone boy from his destitute mother in Tooele Valley. Hamblin recorded several versions of the event, and in one he claimed that the boy's father had been killed by Mormons during recent fighting.[74] Hamblin had also taken part in the conflict before experiencing a profound change of heart. He later recalled that the "Holy Spirit forcibly impressed me that it was not my calling to shed the blood of the scattered remnant of Israel [American Indians], but to be a messenger of peace to them."[75] In subsequent years, Hamblin became a respected missionary and diplomat to Native people in southern Utah and northern Arizona. He eventually married three Paiute women as plural wives and purchased or "redeemed" seven Indigenous children whom he incorporated into his large family.[76]

Hamblin named his new ward Albert and treated him as a son. In writing, Hamblin called Albert "my boy" or "my Indian boy." Albert in turn referred to Hamblin as "father." In 1854, Albert moved with the rest of the family to southern Utah where Hamblin served as missionary to the Paiute. Like other children, Albert provided vital labor for the household economy. During the mid-nineteenth century, the concepts of worker and kin were not mutually exclusive. Albert's main duty was that of a herdsman, but he also joined his adoptive father on various expeditions to explore the country. In 1857, at the age of fourteen, Albert witnessed the horrific Mountain Meadows massacre while Hamblin was away from home. Priscilla, one of Hamblin's wives, recalled that Albert "had a hard time adjusting to life again" after his experience at Mountain Meadows.[77]

But like Sally and Sarah, Albert appears to have fully accepted the Latter-day Saint religion. On one occasion, Albert reported to Hamblin that he had been herding sheep when he saw a personage in a white robe who proceeded to take him on a tour of the heavenly realms. He was told that someday he must "bear witness to all the indians on the earth and try and bring them to occupy the same sphere that this glorious personage did."[78] Thereafter, Albert often expressed a desire to serve a mission to the Shoshone. When Albert was seventeen, Hamblin sent him to Great Salt Lake City for six months under the patronage of Brigham Young. Albert learned to read and write and became very close to Young who ordained him an elder in the priesthood.[79] Although there is no evidence of it, it is not difficult to imagine that Albert met and conversed with Sally while in Young's home.

When Albert returned to southern Utah, he wrote to Young about local affairs. Although Albert always saw himself as an Indian, his letter shows that he identified with his Latter-day Saint family and internalized their values. He explained to Young that the local Paiutes "hav commenced thare old customes abuseing thare squaws the Misionarys had stopt for 4 years. They fit [fought] ove[r] one Squaw here all day stabd hur 3 times. Father and some of the Boys stopt the fuss." Albert continued, "We will be glad to see you when you come here. I hope you will stop to my Father's house when you come." He signed the letter, "your Bro. in the gospel, Albert Hamblin." He also added a postscript to Young. "I prey most every day a lone as you told me."[80]

Two years later, Albert died of pneumonia. Jacob Hamblin was then on a mission to the Hopi people in Arizona. Before Hamblin left, Albert predicted his own death. He told Hamblin that "I shall bloom in another place before you get back. I shall be on my mission!" When Hamblin asked what Albert meant, he responded, "I shall be dead and buried when you get back."[81] The mission that Albert referred to was in the afterlife.

We cannot know for sure all the challenges Albert faced in adapting to a new culture. Although he lived in proximity to Native Americans after his adoption, they were not his people. He always identified with the Shoshone in the north and with his Latter-day Saint family. Had Albert lived, he may or may not have been able to marry and pursue an independent life in Latter-day Saint society. Yet his experience was close to the ideal that Utah legislators imagined when they debated the Indian Indenture Act in 1852. Albert had not been redeemed from Ute raiders, but Hamblin believed that he had saved the boy from poverty and potential starvation. Over the next decade, Albert worked hard for Hamblin. In a eulogy written in 1881, Hamblin recalled, "For a number of years he had charge of my sheep, horses and cattle, and they had increased and prospered in his hands." Yet their relationship was not primarily economic. Albert was less a servant than a trusted member of the family who fulfilled his assigned duties. Most importantly, Albert had become firmly converted to the Latter-day Saint faith. As Hamblin concluded in his eulogy, Albert "was a faithful Latter-day Saint; believed he had a great work to do among his people; had many dreams and visions, and had received his blessings in the house of the Lord."[82]

If the relationship between Jacob and Albert Hamblin represented the ideal behind the Indenture Act, other Mormons were prepared to use the law for profit. David Lewis and Thomas S. Williams were both heavily involved with African American servitude in the territory. Lewis's wife, Duritha, inherited three slaves from her father and ultimately sold two of them, Tampian and Caroline, to Williams. In 1855, Lewis served in the Southern Indian Mission. He became a confidant of Wákara and was ultimately assigned to be an Indian trader at the settlement of Parowan.[83] Lewis was with Wákara when the prominent tribal leader and slave raider died in February of that year. Lewis wrote to Brigham Young that upon Wákara's death, the Ute "killed two Squaws, Piede prisoners, and two Piede children, and about twelve, or fifteen of Walker's best horses," symbols of his status and power.[84]

Earlier that same month, however, evidence indicates that some Latter-day Saints also engaged in the Indigenous slave trade for profit. Missionary Thomas D. Brown recorded, "I met David Lewis, he had arrived with a stock of Goods from Thomas Williams, to trade for Indian children, & some for Mr. Perry to trade for horses."[85] It seems likely that Lewis was leveraging his relationship with Wákara and his band to purchase captive children on behalf of Williams. Williams may have wanted a few Indian servants for his own household, but the implication is that Williams planned to resell the captives in Salt Lake City. If so, the scheme still upheld the general goal of "redeeming" Indian children from their captors where they faced the possibility of torture and death. But it was an obvious attempt to monetize the process. This was little different than the activities of Don Pedro León Luján, whose arrest in 1851 touched off the series of events chronicled here, or countless other men who trafficked in Paiute captives.[86]

9

Slavery, Priesthood Denial, and Brigham Young versus Orson Pratt

As An Act for the Relief of Indian Slaves and Prisoners and An Act in Relation to Service were variously implemented across the Utah Territory, Brigham Young and his colleagues returned to their chief political objective—statehood. Congress denied six applications from Utah over the course of the nineteenth century. Lawmakers in Washington, D.C. did not finally relent until 1896, but only after the Latter-day Saints agreed to abandon polygamy and theocracy. In the late winter of 1856, Young decided that the time was right to try for statehood a second time. The citizens of Utah duly formed a constitutional convention and petitioned Congress to admit Utah into the Union under the name of Deseret. As it turned out, it was not a favorable moment to attempt such an effort. Two years earlier, Congress passed the Kansas-Nebraska Act that organized two new territories under the ambiguous provisions of popular sovereignty. This violated the old Missouri Compromise that prohibited slavery in the Louisiana Purchase north of latitude 36°30'. As a result, Kansas-Nebraska reignited a bitter conflict over slavery from which the nation would not recover. By the summer of 1856, Kansas Territory had collapsed into open conflict between pro- and antislavery forces.[1]

Slavery prompted a passionate debate at Utah's Constitutional Convention as well. Despite Brigham Young's attempts to abate internal conflict over slavery with the Service Act, the convention of 1856 showcased the strong disagreements that continued to exist among the Latter-day Saints—disagreements that were further vented in the Williams Camp hearing several months later. This time, Orson Pratt and Brigham Young were on the same side as they jointly opposed a small faction of Southern delegates who wished to explicitly protect slavery in the proposed constitution. Slave owners, it seems, were not satisfied with the restrictive provisions of the Service Act and wished to abandon the neutral position that Mormon leaders had adopted toward slavery since the late 1840s. Feelings ran so high that some of the delegates actually demanded that their names be recorded as having voted for or against slavery in Deseret.[2]

While those events played out among territorial leaders, Latter-day Saints began to openly discuss the faith's racial priesthood restriction. Orson Pratt and other apostles defended the ban in five newspaper articles published in the 1850s. Those racial restrictions thus became the lasting legacy of the heated debates of that decade, especially after the U.S. Congress outlawed slavery and involuntary servitude in all U.S. territories in 1862. Congress thus brought a legal end to slavery in Utah even though its end in practice—along with that of Native American servitude—remains obscure.

* * *

The 1856 Constitutional Convention gathered at the Council House in Great Salt Lake City, the same building where debates over the Service Act had previously taken place. The delegates consisted of the usual contingent of leading Latter-day Saints, including at least four apostles (Orson Pratt, Parley P. Pratt, George A. Smith, and Ezra T. Benson) and one member of the governing First Presidency, Jedediah M. Grant, who served as convention president. Governor Brigham Young also attended and occasionally spoke. Several non-Mormon territorial officials likewise served as delegates including Chief Justice John F. Kinney of the Territorial Supreme Court, and Dr. Garland Hurt, the Indian agent. Unlike the fictitious constitutional convention of 1849, this assembly involved a series of hard-fought arguments among the delegates, some of which convention reporter John V. Long captured in Pitman shorthand.[3]

The debate began on Friday, March 21. Delegate Seth M. Blair stood to offer an amendment to a proposed declaration of rights. Blair was originally from Missouri, but as a young man he moved to Texas where he fought in the revolution against Mexico before converting to Mormonism. During the Luján trials in 1851–1852, Blair served as U.S. attorney, in which position he unsuccessfully argued to Judge Snow that slavery was legal in Utah. Blair now wished to amend a section of the declaration that read, "In republican governments all men should possess their natural rights."[4] The draft language specified that among those rights were the right of "enjoying and defending their life and liberty."[5] However, Blair proposed to change the statement from one that exhorted what *should* be true in a republican government into a descriptive statement that read, "In *this* Republican government [i.e., the United States] all men possess their natural rights."[6]

Soon thereafter, delegate Orson Pratt addressed the convention. Pratt had lost none of his hatred for slavery nor his characteristic outspokenness since he had scolded the Utah legislature four years before. Pratt now offered an amendment to Blair's language, declaring that in the United States "all *free* persons possess their natural rights."[7] Clearly, Pratt did not believe that enslaved people were in possession of their natural rights, including their right to liberty. Joseph Smith had made a similar argument when drafting a constitution for the Kingdom of God over a decade earlier.[8] Pratt's amendment was seconded by his brother, Parley, although Parley worried that the amended language appeared to be "an abolition doctrine" and would amount to a declaration "before the face and eyes of this government and all governments of [the] earth that we are abolitionists."[9] This would have been a significant change to the neutrality policy that Latter-day Saint leaders had espoused since 1849 and might harm their chances for statehood among Southern lawmakers.

The delegates subsequently engaged in a prolonged debate about whether African American slaves possessed their natural rights. The topic served as surrogate for the broader slavery question, and delegates began to stake out their positions. Thomas S. Williams, who would ultimately claim ownership of several African Americans in Utah, professed, "I believe that [the] Supreme Being gave to the Africa[n] man all the rights that he entitled him to enjoy and that was to be a slave to his superiors."[10] Other delegates also stated that they were in favor of slavery. District Judge George P. Stiles, a lapsed Mormon, declared himself to be a "proslavery man."[11] Others, like Albert Carrington, wished to avoid the question completely, although he admitted that "this country is not adapted to African slavery."[12] Ultimately, both amendments were rejected, and the declaration reverted to the original normative language about natural rights.[13]

As soon as this debate was complete, however, the convention turned to the question of slavery more directly. Seth M. Blair proposed another amendment to the declaration of rights, stipulating, "We recognize the right of the people of this State to adopt and regulate African Slavery, as they in their wisdom may deem proper."[14] As written, this did nothing more than confirm the principle of popular sovereignty under which Utah Territory had been organized and which had been further endorsed by the Kansas-Nebraska Act. It did not indicate whether Deseret would adopt slavery. Rather, it was a continuation of the old neutrality policy and simply pushed the question into the future. George A. Smith, one of the authors of the

Service Act, seconded the motion. However, Thomas S. Williams objected to "the question of slavery or anti-slavery being presented upon neutral grounds."[15] Instead, he argued that the convention should explicitly adopt slavery in Deseret, something that Brigham Young and the territorial legislature had rejected in 1852. Williams acknowledged that "many may suppose that I was tenacious for African slavery and that I go in for African slavery for selfish purposes and pecuniary purposes."[16] Considering his investment in enslaved African Americans, this was not a difficult conclusion to reach. However, he argued that the adoption of slavery was necessary for currying favor with Southerners in Congress and thereby obtaining statehood. This was not far from Almon Babbitt's strategy back in 1849–1850. In fact, Babbitt was then serving as the territorial secretary, and he too was a delegate to the convention.

Orson Pratt would have none of it, and he moved that even Blair's neutral language be stricken from the declaration. Pratt lost this first vote, but he and three other delegates, including his brother Parley, wished it to be noted for the record that they supported removing the provision. However, at least one of these delegates, Enoch Reese, did so because he believed that there was a contradiction between the amendment and other portions of the declaration, and because it did not protect slavery as he would have preferred.[17]

As the debate continued into the next day, Blair altered his amendment. Rather than the original neutral language, his proposed amendment now read, "The people of this State *do* adopt and *will* regulate African Slavery as they in their wisdom may deem proper."[18] Blair declared that he was a "southern man" and condemned what he called the "encroachment of the north," which dated back to the Northwest Ordinance of 1787. "My moral social and religious feelings are this," he said, "that we have a right to go [the] course of the United States and no set of men be who can deprive us of these constitutional rights."[19] This was Brigham Young's nightmare come true. Despite all of his efforts to achieve unity among the Saints, an important community leader like Blair was openly declaring his allegiance to overtly sectional principles. The highly restrictive provisions of the Service Act were apparently not enough to satisfy the territory's pro-slavery minority. Surprisingly, Blair's amendment was again seconded by George A. Smith.[20]

Once more, Orson Pratt stood to address the convention. He attacked Blair's amendment on both religious and political grounds. He admitted that perhaps anciently God had permitted some kind of human bondage as it was recorded in the Bible. But that did not mean God had authorized slavery in the nineteenth century. To support his arguments, Pratt appealed to the revelations of Joseph Smith in the Doctrine and Covenants, a book that Latter-day Saints accepted as scripture. "I read, sir, in that divine book [that] 'it is not right that any man should be in bondage,'" Pratt declared. "You will find it, sir, in a revelation to the people whom we call our constituents that elected us to this convention. It will be found in a revelation that was given in December some 23 years ago, contained in that book, [which is] believed in by the most of our constituents, that 'it is not right that any man should be in bondage [to] another.'"[21]

Pratt then attempted to solidify his point with an appeal to the religious beliefs of the majority of Utahns. It was a blending of religion and politics, but one that Pratt pressed to his advantage. "This being the views then of the constituents [who we represent], I feel to have this boldness to come before this honorable body and advocate the views of this [revelation to this] honorable body. If it be not right that one man should be in bondage to another then I am opposed sir to adopting this [in our constitution]. It is contrary to the views of our constituents that we should adopt this. Our constituents that have sent us here sir would not accept the constitution if we were to adopt views which they as a great mass do not believe."[22]

Pratt then went one step further to argue that slavery was not in fact protected by the U.S. Constitution. Moreover, he again rejected the notion that slavery was justified by the curse of Cain, something that had been hinted at by other delegates. "We have no proof that the Africans are the descendants of old Cain who was cursed," he said, "and even if we had that evidence we have not been ordered to inflict that [curse] upon that race."[23] This was an expansion of arguments that Pratt had made to the legislature four years earlier. He still refused to accept Brigham Young's argument that people of African descent were subject to the curses laid out in Genesis. Pratt did not believe that the Latter-day Saints could enforce a curse against anyone without explicit authority from God—that is, a revelation. Yet he indicated that the Saints had not received such a revelation. He also attacked the prevailing wisdom that Black Africans were literally descended from Cain.[24]

At last, a vote was called on Blair's amendment to adopt slavery. It was a significant defeat for the pro-slavery faction, 26-5 against the measure. Judge John F. Kinney, perhaps sensing the importance of the event, asked for the ayes and nays to be recorded in the convention journal. Those who supported the slavery amendment included Almon Babbitt, Seth M. Blair, Thomas S. Williams, Judge George P. Stiles, and apostle George A. Smith, who may have changed his vote during the roll call to support the amendment.[25] Those who voted against the amendment included apostles Orson and Parley Pratt, Apostle Ezra T. Benson, future apostle Daniel H. Wells, future president of the LDS Church Lorenzo R. Snow, Judge Kinney, and others. However, not all of those who opposed the amendment did so out of antislavery sentiment. Delegates Garland Hurt and William Hooper both stated that "if the question was for or against the principle of slavery they would have voted in favor of slavery; but being in favor of leaving the question of adoption or non-adoption to be settled by the people, they so voted against the motion."[26]

This was not the end of the debate over slavery, however. Thomas S. Williams immediately proposed an amendment to the declaration of rights that would prohibit the legislature of Deseret from taking action to emancipate enslaved people without the consent of their owners or providing full compensation. The amendment would likewise prohibit the legislature from barring the importation of individuals who were deemed to be slaves in other jurisdictions. Williams did not wish to endanger his personal trade in African Americans, and he may have planned to bring more into Utah in the future. The amendment was seconded by Seth M. Blair but was quickly laid on the table. Dr. Hurt also gave notice that before the end of the session, he would "introduce an article providing to submit the subject of Slavery to a vote of the people to decide its adoption or prohibition," although delegates did not pass such a proposal.[27]

Several days later, Williams proposed two amendments to limit the franchise to white men, both of which were decisively defeated. Unlike the Constitution of 1849, the new instrument stipulated that all male citizens over twenty-one were entitled to vote after six months of residence, a modification that might have allowed Black men to vote in Utah as Orson Pratt had advocated in 1852.[28]

There is no record of Brigham Young's view on this matter, but in 1869 he notified his influential friend Thomas L. Kane that Latter-day Saints would not have to modify their attitudes on Black suffrage in order to conform to the newly passed Fifteenth Amendment to the Constitution that codified the practice nationwide. "I will call your attention to Article 7, Amended Constitution, State of Deseret, passed Feb. 4, 1867," Young wrote Kane. Young then quoted the words of that amendment, which read, "'All male citizens of the United States over 21 years of age, having a residence of 6 months in this State shall be entitled to vote'; the words 'free, white, male,' having been stricken out." Young even specified that the "number of votes polled on this amendment was 14000 for, & 30 against," an indication that it must have been put to a public vote.[29]

More importantly, Young's position on the matter seemed to have changed over time. Young did not express the same forceful opposition to Black male voting rights in 1869 that he had in 1852. In fact, he almost seemed pleased to report Utah's stance on the matter to Kane. Gone was Young's insistence that being barred from priesthood ordination automatically precluded Black men from voting. Even though he modified his position on Black suffrage, however, his stand on the priesthood restriction remained fixed.[30]

Black male suffrage aside, Brigham Young was deeply concerned by the debates in the 1856 convention over slavery. He believed that the issue had been satisfactorily resolved by the Service Act in 1852. But according to the available record, the Service Act was not even mentioned during the debates. This omission is telling. It seems likely that if the pro-slavery faction believed that slavery was already legal in Utah, they would have appealed to the Service Act as precedent. Yet they did not. Instead, they argued over whether they should abandon the old posture of neutrality toward slavery and expressly adopt the institution. In fairness, antislavery advocates such as Orson Pratt did not mention the Service Act either. Instead, the law remained quietly in the background as the debates went on.

Young would have preferred the convention to simply adopt the Constitution of 1849, which did not mention slavery at all. He was horrified by proposals that Deseret should enter the Union as a slave state, especially those coming from George A. Smith. On the evening of Sunday, March 23, he told a small leadership council that if Smith was in favor of forming a slave state, he should not be allowed to transmit the new Constitution to Congress. Young speculated that Smith was playing devil's advocate and "[he] don't believe [a] word [of] it."[31]

When Smith arrived at the meeting later, Young demanded to know his views on the subject. Smith admitted that he wished to protect the property rights of slave owners, but that he also wished to regulate the practice. "I don't consider that any one [has] made slaves [in a] right wa[y]," Smith said, "but laws sho^d [be] thrown around [the] Slave [and] we sho^d [have] it [in the] Constitution." In an oblique reference to the Service Act, Young told Smith that "if men bring slaves [to Utah] they must not sell them but treat them well [and] send them [to] school." As always, Young strongly objected to treating African Americans as property. Although Smith tried to defend his position, he ultimately told Young that "when [the] Convention voted they did not want slavery, it was [an] end to me." Young accepted Smith's response but reiterated that he did not want slaves nor slavery in Deseret. "We won't [have] them here [and I] wish we were rid [of] them.... If you were [to] carry out Slavery [as] they do [in the] South it wo^d soon sink us. They r [a] curse [to] any men."[32] Young was relieved by the final Constitution that, as he hoped, did not mention slavery and preserved the territory's political neutrality. An irate Thomas S. Williams, in contrast, refused to even sign the document.

In April 1856, soon after the Constitutional Convention finished its work, Brigham Young wrote to Thomas L. Kane to ask for his support. As in 1849, Young reported to Kane that the "constitution is silent upon the subject of slavery, leaving that question where Congress has left it with the People, but neither our climate, soil, productions, nor minds of the people are congenial to African slavery. Our past experience in this Territory exemplifies the fact that it cannot exist with us as an institution." Young pointed to the Service Act as an example of what Congress might expect if Deseret was admitted to the Union. "It is our object and wishes to leave our Legislature free to enact all such laws, as the nature of the case may require upon that subject," he explained. "We now have a Law probably as suitable to our circumstances upon that subject as one could be made, and under which, that institution does not seem to flourish. This may be taken as an indication of the true state of the case, and should prove satisfactory to all parties, when the subject of adopting slavery was voted upon in the Convention; there were few found in its favor."[33]

Brigham Young still believed that the Service Act of 1852 laid a foundation for Utah to enter the Union as a free state. Even after the Supreme Court handed down the *Dred Scott* decision in 1857, he would reiterate this point to newspaperman Horace Greeley.[34] In Young's mind, the law permitted a small number of Mormon enslavers to continue to exercise limited authority over their African American servants, not to hold them as property. The debates that took place during the Constitutional Convention of 1856 indicate that at least some pro-slavery delegates agreed with Young's assessment. Their ability to profit from the labor of enslaved people had already been significantly limited by the Service Act, and they feared that a future antislavery legislature would further restrict their property rights. Moreover, some may have genuinely believed that appealing to Southern congressmen would improve the chances of the admission of Deseret. Consequently, they demanded explicit constitutional protections for slavery. But the vast majority of delegates refused. As Orson Pratt argued so forcefully, such a policy was against the wishes of their constituents.

* * *

Even as the debates over slavery continued to unfold, Latter-day Saints began to openly discuss the faith's emerging racial priesthood restriction. Evidence indicates that the restriction was in operation sometime before 1852. Even still, 1852 became an important turning point in the faith's open acknowledgement of it. Although one Latter-day Saint apostle, Parley P. Pratt had referred to a priesthood "curse" as early as 1847 and leaders had discussed the matter in a private meeting in 1849, it was still not publicly acknowledged until 1852.[35] At the legislative session that year Young became the first Church president to openly articulate a rationale for the restriction. Legislator Orson Spencer also mentioned the priesthood ban, but he did so as an understood fact, not as something he was hearing about for the first time.

Other evidence from the period bears this out. Government explorer John W. Gunnison, for example, wrote of the racial restriction in his book *The Mormons*, which was published for a national audience in 1852. The timeline of Gunnison's publication and the information contained in his book make it evident that he did not learn of the racial restriction from Young's speeches to the legislature. Gunnison likely came to his understanding through his friendship with Latter-day Saint Albert Carrington who served as an assistant for one of Gunnison's expeditions as well as a consultant for his book. Gunnison had spent the winter of 1849–1850 in Salt Lake City as a member of the Howard Stansbury surveying expedition, and his friendship with Carrington grew out of that experience. Carrington is the most probable source of Gunnison's understanding of Latter-day Saint teachings on a variety of topics, including the racial priesthood restriction.[36]

In *The Mormons* Gunnison explained that the "Negro is cursed as to the priesthood" according to Latter-day Saint teachings "and must always be a servant wherever his lot is cast." He also indicated that a system of Black "involuntary labor" operated in Utah but that it took place in the absence of "any law on the subject," an indication that Gunnison wrote his assessment before the legislature passed An Act in Relation to Service. Gunnison further reported that "Negro caste springs naturally from their doctrine of blacks being ineligible to the priesthood."[37]

Gunnison would have arrived at his understanding of Latter-day Saint racial beliefs sometime between 1849 and 1852, not as a result of Young's speeches to the legislature. In fact, Young's speeches were not published in the *Deseret News* or in the *Journal of Discourses*, typical periodicals where Latter-day Saint leaders made their sermons available to a reading audience. It is thus unclear how widespread knowledge of the restriction was by midcentury. If missionaries who were sent to Jamaica in 1853 were aware of the ban, for example, none of them mentioned it in their letters, journals, or diaries. Those missionaries endeavored to spread the Latter-day Saint message to an island population dominated by Black people, but they did not refer to a racial restriction as they attempted to do so.[38] News of the restriction thus appears to have dispersed unevenly, and the reasons offered to justify it were also not unified.

In the wake of the legislative session, five Latter-day Saint newspapers published articles in the 1850s on the racial priesthood restriction, beginning with the *Deseret News* in April 1852 and ending with *The Mormon*, a New York City–based organ that discussed the ban in September 1857.[39] For whatever reason, the legislative session thus marked a transition in the Saint's willingness to openly discuss the priesthood restriction and to offer their justifications for the practice to fellow congregants and curious outsiders.

Three of the five articles drew on language from the Book of Abraham to justify a racial priesthood restriction. Joseph Smith produced the Book of Abraham that was first published in 1842 in the *Times and Seasons*, a Latter-day Saint newspaper in Nauvoo, Illinois.[40] Even though there is no contemporary evidence that Smith interpreted the verses in Abraham to establish a restriction, Latter-day Saint leaders after him did draw on it for justification.[41]

The book speaks of a "king of Egypt" who was a "descendant from the loins of Ham, and was a partaker of the blood of the Canaaintes by birth." It goes on to describe a daughter of Ham, a woman named Egyptus, whose son became Pharaoh. The Pharaoh was "righteous" and established his kingdom based on wise and just principles. Yet he tried to "imitate" a patriarchal order with his own matriarchal descent. He was not, in other words, the first-born son of a presiding patriarch, but was the son of Egyptus, a matriarch. As the Book of Abraham explained, Pharaoh was "of that lineage by which he could not have the right of Priesthood" even though he attempted to claim it through Noah. He was thus "cursed . . . as pertaining to the Priesthood" (Abraham 1:21–27).

The Book of Abraham portrays the problem in part as matriarchal descent but suggests that the real issue was the Pharaoh's idol worship. Patriarchal descent on its own would not have guaranteed the Pharaoh priesthood but repentance might have. Abraham abandoned the idol worship of his fathers and desired to "keep the commandments of God" that made him "a rightful heir, a High Priest, holding the right belonging to the fathers" (Abraham 1:2). Repentance made Abraham eligible for the priesthood, not lineage. Leaders like Pratt who were immersed in a fraught nineteenth-century racial culture, however, understood the problem racially instead.[42] In doing so they used the phrase from the Book of Abraham—"cursed as pertaining to the priesthood"—as shorthand language to justify a racial restriction.

Brigham Young, however, did not use the same phrase and only drew on the Bible and Cain's murder of Abel as his explanation. The Book of Abraham, in fact, was not canonized in Young's lifetime. Latter-day Saints added it to their scriptural canon in 1880, three years after Young's death. It nonetheless offered ready justification for the racial restriction, both before and after its canonization.[43]

Prominent Latter-day Saint leaders edited all five periodicals that mentioned the racial restriction in the 1850s. The articles they published were unsigned but were most likely penned by each newspaper's respective editor. While they all attempted to justify a racial priesthood restriction, they were by no means unified in their reasons.

Willard Richards, then a member of the faith's First Presidency, its highest governing body, edited the *Deseret News* in 1852 when it ran a long column across several editions titled "To the Saints." On April 3, 1852, that column first addressed the racial restriction and echoed many of the points Brigham Young made just three months earlier to the legislature. Even still, Richards organized his understanding of the racial curse around the confounding of languages and scattering of peoples associated with the Tower of Babel. It was a unique twist to the story that did not persist among other leaders. Like Young, he also used Cain's murder of his brother Abel as the central reason for the "curse" with its associated priesthood restriction.[44]

Richards acknowledged that "God hath made of one blood all nations, kindreds, and tongues that dwell upon the face of the whole earth" (a paraphrase of Acts 17:26) and that the human family began as a unified entity with "one language." Yet fallen "men had corrupted their ways before the Lord, by shedding innocent blood, and committing all manner of abominations." In response, "the heavens were displeased, and the inhabitants of the earth were cursed; some with a skin of blackness, some with darkness, and all with confusion of languages."[45]

Richards then lamented the loss of unity that such wickedness produced. One language and one color were his stated ideals, while diversity of languages and colors were a lamentable deterioration from unity and faith. "And if this increase in diversity of color and language continue, how long will it take to restore the inhabitants of the earth back to their original oneness?" he asked. For Richards oneness meant "*one in all things*; one in language, one in color, one in faith, and one in act[ion]."[46]

People of Black African descent were the most significant disruption to the unity for which Richards hoped. As he saw it, people with black skin were a formidable barrier that stood in unity's way. "The descendants of Cain cannot cast off their skin of blackness, at once, and immediately," he lamented, even if "every soul of them should repent, obey the gospel, and do right, from this day forward. The mark was put upon Cain, by God himself, because Cain killed his brother Abel thereby hoping to get the birthright, and secure to himself the blessings which legally belonged to Abel." It was an echo of Brigham Young's speech from two months earlier. "Cain and his posterity must wear the mark which God put upon them," Richards insisted. Even if white people "wash the race of Cain with fuller's soap every day they cannot wash away God's mark." Skin color for Richards was a curse, one that even repentance and gospel living could not erase. Thus, like Young, Richards argued that Black people were welcomed into the Latter-day Saint fold but were not eligible for its lay priesthood. "The Canaanite may believe the gospel, repent, and be baptized, and receive the Spirit of the Lord, and if he continue faithful until Abel's race is satisfied with his blessings, then may the race of Cain receive a fullness of the priesthood, and become satisfied with blessings, and the two become as one again, when Cain has paid the uttermost farthing." As with Young, there was a promised future redemption, but the terms were ambiguous and the price was high.[47]

Like Young, Richards failed to account for how agency factored into his explanation. Joseph Smith taught that people would be accountable for their own sins and not for Adam's transgression; yet Richards, like Young, held all Black people responsible for a murder in which they took no part.[48] It was a violation of a fundamental Latter-day Saint doctrine that Young and Richards failed to reconcile.

One year later, apostle Orson Pratt weighed in on the matter in an article in *The Seer*, a New York City–based newspaper he edited. His explanation honored the principle of agency and avoided divine curses. Pratt did not mention the priesthood restriction in the 1852 legislative session or in his speech at the 1856 Constitutional Convention, although he clearly challenged the notion of multigenerational curses in both speeches. Yet in 1853 he openly supported the priesthood ban but anchored his rationale in poor choices that Black people supposedly made as spirits in their pre-mortal existence. It was a rationale designed to alleviate the theological pressure point that Young's explanation created. Pratt's description became a key alternative justification to divine curses even though both reasonings continued to animate Latter-day Saint leaders' explanations for the restrictions for the next 130 years. Pratt also used the Book of Abraham shorthand, "cursed, pertaining to the priesthood," to shore up his position.[49]

For Pratt, the central question he hoped to address was the various conditions of human birth, with some born to wealth and privilege and others to poverty and deprivation. "Some are born among the people of God and are brought up in the right way; others are born among the heathen, and taught to worship idols," he explained. "Some spirits take bodies in the lineage of the chosen seed, through whom the priesthood is transferred, others receive bodies among the African negroes or in the lineage of Canaan whose descendants were cursed, pertaining to the priesthood," Pratt said.[50]

It was an argument that was not entirely consistent with his position from 1852 and the stance that he would again take in 1856: ancient curses were not applicable in modern times. He then suggested that the Latter-day Saint teaching that all human beings were eternal and had existed as spirits before obtaining mortal bodies was an important understanding that helped account for the various circumstances in which they entered mortality. Their choices in the pre-earth life, he believed, accounted for the conditions in which they were born on earth. "If rewards and punishments are the results of good and evil actions, then it would seem that the good and evil circumstances under which the spirits enter this world must depend upon the good and evil actions which they had done in the previous world."[51]

Unlike Brigham Young's insistent tone in 1852, Pratt is more tentative. He uses the words "if" and "then" to frame his supposition and "it would seem" to posit a possibility. Importantly, there is no evidence that he returned to a priesthood curse in his later speeches and writings, perhaps an indication of his ongoing reservations.[52]

Despite his spirited rejection of slavery in 1852, his support of Black male voting rights, and his refusal to accept that Black people were cursed descendants of Cain, Pratt crafted his own explanation for a priesthood restriction, one that would endure among Latter-day Saints in various forms for more than a century. Pratt's version honored agency, a key component of the Latter-day Saint gospel plan, but imagined that Black people had exercised it in "evil" ways before coming to earth.[53]

Pratt's explanation was an expansion of an argument that fellow apostle Orson Hyde made in 1845. Hyde did not mention priesthood but did suggest that decisions in the pre-mortal realm accounted for the origins of the "African race." In Hyde's explanation "those spirits in heaven" that did not "take a very active part" in the war between Satan and Jesus were "required to come into the world and take bodies in the accursed lineage of Canaan; and hence the negro or African race."[54]

In 1869, the same year that he appeared to support Black suffrage in a letter to Thomas Kane, Brigham Young denounced the idea of neutrality in the pre-mortal realm as an explanation for black skin or the African race. He taught that "there was No Nutral spirits in Heaven at the time of the Rebellion. All took sides.... All spirits are pure that Come from the presence of God." He then reasserted his standard explanation for black skin: "The posterity of Cane are Black Because He commit[ted] Murder. He killed Abel & God set a Mark upon his posterity."[55]

The debate between Brigham Young and Orson Pratt that began in the 1852 legislative session thus gave rise to the two competing ideas for the racial restrictions that continued to exist in tension with each other until officially disavowed by the Latter-day Saint First Presidency and Quorum of Twelve Apostles in 2013.[56] Both explanations were grounded in an underlying assumption that Black people were inferior to white people and that white skin was normal and black skin was a deterioration from whiteness.[57]

In 1855, apostle Erastus Snow weighed in next in *The St. Louis Luminary*, a publication he edited in St. Louis, Missouri. Unlike Richards and Pratt, Snow anchored his justification in the curse of Ham and a fear of race mixing. "Whatever may be said by abolitionists to the contrary," Snow wrote, "it is a fact as clear as the noon-day sun that the children of Ham are accursed, and are doomed to be servants to their brethren." He then asserted that the central issue was interracial sex. "Those who degrade themselves by sexual intercourse with [the children of Ham], will partake of their curse, and their seed will be doomed to servitude and bondage as long as labor is needful and service demanded." Black people were welcome into the Latter-day Saint gospel and could thereby receive a "remission of sins" for those sins "they have committed in the flesh," Snow indicated, "but they cannot receive the Holy Priesthood and govern in the kingdom of God, but must be servants to their brethren." In Snow's mind, then, the priesthood restriction was linked to the curse of Ham, not Cain. Being "servants to their brethren" meant that Black people could not "govern in the kingdom of God," an explanation that failed to account for the fact that free Black Latter-day Saints such as Elijah Able and Q. Walker Lewis were already ordained to the priesthood and served in leadership roles.[58]

Two years later, George Q. Cannon, then serving as mission president over Oregon and California, entered the conversation in *The Western Standard*, a San Francisco–based newspaper he edited. Like Snow, Cannon cited the curse of Ham but linked it to the Book of Abraham. Cannon's article responded to a report from Dr. David Livingstone, a medical missionary for the London Missionary Society who had been stationed in Africa for over a decade and had explored portions of the continent. Livingstone was an ardent abolitionist who came to respect the African societies and cultures he encountered. In 1857 he published *Missionary Travels and Researches in South Africa*, a chronicle of his work and explorations.[59]

Cannon noted that Livingstone's "travels have thrown a flood of geographical and interesting light on the interior of the continent of Africa, and shows, that though the descendants of Ham have been cursed as pertaining to the Priesthood, they have been blessed with the blessings of the earth pronounced upon their progenitor by his father Noah." It was another shorthand reference to the Book of Abraham that Cannon then made explicit when he noted that Africans "have not only been blessed with the blessings of the earth but have been blessed with the blessings of wisdom, which the book of Abraham informs us, were also conferred upon Ham by Noah."[60] It was an early instance in which Cannon used the Book of Abraham by name to substantiate the racial restriction, something he would return to in 1900 to again demonstrate that "negroes were debarred from the priesthood."[61]

Finally, also in 1857, apostle John Taylor's assistant editor William I. Appleby, also drew on the curse of Ham and the Book of Abraham to justify the priesthood ban in an article published in *The Mormon*, a newspaper they edited in New York. Taylor left New York in May 1857 and likely did not contribute to the newspaper through September of that year.[62] Appleby was thus the probable author of an article that took aim at abolitionist Joshua R. Giddings, who had recently written a letter to the editor of the *National Anti-Slavery Standard* in which he advocated an end to slavery. "As it regards slavery," Appleby began, "we have but little to say either for or against it; but there is one question we would like to ask Mr. Giddings:—If he or all the abolitionists in the world, calculates or expects to remove the '*curse*' of bondage and blackness from the negro, until He who permitted the same to come upon them sees proper to remove the curse?" In his estimation, bondage and blackness were both aspects of the same curse. Appleby wanted Giddings to explain exactly how humans could end a curse God had instigated. More directly, he prodded Giddings to explain the origin of blackness and bondage. "What is the cause of the negro's deformity, bondage, or of their spirits having to take bodies or tabernacles cursed with bondage and blackness?" he demanded. "Mr. Giddings, declare unto us, if you have understanding. Know ye not that there must be a cause to produce an effect? The effect is apparent; but what is the cause?"[63]

Appleby then proceeded to answer his own questions, using the Book of Abraham as the source. "Noah, after he came out of the ark, and lay inebriated in his tent, was made sport of by his son Ham: Noah, thereupon conferred the Patriarchal order and Priesthood upon Shem, blessed Japhet, to be enlarged of the Lord, and to dwell in the tents of Shem," he explained. It was a standard interpretation of the biblical story with a Latter-day Saint twist used to describe patriarchal priesthood. As Appleby then clarified, Noah "also blessed Ham with the blessings of the earth, and with wisdom, but cursed him as appertaining to the Priesthood."[64] Appleby thus offered an ongoing justification for slavery that echoed Joseph Smith's stance from 1836 but failed to acknowledge Smith's plan for compensated emancipation from 1844. Appleby also justified priesthood denial using the Book of Abraham like Pratt and Cannon had done before.[65]

Certainly, 1852 marked a turning point in the public acknowledgment of the racial priesthood restriction among the Latter-day Saints. Beginning that year they openly defended it in five different newspapers over the next five years. Even though the authors of the five articles were unified in the fact of the ban itself, they were scattered in their justifications. Three of the five articles drew on the Book of Abraham but in different ways. Pratt honored agency in his explanation but suggested that Black people exercised it poorly in the pre-mortal realm. Other articles evoked the curse of Ham, the confounding of languages at the Tower of Babel, and the curse of Cain. Some of the articles blended fears of race mixing with biblical curses to justify both slavery and priesthood denial. The slavery justifications disappeared after the Civil War, while priesthood denial persisted well into the twentieth century.

* * *

In many regards the legislative and religious debates that played out among the Latter-day Saints in the 1850s are a microcosm of similar arguments then dividing the nation. Brigham Young and Orson Pratt squared off as Latter-day Saint leaders who represented two strands in a tangled web of political and religious positions then attempting to peacefully solve questions that the nation would only resolve through war. Young attempted to occupy a middle ground, somewhere between the immediate abolitionists on the one hand and the slaveholders of the South on the other hand. Orson Pratt, in contrast, represented an emerging free labor ethic that prompted him to decry both bills introduced in the 1852 legislative session as "this abominable slavery." An assessment of both men's positions thus lays bare how the legislative debates in remote Utah Territory were politically and religiously central to the national arguments then tearing at the fabric of Union.

Gradual emancipationists believed that "by ending slavery over time, basic justice would supposedly be done to masters and slaves alike." Masters would be compensated for their property with the labor of the enslaved, and the rising generation of slaves would gain their freedom at some point, typically as adults.[66] It was a moderate approach to the problem and Brigham Young subscribed to it. Understanding that basic idea regarding Young's position on slavery in the 1850s helps account for why his views on the subject sometimes appeared contradictory. In fact, despite one biographer describing Young as a "bundle of contradictions" in his stance on slavery, he remained remarkably consistent throughout the decade.[67] Like several Protestant moderates of his day, Young attempted to thread a needle between what he considered the sin of holding people as property and the confrontational tactics of immediate abolitionists.[68]

When Southern Saints brought enslaved people with them to the Great Basin, Young noted that "a strong abolitionist feeling [prevails]" and complained that "the devil [is] raised" in response.[69] His overarching task in the wake of his predecessor Joseph Smith's murder had been to preserve a united people, especially as Smith's former followers evaluated several competing claims over prophetic authority and the movement risked fracturing along a variety of fault lines. Questions over race and slavery were two of the fault lines that had threatened the upstart movement from its beginnings, and Young now attempted to smooth them over with a moderate approach.

In fact, even during the Civil War Young continued to defend the middle ground. "I am neither an abolitionist nor a pro-slavery man," he declared, but if forced to choose, "I should certainly be against the pro-slavery side of the question." He railed against both the "rank, rabid abolitionists" as well as the "avarice, blindness, and ungodly actions" of the pro-slavery side.[70] It was a consistent stance for Young that placed him alongside Protestant antislavery moderates who "hoped that, by relying on the peaceful and harmonious tactic of moral persuasion, they could end slavery without dividing the churches and the nation."[71]

This had likewise been the hope of men like Thomas Eddy and John Jay who had initiated the process of gradual emancipation in the late eighteenth century. They believed that moral enlightenment was an incremental process and any attempt to hurry it along would only bring disaster. In the North, their plan to abolish slavery gradually succeeded without war or bloodshed. Yet it kept the enslaved in fetters for decades and left an enduring racism in its wake. Brigham Young was the living embodiment of that legacy.

"The Southerners make the negroes," Young said in 1863, "and the Northerners worship them; this is all the difference between slaveholders and abolitionists."[72] Young spoke these words in the midst of a bloody Civil War that he blamed on belligerent attitudes among Northern abolitionists as well Southern fire-eaters. In Young's estimation, the war was the result of extremists on both sides who refused to compromise. Young thus implied that immediate abolitionism and enslavement were equally unacceptable and that the middle ground was the only suitable space to occupy.

In doing so Young created a caricature of abolitionists that ignored the work they did to end slavery in real and practical ways. Whether they were immediate abolitionists or antislavery advocates of some other stripe, they initiated freedom suits to help enslaved people gain their liberty in court cases, they helped escaped slaves integrate into society and find paid employment, they wrote petitions and lobbied lawmakers, they gave speeches and published newspapers and, like Young, they purchased the freedom of some enslaved people and insisted that human beings were not property. Black enslaved people escaped and rebelled, conducted work slowdowns, and sabotaged plantation production. Free Black people became abolitionists and outspoken advocates of freedom.[73] In Vermont in 1777, antislavery proponents approved "the first written constitution in history to ban adult slavery," and by 1790 freedom suits in Massachusetts "battered slavery's legal supports" to the point that the census that year reported no slaves at all in the state.[74] To write off antislavery advocates as "rank, rabid abolitionists" and negro worshippers ignores the real work they did. Young's middle ground suggested that there was equal distance between two equivalent evils when there was not.

Young's dislike of abolitionists was in part grounded in a defense of polygamy. National politicians and other commentators sometimes linked slavery and polygamy as two of the nation's domestic institutions in need of eradication. In 1855, one dime novel for example called polygamy "white slavery" and said that Latter-day Saint women were "treated as but little better than slaves."[75] Such conflations persisted throughout the 1850s and gained steam following the Civil War. After the war one writer urged that polygamy "receive its death-blow" "by the sword" like "slavery in the great Rebellion."[76]

Abolitionists argued that the government had a right to interfere with the domestic institution of slavery. If Young gave ground on that point, certainly polygamy would be next. By 1856, the Republican Party linked the two "relics of barbarism" in its platform and insisted that Congress had a right and "imperative duty" to eradicate both relics in the territories.[77] It was a political promise that Republicans actually kept: in 1862 they passed two laws within weeks of each other that outlawed slavery and polygamy in the territories. Young's outspoken stance against the abolitionists was thus likely calculated to defend polygamy against its frequent conflation with slavery in national politics.[78]

Young's middle ground was also intended to keep his flock from splitting asunder as had the Methodists, Presbyterians, and Baptists during the previous decades.[79] But in doing so, he sought to conciliate an enslaver minority over a Northern and foreign-born majority who were decidedly opposed to slavery. The 1860 census counted a total of only twelve enslavers in Utah Territory. When their spouses and families and other converts from the South who may have been sympathetic to slavery are included, the population who approved of the practice was undoubtedly higher than that.[80] In fact, the number included some important community leaders such as Seth M. Blair, Thomas S. Williams, Almon Babbitt, and William Hooper. Even still, pro-slavery sentiment among the Saints was never high enough to threaten a division as pronounced as that experienced by the Methodists, who saw a half-million adherents leave the fold and join the newly created Methodist Episcopal Church, South.[81]

The stakes were much lower among the Latter-day Saints. Forcing the issue may have risked offending its white membership from the South, but it likely would have endeared its Black membership, both free and enslaved, that much more tightly to the faith. At least thirty Black Saints had converted by 1852, and more would follow over the coming decade before the Civil War.[82] Young's moderate approach favored white Latter-day Saints over their Black brothers and sisters.

Even still, Young and territorial legislators balanced their deference to enslavers with provisions designed to offer protections to the enslaved. Young was clear that he opposed the idea of property in man and refused to allow human beings to be either categorized or treated as chattel. To do so, in his words, was "not consistent or compatible with the true principles of government."[83] The Service Act required that Black (and white) servants receive at least eighteen months of education and that they be provided "comfortable habitations, clothing, bedding, sufficient food, and recreation." More significantly, it granted them the right to consent to a variety of decisions, even though such consent is difficult to imagine in practice. The law insisted that Black servants arrive in the territory "of their own free will and choice" and honored their right to refuse to be taken from the territory against their will (as in the Dan Camp case) or to be sold without consent.[84]

The principle of consent was key. In granting enslaved people consent over such crucial decisions in their lives, Utah lawmakers elevated them above the level of mere property in the eyes of the law. They were people with agency, strictly limited though it be. From the perspective of Young and his supporters, the Service Act legally transformed these men and women from slaves into servants and from property into human beings.

The law offered a number of additional protections to Utah's enslaved people. Partly based on fears of miscegenation, Black servants were expressly shielded from sexual exploitation by their masters. Moreover, Young suggested that if enslavers violated the provisions of An Act in Relation to Service, the enslaved should be set free, and at his insistence the bill was modified to reflect his position.[85] Although the Service Act recognized a form of lifetime servitude, it also implied that this condition would not pass on to the children of enslaved parents. As such, the Service Act could have become a means of gradual emancipation similar to free womb laws then in operation in Mexico or the indenture laws in the Old Northwest.

Young's moderate antislavery policies notwithstanding, the legislative session revealed an underlying racism that animated his views. His desire to maintain political neutrality and to keep Southern enslavers in the fold by honoring their perceived property rights in slavery ignored the fact that at least some of those enslaved people were also Latter-day Saints. Young's desire to appease white enslavers thus came at the expense of their Black enslaved. In his speech on January 5, 1852, Young argued that enslaved African Americans should be "redeemed from servile bondage, both mental and physical, and placed upon a platform upon which they can build, and extend forth as far as their capability and natural rights will permit."[86] A few weeks later, he told the legislature: "As far as [the] comforts [of] salvation, light, truth, enjoyment, [and] understand[ing] [are concerned] the blacks have the same privilege [as] white [men]."[87]

Young believed that all people were capable of moral and intellectual progress. His paternalistic attitude toward African Americans was based on that premise. He accepted that white Latter-day Saints had a moral duty to baptize, educate, and care for people of African descent. But for Young, the curses supposedly pronounced on Africans in the book of Genesis erected a wall beyond which they could not pass until God himself intervened. As a result, he utterly refused to allow African Americans to hold positions of authority within the Church he led.

The same held true for voting rights. Legislator and apostle Orson Pratt advocated Black male voting rights in Utah Territory while Young argued against it. "[We] just [as well] make [a] bill here for mules to vote as Negroes [and] Indians," Young declared. Black people were racially cursed in his estimation and therefore were not qualified to hold the Latter-day Saint priesthood or capable of exercising the right to vote. Young refused to see Black people as equal to white people and even insisted that his "voice shall be against [it] all the day long."[88]

Young thus placed his prejudice on full display before the territorial legislature. He unabashedly insisted on the racial inferiority of Black people, a position he did not moderate over time. In 1856, in a meeting with Latter-day Saint bishops he again indicated his bias. "I say, 'put no Black to rule over me,'" Young told the gathered bishops. He used the phrase as a metaphor to decry the hypocrisy of those who "get up in our midst, and preach and Thunder away at the people upon the very things that they themselves are most guilty of." He then compared such men to "the nigger slave driver[s]" who in his estimation were "the most unmerciful kind of drivers the poor black can have."[89]

Young's opposition to the possibility of a Black man ruling over him clearly animated his views during the 1852 legislative session and beyond. It informed his position on slavery and voting rights in Utah Territory as well as on priesthood ordination in the Church he led. By 1869, Young had come to terms with Black male voting rights, but he refused to budge on priesthood ordination. After a decade, Congress overruled his approach to slavery in the territories, but his position against priesthood ordination lasted for nearly 130 years and became so entrenched in Latter-day Saint belief and practice that it required God to overrule him—but not until 1978.[90]

Young's racial inclinations notwithstanding, he insisted that if admitted into the Union, Utah would be free. He was not being duplicitous in making such claims any more than it was duplicitous to call states such as New York, Pennsylvania, and New Jersey "free" while gradual emancipation ran its course in those locations. Utah's 1856 Constitutional Convention supported Young's stance. Delegates there voted decisively against application as a slave state. Soon afterward, Young wrote to Thomas Kane that the results of the Constitutional Convention offered evidence that Utah would never adopt slavery.[91] By the time newspaperman Horace Greeley interviewed Young in 1859, he was resolute. Utah "will be a free State," Young insisted. "Slavery here would prove useless and unprofitable." Yet in the same interview he called slavery a "Divine institution" and referred to the curse of Ham. It was a perfect encapsulation of Young's views across the decade.[92]

Men like Brigham Young, George A. Smith, and Orson Spencer held traditional American views in regard to labor. Although these men generally supported a free labor ethic, they understood various degrees of unfreedom to be perfectly compatible with a free and well-ordered society. In their experience, unfree labor was a legitimate method to care for the most vulnerable members of a given community. Except for Smith's strange defection during the 1856 Constitutional Convention, these men were Northerners who had lived through gradual emancipation and rejected chattel slavery. They believed that servitude and slavery were two different things. In this sense, law and historical practice were in their favor.

Thus, legislation like the Service Act or the Indian indenture bill appeared to them like reasonable compromises to maintain political neutrality and avoid internal dissension concerning slavery. In their minds, these statutes transformed enslaved Native Americans or African Americans into servants who would receive care, education, and, ideally, the Latter-day Saint gospel. These men did not believe that they were perpetuating slavery in Utah. In fact, quite the opposite. As Smith said of the Indian indenture bill, "The object of the bill is to abolish slavery."[93]

In contrast, legislator Orson Pratt perhaps captures as clearly as anyone in the legislative session a sense of what was at stake in the long view of history.

Pratt represented the emerging view of labor in the United States. He did not wholly reject unfree labor. He did not apparently object to apprenticeship for children, nor to indentured servitude for European immigrants. But he had a far broader understanding of what constituted slavery. For him, the forms of servitude contemplated by the Service Act and the Indian Indenture Bill were little different from the "abominable slavery" practiced in the American South. In his estimation, perpetuating Black or Native American slavery in Utah territory would bring God's judgment on the Latter-day Saints.

Latter-day Saint scriptural ideals suggested that all people were "alike" in the eyes of God, that "it is not right that any man should be in bondage one to another," and that Jesus claimed "all flesh" as his own.[94] On one level, the proceedings of the 1852 legislature represented a theological debate among Latter-day Saint leaders about how these tenets should be interpreted. Did "alike" mean "equal in all ways?" What precisely constituted "bondage?" Orson Pratt took a liberal view on both questions. For Pratt, the racial hierarchies proposed by Brigham Young were an affront to fundamental religious values. Consequently, Pratt stood his ground. He described the Indian indenture bill and An Act in Relation to Service as forms of slavery and argued against them. He advocated for Black male voting rights in 1852 and refused to relent on slavery or servitude. By 1853, he nonetheless publicly supported his faith's racial priesthood restriction even though he did not tolerate Brigham Young's rationale for it.[95] He again rejected slavery in 1856 and drew on Latter-day Saint scripture to do so. He further undermined Young's key justification for the racial priesthood restriction when he insisted that there was "no proof" that Africans were descendants of Cain.[96]

Pratt thus staked out a position grounded in moral principles on which he refused to relent. His stance in relation to Native American indentures was markedly different, however, than his position toward Black slavery. In the case of Indian children being offered for sale to Mormon settlers, Pratt was motivated by humanitarian impulses and a white paternalistic desire "for the redemption of that people." Pratt argued that Mormon settlers should "use every means in [our] power to benefit the Indians." Pratt believed Mormons had a moral obligation to save Indian captives from their Native American captors. "I believe in the philanthropic principles that exists in [the] bosoms of [church] members towards that race," he said.[97]

Pratt in sum attempted to embrace a free labor ethic in Utah even as other legislators clung to various forms of unfree labor from their upbringing. Pratt was attuned to the free labor trends of his day and was intent on pushing them forward. The debates chronicled here thus make it clear that lawmakers had choices. As judge Zerubbabel Snow indicated in the Luján case, the act that created Utah Territory included "a clause giving to the people here the right to introduce slavery, or reject it."[98]

Utah lawmakers chose to perpetuate several related systems of unfree labor. They could have spurned the idea "with indignation" as Pratt urged, but they chose forms of bondage instead.[99] Pratt was on the right side of history, a fact that he attempted to make clear to his fellow legislators. Slavery was on its way out across the globe, and he shuddered at the thought of sanctioning it in Utah. "Shall we hedge up the way before us by introducing this abominable slavery? No! My voice shall be against it from this time until the bill shall pass if you are determined to pass it." Although legislators made several important revisions to the bill that Pratt wanted rejected, they were ultimately determined to pass it. As Pratt contended, it was "enough to cause the angels in heaven to blush!"[100]

It is difficult to know what might have happened if legislators had opted for immediate emancipation in Utah, or if they simply refused to legally recognize unfree relationships as had been the case from 1847 to 1851. Proposals to strip slave owners of the wealth that they held in the bodies of their slaves had always been controversial, even among those who wished to end slavery. With this in mind, Joseph Smith had proposed government-funded compensation to enslavers as a method of emancipation. Even the British model was grounded in compensation to enslavers for their lost "property," a costly endeavor for the British Empire and not a feasible option in Utah Territory. Young became governor of the territory in 1850, a suspect political entity that Congress kept a wary eye on from its inception. As governor he did not have the financial means or the political capital to draw on federal funds to compensate the territory's enslavers. Instead, Young honored an enslaver's perceived right to the labor of the enslaved, even for life.

Had legislators chosen immediate emancipation in 1852, would it have led to an exodus of Southern converts from the Church? Certainly, the outcome of the 1856 Constitutional Convention four years later deeply angered men such as Thomas S. Williams who eventually became disaffected from the Church. It is hard to believe that such a policy would not have had some effect within the Southern minority, both in Utah and the Southern states. Yet other pro-slavery delegates like William Hooper and Seth M. Blair remained stalwart members of the Church despite the positions lawmakers and delegates adopted in 1852 and 1856. Furthermore, Black people were

Latter-day Saints too, both free and enslaved. Any detrimental effect among enslavers and their sympathizers might have been balanced by a favorable reaction among Black people as well as abolitionists.

Young accepted a prevailing sentiment among gradualists that in setting Black people free all at once it would turn loose on society a group of men and women with no means of support, or worse. When the Civil War erupted, Young feared that "the Abolitionists would let the negroes loose to massacre every white person."[101] Short of that, they might become vagrants and drain public coffers or otherwise disrupt the social order. Young believed that it was thus better to eradicate slavery slowly and individually rather than universally and immediately.[102] Individual manumission would likely have been Young's preferred method of emancipation. It was a procedure that he personally utilized in the case of Green Flake and others. Indeed, he urged abolitionists to "purchase [slaves] into FREEDOM."[103] But this was a policy that needed willing participants to succeed. As the debate and vote over slavery at the 1856 Constitutional Convention indicated, some Southerners were not willing participants.

There was also an important distinction between the possibilities of emancipation for the nation versus those for Utah Territory. The scale of the challenge to immediate abolitionism was greater for the country than it was for Utah Territory. As the Civil War and Reconstruction demonstrated, the challenges of integrating 4 million enslaved people into a free labor economy were not easily resolved. But Utah Territory had roughly thirty-five enslaved people in the 1850s, not 4 million. Latter-day Saints were accustomed to welcoming hundreds of emigrants from Europe and the eastern United States every year and absorbing them into a barter-based economy. Integrating thirty-five freed people into the same system should have been no more of a challenge.

The difference between integrating European converts from migrant trains and absorbing freed Black people, however, was racial. Unlike some states and territories, Utah did not pass a law prohibiting free or enslaved Black people from migrating there. All were welcome. Moreover, Latter-day Saints in Utah participated in integrated worship services, and their notion of "gathering to Zion" was racially inclusive. However, integration had its limits, and Young forcefully articulated them. It is no coincidence that An Act in Relation to Service criminalized sex between white and Black people, and Young made some of his most pointed comments during the legislative session against race mixing. "Let my seed mingle with [the] seed of Cain," Young warned, "[and it] brings the curse upon me and my generations."[104] Fear of race mixing undergirded Young's position on emancipation and animated his stance against priesthood ordination for Black men.

Political calculations also weighed in the balance. Young feared that taking a strong position on slavery would block Utah's path to statehood. Although Thomas Kane was an antislavery man through and through, he consistently urged Latter-day Saint leaders to remain neutral concerning slavery for just this reason. In retrospect, however, the Latter-day Saints' public announcement of polygamy in 1852 and subsequent disputes with federal officials over theocracy in the territory were probably far more consequential.[105] Indeed, by 1859, Young openly declared that Utah would be a free state.[106]

Even still, a key impasse remained, both nationally and in Utah: enslavers insisted that slaves were property and no government could interfere with a person's property. Slavery's opponents just as adamantly argued that freedom was an inalienable right that was superior to property claims. All people had a right to own themselves and their own labor, abolitionists demanded.[107]

The 1850s thus revealed a nation that was deeply divided over the institution of slavery and Utah Territory was no different. Even in the American West, the practice of human bondage threatened to pull the thin fabric of the Union apart. Pro-slavery forces in California attempted to carve off the southern portion of that state to legalize slavery there. Kansas Territory split into rival factions and deteriorated into bloodshed while Southern sympathizers in New Mexico formed a territory named Arizona and joined a Confederacy dedicated to the perpetuation of slavery. For the nation as a whole it ultimately took a bloody civil war to resolve the standoff in favor of freedom. Perhaps, then, the remarkable nature of the Utah experience was that despite its frayed edges, lawmakers there managed to craft an untidy center that held.

10
Utah's Juneteenth

On June 13, 1862, John M. Bernhisel, Utah Territory's delegate to Congress, wrote to Brigham Young to fill him in on legislative happenings in Washington, D.C. Bernhisel informed Young of his ongoing efforts to win statehood for Utah and told him of other political matters then playing out in the nation's capital. Sandwiched in between an update on Bernhisel's effort to secure financial compensation for Young's claims on his "Indian accounts" and information on newly approved U.S. mail routes in Utah, Bernhisel told Young that "Congress has passed a bill abolishing slavery in all the Territories of the United States, and only requires the sanction of the Executive to become a law." He also let Young know that "[t]he polygamy bill has passed both Houses" of Congress.[1] Young thus learned that within weeks of each other, Republicans in Congress had made good on their 1856 pledge to "prohibit in the territories, those twin relics of barbarism, polygamy and slavery."[2]

On June 20, President Abraham Lincoln signed into law An Act to Secure Freedom to All Persons within the Territories of the United States, and in doing, so he ostensibly freed Utah's remaining roughly thirty-five slaves. On July 2, the Church-owned *Deseret News* reported that fact without elaboration. There was no banner headline or extensive story about what the law's passage meant to Utah's enslavers or to those whom they enslaved. There were no instructions that accompanied the news; Latter-day Saint leaders or government officials did not tell Utah's enslavers to emancipate their slaves or in any way establish guidelines or expectations. There was no sense of relief or feelings of joy expressed over the legal end of slavery in the territory. In fact, the announcement in the *Deseret News* would have been easy to miss. It was published on page four, tucked into the middle of a column titled "From Washington," with no fanfare or commentary whatsoever. Nothing drew the reader's eye to the column and no sense of adulation accompanied the report. The paper simply informed its readers that the "President approved the bill prohibiting slavery in the Territories."[3] That was it.

There is no surviving evidence to indicate how or when news of the Freedom Act's passage might have made it into the hands of the territory's enslavers, let alone into the hands of those whom they enslaved. There is no indication to date as to how or when Utah's remaining enslaved population actually gained their freedom. The July 2 newspaper article is the earliest public announcement of the new law, but thus far the written record offers no indication of a concerted effort to communicate news of freedom to the people to whom it mattered most, the territory's enslaved women and men. Thus, while the congressional statute ostensibly marked an end to Utah's decade-long legalization of servitude, its end in practice remains obscure.

In other locations across the United States, previously enslaved people had few economic options, especially as their former enslavers used a variety of coercive means to keep them working on their plantations. In Galveston, Texas, for example, news of freedom did not arrive until June 19, 1865, two months after the end of the Civil War. Even then, it would take the arrival of federal troops and Freedman's Bureau officers to enforce it, and they did so unevenly. Freed people faced coercion, violence, and "Black Codes" designed to keep them working on their former plantations.[4]

Henrietta Wood, for example, was a formerly enslaved woman who agreed to work on her former plantation in Natchez, Mississippi, for three years in exchange for food, one pair of shoes, two suits of clothing, shelter, and $10 per month in wages. Yet after three years she had only managed to save $25, the proceeds from her own efforts at raising pigs and poultry, not wages from her employer. In fact, she recounted that her former enslaver "never paid her a cent." She eventually used her hard-earned money to move to Ohio and find paid employment there. Other former slaves continued to face coercion, intimidation, and violence that kept them working as sharecroppers on their former plantations.[5]

In Utah, two former slaves, Marinda Redd and her husband Alex Bankhead, later in life remembered with fondness the "joyful expressions which were upon the faces of all the slaves when they ascertained that they had acquired their freedom through the fortunes of war."[6] Their remembrance however fails to indicate when they both learned of the news or how they found out that they were free. Marinda had already gained her freedom sometime after 1858 when her enslaver John Hardison Redd died. Redd had remembered Marinda in his will with an unusual bequest. Along with his white descendants, Marinda received equal shares of land, animals, grain, and household goods, a possible indication that Redd was her biological father. A DNA study revealed that Redd had fathered a son with one of his enslaved women, but that study did not include Marinda and her descendants. In either case she gained her freedom, along with a land inheritance, by 1859.[7]

For Marinda, however, freedom did not necessarily mean a life without continued exploitation. In the 1860s, before she married Alex, she gave birth to two children out of wedlock. White men in the small farming community of Spanish Fork fathered both children. Such relationships earned the ire of local bishop Albert King Thurber who railed against "whoredoms" and race mixing from the pulpit. Thurber warned that "if there was any more whoring with black folks both black and white shall be killed."[8]

Marinda and Alex married around 1870 and established a twenty-acre farm in Spanish Fork. A news article published in 1899 described them as "devout and strict Mormons" and noted that Marinda "belongs to the Ladies' Relief Society of her Ward and takes an active part with her white sisters in all work of that character."[9] As property owners, the Bankheads were able to pass an inheritance on to Marinda's surviving son when they died in the early twentieth century.[10]

Green Flake (see figure 10.1), one of the three enslaved men who entered the Salt Lake Valley in July 1847, two days ahead of Brigham Young, offers another example. After Brigham Young freed him around 1852, Flake married Martha Ann Morris, a formerly enslaved woman, and the couple moved to Union, at the mouth of Big Cottonwood Canyon in the Salt Lake Valley. There Flake worked as a day laborer; owned a farm; prospected for mines in the nearby canyons; and with Martha raised their two children, Lucinda and Abraham, as Latter-day Saints.[11]

By the 1880s Flake had become an honored member of the annual Pioneer Day celebrations in Utah that commemorated the arrival of the 1847 settlers in the Salt Lake Valley. He was frequently invited to speak at such events and was revered for his role in the overland trek to the Great Basin. He was mentioned as an esteemed pioneer in at least nineteen newspaper articles over the years. At the 1894 observance, the *Deseret Weekly News* called him "the only survivor of the three colored men who were numbered among the Pioneers of 1847." It further noted that he "gave a short speech in which he said that he had always felt proud of the distinction of being one of the Pioneers of Utah" and that he "had watched with great interest the improvements made since 1847."[12]

After Martha died, Flake moved to Idaho to be with his son Abraham, but he sometimes still attended the annual celebrations in Utah. In 1897, the *Salt Lake Tribune* described him as "a vigorous, broad-shouldered,

Figure 10.1 Green Flake (1828–1903) was an original Latter-day Saint settler in the Salt Lake Valley in 1847, arriving as an enslaved man two days ahead of Latter-day Saint leader Brigham Young. He was celebrated in his later life for his status as an 1847 pioneer. Used by permission, Utah Historical Society.

good-natured, bright old gentleman, long a resident of Salt Lake County, but now living at John Gray's Lake, Idaho."[13]

When Flake died in 1903, the *Deseret Evening News* announced his passing on its front page. The *Salt Lake Tribune* and *Herald* along with the *Ogden Standard* also ran stories about him. The *Standard* described him as a "well known... pioneer of 1847" and suggested that he was "one of the few colored men who accepted the faith of the Latter-day Saints in the early days and who joined the pioneer band in its pilgrimage to the barren west." The *Tribune* noted that Flake "always remained a firm believer in the Mormon faith." The stories mentioned both his faith and his race, but none of them recalled that when he arrived in the valley in 1847, he was enslaved to another man.[14] By the time Flake died, slavery in Utah Territory had become a distant memory, replaced in his case with stories of pioneering fortitude.

Other former slaves did not fare as well as Flake and were hardly remembered at all. Such was the case for Betsy Brown Fluellen. She was eleven years old in 1848 when her enslavers John and Elizabeth Crosby Brown took her to Utah Territory, where she grew up far removed from family and friends in Missouri or Mississippi where the Brown family purchased her. When she was eighteen she accepted baptism into the Latter-day Saint faith and continued to perform domestic labor for the Brown family at least until 1862 when Congress freed enslaved people in all U.S. territories.[15]

For Betsy Brown freedom meant an opportunity to marry and raise a family, as well as a chance to find paid employment. In the1870s she found work as a domestic servant and washer woman in Corinne, Utah, a railroad town north of Salt Lake City. She married a barber there, John Fluellen, and the couple had three children together, only one of whom survived infancy. After John died, Betsy struggled. She ended up in the Salt Lake City Poorhouse by 1893 where a judge declared her legally insane and committed her to the state mental hospital. She died there in 1900, after spending the last seven years of her life institutionalized. Freedom for Betsy did not mean unbounded opportunity.[16] Had Congress not intervened in 1862, or the Thirteenth Amendment to the Constitution passed in 1865 (only after a Civil War cost the nation over 600,000 lives), it is possible that her bondage might have extended until Betsy died in 1900. That is how far into the future gradual emancipation might have lasted in Utah if left to play out of its own accord.

Alex's, Marinda's, Green's, and Betsy's experiences only offer vague glimpses into the ways that the transition from enslavement to freedom played out in practice. Federal troops did not arrive in Utah to enforce or even announce passage of the June 1862 law. In 1863, the Emancipation Proclamation freed enslaved people in states that were in rebellion against the federal government and so did not apply to Utah. It was not until December 1865 that the Thirteenth Amendment to the Constitution outlawed slavery and involuntary servitude everywhere. By that point, Utah's enslaved people had arguably been free for over three years—that is if they knew about it.

Part of the problem was the ambiguity that had always surrounded slavery in Utah. An Act to Secure Freedom which Congress passed in 1862 stipulated that "there shall be neither slavery nor involuntary servitude in any of the Territories of the United States now existing, or which may at any time hereafter be formed or acquired by the United States, otherwise than in punishment of crimes whereof the party shall have been duly convicted."[17] This language was a direct attack on the *Dred Scott* decision of 1857, which held that Congress did not have the power to ban slavery in a U.S. territory. It was not immediately obvious, however, that this legislation nullified the decade-old Service Act.

The legislative debates of 1852 had centered on the distinction between servitude and slavery. Men like Brigham Young and Orson Spencer had never believed that the Service Act legalized chattel slavery in Utah. They viewed the "servitude" permitted by the law as a kind of long-term apprenticeship. In fact, the law's requirement for consent could be interpreted to mean that it did not authorize involuntary servitude at all. Moreover, the Service Act applied to European immigrants as well as African Americans. A reasonable argument could be made that the Service Act, or at least a significant portion of it, was still good law even after 1862. It is therefore possible that political leaders in Utah simply did not know how to respond when Congress passed An Act to Secure Freedom. For a decade Utah lawmakers had argued that servitude and slavery were not the same thing. They had even continued to uphold the Service Act after the *Dred Scott* decision ostensibly legalized slavery in all U.S. territories. The only clue suggesting that legislators ultimately acknowledged the Service Act was no longer in force is the fact that the statute was not reprinted in an 1866 compilation of territorial laws.[18]

A similar debate took place in other parts of the West. After 1862, landowners in New Mexico continued to practice peonage in the belief that it was a form of voluntary servitude and therefore not prohibited by An Act to Secure Freedom. Even after the conclusion of the Civil War and passage of the Thirteenth Amendment, members of Congress could not agree whether peonage constituted involuntary servitude. U.S. lawmakers finally responded by passing the Anti-Peonage Act of 1867 that prohibited both voluntary and involuntary forms of servitude.

The termination of Utah's Native American Indenture Act is also vague. If Utah legislators ultimately understood Congress to outlaw the enslavement of African Americans in Utah Territory in 1862, evidence suggests they did not believe that the law Congress passed also nullified An Act for the Relief of Indian Slaves and Prisoners. In fact, historians have documented over 400 Indigenous children who lived in Latter-day Saint homes between 1847 and the early 1900s.[19] The Indenture Act remained in force in Utah perhaps as

230 THIS ABOMINABLE SLAVERY

late as 1876 when it no longer appeared in a compilation of territorial statutes.[20] After that, Latter-day Saints may have continued to purchase or accept Indigenous children into their homes on an ad hoc basis, according to long-standing customs.

The legal ends to slavery and servitude in Utah Territory were thus distinct from their more ambiguous ends in practice.

APPENDIX 1

Legislative Chronology, 1852

This chronology provides a timeline of events for the 1852 Utah territorial legislative session. It is not comprehensive; rather, it follows the key bills discussed in this volume through their various stages, from introduction to passage, and includes the dates of the corresponding debates and speeches.

January 5 (Monday)

- Thomas Bullock, Young's secretary, reads a prepared speech to a joint session of the legislature. It includes Young's views on a variety of issues, including Black slavery and the Indian slave trade.[1]
- George D. Watt elected reporter for the Council on motion of Orson Pratt. He was also elected reporter for the House.[2]

January 23 (Friday)

Council

- George A. Smith reports An Act in Relation to African Slavery (returned to committee, instructed to create preamble).[3]
- Brigham Young delivers first speech on slavery/priesthood and changes name of Smith's bill to An Act in Relation to Service.[4]
- George A. Smith reports "An Act for the Protection of the Rights of Indians, returned to committee for a preamble and resolutions.[5]
- Perhaps debate on Indian servitude begins, but no date is given in Watt's record.[6]

House

- An Act Concerning Masters and Apprentices read twice and laid on the table until Monday, January 26.[7]

January 24 (Saturday)

Council

- 10 a.m.—Orson Spencer reports preamble in relation to servitude; George A. Smith motions report be accepted, and Spencer continues labors.[8]

January 26 (Monday)

Council

- 10 a.m.—George A. Smith reports preamble of An Act for the Relief of Indians and An Act in Relation to Service. Both laid on the table for further consideration.[9]
- An Act in Relation to Justices of the Peace allows individuals to be involuntarily hired out for labor in order to pay fines.[10]
- 2 p.m.—A preamble and resolution for the Relief of Indians taken up and read twice before adjournment.[11]

January 27 (Tuesday)

Council

- 10 a.m.—Debate over An Act for the Relief of the Indians resumed.[12]
- George Watt records that "An act for the relief of Indians was read by the clerk. Motioned and second[ed]."[13] Orson Pratt motions that the act be postponed indefinitely and loses 6-4. Pratt's motion to strike out sec. 1 loses 6-4. Debate resumes on its second reading.[14]
- 2 p.m.—An Act for the Relief of Indians referred to committee on Indian affairs.[15]
- "An Act in Relation to Service read twice, accepted, referred back to committee on motion of Orson Spencer.[16]
- Orson Pratt delivers speech in vehement opposition to slavery and An Act in Relation to Service but does not mention priesthood ban.[17]
- Orson Spencer delivers speech in opposition to slavery and mentions priesthood ban.[18]
- Brigham Young speaks briefly and argues that if a master forfeits his or her rights to her or his servant by violating provisions of the act, rather than allow the servant to be sold to a new master, "let them be free, [the] same as white people."[19]
- Charles R. Dana reports An Act Regulating Elections that is accepted and laid on the table.[20]

January 29 (Thursday)

- Brigham Young delivers speech to the legislature about the need to pass bills, not just criticize them.[21]

Council

- 10 a.m.—Charles R. Dana reports back An Act Regulating Elections with two additional sections.[22]
- 2 p.m.—An Act Regulating Elections read twice and referred back to committee for amendments.[23]

January 30 (Friday)

Council

- 10 a.m.—Charles R. Dana reports back An Act Regulating Elections—referred to Engrossing Committee on motion of Orson Pratt.[24]

Joint Session (10:30 a.m.)

- Brigham Young presents newspaper articles about runaway judges.[25]
- Voted for Council and House to sit in joint session for remainder of term.[26]
- Houses go into "secret secion."[27]

January 31 (Saturday)

Joint Session

- Acts in relation to minors/guardians/masters and apprentices passed.[28]
- Preamble and Act for Relief of Indian Slaves and Prisoner signed.[29]

February 2 (Monday)

Joint Session

- Act in Relation to Service read three times and passed.[30]
- 2 p.m.—At second reading Section 4 slightly amended on motion of Joseph A. Young, passes on motion of James Brown.[31]

February 4 (Wednesday)

Joint Session

- Brigham Young speaks to joint session regarding the mix between church and state.[32]
- Heber C. Kimball speaks, endorses Young's speech.[33]
- An Act in Relation to Elections read three times and passed.[34]
- Brigham Young signs An Act in Relation to Service into law.[35]

February 5 (Thursday)

Joint Session

- Brigham Young delivers his most complete sermon on the priesthood ban/slavery/who should rule, as well as his view of white over Black.[36]
- Orson Pratt votes against all acts prohibiting Black men from voting.[37]
- An act to incorporate Cedar City is read three times and passed, "Councilor Pratt voting in the negative."[38]
- An act to incorporate Fillmore City is read three times and passed, "Councilor Pratt opposed the bill on the ground that colored people were there prohibited from voting."[39]

February 17 (Tuesday)

Joint Session

- On motion from Orson Pratt, an act authorizing Pratt to lead topographical and exploring committee rejected.[40]

February 19 (Thursday)

Joint Session

- Special session of legislature opens.[41]
- Brigham Young and Orson Pratt speak on duty of legislators "to be humble and enjoy the spirit of God and act as Elders of Israel."[42]

February 26 (Thursday)

Joint Session

- Act in relation to unlawful assembling of Indians in vicinity of settlements passed.[43]

February 27 (Friday)

Joint Session

- Wells reported an act in relation to Indian prisoners; on motion of Woodruff the bill laid on the table.[44]
- Memorial to form a state government referred back to committee for revision.[45]

February 28 (Saturday)

Joint Session

- Memorial to form a state government adopted.[46]
- Act in Relation to Indian Slaves and Children passed and then "vote recinded"; adjourned until 10 a.m. Monday, 1 March.[47]

March 3 (Wednesday)

Joint Session

- Act in relation to unlawful assembling of Indians in vicinity of settlements approved.[48]

March 4 (Thursday)

- Legislative Ball attended by "some 65 men and over 100 women. The supper consisted of the best to be produced in this place & plenty for all." The party began at 1 p.m. and continued till 2 a.m.[49]

March 6 (Saturday)

Joint Session

- Act for the Relief of Indian Slaves and Prisoners approved.[50]

Legislature adjourns.[51]

APPENDIX 2

Preamble and An Act for the Further Relief of Indian Slaves and Prisoners[*]

Whereas, By reason of the acquisition of Upper California and New Mexico, and the subsequent organization of the Territorial Governments of New Mexico and Utah, by the acts of the Congress of the United States; these Territories have organized Governments within and upon what would otherwise be considered Indian Territory and which really is Indian Territory so far as the right of soil is involved; thereby presenting the novel feature of a white legalized Government on Indian lands; and

Whereas, The laws of the United States in relation to intercourse with Indians are designed for, and only applicable to Territories, and Countries under the sole and exclusive jurisdiction of the United States; and

Whereas, From time immemorial, the practice or purchasing Indian women and children, of the Utah tribe of Indians by Mexican traders, has been indulged in, and carried on by those respective people; until, the Indians consider it an allowable traffic, and frequently offer their prisoners or children for sale; and

Whereas, It is a common practice among these Indians to gamble away their own children and women; and it is a well established fact, that women and children thus obtained, or obtained by war, or theft, or in any other manner, are by them frequently carried from place to place; packed upon horses or mules, larietted out to subsist upon grass, roots, or starve; and are frequently bound with thongs made of raw hide, until their hands and feet become swollen, mutilated, inflamed with pain, and wounded; and when with suffering, cold, hunger, and abuse, they fall sick, so as to become troublesome, are frequently slain by their masters to get rid of them; and

Whereas, They do frequently kill their women and children taken prisoners, either in revenge, or for amusement, or through the influence of tradition, unless they are tempted to exchange them for trade, which they usually do if they have an opportunity; and

Whereas, One family frequently steals the children and women of another family, and such robberies and murders are continually committed, in times of their greatest pesce [sic], and amity; thus dragging free Indian women and children into Mexican servitude and slavery, or death, to the most entire extirpation of the whole Indian race; and

Whereas, These inhuman practices are being daily enacted before our eyes in the midst of the white settlements, and within the organized counties of the Territory, and when the inhabitants do not purchase or trade for those so offered for sale, they are generally doomed to the most miserable existence; suffering the torture of every species of cruelty until death kindly relieves them and closes the revolting scenery:

Wherefore, When all these facts are taken into consideration, it becomes the duty of all humane and Christian people to extend unto this degraded and downtrodden race, such

---

[*] Preamble and an Act for the Relief of Indian Slaves and Prisoners, in *Acts, Resolutions, and Memorials, Passed by the First Annual, and Special Sessions, of the Legislative Assembly of the Territory of Utah, Begun and held at Great Salt Lake City, on the 22nd day of September, A. D., 1851* (Great Salt Lake City: Brigham H. Young, Printer, 1852), 91–93.

relief as can be awarded to them, according to their situation and circumstances; it therefore becomes necessary to consider;

First; The circumstances of our location among these savage tribes under the authority of Congress, while yet the Indian title to the soil is left unextinguished; not even a treaty having been held, by which a partition of territory or country has been made, thereby bringing them into our door yards, our houses, and in contact with our every avocation.

Second; Their situation, and our duty towards them, upon the common principles of humanity.

Third; The remedy or what will be the most conducive to ameliorate their condition, preserve their lives, and their liberties, and redeem them from a worse than African bondage; it suggests itself to your committee that to memorialize Congress to provide by some act of National Legislation for the new and unparalleled situation of the inhabitants of this Territory, in relation to their intercourse with these Indians, would be one resource, prolific in its results for our mutual benefit; and further, that we ask their concurrence in the following enactment, passed by the Legislature of the Territory of Utah, January 31, A. D. 1852; entitled,

AN ACT FOR THE RELIEF OF INDIAN SLAVES AND PRISONERS

Sec. 1. Be it enacted by the Governor and Legislative Assembly of the Territory of Utah, That whenever any white person within any organized county of this Territory, shall have any Indian prisoner, child or woman, in his possession, whether by purchase or otherwise; such person shall immediately go, together with such Indian prisoner, child, or woman, before the Select men or Probate Judge of the county. If in the opinion of the Select men or Probate Judge the person having such Indian prisoner, child, or woman; it shall be his or their duty to bind out the same by indenture for the term of not exceeding twenty years, at the discretion of the Judge or Select men.

Sec. 2. The Probate Judge or Select men shall cause to be written in the indenture; the name, and age; place where born, name of parents if known, tribe to which said Indian person belonged; name of the person having him in possession; name of Indian from whom said person was obtained; date of the indenture, a copy of which shall be filed in the Probate Clerk's office.

Sec. 3. The Select men in their respective counties, are hereby authorized to obtain such Indian prisoners children, or women, and bind them to some useful avocation.

Sec. 4. The master to whom the indenture is made is hereby required to send said apprentice to school, if there be a school in the district or vicinity, for the term of three months in each year; and at a time when said Indian child shall be between the ages of seven years and sixteen. The master shall clothe his apprentice in a comfortable and becoming manner, according to his, said master's condition in life.

Approved, March 6, 1852.

APPENDIX 3

An Act in Relation to Service

A Comparison of an Early Draft and the Final Version of An Act in Relation to Service[*]

(changes in bold)

An Act in Relation to Service[a] SEC. 1 Be it enacted by the Governor and Legislative Assembly of the Territory of Utah, That any person or persons coming to this Territory and bringing with them servants justly bound to them, arising from special contract or otherwise, said person or persons shall be entitled to such service or labor by the laws of this Territory: Provided, That he shall file in the office of the Probate Court written and satisfactory evidence that such service or labor is due.	An Act in Relation to Service[b] SEC. 1. Be it enacted by the Governor and Legislative Assembly of the Territory of Utah, that any person or persons coming to this Territory and bringing with them servants justly bound to them, arising from special contract or otherwise, said person or persons shall be entitled to such service or labor by the laws of this Territory. Provided, That he shall file in the office of the Probate Court written and satisfactory evidence that such service or labor is due.
SEC. 2. That the Probate Court shall receive as evidence any contract properly attested in writing or any well proved agreement wherein the party or parties serving have received or are to receive a reasonable compensation for his, her, or their services: Provided, that no contract shall bind the heirs of the servant or servants to service for a longer period than will satisfy the debt due his, her, or their master or mistress.	SEC. 2. That the Probate Court shall receive as evidence any contract properly attested in writing or any well proved agreement wherein the party or parties serving have received or are to receive a reasonable compensation for his, her, or their services: Provided, **That** no contract shall bind the heirs of the servant or servants to service for a longer period than will satisfy the debt due his, her, or their master or mistress.

---

[*] Nathaniel R. Ricks, "A Peculiar Place for the Peculiar Institution: Slavery and Sovereignty in Early Territorial Utah" (Master's thesis, Brigham Young University, 2007), 160–162, offers a similar comparison. The parallel columns below are based on our transcript of the handwritten bills in the Territorial Legislative Record and the draft version of the bill found at the LDS Church History Library. For the original draft of the bill see Territorial Legislative Records, 1851–1894, series 3150, reel 1, box 1, folder 55, 700–703, UDARS. For the final draft see pp. 704–706 of the same source. For the working draft of the bill see, Utah Territory Legislative Assembly Papers, 1851–1872, MS 2919, First Session, 1851–1852, Acts numbers 15–39, box 1, folder 3, CHL.

SEC. 3. That any person bringing a servant or servants, and his, her, or their children from any part of the United States, and shall place in the Office of the Probate Court the certificate of any court of Record under seal, properly attested that he, she, or they **is or** are entitled lawfully to the service of such servant or servants, and his, her, or their children, the Probate Justice shall record the same, and the Master or Mistress, or his, her, or their heirs shall be entitled to the services of the said servant or servants **and his, her, or their children, until the curse of servitude is taken from the descendants of Canaan** unless forfeited as hereinafter provided, if it shall appear that such servant or servants came into the Territory of their own free will or choice.

SEC. 4. That if any master or mistress shall have sexual or carnal intercourse with **any of** his or her servants of the African race he or she shall forfeit all claim to said servants **and the Probate Court is hereby required to declare as soon as the fact is proven before him that all claim of said master or mistress is at an end. The Court shall Indenture said servant or servants and his or her children to such other master or mistress as in his opinion will set before his servants a moral example** and if any white person shall be guilty of sexual intercourse with any of the African race, they shall be subject on conviction thereof to a fine of not exceeding one thousand dollars, nor less than five hundred; and imprisonment not exceeding three years, **and forfeiture of all right of service they may hold or may afterwards descend to them by heirship; and in case of males offending as herein provided, they shall be disqualified from holding any office under the laws of this Territory or from voting at any election.**

SEC. 3. That any person bringing a servant or servants, and his, her, or their children from any part of the United States, **or other country**, and shall place in the office of the Probate Court the certificate of any Court of record under seal, properly attested that he, she, or they are entitled lawfully to the service of such servant or servants, and his, her, or their children, the Probate Justice shall record the same, and the master or mistress, or his, her, or their heirs shall be entitled to the services of the said servant or servants unless forfeited as hereinafter provided, if it shall appear that such servant or servants came into the Territory of their own free will **and** choice.

SEC. 4. That if any master or mistress shall have sexual or carnal intercourse with his or her **servant or** servants of the African race, he or she shall forfeit all claim to said **servant or** servants **to the commonwealth;** and if any white person shall be guilty of sexual intercourse with any of the African race, they shall be subject on conviction thereof to a fine of not exceeding one thousand dollars, nor less than five hundred, **to the use of the Territory,** and imprisonment not exceeding three years.

SEC. 5. **That the title of master to whom said servant is indentured shall be as <u>bona fide</u> in law, to his heirs and assignee, as if he had been the original master; provided that no servant shall be compelled to leave the Territory without his or her consent.**

[Section 5 was removed from the final bill]

SEC. 6. It shall be the duty of masters or mistresses, to provide for his or their servants comfortable habitations, clothing, bedding, sufficient food, and recreation. And it shall be the duty of the servant in return therefor to labor faithfully all reasonable hours, and do such service with fidelity as may be required by his or her master or mistress.

SEC. 5. It shall be the duty of masters or mistresses, to provide for his, **her**, or their servants comfortable habitations, clothing, bedding, sufficient food, and recreation. And it shall be the duty of the servant in return therefor to labor faithfully all reasonable hours, and do such service with fidelity as may be required by his, or her master or mistress.

SEC. 7. It shall be the duty of the master to correct and punish his servant in a reasonable manner when it may be necessary, being guided by prudence and humanity; and if he shall be guilty of cruelty or abuse, or neglect to feed, clothe or shelter his servants in a proper manner, the Probate Court may declare the contract between Master and servant or servants void, **and indenture them to another Master or Mistress,** according to the provisions of the fourth section of this act.

SEC. 6. It shall be the duty of the master to correct and punish his servant in a reasonable manner when it may be necessary, being guided by prudence and humanity; and if he shall be guilty of cruelty or abuse, or neglect to feed, clothe, or shelter his servants in a proper manner, the Probate Court may declare the contract between master and servant or servants void, according to the provisions of the fourth section of this act.

SEC. 8. That servants may be transferred from one Master or Mistress to another by consent and approbation of the Probate Court, who shall keep a Record of the same in his office; but no transfer shall be made without the consent of the servant given to the Probate Judge in the absence of his Master or Mistress.

SEC. 7. That servants may be transferred from one master or mistress to another by **the** consent and approbation of the Probate Court, who shall keep a record of the same in his office; but no transfer shall be made without the consent of the servant given to the Probate Judge in the absence of his master or mistress.

SEC. 9. Any person transferring a servant or servants contrary to the provisions of this act, or taking one out of the Territory contrary to his will, except by decree of **the** Court in case of a fugitive from labor, shall be on conviction thereof, subject to a fine, not exceeding five thousand dollars, and imprisonment, not exceeding five years, or both, at the discretion of the Court, and shall forfeit all claims to the services of such servant or servants.

SEC. 8. Any person transferring a servant or servants contrary to the provisions of this Act, or taking one out of the Territory contrary to his, **or her** will, except by decree of Court in case of a fugitive from labor, shall be on conviction thereof, subject to a fine, not exceeding five thousand dollars, and imprisonment, not exceeding five years, or both, at the discretion of the Court, and shall forfeit all claims to the services of such servant or servants, **as provided in the fourth section of this act.**

SEC. 10. ~~Be it further enacted that~~ It shall further be the duty of all Masters or Mistresses to send their servant or servants to school not less than eighteen months between the ages of six years and twenty years.

SEC. 9. It shall further be the duty of all masters or mistresses, to send their servant or servants to school, not less than eighteen months between the ages of six years and twenty years.

---

[a] Territorial Legislative Records, 1851–1894, series 3150, reel 1, box 1, folder 55, 700–703, UDARS. See also, Utah Territory Legislative Assembly Papers, 1851–1872, MS 2919, First Session, 1851–1852, Acts numbers 15–39, box 1, folder 3, CHL.

[b] Territorial Legislative Records, 1851–1894, series 3150, reel 1, box 1, folder 55, 704–706, UDARS. See also, Utah Territory Legislative Assembly Papers, 1851–1872, MS 2919, First Session, 1851–1852, Acts numbers 15–39, box 1, folder 3, CHL.

Notes

Introduction

1. W. Randall Dixon, "From Emigration Canyon to City Creek: Pioneer Trail and Campsites in the Salt Lake Valley in 1847," *Utah Historical Quarterly* 65, no. 2 (Spring 1997): 155–164. The Church of Jesus Christ of Latter-day Saints is the official name of the Church under study here. We refer interchangeably to adherents to that faith as Latter-day Saints, Saints, and, in historical context, Mormons.
2. The three enslaved men arrived in the valley under the oversight of John Brown, a Southern convert who agreed to take them to the valley where they were to establish crops and shelters for their white enslavers who would arrive in subsequent migrations. Hark Wales (1825–c. 1880s) was enslaved to Sytha Crosby and William Lay when he arrived in the Salt Lake Valley in 1847 and was known in records of the period as Hark Lay. He chose the last name of Wales after his emancipation. Sytha Crosby Lay joined the Church of Jesus Christ of Latter-day Saints in Mississippi, but her husband William never did. A Crosby family remembrance suggested that Hark was baptized in Mississippi when many of the Crosby family converted. That assertion is borne out by a document created on April 20, 1851, in Parowan Utah. Leaders of a Latter-day Saint colonizing mission to San Bernardino, California, asked colonizers to pledge their loyalty to the mission before departing from Parowan. Those who were willing to do so listed their names, with those who were not members of the LDS Church specified in the document as "not member." Hark is listed as one who pledged his loyalty, with "Col'd" listed next to his name for "colored" but nothing to indicate he was not LDS. See California Papers, 1851–1857, Charles C. Rich Collection, MS 889, box 3, folder 18, 1, CHL; we are indebted to Kristine Shorey Forbes for drawing our attention to this source; for the family remembrance see Charmaine Lay Kohler, *Southern Grace: A Story of the Mississippi Saints* (Boise, ID: Beagle Creek Press, 1995), 60. Even still no baptismal record for Hark has been found; moreover, in the 1880 Utah census, which includes religious designations in the margins of the document, Hark is noted as a "gentile," a designation that meant he had never been a Latter-day Saint. He eventually returned to Utah and engaged in mining and died there sometime in the 1880s. See Megan Weiss, "Hark Wales," Century of Black Mormons, https://exhibits.lib.utah.edu/s/century-of-black-mormons/page/wales-hark and Amy Tanner Thiriot, *Slavery in Zion: A Documentary and Genealogical History of Black Lives and Black Servitude in Utah Territory, 1847–1862* (Salt Lake City: University of Utah Press, 2022), 234–236. Oscar Smith (1815–1872) was enslaved to William Crosby when he entered the Salt Lake Valley and was known as Oscar Crosby. He was rebaptized after his arrival in the valley and, like Hark, pledged his loyalty to the San Bernardino mission. He took the last name of Smith after gaining his freedom. He died in Los Angeles in 1872. See Thiriot, *Slavery in Zion*, 203–205. Green Flake (1828–1903) was enslaved to James Madison Flake when he entered the valley. He was also rebaptized after his arrival. Brigham Young eventually freed Flake, and he worked as a farmer and miner. He eventually moved to Idaho where he died in 1903. See Benjamin Kiser, "Green Flake," Century of Black Mormons, https://exhibits.lib.utah.edu/s/century-of-black-mormons/page/flake-green and Thiriot, *Slavery in Zion*, 220–226.
3. Sondra Jones, *The Trial of Don Pedro León Luján: The Attack against Indian Slavery and Mexican Traders in Utah* (Salt Lake City: University of Utah Press, 2000); Sondra Jones, *Being and Becoming Ute: The Story of an American Indian People* (Salt Lake City: University of Utah Press, 2019), chapters 4–6; Virginia Kerns, *Sally in Three Worlds: An Indian Captive in the House of Brigham Young* (Salt Lake City: University of Utah Press, 2021); Stephen P. Van Hoak, "Waccara's Utes: Native American Equestrian Adaptations in the Eastern Great Basin, 1776–1886," *Utah Historical Quarterly* 67, no. 4 (Fall 1999): 309–330; Ronald W. Walker, "Wakara Meets the Mormons: A Case Study in Native American Accommodation, 1848–1852," *Utah Historical Quarterly* 70, no. 3 (Summer 2002): 215–237; Ned Blackhawk, *Violence over the Land: Indians and Empires in the Early American West* (Cambridge, MA: Harvard University

Press, 2009); James A. Brooks, *Captives & Cousins: Slavery, Kinship, and Community in the Southwest Borderlands* (Chapel Hill: University of North Carolina Press, 2002).
4. John R. Alley, Jr., "Prelude to Dispossession: The Fur Trade's Significance for the Northern Utes and Southern Paiutes," *Utah Historical Quarterly* 50 (Spring 1982): 104–123.
5. Jones, *The Trial of Don Pedro León Luján*, 101–102; Kerns, *Sally in Three Worlds*, chapters 6 and 7.
6. Brigham Young, testimony in *U.S. v. Pedro León* case of libel, January 15, 1852, First District Court, Minute Book, 1851–1896, series 10035, reel 1, 46, UDARS.
7. Matthew J. Grow et al., eds., *Council of Fifty, Minutes, March 1844–January 1846*, vol. 1 of the Administrative Records series of *The Joseph Smith Papers*, ed. Ronald K. Esplin, Matthew J. Grow, and Matthew C. Godfrey (Salt Lake City: Church Historian's Press, 2016), 352, 354–355.
8. Brigham Young, Mt. Pisgah, Iowa, to Samuel Bent and the Saints at Garden Grove, Iowa, July 7, 1846, Brigham Young Office Files, CR 1234 1, CHL; Brigham Young, Omaha Nation, to James K. Polk, Washington D.C., August 8, 1846, Brigham Young Office Files, CR 1234 1, CHL.
9. Edmund S. Morgan, *American Slavery, American Freedom: The Ordeal of Colonial Virginia* (New York: W. W. Norton, 1975).
10. Sean Wilentz, *No Property in Man: Slavery and Antislavery at the Nation's Founding* (Cambridge, MA: Harvard University Press, 2018), chapters 1 and 2.
11. Wilentz, *No Property in Man*, 44–45, 52–53.
12. Mark J. Stegmaier, "A Law That Would Make Caligula Blush?: New Mexico Territory's Unique Slave Code, 1859–1861," *New Mexico Historical Review* 87 (Spring 2012): 209–242.
13. Stacey L. Smith, *Freedom's Frontier: California and the Struggle over Unfree Labor, Emancipation, and Reconstruction* (Chapel Hill: University of North Carolina Press, 2013), 39–42.
14. Leonard L. Richards, *The California Gold Rush and the Coming of the Civil War* (New York: Vintage Books, 2008), 93, 128–129, 228; Brian McGinty, *Archy Lee's Struggle for Freedom: The True Story of California Gold, the Nation's Tragic March toward Civil War, and a Young Black Man's Fight for Liberty* (Guilford, CT: Lyons Press, 2020).
15. Smith, *Freedom's Frontier*; McGinty, *Archy Lee's Struggle for Freedom*; Richards, *The California Gold Rush and the Coming of the Civil War*; Stegmaier, "A Law That Would Make Caligula Blush?"; Brooks, *Captives & Cousins*; William S. Kiser, *Borderlands of Slavery: The Struggle over Captivity and Peonage in the American Southwest* (Philadelphia: University of Pennsylvania Press, 2017).
16. Andrés Reséndez, *The Other Slavery: The Uncovered Story of Indian Enslavement in America* (Boston and New York: Houghton Mifflin Harcourt, 2016) and Kevin Waite, *West of Slavery: The Southern Dream of a Transcontinental Empire* (Chapel Hill: University of North Carolina Press, 2021) are two recent exceptions that integrate Utah into the national story. Reséndez and Waite, however, lacked access to the documents examined here. Newell G. Bringhurst, *Saints, Slaves, and Blacks: The Changing Place of Black People within Mormonism* (Westport, CT: Greenwood Press, 1981; 2nd ed.: Salt Lake City: Greg Kofford Books, 2018) is the standard interpretation. For a recent study from the vantage point of the enslaved see Thiriot, *Slavery in Zion*. See also Christopher B. Rich, Jr., "The True Policy for Utah: Servitude, Slavery, and 'An Act in Relation to Service,'" *Utah Historical Quarterly* 80 (Winter 2012): 54–74; Nathaniel R. Ricks, "A Peculiar Place for the Peculiar Institution: Slavery and Sovereignty in Early Territorial Utah" (Master's thesis, Brigham Young University, 2007); Ronald G. Coleman, "Utah's Black Pioneers, 1847–1869," *Umoja: A Scholarly Journal of Black Studies* 11 (Summer 1978): 95–110; Ronald G. Coleman, "A History of Blacks in Utah, 1825–1910," (PhD diss., University of Utah, 1980); and Dennis L. Lythgoe, "Negro Slavery in Utah," *Utah Historical Quarterly* 39 (Winter 1971): 40–54.
17. D. Michael Quinn, *The Mormon Hierarchy: Origins of Power* (Salt Lake City: Signature Books, 1994), 659; Shirley Ann Wilson Moore, *Sweet Freedom's Plains: African Americans on the Overland Trails, 1841–1869* (Norman: University of Oklahoma Press, 2016), 45; Newell G. Bringhurst, "The Mormons and Slavery—A Closer Look," *Pacific History Review* 50 (August 1981): 329.
18. W. Paul Reeve, *Religion of a Different Color: Race and the Mormon Struggle for Whiteness* (New York: Oxford University Press, 2015).
19. W. Paul Reeve, *Let's Talk about Race and Priesthood* (Salt Lake City: Deseret Book, 2023).
20. Rich, "The True Policy for Utah."
21. Thiriot, *Slavery in Zion*.
22. Utah Territorial Census, 1851, Utah, Salt Lake, and Davis Counties, Schedule 2, MS 2672, box 1, folder 6, 10, 23, CHL.

23. Thiriot, *Slavery in Zion*, 74–76, 88, 93, 95, 124. For a table and discussion on various prior estimates see Bringhurst, *Saints, Slaves, and Blacks*, 2nd ed., 219. See also Coleman, "Utah's Black Pioneers, 1847–1869," 98, 107n9 and "A History of Blacks in Utah, 1825–1910," 69n56.
24. Matthew J. Grow and Ronald W. Walker, *The Prophet and the Reformer: The Letters of Brigham Young and Thomas L. Kane* (New York: Oxford University Press, 2015), 68–69; Dan Vogel, ed., *The Wilford Woodruff Journals*, Typescript, 6 vols. (Salt Lake City: Benchmark Books, 2020), 2:402–403.
25. "From Utah," *National Era* (Washington, D.C.), January 23, 1851; Reeve, *Religion of a Different Color*, 142.
26. Jones, *The Trial of Don Pedro León Luján*, 81–82.
27. "First Judicial Court," *Deseret News*, March 6, 1852, 4.
28. Alley, Jr., "Prelude to Dispossession"; Van Hoak, "Waccara's Utes"; Sondra Jones, "'Redeeming' the Indian: The Enslavement of Indian Children in New Mexico and Utah," *Utah Historical Quarterly* 67 (Summer 1999): 220–241; Jones, *The Trial of Don Pedro León Luján*, chapter 6; Michael Bennion, "Captivity, Adoption, Marriage and Identity: Native American Children in Mormon Homes, 1847–1900" (Master's thesis, University of Nevada-Las Vegas, 2012); Brian Q. Cannon, "'To Buy Up the Lamanite Children as Fast as They Could': Indentured Servitude and Its Legacy in Mormon Society," *Journal of Mormon History* 44 (Spring 2018): 1–36.
29. Jones, *The Trial of Don Pedro León Luján*, chapter 6; Jones, *Being and Becoming Ute*, chapters 5 and 6.
30. Orson Pratt before the Territorial Legislature on Slavery, January 27, 1852, CR 100 912, Church History Department Pitman Shorthand transcriptions, 2013–2021, Addresses and sermons, 1851–1874, Miscellaneous transcriptions, 1869, 1872, 1889, 1848, 1851–1854, 1859–1863, Utah Territorial Legislature, January–February 1852, CHL.
31. Utah Territorial Legislature, Debate on Indian Slavery, possibly beginning January 23, 1852, CR 100 912, Church History Department Pitman Shorthand transcriptions, 2013–2021, Addresses and sermons, 1851–1874, Miscellaneous transcriptions, 1869, 1872, 1889, 1848, 1851–1854, 1859–1863, Utah Territorial Legislature, January–February 1852, CHL.
32. *Journals of the House of Representatives, Council, and Joint Sessions of the First Annual and Special Sessions of the Legislative Assembly of the Territory of Utah. Held at Great Salt Lake City, 1851 and 1852* (Great Salt Lake City: Brigham H. Young, Printer, 1852), 128.
33. Minutes of Utah Constitutional Convention, Council House, March 21–27, 1856, MS 2988, CHL; Orson Pratt, March 22, 1856, before the 1856 Utah Constitutional Convention, Church History Department Pitman Shorthand transcriptions, 2013–2021, Addresses and sermons, 1851–1874, Utah Constitutional Convention, 1856 March, CHL; facsimile transcript, CR 100 912, CHL.
34. Waite, *West of Slavery*, chapter 4.
35. Fred Lockley, "Some Documentary Records of Slavery in Oregon," *Quarterly of the Oregon Historical Society*, 17, no. 2 (June 1916): 107–115; Quintard Taylor, "Slaves and Free Men: Blacks in the Oregon Country, 1840–1860," *Oregon Historical Quarterly* 83, no. 2 (Summer 1982): 153–170.
36. Michael E. Woods, *Bleeding Kansas: Slavery, Sectionalism, and Civil War on the Missouri-Kansas Border* (New York: Routledge, 2016).
37. Howard Roberts Lamar, *The Far Southwest, 1846–1912: A Territorial History* (New Haven, CT: Yale University Press, 1966), 428; Waite, *West of Slavery*, 164–173.
38. On George D. Watt's (1812–1881) place in early Mormonism and his role as "scribe for Zion," see Ronald G. Watt, *The Mormon Passage of George D. Watt: First British Convert, Scribe for Zion* (Logan: Utah State University Press, 2009).
39. For an explanation of Watt's transcription process and the liberties he sometimes took in that process see Gerrit Dirkmaat and LaJean Purcell Carruth, "The Prophets Have Spoken, but What Did They Say? Examining the Differences between George D. Watt's Original Shorthand Notes and the Sermons Published in the *Journal of Discourses*," *BYU Studies* 54, no. 4 (2015): 25–118.
40. The passage of Utah's "servant code" is traditionally described as the context for Young's public announcement of a priesthood restriction. Yet historians remain confused regarding the circumstances and timing of Young's speeches to the legislature and even the content of those speeches. Lester Bush, in his seminal article "Mormonism's Negro Doctrine," called one of Brigham Young's declarations to the legislature "one of the most important statements in the entire history" of the ineligibility of Black men for the LDS priesthood. Yet, Bush misdated Young's speech and quoted Wilford Woodruff's summary as the source: Lester E. Bush, Jr.,

"Mormonism's Negro Doctrine: An Historical Overview," in *Neither White nor Black: Mormon Scholars Confront the Race Issue in a Universal Church*, ed. Lester E. Bush, Jr. and Armand L. Mauss (Midvale, UT: Signature Books, 1984), 65, 70. Woodruff, an apostle, legislator, and future Latter-day Saint prophet, captured only one of Young's speeches in his journal. He failed to date it and only managed to record a truncated and paraphrased version of Young's sentiments: Vogel, *Wilford Woodruff Journals*, 2:510–511. Scholars Newell Bringhurst and Armand Mauss also quoted Woodruff's version of the speech and offered no clear timeline or context other than the debate over the "slave" code: Bringhurst, *Saints, Slaves, and Blacks*, 99, although at 115 Bringhurst quotes the Watt version; Armand L. Mauss, *All Abraham's Children: Changing Mormon Conceptions of Race and Lineage* (Urbana: University of Illinois Press, 2003), 212). Ronald Esplin, in a 1979 *BYU Studies* article, correctly dated Young's speech as February 5, even as he argued that the priesthood restriction originated with Joseph Smith: Ronald K. Esplin, "Brigham Young and Priesthood Denial to the Blacks: An Alternate View," *BYU Studies* 19 (Spring 1979): 394–402. Edward Kimball's 2008 article in *BYU Studies* quoted from Woodruff's version of Young's speech: Edward L. Kimball, "Spencer W. Kimball and the Revelation on Priesthood," *BYU Studies* 47, no. 2 (2008): 15. John Turner's 2012 biography of Brigham Young established a firmer chronology and wider context but still relied on Woodruff for at least a portion of Young's ideas: John G. Turner, *Brigham Young: Pioneer Prophet* (Cambridge, MA: Harvard University Press, 2012), 226. Richard Van Wagoner's *The Complete Discourses of Brigham Young* included two of Young's legislative speeches on race but, unfortunately, misdated Young's February 5 speech as January 5: Richard S. Van Wagoner, *The Complete Discourses of Brigham Young*, vol. 1: *1832 to 1852* (Salt Lake City: Smith-Pettit Foundation, 2009), 468–472, 473–474. Van Wagoner also includes Woodruff's version of the February 5 speech, which allows for comparison between Watt's transcribed version and Woodruff's account. And Max Perry Mueller's *Race and the Making of the Mormon People* again quoted Woodruff, via Lester Bush, and muddied the chronology of events: Max Perry Mueller, *Race and the Making of the Mormon People* (Chapel Hill: University of North Carolina Press, 2017), 147, 188–194. None of this is meant to reflect negatively on the erudition of these respected scholars. Rather, it is meant to highlight the confusion that continues to surround the 1852 territorial legislative session and the chronological unfolding of bills and Brigham Young's speeches. Prior scholars reconstructed confusing timelines and conflated various versions of Young's speeches based on their understanding of a sparse historical record. This book attempts to clarify and contextualize that record according to a flood of new information.

41. *Journals of the House of Representatives, Council, and Joint Sessions*, 104–110; "Governor's Message," *Deseret News*, January 10, 1852, 18. No shorthand is extant for this speech. Watt probably did not record it in shorthand, as a longhand text was already prepared for Bullock to read.
42. Reséndez, *The Other Slavery*, 10–11.
43. Alice L. Baumgartner, *South to Freedom: Runaway Slaves to Mexico and the Road to the Civil War* (New York: Basic Books, 2020), 5, 58.
44. Jones, *The Trial of Don Pedro León Luján*, 103; Reséndez, *The Other Slavery*, 10–11.
45. Here we take Reséndez's point seriously when he writes that "labor practices may have seemed quite distinct to officials and masters at the time, and continue to seem so to researchers today, but they were decidedly less so to the victims themselves, who experienced the everyday reality of labor coercion with little or no compensation." See Reséndez, *The Other Slavery*, 11.
46. Quentin Thomas Wells, *Defender: The Life of Daniel H. Wells* (Boulder, CO: Utah State University Press, 2016), 112.
47. Constance L. Lieber, *Dr. Martha Hughes Cannon: Suffragist, Senator, Plural Wife* (Salt Lake City: Signature Books, 2022).
48. Andrea G. Radke-Moss, "Polygamy and Women's Rights: Nineteenth-Century Mormon Female Activism," in *The Persistence of Polygamy: From Joseph Smith's Martyrdom to the First Manifesto, 1844–1890*, ed. Newell G. Bringhurst and Craig L. Foster (Independence, MO: John Whitmer Books, 2013); Carol Cornwall Madsen, ed., *Battle for the Ballot: Essays on Woman Suffrage in Utah, 1870–1896* (Logan: Utah State University Press, 1997); Lola Van Wagenen, "Sister-Wives and Suffragists: Polygamy and the Politics of Woman Suffrage, 1870–1896" (PhD diss., New York University, 1994).
49. Ricks, "A Peculiar Place for the Peculiar Institution," 92–99.
50. Ricks, "A Peculiar Place for the Peculiar Institution," 93–94 counts five presidents of the Seventy; the three identified here were Joseph Young (1797–1881) from Hopkinton, Massachusetts; Levi

W. Hancock (1803–1882) from Springfield, Massachusetts; and Albert P. Rockwood (1805–1879) from Holliston, Massachusetts; all three were members of the House of Representatives.

51. John Rowberry (1823–1884) was born in Herefordshire, England, and served as bishop in Tooele County; Gideon Brownell (1789–1871), a native of Danby, Vermont, served as bishop of the Farmington Ward in Davis County; David Evans (1804–1883) was born in Maryland and was bishop of the Lehi Ward in Utah County; and Aaron Johnson (1806–1877) was from Haddom, Connecticut, and served as bishop of the Springville Ward in Utah County. Lorin Farr (1820–1909) was from Waterford, Vermont, and served as president of the Weber Stake, with fellow legislator Charles R. Dana (1802–1868) from Schenectady, New York, serving as his counselor. Similarly, Daniel Spencer (1794–1868) from West Stockbridge, Massachusetts, served as president of the Salt Lake Stake with legislator David Fullmer (1803–1879) from Chillisquaque, Pennsylvania, serving as his counselor.

52. Ricks, "A Peculiar Place for the Peculiar Institution," 99–103, has slightly different numbers (twenty-nine from Northern states and three foreign born); on states with gradual emancipation codes see Arthur Zilversmit, *The First Emancipation: The Abolition of Slavery in the North* (Chicago: University of Chicago Press, 1967), 123–124, 128–129, 180–182, 193.

53. "From Washington," *Deseret News*, July 2, 1862, 4; John M. Bernhisel, Washington, D.C., to Brigham Young, Salt Lake City, June 13, 1862, CR 1234 1, reel 71, box 61, folder 6, CHL.

54. Reeve, *Religion of a Different Color*, chapters 4–7. The Church of Jesus Christ of Latter-day Saints includes a dual worship structure in which Sunday services are open to all people, even those of other faiths or of no faith tradition. Temple worship takes place during the week but not on Sunday and is available only to baptized members of the faith who meet certain standards. From roughly 1852 to 1978, leaders of the Church restricted temple worship and priesthood ordination from people of Black African descent but still admitted them into membership through baptism, confirmation, and integrated Sunday worship.

Chapter 1

1. Thomas Eddy to J. Griscom, July 8, 1818, in Samuel L. Knapp, *The Life of Thomas Eddy; Comprising an Extensive Correspondence with Many of the Most Distinguished Philosophers and Philanthropists of This and Other Countries* (New York: Conner & Cooke, 1834), 282–283; see also David N. Gellman, *Emancipating New York: The Politics of Slavery and Freedom, 1777–1827* (Baton Rouge: Louisiana State University Press, 2006), 189.
2. Paul J. Polgar, *Standard Bearers of Equality: America's First Abolition Movement* (Chapel Hill: University of North Carolina Press, 2019), 44–63.
3. Christopher Levenick, "Thomas Eddy," Philanthropy Roundtable, https://www.philanthropyroundtable.org/resource/thomas-eddy/; Gellman, *Emancipating New York*, chapters 8–9.
4. John Jay to the English Anti-Slavery Society, June 1788, in *The Correspondence and Public Papers of John Jay*, vol. 3: *1782–1793*, ed. Henry P. Johnston (New York: G.P. Putnam's Sons, 1891), 341–344.
5. David Brion Davis, *Inhuman Bondage: The Rise and Fall of Slavery in the New World* (New York: Oxford University Press, 2006), 194.
6. For a recent account of antislavery politics in the United States, see Sean Wilentz, *No Property in Man: Slavery and Antislavery at the Nation's Founding* (Cambridge, MA: Harvard University Press, 2018).
7. Polgar, *Standard Bearers of Equality*, passim. John Jay epitomized the contradictions of his age. Despite his commitment to the abolition of slavery, he and other members of the New York Manumission Society owned slaves. In fact, Jay routinely purchased enslaved people with the intention of setting them free after they had worked off their purchase price. Gellman, *Emancipating New York*, 56–67.
8. John Jay to the English Anti-Slavery Society, June 1788, in Johnston, *Correspondence and Public Papers of John Jay*, 341–344.
9. Robert J. Steinfeld, *The Invention of Free Labor: The Employment Relation in English & American Law and Culture, 1350–1870* (Chapel Hill: University of North Carolina Press, 1991); Wilentz, *No Property in Man*, 27; Gellman, *Emancipating New York*, chapter 2.
10. Here, specific performance is used in a general sense to mean that a servant could be forced to comply with the conditions of a labor contract through various strategies. This should not be confused with the more technical meaning of specific performance: an equitable injunction requiring a party who breaches a contract to perform the contract. During the nineteenth century there was no equitable remedy for the breach of a personal service contract. Although this

was originally due to the doctrinal limits of equity courts, it was later justified in terms of free labor ideology. We thank Nathan Oman for making this point clear.
11. Steinfeld, *Invention of Free Labor*, 3–9.
12. Steinfeld, *Invention of Free Labor*, 67.
13. E.g., in 2017 the *Atlantic* magazine published an article concerning a Filipino family that lived in the United States with a dependent servant that was provocatively entitled "My Family's Slave." Alex Tizon, "My Family's Slave," *Atlantic*, June 2017, https://www.theatlantic.com/magazine/archive/2017/06/lolas-story/524490/.
14. Gellman, *Emancipating New York*, 184.
15. In his otherwise brilliant study of colonial labor systems, Andrés Reséndez purposely uses an extremely broad definition of slavery that encompasses a variety of unfree statuses based on their "ultimate purpose, which was to forcibly extract labor from Natives." He likewise settles on this broad usage to honor the experience of the victims and to tie these historical practices with contemporary forms of bondage. Nevertheless, within the text he is often far more nuanced, arguing, e.g., that the early *encomienda* system in central Mexico "was not tantamount to slavery." Andrés Reséndez, *The Other Slavery: The Uncovered Story of Indian Enslavement in America* (Boston and New York: Houghton Mifflin Harcourt, 2016), 10–11, 62. In contrast, William Kiser argues that debt peonage in New Mexico constituted a "hybridized form of slavery, servitude, and serfdom" but is at pains to distinguish peonage from Indian captivity and chattel slavery. William S. Kiser, *Borderlands of Slavery: The Struggle over Captivity and Peonage in the American Southwest* (Philadelphia: University of Pennsylvania Press, 2017), 16–22.
16. Hendrik Hartog, *The Trouble with Minna: A Case of Slavery and Gradual Emancipation in the Antebellum North* (Chapel Hill: University of North Carolina Press, 2018), 6–8.
17. Steinfeld, *Invention of Free Labor*, 13–14, 53–54, 138–149.
18. Steinfeld, *Invention of Free Labor*, 122–146.
19. James Gray Pope, "Contract, Race, and Freedom of Labor in the Constitutional Law of 'Involuntary Servitude,'" *Yale Law Journal* 119, no. 7 (May 2010): 1474–1567.
20. U.S. Const. amend. XIII.
21. Pope, "Contract, Race, and Freedom of Labor," 1478.
22. Steinfeld, *Invention of Free Labor*, 148–152.
23. Bailey v. Alabama, 219 U.S. 219, 241 (1911).
24. Even as state legislatures severely restricted unfree relationships such as indentured servitude, Anglo-American law still recognized a liminal space between free labor and unfree labor. For instance, as late as the 1830s, the common law presumed that a labor contract had a term of one year unless the parties agreed otherwise. We are indebted to Nathan Oman for this insight.
25. Steinfeld, *Invention of Free Labor*; Eric Foner, *Free Soil, Free Labor, Free Men: The Ideology of the Republican Party before the Civil War* (New York: Oxford University Press, 1995).
26. We are indebted to Nathan Oman for this insight.
27. Many prominent men of the Jacksonian period began their careers as apprentices, including the famed trapper and Indian fighter Kit Carson, newspaperman Horace Greeley, abolitionist William Lloyd Garrison, and even President Millard Fillmore. W. J. Rorabaugh, *The Craft Apprentice: From Franklin to the Machine Age in America* (New York: Oxford University Press, 1986), 43, 69–70, 78–85, 100–102; Hampton Sides, *Blood and Thunder: The Epic Story of Kit Carson and the Conquest of the American West* (New York: Anchor Books, 2006), 13–15.
28. John G. Turner, *Brigham Young: Pioneer Prophet* (Cambridge, MA: Harvard University Press, 2012), 7–8, 14; Richard F. Palmer and Karl D. Butler, *Brigham Young: The New York Years* (Provo, UT: Charles Redd Center for Western Studies, 1982), 11–16.
29. Stanley B. Kimball, *The Life of Heber C. Kimball: Mormon Patriarch and Pioneer* (Urbana: University of Illinois Press, 1981), 8–10.
30. Biography of Edward Partridge, History, 1838–1856, vol. A-1, 94, Joseph Smith Papers, https://www.josephsmithpapers.org/paper-summary/history-1838-1856-volume-a-1-23-december-1805-30-august-1834/100.
31. John Taylor, Autobiography, 1858, CR 100 93, 2–3, CHL.
32. In the United States, apprenticeship was most widely practiced in New England. Rorabaugh, *Craft Apprentice*, 9; Christopher Tomlins, *Freedom Bound: Law, Labor, and Civic Identity in Colonizing English America, 1580–1865* (Cambridge: Cambridge University Press, 2010), 240–258. Nevertheless, one study finds that nearly 23 percent of white males in Frederick County, Maryland, between ages fifteen and twenty were indentured in 1814. Despite massive declines in the apprentice population over the next several decades, that figure was still approximately

6 percent in 1844. Rorabaugh, *Craft Apprentice*, 211. Another study analyzing records from Montreal, Quebec, found a similar drop in apprenticeships after the War of 1812. Nevertheless, as late as 1843 some 16 percent of craftsmen listed in the city directory had entered an apprentice contract as master prior to that year. Gillian Hamilton, "The Decline of Apprenticeship in North America: Evidence from Montreal," *Journal of Economic History* 60, no. 3 (September 2000): 12, 16, 50.

33. William W. Phelps, Kirtland, OH, to Sally Phelps, Liberty, MO, 14 Nov. 1835, in Historical Department, Journal History of the Church, 14 Nov. 1835, CHL.
34. Minutes, Nauvoo Legion, 8 July 1843, p. 52, sec. 29, Joseph Smith Papers, https://www.josephsmithpapers.org/paper-summary/minutes-nauvoo-legion-8-july-1843/14.
35. Between 1783 and 1799, at least twelve states passed laws limiting apprenticeship to minors and made a number of other modifications to colonial statutes. Rorabaugh, *Craft Apprentice*, 51.
36. Lawrence W. Towner, "The Indentures of Boston's Poor Apprentices: 1734–1805," *The Colonial Society of Massachusetts* 43 (March 1962), 420; Rorabaugh, *Craft Apprentice*, 38; Steinfeld, *Invention of Free Labor*, 56–58.
37. Tomlins, *Freedom Bound*, 322.
38. Janet L. Dolgin, "Transforming Childhood: Apprenticeship in American Law," *New England Law Review* 31 (Summer 1997), 1123–1126, 1128; Steinfeld, *Invention of Free Labor*, 55–60.
39. Steinfeld, *Invention of Free Labor*, 55–60.
40. Rorabaugh, *Craft Apprentice*, 10–15.
41. Quoted in Richard Lyman Bushman, *Joseph Smith: Rough Stone Rolling* (New York: Alfred A. Knopf, 2005), 10.
42. Turner, *Brigham Young*, 8.
43. James Kent, *Commentaries on American Law*, vol. 2 (New York: O. Halsted, 1832), 261, lecture 32.
44. Rorabaugh, *Craft Apprentice*, 32.
45. U.S. Const. art. IV, sec. 2, cl. 3; Tomlins, *Freedom Bound*, 397; Wilentz, *No Property in Man*, 101–112. One 1788 statute from New York stated that a runaway might be "compelled to serve his or her said master or mistress, for double the time he or she shall have so absented him or herself from such service." If a recaptured apprentice still refused to serve her master, she could be jailed until she submitted. The legislature renewed these provisions some forty years later after many of the early Mormon leaders had already begun to establish themselves in business. Nevertheless, courts generally softened the severe measures permitted by statute. An Act Concerning Apprentices and Servants, New York, February 6, 1788, in *Laws of the State of New York*, vol. 1 (Albany: Weed Parsons, 1886), 16, 620–625; *Revised Statutes of the State of New York*, vol. 2 (Albany: Packard and Van Benthuysen, 1829), 159; Christine Daniels, "'Liberty to Complaine': Servant Petitions in Maryland, 1652–1797," in *The Many Legalities of Early America*, ed. Christopher L. Tomlins and Bruce H. Mann (Chapel Hill: University of North Carolina Press, 2001), 219–249.
46. Rorabaugh, *Craft Apprentice*, 211; Hamilton, "Decline of Apprenticeship in North America," 12, 16, 50.
47. Rorabaugh, *Craft Apprentice*, 124–127, 128–129, 131, 157–158, 166–171, 206–211.
48. Dolgin, "Transforming Childhood," 1174–1188.
49. Rorabaugh, *Craft Apprentice*, 24–25, 32, 37–38, 67–75, 90, 139–140, 159–160, 207–208; Hamilton, "Decline of Apprenticeship in North America," 31–32; Dolgin, "Transforming Childhood," 1166–1169; Steinfeld, *Invention of Free Labor*, 160–163.
50. Rorabaugh, *Craft Apprentice*, 24–25, 32, 37–38, 90, 139–140, 159–160, 207–208.
51. Rorabaugh, *Craft Apprentice*, 32–36, 58–67, 76–77, 89–90, 102–103, 132–133, 136–139.
52. Leonard J. Arrington, *From Quaker to Latter-day Saint: Bishop Edwin D. Woolley* (Salt Lake City: Deseret Book, 1976), 15–29.
53. See Tomlins, *Freedom Bound*, 245; David W. Galenson, "The Rise and Fall of Indentured Servitude in the Americas: An Economic Analysis," *Journal of Economic History* 44, no. 1 (March 1984): 6n19; Daniels, "'Liberty to Complaine,'" 221.
54. Steinfeld, *Invention of Free Labor*, 10; Tomlins, *Freedom Bound*, 30–35, 64–66; Galenson, "Rise and Fall of Indentured Servitude," 1.
55. Farley Grubb, "The Market for Indentured Immigrants: Evidence on the Efficiency of Forward-Labor Contracting in Philadelphia, 1745–1773," *Journal of Economic History* 45, no. 4 (December 1985): 859.
56. Steinfeld, *Invention of Free Labor*, 164; Galenson, "Rise and Fall of Indentured Servitude," 14.

57. Steinfeld, *Invention of Free Labor*, 89.
58. "Documents: Diary of John Harrower, 1773–1776," *The American Historical Review* 6 (October 1900): 77.
59. Edmund S. Morgan, *American Slavery, American Freedom: The Ordeal of Colonial Virginia* (New York: W. W. Norton, 1975), 236, 339–340.
60. Gottlieb Mittelberger, *Journey to Pennsylvania in the Year 1750 and Return to Germany in the Year 1754*, trans. Carl Theo Eben (Philadelphia: John Jos. McVey, 1898), 26, 28.
61. Mittelberger, *Journey to Pennsylvania*, 27–28.
62. An Act Relative to German and Swiss Redemptioners, in *Laws Made and Passed by the General Assembly of the State of Maryland, at a Session Begun and Held at the City of Annapolis* (Annapolis, MD: Jonas Green, Printer to the State, 1818), 223; An Act for Regulating the Importation of German and Other Passengers, in *Laws of the Commonwealth of Pennsylvania from the Fourteenth Day of October One Thousand Seven Hundred*, vol. 7 (Philadelphia: John Bioren, 1822), 29–34.
63. Galenson, "Rise and Fall of Indentured Servitude," 16–24; Tomlins, *Freedom Bound*, 78–80, 263; Morgan, *American Slavery, American Freedom*, 236–239, 295.
64. Grubb, "Market for Indentured Immigrants," 855; Jackie Hill, "Case Studies in Indentured Servitude in Colonial America," *Constructing the Past* 9, no. 1 (Spring 2008): 55–62. Some scholars emphasize that indentured servitude was also an important model for mobilizing the labor of poor youths and other surplus or otherwise undesirable individuals to support English colonization efforts. Tomlins, *Freedom Bound*, 78–80, 263; Morgan, *American Slavery, American Freedom*, 236–239, 295.
65. Morgan, *American Slavery, American Freedom*, 176–179.
66. Morgan, *American Slavery, American Freedom*, 224–225; Steinfeld, *Invention of Free Labor*, 90, 121, 131–132; Tomlins, *Freedom Bound*, 273, 290–291, 326; David J. Silverman, "The Impact of Indentured Servitude on the Society and Culture of Southern New England Indians, 1680–1810," *New England Quarterly* 74, no. 4 (December 2001): 636–640; Joanne Pope Melish, *Disowning Slavery: Gradual Emancipation and "Race" in New England, 1780–1860* (Ithaca, NY: Cornell University Press), 77–79.
67. An Act Against Adultery and Fornication, in *The Statutes at Large of Pennsylvania from 1682–1801*, vol. 2, chapter CXXII (PA: State Printer, Clarence M. Busch, 1896); An Act for the Preventing of Clandestine Marriages, in *The Statutes at Large of Pennsylvania from 1682–1801*, vol. 2, chapter CIX (1701).
68. See, e.g., An Act Reducing into One the Several Acts Concerning Servants, in *A Collection of All Such Acts of the Commonwealth of Virginia*, chapter CXXXII (1792).
69. In an infamous 1634 case in Virginia, two servants died as a result of beatings administered by their master that included up to 500 lashes. Morgan, *American Slavery, American Freedom*, 127.
70. The English jurist William Blackstone explained in the mid-eighteenth century that "every master has by his contract purchased, for a valuable consideration, the service of his domestics for a limited time.... [T]he master has by his contract acquired [property] in the labour of the servant." St. George Tucker, ed., *Blackstone's Commentaries: With Notes of Reference* (Philadelphia: William Young Birch and Abraham Small, 1803), 4:142.
71. Mary Sarah Bilder, "The Struggle over Immigration: Indentured Servants, Slaves, and Articles of Commerce," *Missouri Law Review* 61, no. 4 (Fall 1996): 743, 767–770.
72. Steinfeld, *Invention of Free Labor*, 88, 90.
73. Morgan, *American Slavery, American Freedom*, 128–129. In seventeenth-century Virginia, it was not unheard of for men to gamble using their servants as stakes.
74. Morgan, *American Slavery, American Freedom*, 128.
75. An Act for the Better Regulation of Servants in the Province and Territories, in *The Statutes at Large of Pennsylvania from 1682–1801*, vol. 2, chapter XLIX.
76. An Act Reducing into One the Several Acts Concerning Servants, in *A Collection of All Such Acts of the Commonwealth of Virginia*, chapter CXXXII (1792); Tucker, *Blackstone's Commentaries*, 2:425n4.
77. There is considerable argument concerning the nature of the property right underlying both indentured servitude and slavery. Blackstone argued that even in the case of slavery, a master merely owned the labor of the slave. Tucker, *Blackstone's Commentaries*, 1:410–420.
78. See, e.g., An Act Reducing into One, the Several Acts Concerning Servants, in *A Collection of All Such Acts of the General Assembly of Virginia of a Public or Permanent Nature as Are Now in Force* (1794), chapter CXXXII; Brandon Paul Righi, "The Right of Petition: Cases of

Indentured Servants and Society in Colonial Virginia, 1698–1746" (master's thesis, College of William and Mary, 2010); Alexa Silver Cawley, "A Passionate Affair: The Master-Servant Relationship in Seventeenth-Century Maryland," *Historian* 61, no. 4 (June 1999): 754. Servants often prevailed in these lawsuits as courts sought to ensure that masters adequately performed their duties toward persons who amounted to their legal dependents. Daniels, "'Liberty to Complaine."

79. Steinfeld, *Invention of Free Labor*, 98–103, 121–149.
80. Farley Grubb, "The End of European Immigrant Servitude in the United States: An Economic Analysis of Market Collapse, 1772–1835," *Journal of Economic History* 54, no. 4 (December 1994): 815–818.
81. Steinfeld, *Invention of Free Labor*, 132–136; Rorabaugh, *Craft Apprentice*, 51. Christopher Tomlins has argued that indentured servitude was almost always associated with youthful immigrants, and consequently the American Revolution did not create any major breaks concerning the practice. He asserts that the true transition from freedom to unfreedom for the white adult population of British North America was the transition to African slavery at the end of the seventeenth century. Tomlins, *Freedom Bound*, 64–66.
82. Of Masters, Apprentices, and Servants, in *Revised Statutes of New York*, vol. 2, chapter VIII, Title IV (1829); Steinfeld, *Invention of Free Labor*, 133.
83. United States, 1820 Census, New York State.
84. Palmyra did not become a part of Wayne County until 1823. United States, 1820 Census, Palmyra Township, Ontario County, New York.
85. United States, 1820 Census, Cayuga County, New York.
86. Brigham Young, "Testimony to the Divinity of Joseph Smith's Mission—Elders Should Go Their Missions without Purse or Scrip—The Lord Deals with the Saints—Jesus Their President—Satan Angry," August 31, 1856, *Journal of Discourses*, vol. 4 (Liverpool: Latter-day Saints' Book Depot, 1857), 39.
87. Joseph Smith Jr., *General Smith's Views of the Powers and Policy of the Government of the United States* (Nauvoo, IL: J. Taylor Printing, 1844), 7.
88. Young, "Testimony to the Divinity," 39.
89. In England, the slave trade was outlawed soon after the Norman Conquest of 1066, and chattel slavery died out soon thereafter. Still, English law did permit a form of unfree labor that has been labeled "slavish servitude" or "near-slavery," which functioned as a kind of indentured servitude for life. By the mid-seventeenth century this had been extended to enslaved Africans who were brought to England from the colonies. The English also theorized about the rehabilitative or redemptive benefits of slavery, and for a brief time in the 1540s, Parliament legalized slavery for up to two years as a criminal punishment. William M. Wiecek, "The Origins of the Law of Slavery in British North America," *Cardozo Law Review* 17, no. 6 (May 1996): 1711, 1715–1718; George Van Cleve, "*Somerset's Case* and Its Antecedents in Imperial Perspective," *Law and History Review* 24, no. 3 (Fall 2006): 601–645; Krista J. Kesselring, "Slavery and Cartwright's Case before Somerset," Legal History Miscellany, October, 10, 2018, https://legalhistorymiscellany.com/2018/10/10/slavery-and-cartwrights-case-before-somerset/; Michael Guasco, "To 'doe some good upon their Countrymen': The Paradox of Indian Slavery in Early Anglo-America," *Journal of Social History* 41, no. 2 (Winter 2007): 394, 399–402.
90. In 1667, the Virginia Burgesses concluded that "the conferring of baptisme doth not alter the condition of the person as to his bondage or ffreedom; that diverse masters, ffreed from this doubt, may more carefully endeavour the propogation of christianity." Four years later, the Maryland legislature likewise provided that baptism would not free any "Negroe or Negroes Slaue or Slaues or any [of] his or their Issue or Issues from his her their or any of their Servitude or Servitudes." William Walter Hening, ed., *Statutes at Large; Being a Collection of All the Laws of Virginia*, vol. 2 (New York: R & W & G Bartow, 1823), 260; William Hand Browne, ed., *Archives of Maryland Proceedings and Acts of the General Assembly of Maryland, April 1666–June 1676* (Baltimore: Maryland Historical Society, 1884), 272.
91. Early modern legal authorities maintained that an individual could consensually enter a state of slavery or be condemned to slavery as a criminal punishment. This was reflected in early colonial statutes such as the 1641 Body of Liberties in Massachusetts and the 1665 Duke's Laws in New York. There are a number of documented cases in which Englishmen and women were "enslaved" for a term. Later commentators such as John Locke and Blackstone denied that it was possible to sell oneself into slavery. But as late as the Civil War, some Southern states passed laws allowing free African Americans to voluntarily become slaves. Wiecek, "Origins

of the Law of Slavery in British North America," 1745; Tomlins, *Freedom Bound*, 480; Guasco, "To 'doe some good upon their Countrymen,'" 394, 399–401; *The Colonial Laws of New York from the Year 1664 to the Revolution* (Albany: James B. Lyon, 1894), 1:18.

92. The Indian slave trade diminished significantly after the 1720s and was further circumscribed by legislative and judicial action. In Virginia, statutes enacted in 1691 and 1705 were later interpreted to mean that it was illegal to enslave an Indian in the colony from that time forward. In the 1806 case of *Hudgins v. Wright*, the Virginia Court of Appeals went so far as to free a slave who claimed to be descended from Native Americans. The court further held that all Indians who came into the state were legally presumed free. Four years earlier, a North Carolina court likewise held that Indians were presumed free under the law. Nevertheless, the court continued that there was a legal presumption of "every black person being a slave ... because the negroes originally brought to this country were slaves, and their descendants must continue slaves until manumitted by proper authority." By 1848, one authority in South Carolina declared that the "race of slave Indians ... is extinct." Hening, *Statutes at Large*, 3:69; Thomas D. Morris, *Southern Slavery and the Law, 1619–1860* (Chapel Hill: University of North Carolina Press, 1996), 20–21; Jacob D. Wheeler, *A Practical Treatise on the Law of Slavery* (New York: Allan Pollock, Jr., 1837) 18–19; Gobu v. Gobu, 1 N.C. 188 (N.C. Super. 1802).

93. Since ancient times, slavery has primarily been defined by the legal right of one individual to own another person. As far back as the second century A.D., the Roman jurist Florentinus explained that slavery "is a product of the [law of nations], whereby someone against nature is made subject to the ownership of another." Quoted in John W. Cairns, "The Definition of Slavery in Eighteenth-Century Thinking: Not the True Roman Slavery," in *The Legal Understanding of Slavery: From the Historical to the Contemporary*, ed. Jean Allain (New York: Oxford University Press, 2012), 61.

94. James W. C. Pennington, *The Fugitive Blacksmith; or, Events in the History of James W. C. Pennington, Pastor of a Presbyterian Church, New York, Formerly a Slave in the State of Maryland, United States* (London: Charles Gilpin, 1849), iv–v. The Slavery Convention of 1926 defined slavery as "the status or condition of a person over whom any or all of the powers attaching to the right of ownership are exercised." Slavery Convention of 1926, art. 1 found at http://www.ohchr.org/EN/ProfessionalInterest/Pages/SlaveryConvention.aspx.

95. Morris, *Southern Slavery and the Law*, 61–80; Thomas D. Morris, "Slaves and the Rules of Evidence in Criminal Trials," in *Slavery and the Law*, ed. Paul Finkelman (Madison, WI: Madison House, 1997), 209.

96. Thomas R. R. Cobb, *An Inquiry into the Law of Negro Slavery in the United States of America*, vol. 1 (Philadelphia: T. & J. W. Johnson, 1858), 83.

97. See Cobb, *Inquiry into the Law of Negro Slavery*, 226–262. According to the philosopher Aristotle, a slave is a "living possession" or, translated differently, "thinking property." Aristotle, *Politics*, book 1, chapter 4; Alan Watson, "Thinking Property at Rome," in Finkelman, *Slavery and the Law*, 419. The Tennessee Supreme Court opined in 1835 that a slave "is an intelligent moral agent, capable of being a subject of government, and, like all other men, liable to answer for his own wrongs to the injured party, but for the fact that all his personal rights as a citizen, and his liabilities as such, are destroyed and merged in the ownership of the master, who controls his person, owns his property, and is entitled to the fruits of his labor." Wright v. Weatherly, 15 Tenn. (7 Yer.) 367, 378–80, quoted in Jacob I. Corré, "Thinking Property at Memphis," in Finkelman, *Slavery and the Law*, 437, 440. There were exceptions to this, however. For instance, in eighteenth-century New England, enslaved persons were able to own property. Melish, *Disowning Slavery*, chapter 1.

98. Some courts went so far to suggest that these concessions transformed an enslaved person or her children into indentured servants, while others contended that such a person actually remained in a kind of "limited slavery." Morris, *Southern Slavery and the Law*, 400–423.

99. Steinfeld, *Invention of Free Labor*, 99, 101n23; Cairns, "Definition of Slavery," in *Legal Understanding of Slavery*, ed. Jean Allain, 75–78. In New York, the 1665 Duke's Laws provided that lifetime servitude based on a contract was distinct from slavery. The act expressly acknowledged that claims of a "Master or Dame who shall by any Indenture or Covenant take Apprentices for Terme of Years, or other Servants for Term of years or Life." However, there is no existing record of a self-sale for life in New York. *Colonial Laws of New York*, 18; Wiecek, "Origins of the Law of Slavery in British North America," n217.

100. Van Cleve, "*Somerset's Case* and Its Antecedents in Imperial Perspective."

101. Blackstone declared that "the law of England . . . will not endure the existence of slavery within this nation. . . . [A] slave or negro, the instant he lands in England, becomes a freeman." Blackstone opined that this reclassification would "protect him in the enjoyment of his person, and his property." Nevertheless, Blackstone contended that a former slave would remain in servitude for life. "[W]ith regard to any right which the master may have lawfully acquired to the perpetual service of [an individual]," Blackstone explained, "this will remain exactly in the same state as before: for this is no more than the same state of subjection for life, which every apprentice submits to for the space of seven years, or sometimes for a longer term." Tucker, *Blackstone's Commentaries*, 2:424. See also Edward Chamberlayne, *Angliæ Notitia, or The Present state of England together with divers reflections upon the antient state thereof* (London: printed by T.N. for John Martyn, 1669), 325–326. As Chamberlayne put it, "A Foreign Slave brought into England, is upon landing *ipso facto* free from Slavery, but not from ordinary service." In 1772, the celebrated *Somerset's Case*, although delivering a blow against chattel slavery, almost certainly upheld this parallel form of bondage under English law. Van Cleve, "*Somerset's Case* and Its Antecedents in Imperial Perspective," 633–639, 642–645.

102. United States, 1800 Census, New York, New Jersey.

103. Gellman, *Emancipating New York*, 169–176; Hartog, *Trouble with Minna*, 5, 28.

104. Manisha Sinha, *The Slave's Cause: A History of Abolition* (New Haven, CT: Yale University Press, 2016), chapter 3.

105. Some scholars have viewed this compromise skeptically, while others have defended it as a practical necessity. For various interpretations of gradual emancipation, see Gary B. Nash and Jean R. Soderland, *Freedom by Degrees: Emancipation in Pennsylvania and Its Aftermath* (New York: Oxford University Press, 1991); Robert William Fogel and Stanley L. Engerman, "Philanthropy at Bargain Prices: Notes on the Economics of Gradual Emancipation," *The Journal of Legal Studies* 3, no. 2 (June 1974): 377–401; Melish, *Disowning Slavery*, chapters 2 and 3; Polgar, *Standard-Bearers of Equality*, chapters 2 and 3; Gellman, *Emancipating New York*, 175.

106. Alice Baumgarten, *South to Freedom: Runaway Slaves to Mexico and the Coming of the Civil War* (New York: Basic Books, 2021), 5, 58.

107. Daniel Walker Howe, *What Hath God Wrought: The Transformation of America, 1815–1848* (New York: Oxford University Press, 2007), 148–149, 155, 325–327; Kentucky Senator Henry Clay advocated gradual emancipation for decades and blamed its ultimate failure on Northern abolitionists who demanded immediate, uncompensated emancipation. In 1839 Clay dejectedly concluded that the number of Kentuckians "who would now favor gradual emancipation is probably less than it was in the years 1798–99." *Appendix to the Congressional Globe*, 25th Cong., 3rd Sess. (Washington D.C.: Blair and Rives, 1839), 358.

108. Howe, *What Hath God Wrought*; Sean Wilentz, *The Rise of American Democracy: Jefferson to Lincoln* (New York: W. W. Norton, 2005).

109. Eric Foner, *The Fiery Trial: Abraham Lincoln and American Slavery* (New York: W. W. Norton, 2010), 239, 269–270.

110. Melish, *Disowning Slavery*, 79–80. Elsewhere Melish uses the term "statutory slavery" to emphasize some of the slave-like conditions that attached to the status. However, under the gradual emancipation statutes, the children of slaves were considered free. For a case study demonstrating how gradual emancipation laws operated in New Jersey, see Hartog, *Trouble with Minna*.

111. Christopher B. Rich Jr., "The True Policy for Utah: Servitude, Slavery, and 'An Act in Relation to Service,'" *Utah Historical Quarterly* 80, no. 1 (Winter 2012): 54–74; Hartog, *Trouble with Minna*. In 1850, four years after slavery was abolished, the census still listed 236 slaves in New Jersey. However, most of them were probably "perpetual apprentices" as designated by the legislature. Indeed, more than 80 percent of those enumerated as slaves were over the age of fifty, and at least seventy-one individuals were over the age of seventy. In other words, individuals the legislature deemed likely to become paupers if they were freed. United States, 1850 Census, New Jersey.

112. As early as 1777, the same year that Vermont abolished slavery, Gouverneur Morris introduced an amendment during the New York Constitutional Convention endorsing some kind of gradual emancipation program. His proposed language merely recommended that future legislatures "take the most effectual measures consistent with the public safety, and the private property of individuals, for abolishing domestic slavery within the same." However, even this hortatory statement was too much for the convention and it was defeated. *Journals of the*

Provincial Congress, Provincial Convention, Committee of Safety and Council of Safety of the State of New-York: 1775–1776–1777 (Albany: Thurlow Weed, 1842), 1:887, 889; Gellman, *Emancipating New York*, 33–34.

113. Gellman, *Emancipating New York*, chapters 3, 4, and 8.
114. An Act for the Gradual Abolition of Slavery, March 29, 1799, in *Laws of the State of New York, Passed at the Twenty-Second Session, Second Meeting of the Legislature Begun … the Second Day of January, 1799* (Albany: Loring Andrews, 1799).
115. Windsor v. Hartford, 2 Conn. 355 (1817), quoted in David Menschel, "Abolition without Deliverance: The Law of Connecticut Slavery 1784–1848," *Yale Law Journal* 111, no. 1 (October 2001): 217.
116. Menschel, "Abolition without Deliverance," 217; Melish, *Disowning Slavery*, 81–93.
117. Menschel, "Abolition without Deliverance," 215–216; Hartog, *Trouble with Minna*, 51.
118. Hartog, *Trouble with Minna*, 5.
119. An Act Relative to Slaves and Servants, March 31, 1817, in *Laws of the State of New York Passed at the Fortieth Session of the Legislature, Begun and Held at the City of Albany, the Fifth Day of November, 1816* (Albany: J. Buel, 1817), 136–144.
120. Tragically, enslaved people and their children were vulnerable to removal from gradual emancipation states to jurisdictions that fully recognized chattel slavery. State legislatures enacted numerous laws designed to provide these individuals with some protection. For instance, in 1798 New Jersey prohibited the removal of an enslaved person from the state without his or her consent. Yet some enslavers simply broke the law in an attempt to obtain a measure of financial compensation. In the summer of 1818, New York and New Jersey newspapers reported a conspiracy to transfer more than one hundred enslaved adults and their children from New Jersey to Louisiana and Alabama. Documents purporting to verify consent on the part of these individuals were likely forged with the connivance of a local judge. An Act Respecting Slaves, March 14, 1798, in New Jersey Session Law, Legislature Number 22, Session No. 2, 1798, at 369; Menschel, "Abolition without Deliverance," 209–213; Hartog, *Trouble with Minna*, 69–82; Gellman, *Emancipating New York*, 108, 204–205; W. Caleb McDaniel, *Sweet Taste of Liberty: A True Story of Slavery and Restitution in America* (New York: Oxford University Press, 2019).
121. Paul Finkelman, *An Imperfect Union: Slavery, Federalism, and Comity* (Chapel Hill: University of North Carolina Press, 1981), 73.
122. Polgar, *Standard-Bearers of Equality*, chapter 3; Gellman, *Emancipating New York*, 72–77, 156–159, Melish, *Disowning Slavery*, 137–149.
123. Polgar, *Standard-Bearers of Equality*, chapters 5 and 6; Gellman, *Emancipating New York*, 199–213; Davis, *Inhuman Bondage*, 255–260; Melish, *Disowning Slavery*, chapter 4.
124. Melish, *Disowning Slavery*, 97–100, 109–110, 122–137, 189–209; Howe, *What Hath God Wrought*, 260–266; Alexander Keyssar, *The Right to Vote: The Contested History of Democracy in the United States* (New York: Basic Books, 2000), 54–55.
125. Nathaniel H. Carter and William L. Stone, *Reports of the Proceedings and Debates of the Convention of 1821, Assembled for the Purpose of Amending the Constitution of the State of New-York* (Albany: E and E. Hosford, 1821), 280.
126. Gellman, *Emancipating New York*, 179–180.
127. Carter and Stone, *Reports of the Proceedings*, 184.
128. Carter and Stone, *Reports of the Proceedings*, 191.
129. New York Constitution of 1821, art. II, sec. 1; Howe, *What Hath God Wrought*, 239–240.
130. Finkelman, *Imperfect Union*, 46–69, quotation at 56. In 1788, the law was amended to remove the six-month grace period for new residents to enter indenture contracts with their slaves. An 1832 case confirmed that indenture contracts with enslaved persons had to be executed outside the state. Over the years, case law gradually tightened restrictions on the ability to indenture slaves in Pennsylvania. An Act for the Gradual Emancipation of Slavery and An Act to Explain and Amend an Act Entitled "An Act for the Gradual Abolition of Slavery," in *The Statutes at Large of Pennsylvania from 1682 to 1801*, James T. Mitchell and Henry Flanders, comps. (n.p.: Wm Stanley Ray, 1899), vol. 10 (1779–1781), 67–73; vol. 13 (1787–1790), 52–56.
131. Paul Finkelman, "Evading the Ordinance: The Persistence of Bondage in Indiana and Illinois," *Journal of the Early Republic* 9, no. 1 (Spring 1989): 25–34; Howe, *What Hath God Wrought*, 136–137; M. Scott Heerman, "In a State of Slavery: Black Servitude in Illinois, 1800–1830," *Early American Studies: An Interdisciplinary Journal* 14, no. 1 (Winter 2016): 119–122.

132. Finkelman, "Evading the Ordinance," 38–39; An Act Concerning the Introduction of Negroes and Mulattoes into This Territory, in *Laws of Indiana Territory, 1801–1809*, ed. Francis S. Philbrick (Springfield, IL: n.p., 1930), 523–526.
133. An Act Concerning the Introduction of Negroes and Mullattoes into This Territory, 523–526.
134. Allison Mileo Gorsuch, "To Indent Oneself: Ownership, Contracts, and Consent in Antebellum Illinois," in *Legal Understanding of Slavery*, ed. Jean Allain, 136. Consent was one of the key elements that differentiated an indentured servant from a slave. As John Locke once argued, when a master entered a contract or agreement with his or her slave "for a limited power on the one side, and obedience on the other, the state of war and slavery ceases, as long as the Compact endures." John Locke, *Two Treatises of Government* (London: Thomas Tegg, 1823), 115.
135. In one 1796 petition to Congress, several citizens from the Illinois Country specifically referenced Blackstone's *Commentaries* in making the case that "any person purchasing, or otherwise acquiring a slave in any of the States, is entitled to his perpetual service in this Territory as a servant [for life]." "The Petition of 1796," in Jacob Piatt Dunn, *Slavery Petitions and Papers* (Indianapolis: Bowen-Merrill, 1894), 5–10; Finkelman, "Evading the Ordinance," 27–28.
136. Of the indentures executed in St. Claire County, Illinois Territory between 1809 and 1818, at least five were for a term of ninety-nine years. Approximately one-third of the contracts specified terms of at least thirty years, while another one-fifth of the contracts specified terms of twenty to thirty years. Gorsuch, "To Indent Oneself," 142, 147.
137. Heerman, "In a State of Slavery," 114–139, 124–128; Gorsuch, "To Indent Oneself," 144–148.
138. An Act Concerning the Introduction of Negroes and Mullattoes into this Territory, 523–526.
139. An Act Concerning the Introduction of Negroes and Mullattoes into this Territory, 523–526.
140. An Act Concerning Servants, in *Laws of Indiana Territory, 1801–1809*, 463–464. The law likely applied to a broad spectrum of indentured servants. Sec. 1 of the statute referenced "negroes, mulattoes, (and other persons not being citizens of the United States)." Presumably, this included European indentured servants (who under the Naturalization Act of 1802 could not become citizens until they had resided in the country for at least five years) and Native Americans. However, sec. 7 of the statute also referenced "servants, being citizens of any of the United States of America." The children of registered servants who were born in Indiana were instead governed by An Act Respecting Apprentices.
141. An Act Concerning Executions, in *Laws of Indiana Territory, 1801–1809*, 540–541. See also *Nance, a girl of color v. John Howard*, 1828, in Sidney Breese, *Reports of Cases at Law and in Chancery Argued and Determined in the Supreme Court of the State of Illinois* (Hartford, CT: n.p., 1861), 1:242–247.
142. Constitution of Indiana 1816, art. XI, sec. 7.
143. One scholar has identified over 350 indenture contracts signed by adult slaves entering Illinois, most from the period 1807–1818. Heerman, "In a State of Slavery," 124–125n37.
144. Constitution of Illinois 1818, art. VI. In addition to indentured servitude, the Constitution protected de jure slavery for persons who were enslaved prior to 1787 or their descendants. The state supreme court did not free the descendants of the pre-1787 slaves until 1845. It further allowed the use of out-of-state slaves at the salt works near Shawneetown until 1825. Finally, Illinois continued to liberally extend comity to slave states that allowed masters to travel through the state with their human property. Finkelman, *Imperfect Union*.
145. In 1836, the Supreme Court of Illinois held that any indenture that was not entered strictly in conformity with the provisions of the act of 1807 was void. Choisser v. Hargrave, 1 Scam. 317, 2 Ill. 317 (Ill. 1836). That same year the court declared that the children of registered servants who were born in Indiana were not subject to any form of servitude whatsoever and were free at birth. Boon v. Juliet, 1 Scam. 258, 2 Ill. 258, (Ill. 1836). In 1841, in a case argued by Abraham Lincoln, the Illinois Supreme Court held that there was a legal assumption in the state that all persons were free regardless of color. This placed the burden on masters to prove that an individual was bound to service rather than forcing that individual to prove that he was free. Bailey v. Cromwell et al., 3 Scam. 341, 5 Ill. 341, (Ill. 1841).
146. Illinois Constitution 1848, art. XIII, sec. 16.
147. Illinois Constitution 1848, art. XIV.
148. John Reynolds, *My Own Times, Embracing also, the History of My Life* (Illinois: n.p., 1855), 208. Governor Thomas Ford of Illinois (1842–1846) emphasized in his memoirs that slaves who were brought into the region were in fact "indentured and registered servants." Thomas Ford, *A History of Illinois from Its Commencement as a State in 1818 to 1847* (New York: S. C. Griggs, 1854), 32

149. Douglas's immediate purpose in making this statement was to refute John C. Calhoun's assertions that the Northwest Ordinance was the first incident of "northern aggressions" that deprived the South of its "due share in the territories." *Appendix to the Congressional Globe*, 31st Cong., 1st Sess. (Washington D.C.: John C. Rives, 1850), 369.

150. Peoria Speech, October 16, 1854, Collected Works of Abraham Lincoln, https://quod.lib.umich.edu/cgi/t/text/textidx?c=lincoln;cc=lincoln;rgn=div2;view=text;idno=lincoln2;node=lincoln2:282.1.

151. M. Scott Heerman, *The Alchemy of Slavery: Human Bondage and Emancipation in Illinois Country, 1730–1865* (Philadelphia: University of Pennsylvania Press, 2018), 89. Heerman argues that that the system of Black servitude that existed in Illinois cannot be considered a form of *post-nati* gradual emancipation since the law "set no fixed date after which children would be born free." There is no question that the Illinois system differed in some important respects from gradual emancipation laws in New York or Pennsylvania. Yet the condition of statutory servitude imposed upon the children of slaves in those jurisdictions was in many ways comparable to the condition of servitude imposed upon the children of slaves who immigrated to Illinois with their masters. In either case, the child was not legally considered a slave but a kind of apprentice or indentured servant. Moreover, the child would be freed after a defined period of servitude. Unlike gradual emancipation laws in the eastern states, the Illinois statute did not propose to wholly end slavery or involuntary servitude in the territory. In fact, the subsequent Constitution of 1818 only prohibited the *further* introduction of enslaved people, with several important caveats. Nevertheless, the law ensured that certain categories of slaves or their descendants would be emancipated over time.

152. Finkelman, "Evading the Ordinance," 35.

153. Gorsuch, "To Indent Oneself," 138.

154. The term "involuntary servitude" first appeared in a 1784 report issued by Thomas Jefferson's Committee for the Western Territory. The report recommended that after the year 1800, "slavery and involuntary servitude" should be prohibited in any new states formed from lands ceded to the United States. Three years later, Congress adopted portions of this language in the Northwest Ordinance. "III. Report of the Committee, 1 March 1784," Founders Online, National Archives, https://founders.archives.gov/documents/Jefferson/01-06-02-0420-0004.

155. Robert Steinfeld has argued that Ohio, Illinois, and Indiana formulated three separate conceptions of involuntary servitude, although by 1830 each had concluded that a long-term indenture contract between a master and a slave was involuntary. Steinfeld contends that Ohio considered whether a labor contract was entered voluntarily, if the contract included compensation, as well as the prospective duration of the contract. Illinois also looked to the voluntariness of the contract when it was first executed but without reference to the length of service or other considerations. On the other hand, Indiana determined that even if a contract was entered voluntarily, the moment that a servant no longer wished to serve and was compelled to do so, the relationship became involuntary. This was a major shift from traditional understandings of unfree labor. Steinfeld continues that while the Indiana tradition ultimately became the rule in the United States, the Illinois tradition retained vitality until the early twentieth century. Robert J. Steinfeld, *Coercion, Contract, and Free Labor in the Nineteenth Century* (Cambridge: Cambridge University Press, 2001), 255–285. In contrast, legal scholar Nathan Oman has emphasized the continuity between these conceptions of unfree labor. He asserts that when read together, the jurisprudence of Ohio, Illinois, and Indiana shows a "unified approach" to involuntary servitude that asked if a particular labor contract was entered in "a state of perfect freedom," if it included compensation, the length of service associated with the contract, and if it permitted a master to completely dominate his or her servant. Nathan B. Oman, "Specific Performance and the Thirteenth Amendment," *Minnesota Law Review* 93, no. 6 (2009): 2020, 2047–2048. See also James Gray Pope, "Contract, Race, and Freedom of Labor in the Constitutional Law of 'Involuntary Servitude,'" *Yale Law Journal* 119, no. 7 (May 2010): 1481–1485.

156. Pheobe, a woman of color v. Jay, 1 Ill. 268 (Ill. 1828).

157. Borders, a woman of color v. Borders, 4 Scam. 341, 5 Ill. 341 (Ill. 1843).

158. Howard Lamar, "From Bondage to Contract: Ethnic Labor in the American West, 1600–1890," in *The Countryside in the Age of Capitalist Transformation: Essays in the Social History of Rural America*, ed. Steven Hahn and Jonathan Prude (Chapel Hill: University of North Carolina Press, 1985), 293–326.

159. Kevin Waite, *West of Slavery: The Southern Dream of a Transcontinental Empire* (Chapel Hill: University of North Carolina Press, 2021).
160. Stacey L. Smith, *Freedom's Frontier: California and the Struggle over Unfree Labor, Emancipation, and Reconstruction* (Chapel Hill: University of North Carolina Press, 2013); Kiser, *Borderlands of Slavery*, 16–22.

Chapter 2

1. John Brown, Reminiscences and Journal, vol. 1, 31, MS 1636, CHL; Ami Chopine, "Charlotte," Century of Black Mormons, https://exhibits.lib.utah.edu/s/century-of-black-mormons/page/charlotte.
2. These numbers are based on evidence gathered by researchers working on the Century of Black Mormons data base. Once the biographies of all of the enslaved people are complete, they will be posted at http://centuryofblackmormons.org.
3. Molly Oshatz, *Slavery and Sin: The Fight against Slavery and the Rise of Liberal Protestantism* (New York: Oxford University Press, 2012).
4. C. C. Goen, *Broken Churches, Broken Nation: Denominational Schisms and the Coming of the American Civil War* (Macon, GA: Mercer University Press, 1985).
5. Goen, *Broken Churches, Broken Nation*, 82–83.
6. Goen, *Broken Churches, Broken Nation*, 83.
7. Anson West, *A History of Methodism in Alabama* (Nashville, TN: Methodist Episcopal Church, South, 1893), 641–642.
8. Goen, *Broken Churches, Broken Nation*, 4, 66–67.
9. J. Spencer Fluhman, *"A Peculiar People": Anti-Mormonism and the Making of Religion in Nineteenth-Century America* (Chapel Hill: University of North Carolina Press, 2012); David Sehat, *The Myth of American Religious Freedom* (New York: Oxford University Press, 2011).
10. Matthew McBride, "Peter," Century of Black Mormons, https://exhibits.lib.utah.edu/s/century-of-black-mormons/page/peter.
11. Wilford Woodruff, Membership Record Book, 1835, Wilford Woodruff Collection, MS 5506, box 2, folder 6, CHL; W. Paul Reeve, "John Burton," Century of Black Mormons, https://exhibits.lib.utah.edu/s/century-of-black-mormons/page/burton-john.
12. Quincy D. Newell, *Your Sister in the Gospel: The Life of Jane Manning James, A Nineteenth-Century Black Mormon* (New York: Oxford University Press, 2019); W. Paul Reeve, "'I Dug the Graves': Isaac Lewis Manning, Joseph Smith, and Racial Connections in Two Latter-day Saint Traditions," *Journal of Mormon History* 47, no. 1 (January 2021): 29–67.
13. See, e.g., Benjamin Kiser, "Green Flake," Century of Black Mormons, https://exhibits.lib.utah.edu/s/century-of-black-mormons/page/flake-green; Jeffrey D. Mahas, "Hager," Century of Black Mormons, https://exhibits.lib.utah.edu/s/century-of-black-mormons/page/hager; Amy Chopine, "Jack," Century of Black Mormons, https://exhibits.lib.utah.edu/s/century-of-black-mormons/page/jack; Amy Chopine, "Maron," Century of Black Mormons, https://exhibits.lib.utah.edu/s/century-of-black-mormons/page/maron.
14. Brown, Reminiscences and Journal, vol. 1, 31; Chopine, "Charlotte"; "Minutes of the first annual Conference held in the district of Alabama, Tuscaloosa county, Feb'y 15th, 1845," *Times and Seasons*, vol. 6 (Nauvoo, IL, 1845–1846), 843–844.
15. On priesthood ordinations in the North see W. Paul Reeve, "Elijah Able," Century of Black Mormons, https://exhibits.lib.utah.edu/s/century-of-black-mormons/page/able-elijah; and Jordan T. Watkins, "Quack Walker Lewis," Century of Black Mormons, https://exhibits.lib.utah.edu/s/century-of-black-mormons/page/lewis-quack-walker. For an early priesthood holder of Black African ancestry who passed as white, see Jeffrey D. Mahas, "Joseph T. Ball," Century of Black Mormons, https://exhibits.lib.utah.edu/s/century-of-black-mormons/page/ball-joseph-t. See also, W. Paul Reeve, *Religion of a Different Color: Race and the Mormon Struggle for Whiteness* (New York: Oxford University Press, 2015), chapters 4–7.
16. Reeve, *Religion of a Different Color*, 116–122; "Free People of Color," *The Evening and the Morning Star*, July 1833.
17. "Free People of Color."
18. P. J. Staudenraus, *The African Colonization Movement, 1816–1865* (New York: Columbia University Press, 1961); Eric Foner, *The Fiery Trial: Abraham Lincoln and American Slavery* (New York: W. W. Norton, 2010); Elise Lemire, *"Miscegenation": Making Race in America* (Philadelphia: University of Pennsylvania Press, 2002); "The Elders Stationed in Zion to the

Churches Abroad, in Love Greeting," *The Evening and the Morning Star*, July 1833; Reeve, *Religion of a Different Color*, 118.
19. *The Evening and the Morning Star Extra*, July 16, 1833; Reeve, *Religion of a Different Color*, 118–119; W. Paul Reeve, *Let's Talk about Race and Priesthood* (Salt Lake City: Deseret Book, 2023), 28–29.
20. "Regulating the Mormonites," *Erie Gazette* (Erie, PA), September 5, 1833; "Regulating the Mormonites," *Daily Missouri Republican* (St. Louis, MO), August 9, 1833; Reeve, *Religion of a Different Color*, 119–120; Reeve, *Let's Talk about Race*, 29.
21. "The Outrage in Jackson County Missouri," *Evening and the Morning Star* (Kirtland, OH), January 1834.
22. Reeve, *Religion of a Different Color*, 119–128.
23. Henry Mayer, *All on Fire: William Lloyd Garrison and the Abolition of Slavery* (New York: St. Martin's Press, 1998); Reeve, *Religion of a Different Color*, 115–116; Reeve, *Let's Talk about Race*, 27, 34.
24. Lemire, *Miscegenation*, 55–61.
25. Larry E. Tise, *Proslavery: A History of the Defense of Slavery in America, 1701–1840* (Athens: University of Georgia Press, 1987), 267–268; Donald G. Mathews, *Slavery and Methodism* (Princeton, NJ: Princeton University Press, 1965), 142; Ryan Jordan, *Slavery and the Meeting House: The Quakers and the Abolitionists Dilemma, 1820–1865* (Bloomington: Indiana University Press, 2007); Brycchan Carey and Geoffrey Plank, eds., *Quakers and Abolition* (Urbana: University of Illinois Press, 2014), 1–12, 43–55; Richard J. Carwardine, *Evangelicals and Politics in Antebellum America* (New Haven, CT: Yale University Press, 1993), 139; Reeve, *Religion of a Different Color*, 122; see also Reeve, *Let's Talk about Race*, 34–35.
26. The declaration was first published in *Latter Day Saints' Messenger and Advocate* (Kirtland, OH), August 1835, under the heading "General Assembly"; it was also included as sec. 102 in Doctrine and Covenants, 1835, pp. 252–254, Joseph Smith Papers, https://www.josephsmithpapers.org/paper-summary/doctrine-and-covenants-1835/262, and eventually became sec. 134 in more recent versions of the Doctrine and Covenants. Reeve, *Religion of a Different Color*, 122; Reeve, *Let's Talk about Race*, 34–36.
27. Doctrine and Covenants 101:79.
28. John L. Myers, "Anti-Slavery Activities of Five Lane Seminary Boys in 1835–36," *Bulletin of the Historical and Philosophical Society of Ohio* 21 (April 1963): 99–102; "Anti-Slavery Intelligence," *Philanthropist* (Cincinnati, OH), April 22, 1836; Newell G. Bringhurst, *Saints, Slaves and Blacks: The Changing Place of Black People within Mormonism*, 2nd ed. (Salt Lake City: Greg Kofford Books, 2018), 13–14; Leonard L. Richards, *"Gentlemen of Property and Standing": Anti-Abolition Mobs in Jacksonian America* (New York: Oxford University Press, 1970), chapter 1, 78–79, 156–157; Reeve, *Religion of a Different Color*, 123.
29. Joseph Smith Jr., "For the Messenger and Advocate," *Latter Day Saints' Messenger and Advocate* (Kirtland, OH), April 1836; Reeve, *Religion of a Different Color*, 124–126.
30. Smith Jr., "For the Messenger and Advocate"; Reeve, *Let's Talk about Race*, 34–36.
31. Smith Jr., "For the Messenger and Advocate."
32. Smith Jr., "For the Messenger and Advocate"; Reeve, *Let's Talk about Race*, 35–36.
33. *Elders' Journal* (Far West, Caldwell Co., MO), July 1838, 43; Reeve, *Let's Talk about Race*, 36.
34. Bringhurst, *Saints, Slaves, and Blacks*, 52–56; Richards, *"Gentlemen of Property and Standing,"* 156–170; Reeve, *Let's Talk about Race*, 36.
35. Reeve, *Religion of a Different Color*, 126; Reeve, *Let's Talk about Race*, 36–37.
36. Andrew H. Hedges, Alex D. Smith, and Richard Lloyd Anderson, eds., *The Joseph Smith Papers: Journals*, vol. 2: *December 1841–April 1843* (Salt Lake City: Church Historian's Press, 2011), 212; Reeve, *Let's Talk about Race*, 37. Smith's position here was similar to those espoused by first movement abolitionists prior to the colonization movement.
37. Spencer W. McBride, *Joseph Smith for President: The Prophet, the Assassins, and the Fight for American Religious Freedom* (New York: Oxford University Press, 2021); this and the next five paragraphs are derived from Reeve, *Let's Talk about Race*, 37–39.
38. Marika Sherwood, *After Abolition: Britain and the Slave Trade Since 1807*, (London: I.B. Tauris, 2007); Claudius K. Fergus, *Revolutionary Emancipation: Slavery and Abolitionism in the British West Indies* (Baton Rouge: Louisiana State University Press, 2013); James Latimer, "The Apprenticeship System in the British West Indies," *The Journal of Negro Education* 33, no. 1 (1964): 52–57.

39. Joseph Smith, *General Smith's Views of the Powers and Policy of the Government of the United States* (Nauvoo, IL), February 7, 1844, 9, 11; Reeve, *Let's Talk about Race*, 38.
40. Smith, *General Smith's Views*, 9.
41. Andrew F. Ehat and Lyndon W. Cook, *The Words of Joseph Smith: The Contemporary Accounts of the Nauvoo Discourses of the Prophet Joseph* (Orem, UT: Grandin Book, 1991), 325–326.
42. Smith, *General Smith's Views*, 3; Reeve, *Let's Talk about Race*, 38–39.
43. Smith, *General Smith's Views*, 3–4; Reeve, *Let's Talk about Race*, 39. How committed Smith was to racial equality in practice is difficult to determine when one factors in interracial marriage, voting rights, and the integration of freed slaves in American society.
44. George Miller, Biography, Joesph Smith Papers, https://www.josephsmithpapers.org/person/george-miller. Lyman Wight, Biography, Joesph Smith Papers, https://www.josephsmithpapers.org/person/lyman-wight.
45. *Council of Fifty, Minutes, March 1844–January 1846*, ed. Matthew J. Grow, Ronald K. Esplin, Mark Ashurst-McGee, Jeffrey D. Mahas, Matthew C. Godfrey, and Gerrit J. Dirkmaat (Salt Lake City: Church Historian's Press, September 2016), 30–31.
46. *Council of Fifty*, 34–35.
47. Walter Johnson, *Soul by Soul: Life Inside the Antebellum Slave Market* (Cambridge, MA: Harvard University Press, 2001); Edward E. Baptist, *The Half Has Never Been Told: Slavery and the Making of American Capitalism* (New York: Basic Books, 2014).
48. Melvin C. Johnson, *Polygamy on the Pedernales: Lyman Wight's Mormon Village in Antebellum Texas* (Logan: Utah State University Press, 2006).
49. Sidney Rigdon, "To the Honorable, the Senate and House of Representatives of Pennsylvania, in Legislative Capacity Assembled," *Times and Seasons* (Nauvoo, IL), February 1, 1844, 422.
50. *Council of Fifty*, 106.
51. *Council of Fifty*, 111–113; Reeve, *Let's Talk about Race*, 39.
52. *Council of Fifty*, 117–118.
53. "Editorial," *Latter Day Saints Millennial Star*, vol. 4, September 1843, 77.
54. "Slave Trade of the Sectarians!," *Prophet of the Jubilee* (Merthyr Tydfil, Wales) August 1849, in *Prophet of the Jubilee*, trans. and ed. Ronald D. Dennis (Provo, UT: Religious Studies Center, 1997), 187.
55. Dean L. May, "A Demographic Portrait of the Mormons, 1830–1980," in *The New Mormon History: Revisionist Essays on the Mormon Past*, ed. D. Michael Quinn (Salt Lake City: Signature Books, 1992), 124.
56. Brigham Young before Territorial Legislature, January 23, 1852, CR 100 912, Church History Department Pitman Shorthand transcriptions, 2013–2021, Addresses and sermons, 1851–1874, Miscellaneous transcriptions, 1869, 1872, 1889, 1848, 1851–1854, 1859–1863, Utah Territorial Legislature, January–February 1852, CHL.
57. Reeve, *Let's Talk about Race*, 40.
58. "Report from the Presidency," *Times and Seasons* (Nauvoo, IL), October 1840, 188.
59. Smith, *General Smith's Views*, 11.
60. *Council of Fifty*, 268.

Chapter 3

1. James R. Clark, comp., *Messages of the First Presidency*, 6 vols. (Salt Lake City: Bookcraft, 1965), 1:299.
2. Virginia Kerns, *Sally in Three Worlds: An Indian Captive in the House of Brigham Young* (Salt Lake City: University of Utah Press, 2021).
3. Amy Tanner Thiriot, *Slavery in Zion: A Documentary and Genealogical History of Black Lives and Black Servitude in Utah Territory, 1847–1862* (Salt Lake City: University of Utah Press, 2022), chapters 1–4.
4. Manisha Sinha, *The Slave's Cause: A History of Abolition* (New Haven, CT: Yale University Press, 2016), 481–485.
5. Although the Wilmot Proviso only affected land obtained from Mexico, it significantly influenced discussions concerning the organization of the Oregon Country lately acquired from Great Britain. In August 1848, Congress ratified Oregon's existing ban on slavery and involuntary servitude. Even so, a number of slave owners in the territory retained their slaves in contravention of the organic act. Others may have entered indenture contracts with their slaves. When Oregon passed a state constitution in 1857, a significant minority of the electorate voted for Oregon to enter the Union as a slave state. Although this proposal failed, over three-fourths

of the electorate voted for Oregon to prohibit free African Americans from residing within its boundaries. R. Alton Lee, "Slavery and the Oregon Territorial Issue: Prelude to the Compromise of 1850," *Pacific Northwest Quarterly* 64, no. 3 (July 1973): 112–119; Fred Lockley, "Some Documentary Records of Slavery in Oregon," *Quarterly of the Oregon Historical Society* 17, no. 2 (June 1916): 107–115; Quintard Taylor, "Slaves and Free Men: Blacks in the Oregon Country, 1840–1860," *Oregon Historical Quarterly* 83, no. 2 (Summer 1982): 153–170.
6. Historian's Office, General Church Minutes, 1839–1877, March 26, 1847, CHL; W. Paul Reeve, *Religion of a Different Color: Race and the Mormon Struggle for Whiteness* (New York: Oxford University Press, 2015), 131.
7. General Church Minutes, December 3, 1847, CHL.
8. Reeve, *Religion of a Different Color*, 106–139.
9. Reeve, *Religion of a Different Color*, 128–148; Newell G. Bringhurst, *Saints, Slaves and Blacks: The Changing Place of Black People within Mormonism*, 2nd. ed. (Salt Lake City: Greg Kofford Books, 2018), 77–100.
10. Thiriot, *Slavery in Zion*, 110.
11. Ordinances of the High Council, December 27, 1847, in Dale L. Morgan, *The State of Deseret* (Logan: Utah State University Press, 1987), 196;Peter L. Crawley, "The Constitution of the State of Deseret," *BYU Studies* 29, no. 4 (Fall 1989): 8.
12. Ordinances of the High Council, in Morgan, *State of Deseret*; Christopher B. Rich Jr., "The True Policy for Utah: Servitude, Slavery, and 'An Act in Relation to Service,'" *Utah Historical Quarterly* 80, no. 1 (Winter 2012): 61.
13. Hosea Stout, *On the Mormon Frontier: The Diary of Hosea Stout, 1844–1861*, ed. Juanita Brooks, 2 vols. (Salt Lake City: University of Utah Press and Utah State Historical Society, 1964), 2:375; An Ordinance to Incorporate Great Salt Lake City, January 9, 1851, and An Ordinance, in Reference to Vagrants, February 10, 1851, in Morgan, *State of Deseret*, 163–169, 192.
14. Stout, *On the Mormon Frontier*, 2:348; Robert Glass Cleland and Juanita Brooks, eds., *A Mormon Chronicle: The Diaries of John D. Lee, 1848–1876* (San Marino, CA: Huntington Library, 1955); Historical Department Journal History of the Church, March 2–4, 1849, CR 100 137, CHL (hereafter Journal History); John G. Turner, *Brigham Young: Pioneer Prophet* (Cambridge, MA: Harvard University Press, 2012), 185–87.
15. Journal History, January 1, 1849.
16. Morgan, *State of Deseret*, 15–18; Crawley, "Constitution of the State of Deseret," 8; Leonard J. Arrington, *Great Basin Kingdom: An Economic History of the Latter-day Saints, 1830–1900* (Urbana: University of Illinois Press, 2005), chapter 4.
17. Wilford Woodruff to Orson Pratt, March 1, 1849, Journal History, March 1, 1849.
18. James K. Polk, Fourth Annual Message to Congress, December 5, 1848, University of Virginia, Miller Center, Presidential Speeches, https://millercenter.org/the-presidency/presidential-speeches/december-5-1848-fourth-annual-message-congress.
19. *Congressional Globe*, 30th Cong., 2nd Sess. (Washington, D.C.: Blair and Rives, 1849), 33; Fergus M. Bordewich, *America's Great Debate: Henry Clay, Stephen A. Douglas, and the Compromise That Preserved the Union* (New York: Simon & Schuster, 2012), 40.
20. Thomas L. Kane to Willard Richards, April 25, 1847, MS 1490, box 4, folder 9, CHL.
21. Willard Richards to Thomas Kane, June 5, 1848, MS 1490, box 3, folder 9, CHL; Willard Richard to Thomas L. Kane, July 25, 1849, MS 1490, box 3, folder 10, CHL.
22. Matthew J. Grow and Ronald W. Walker, *The Prophet and the Reformer: The Letters of Brigham Young and Thomas L. Kane* (New York: Oxford University Press, 2015), 67–68.
23. Dan Vogel, ed., *The Wilford Woodruff Journals*, Typescript, 6 vols. (Salt Lake City: Benchmark Books, 2020), November 26, 1848, 3:513–515.
24. Crawley, "Constitution of the State of Deseret," 7–22; Morgan, *State of Deseret*.
25. Wilford Woodruff to Thomas L. Kane, November 27, 1849, MS 1352, box 6, folder 4, CHL.
26. "Memorial," in *Report of the Debates in the Convention of California, on the Formation of the State Constitution, in September and October, 1849*, ed. J. Ross Browne (Washington: John T. Towers, 1850), XIV–XXIII, XIX.
27. *Wilford Woodruff Journals*, November 26, 1848, 3:514.
28. Woodruff to Kane, November 27, 1849, CH.
29. Bringhurst, *Saints, Slaves, and Blacks*, 219; Thiriot, *Slavery in Zion*, 88.
30. Benjamin Mathews to Brigham Young, March 31, 1849, Brigham Young Office Files, CR 1234 1, box 21, folder 16, CHL.

31. Francis McKown to Brigham Young, March 31, 1849, Brigham Young Office Files, CR 1234 1, box 21, folder 16, CHL; Thiriot, *Slavery in Zion*, 10, 59, 87, 243–245, 356.
32. Brigham Young to John Bernhisel, July 19, 1849, Brigham Young Office Files, CR 1234 1, box 16, folder 17, CHL.
33. Brigham Young to Orson Hyde, July 19, 1849, Brigham Young Office Files, CR 1234 1, box 16, folder 17, CHL.
34. Willard Richards to Thomas L. Kane, July 25, 1849, CHL; "Sentiment from the Valley by Last Mail," *Frontier Guardian*, September 19, 1849.
35. Brigham Young, Heber C. Kimball, Willard Richards, to Amasa Lyman, September 5, 1849, Brigham Young Office Files, CR 1234 1, box 16, folder 18, CHL.
36. In 1854, Latter-day Saints attempted to bar the common law from being cited as precedent in Utah's territorial courts. The Mormon leadership, particularly Brigham Young, was openly hostile toward Anglo-American legal practices in general. However, the common law's position on bigamy may have been particularly concerning after the public announcement of plural marriage in 1852. See Jerrold S. Jensen, "The Common Law of England in the Territory of Utah," *Utah Historical Quarterly* 60, no. 1 (Winter 1992): 4–26; Michael W. Homer, "The Judiciary and the Common Law in Utah Territory, 1850–61," *Dialogue: A Journal of Mormon Thought* 21, no. 1 (Spring 1988): 97–108.
37. George Van Cleve, "*Somerset's Case* and Its Antecedents in Imperial Perspective," *Law and History Review* 24, no. 3 (Fall 2006): 601–645; Krista J. Kesselring, "Slavery and Cartwright's Case before *Somerset*," *Legal History Miscellany*, October 10, 2018, https://legalhistorymiscellany.com/2018/10/10/slavery-and-cartwrights-case-before-somerset/
38. "From Utah," *National Era* (Washington, D.C.), January 23, 1851; Reeve, *Religion of a Different Color*, 142.
39. Young, Kimball, Richards, to Lyman, September 5, 1849, CHL.
40. Young, Kimball, Richards, to Lyman, September 5, 1849, CHL.
41. "Deseret Asks Admittance to California," *Deseret News*, July 5, 1850; Frederic A. Culmer and John Wilson, "General John Wilson, Signer of the Deseret Petition: Including Letters from the Leonard Collection," *California Historical Society Quarterly* 26, no. 4 (December 1947): 321–348; Rich, "True Policy for Utah," 62.
42. "Slavery and the Mormons," *Frontier Guardian*, January 23, 1850, 2.
43. John Bernhisel to Brigham Young, March 21, 1850, Brigham Young Office Files, CR 1234 1, box 60, folder 9, CHL. Emphasis in original.
44. John Bernhisel to Brigham Young, July 3, 1850, Brigham Young Office Files, CR 1234 1, box 60, folder 10, CHL; see also John Bernhisel to Brigham Young, February 5, 1850; John Bernhisel to Brigham Young, September 7, 1850, Brigham Young Office Files, CR 1234 1, box 60, folder 10, CHL.
45. See, e.g., *Congressional Globe*, 31st Cong., 1st Sess. (Washington, D.C.: John C. Rives, 1850), 233–237.
46. Thomas L. Kane to Brigham Young, February 19, 1851, in Grow and Walker, *Prophet and the Reformer*, 94–106; *Congressional Globe*, 31st Cong., 1st Sess., 1702–1703.
47. New York law then permitted enslavers to temporarily bring enslaved persons into the state for up to six months.
48. *Congressional Globe*, 31st Cong., 1st Sess., 1703; Nathaniel R. Ricks, "A Peculiar Place for the Peculiar Institution: Slavery and Sovereignty in Early Territorial Utah" (Master's thesis, Brigham Young University, 2007), 55–63, 80–86.
49. Lewis Cass to A.P.O. Nicholson, December 24, 1847, originally published as "A Letter from Gen. Cass in Relation to the War and the Wilmot Proviso," *Washington Union* (Washington, D.C.) December 30, 1847, 2.
50. Sean Wilentz, *No Property in Man: Slavery and Antislavery at the Nation's Founding* (Cambridge, MA: Harvard University Press, 2018), 234–235.
51. An Act to Establish a Territorial Government for Utah, September 9, 1850, https://codes.findlaw.com/ut/organic-act-of-the-territory-of-utah/ut-organic-act-territorial-act.html.
52. See, e.g., *Appendix to the Congressional Globe*, 31st Cong., 1st Sess., 372.
53. Bordewich, *America's Great Debate*, 102, 127, 374–375. In 1854, Stephen Douglas and his colleagues determined to extend the still ambiguous concept of popular sovereignty to the new territories of Kansas and Nebraska consisting of the remaining unorganized land in the Louisiana Purchase. In doing so, they consciously abrogated the Missouri Compromise under which these lands would have remained free in perpetuity.

262   NOTES

54. Dred Scott v. Sandford, 60 U.S. 393 (1856). As early as June 1857, Stephen Douglas undertook a campaign to prove Justice Taney wrong. Without repudiating the legitimacy of the Supreme Court or the *Dred Scott* decision, he argued that the residents of a territory could still effectively exclude slavery by failing to enact local "police regulations" to protect it. He more famously annunciated this so-called Freeport Doctrine during a debate with Abraham Lincoln in August 1858 and then in an article in *Harper's Magazine* the next year.
55. John Bernhisel to Brigham Young, November 9, 1850, Brigham Young Office Files, CR 1234 1, box 60, folder 10, CHL; John Bernhisel to Brigham Young, September 12, 1850, Brigham Young Office Files, CR 1234 1, box 60, folder 10, CHL.
56. Bernhisel to Young, July 3, 1850, CHL.
57. Utah Territorial Census, 1850, MS 11309, CHL; Utah Territorial Census, 1851, MS 2672, CHL.
58. United States, 1850 Census, California.
59. Bringhurst, *Saints, Slaves, and Blacks*, 219; Thiriot, *Slavery in Zion*, 88.
60. John W. Gunnison, *The Mormons, or, Latter-day Saints, in the Valley of the Great Salt Lake* (Philadelphia: Lippincott, Grambo, 1852), 143.
61. "From Utah," *National Era*, January 23, 1851.
62. Orson Hyde, "Slavery among the Mormons," *Frontier Guardian*, December 11, 1850, 2.
63. Hyde, "Slavery among the Mormons," 2.
64. Hyde, "Slavery among the Mormons," 2.
65. Hyde, "Slavery among the Mormons," 2.
66. Hyde, "Slavery among the Mormons," 2.
67. Quoted in Paul Finkelman, *An Imperfect Union: Slavery, Federalism, and Comity* (Clark, NJ: Lawbook Exchange, 2000), 174.
68. Stacey L. Smith, *Freedom's Frontier: California and the Struggle over Unfree Labor, Emancipation, and Reconstruction* (Chapel Hill: University of North Carolina Press, 2013) 129–131; "Suit for Freedom," *Los Angeles Star*, February 2, 1856.
69. Finkelman, *Imperfect Union*, 119–123; "Suit for Freedom," *Los Angeles Star*, February 2, 1856.
70. For evidence of freedom suits and other organized abolitionist methods see Manisha Sinha, *The Slave's Cause: A History of Abolition* (New Haven, CT: Yale University Press, 2016), 17, 67–69, 84, 92, 175–176.
71. Duritha Lewis, Slave Registration, Utah Territory, Third District, Probate Court Records, series 373, reel 6, box 5, folder 11, UDARS; Affidavit of Dianah Camp in Regard to Negro Boy Shepherd, filed July 10, 1856, series 373, reel 5, box 4, folder 26, UDARS; Affidavit of Williams Camp in Regard to Negro Boy Shepard, filed July 10 1856, series 373, reel 5, box 4, folder 26, UDARS.
72. William Crosby to Brigham Young, March 12, 1851, Brigham Young Office Files, CR 1234 1, box 22, folder 6, CHL; Brigham Young to William Crosby, March 12, 1851, Brigham Young Office Files, CR 1234 1, box 22, folder 6, CHL.
73. Crosby to Young, March 12, 1851, CHL.
74. Young to Crosby, March 12, 1851, CHL; Turner, *Brigham Young*, 224; Thiriot, *Slavery in Zion*, 98–100, 172, 356–357.
75. Journal History, March 26, 1851; Turner, *Brigham Young*, 224–225; Thiriot, *Slavery in Zion*, 16–18, 19, 36–37, 99–100, 108–114, 151–154, 205–209.
76. Thomas Kane to Brigham Young, February 19, 1851, in Grow and Walker, *Prophet and the Reformer*, 94–106.
77. James M. Monroe to Brigham Young, March 22, 1851, Brigham Young Office Files, CR 1234 1, box 22, folder 9, CHL.
78. Vogel, *Wilford Woodruff Journals*, 2:473; Young referred to Isaac James who worked as his coachman and Jane Manning James who was a servant in his household. See "A List of President Brigham Young's Family Residing in the 18th Ward," March 19, 1855, Brigham Young Office Files, CR 1234 1, Miscellaneous files, 1832–1878, Family information, c. 1853–1858, CHL.
79. A number of antislavery Northerners, such as William Channing, Daniel Webster, and even someone like Moses Stuart held similar views. See Jordan T. Watkins, *Slavery and Sacred Texts: The Bible, the Constitution, and Historical Consciousness in Antebellum America* (Cambridge: Cambridge University Press, 2021).
80. Vogel, *Wilford Woodruff Journals*, 2:473.
81. David M. Goldenberg, *The Curse of Ham: Race and Slavery in Early Judaism, Christianity, and Islam* (Princeton, NJ: Princeton University Press, 2003), 1.

Chapter 4

1. Don Pedro León Luján (1794–after 1870) was born in Abiquiú, New Mexico. He was fifty-seven years old when he set out on his expedition to Utah Territory in 1851. He was of moderate wealth and served in militia campaigns against Navajos in the 1830s. He traded for years among the Ute before his arrest and trial and had christened two Ute Indian boys, one in 1833 and one in 1840, who worked as his servants. Following his trial in Utah, he served as a militia officer in campaigns against Jicarilla Apache in the 1850s. His trial and conviction in Utah Territory did not stop his human trafficking. In 1870 his household included two Paiute boys, one eleven years of age and the other fourteen. See Sondra Jones, *The Trial of Don Pedro León Luján: The Attack against Indian Slavery and Mexican Traders in Utah* (Salt Lake City: University of Utah Press, 2000), chapter 4.
2. Leland Doland, *Aboriginal Slavery on the Northwest Coast of North America* (Berkeley: University of California Press, 1997), 33–34; Orlando Patterson, *Slavery and Social Death: A Comparative Study* (Cambridge, MA: Harvard University Press, 1982), 149; Brett Rushforth, *Bonds of Alliance: Indigenous and Atlantic Slaveries in New France* (Chapel Hill: University of North Carolina Press, 2013), 19–34, 59–65; James A. Brooks, *Captives and Cousins: Slavery, Kinship, and Community in the Southwest Borderlands* (Chapel Hill: University of North Carolina Press, 2002), 47; Christina Snyder, *Slavery in Indian Country: The Changing Face of Captivity in Early America* (Cambridge, MA: Harvard University Press, 2010), 27–28, 35–40; Andrés Reséndez, *The Other Slavery: The Uncovered Story of Indian Enslavement in America* (Boston and New York: Houghton Mifflin Harcourt, 2016), 64–65, 194–195; William S. Kiser, *Borderlands of Slavery: The Struggle over Captivity and Peonage in the American Southwest* (Philadelphia: University of Pennsylvania Press, 2017), 1–2; Pekka Hämäläinen, *The Comanche Empire* (New Haven, CT: Yale University Press, 2008), 11, 26–27, 250–259.
3. This is true of the majority of slaveholding societies throughout history. David Brion Davis, *Inhuman Bondage: The Rise and Fall of Slavery in the New World* (New York: Oxford University Press, 2006), 38; Rushforth, *Bonds of Alliance*, 39–47.
4. Rushforth, *Bonds of Alliance*, 46–47; Brooks, *Captives and Cousins*, 187–193.
5. Brooks, *Captives and Cousins*.
6. Brooks, *Captives and Cousins*, 180n23.
7. Brooks, *Captives and Cousins*, 180–193, 242; Reséndez, *The Other Slavery*, 183; Rushforth, *Bonds of Alliance*, 47–52, 64–70.
8. Rushforth, *Bonds of Alliance*, 70.
9. Ned Blackhawk, *Violence over the Land: Indians and Empires in the Early American West* (Cambridge, MA: Harvard University Press, 2009), 70–80; Brooks, *Captives and Cousins*, 60–64, 71–72; Rushforth, *Bonds of Alliance*, 166–169, 174–180; Hämäläinen, *The Comanche Empire*, 45–46.
10. Brooks, *Captives and Cousins*, 71–72, 89–92, 115–116, 215–217, 225–228; Snyder, *Slavery in Indian Country*, 182–212; Reséndez, *The Other Slavery*, 184; Hämäläinen, *The Comanche Empire*, 244–259.
11. Robert C. Davis, *Christian Slaves, Muslim Masters: White Slavery in the Mediterranean, the Barbary Coast, and Italy, 1500–1800* (New York: Palgrave Macmillan, 2003), 3; Brian Glyn Williams, *The Sultan's Raiders: The Military Role of the Crimean Tatars in the Ottoman Empire* (Washington, D.C.: Jamestown Foundation, 2013), 27; Rushforth, *Bonds of Alliance*, 86, 148–149; Davis, *Inhuman Bondage*, 77–78; Brooks, *Captives and Cousins*, 18–40; Simon Shaw, *Moors in Mesoamerica: The Impact of Al-Andalus in the New World* (PhD diss., University of Bristol, 2010); David J. Weber, *The Spanish Frontier in North America* (New Haven, CT: Yale University Press, 1992), 20–21.
12. Ferdinand and Isabella presided over the enslavement of Muslims, Africans, and even Eastern Europeans, yet they had significant moral and legal reservations about the enslavement of Native Americans. They ultimately commissioned a study by prominent lawyers and theologians to determine if Native Americans could legally be enslaved. The study took five years to complete, and the results have unfortunately been lost. Reséndez, *The Other Slavery*, 25–28, 41–42; Rushforth, *Bonds of Alliance*, 110–114; Davis, *Inhuman Bondage*, 97.
13. Reséndez, *The Other Slavery*, 67–75, 89–90, 128–132, 136–137, 146–147; Brooks, *Captives and Cousins*, 123–124.
14. Brooks, *Captives and Cousins*, 123–127; Kiser, *Borderlands of Slavery*, 4; Reséndez, *The Other Slavery*, 106, 115–123, 140–142, 149–167, 182–183; Rushforth, *Bonds of Alliance*, 344–347.

15. Doland, *Aboriginal Slavery*, 33; Brooks, *Captives and Cousins*, 184–193, 246; Reséndez, *The Other Slavery*, 227–229; Rushforth, *Bonds of Alliance*, 39–71.
16. During the first decade of the eighteenth century, the Navajos and several other tribes even threatened an anti-Spanish revolt if the New Mexicans would not purchase captives from them. Reséndez, *The Other Slavery*, 179.
17. Reséndez, *The Other Slavery*, 177–179.
18. Hämäläinen, *The Comanche Empire*, 45–46.
19. Altamira to the viceroy, January 9, 1751, in *Historical Documents Relating to New Mexico, Nueva Vizeaya, and Approaches Thereto, to 1773*, ed. Charles Wilson Hacket, 3 vols. (Washington, D.C.: Carnegie Institution, 1923–1937), 3:332
20. Hämäläinen, *The Comanche Empire*, 45.
21. Brooks, *Captives and Cousins*, 125.
22. This was also true under the relatively liberal laws of slavery promulgated in medieval Spain. James F. Brooks, "'Lest We Go in Search of Relief to Our Lands and Our Nation': Customary Justice and Colonial Law in the New Mexico Borderlands, 1680–1821," in *The Many Legalities of Early America*, ed. Christopher L. Tomlins and Bruce H. Mann (Chapel Hill: University of North Carolina Press, 2001), 156.
23. Ramón A. Gutiérrez, *When Jesus Came the Corn Mothers Went Away: Marriage, Sexuality, and Power in New Mexico, 1500–1846* (Stanford, CA: Stanford University Press, 1991), 184.
24. Brooks, *Captives and Cousins*, 234–241.
25. Emancipated *genízaros* were granted the right to build their own villages on the frontiers that served as a buffer against attacks by nomadic tribes. They likewise engaged in numerous offensive operations and slave raids as military auxiliaries. Indeed, the term *genízaro* derives from the Janissaries, an elite corps of assimilated Christian slaves who fought on behalf of the Ottomans. Brooks, *Captives and Cousins*, 123–148, 298–299; Brooks, "Lest We Go in Search of Relief," 250–280; Weber, *The Spanish Frontier in North America*, 126–127; Reséndez, *The Other Slavery*, 180.
26. Brooks, *Captives and Cousins*, 234–241.
27. Much like in colonial Virginia, there was very little circulating currency in the frontiers of New Spain. As a result, offering one's labor or the labor of a dependent was perhaps the only method for poor people to secure a loan. Kiser, *Borderlands of Slavery*, 19.
28. Brooks, *Captives and Cousins*, 252, 299, 327–330, 345–349; Reséndez, *The Other Slavery*, 113, 238–240, 246–249, 292–293, 299–300; Howard R. Lamar, *The Far Southwest, 1846–1912: A Territorial History* (Albuquerque: University of New Mexico Press, 2000), 23–25; Kiser, *Borderlands of Slavery*, 11–13, 16–18.
29. Brooks, *Captives and Cousins*, 299.
30. Virginia Kerns, *Sally in Three Worlds: An Indian Captive in the House of Brigham Young* (Salt Lake City: University of Utah Press, 2021), chapters 7–11.
31. For the story of Baptiste and the two teenage captives see Brigham Young, testimony in U.S. v Pedro León case of libel, January 15, 1852, First District Court, Minute Book, 1851–1896, series 10035, reel 1, 46, UDARS; and Kerns, *Sally in Three Worlds*, chapter 1. For information on the Indian slave trade in Utah Territory see Jones, *The Trial of Don Pedro León Luján*, chapters 1 and 3; Michael Bennion, "Captivity, Adoption, Marriage and Identity: Native American Children in Mormon Homes, 1847–1900" (Master's thesis, University of Nevada-Las Vegas, 2012), and Brian Q. Cannon, "'To Buy Up the Lamanite Children as Fast as They Could': Indentured Servitude and Its Legacy in Mormon Society," *Journal of Mormon History* 44 (Spring 2018): 1–36. For a broader understanding of Mormon Indian relations in general see W. Paul Reeve, *Religion of a Different Color: Race and the Mormon Struggle for Whiteness* (New York: Oxford University Press, 2015), chapters 2 and 3; Sondra Jones, *Being and Becoming Ute: The Story of an American Indian People* (Salt Lake City: University of Utah Press, 2019); Brent M. Rogers, *Unpopular Sovereignty: Mormons and the Federal Management of Early Utah Territory* (Lincoln: University of Nebraska Press, 2017), chapter 3; W. Paul Reeve, *Making Space on the Western Frontier: Mormons, Miners, and Southern Paiute* (Urbana: University of Illinois Press, 2006); Jared Farmer, *On Zion's Mount: Mormons, Indians, and the American Landscape* (Cambridge, MA: Harvard University Press, 2008); Gregory Smoak, *Ghost Dances and Identity: Prophetic Religion and American Indian Ethnogenesis in the Nineteenth Century* (Berkley: University of California Press, 2006); Darren Parry, *The Bear River Massacre: A Shoshone History* (Salt Lake City: By Common Consent Press, 2019); John Alton Peterson, *Utah's Blackhawk War* (Salt Lake City: University of Utah Press, 1998); Scott R. Christensen, *Sagwitch: Shoshone Chieftain, Mormon Elder, 1822–1887* (Logan: Utah State

University Press, 1999). Brigham D. Madsen, *The Shoshoni Frontier and the Bear River Massacre* (Salt Lake City: University of Utah Press, 1985); and Blackhawk, *Violence over the Land*.
32. Stephen P. Van Hoak, "Waccara's Utes: Native American Equestrian Adaptations in the Eastern Great Basin, 1776–1886," *Utah Historical Quarterly* 67 (Fall 1999): 309–330; Ronald W. Walker, "Wakara Meets the Mormons: A Case Study in Native American Accommodation, 1848–1852," *Utah Historical Quarterly* 70 (Summer 2002): 215–237; Jones, *Being and Becoming Ute*, chapters 4–6; Blackhawk, *Violence over the Land*, 139–141, 145, 234–245.
33. Brigham Young, testimony in U.S. v Pedro León case of libel, 47, UDARS.
34. Brigham Young, testimony in U.S. v Pedro León case of libel, 45, UDARS.
35. Jones, *The Trial of Don Pedro León Luján*, 4, 66–69.
36. Jones, *The Trial of Don Pedro León Luján*, 61–70.
37. See An Act to Regulate Trade and Intercourse with the Indian Tribes, and to Preserve Peace on the Frontiers, June 30, 1834, in *Statutes at Large*, vol. 4, 23rd Cong., 1st Sess. (Boston: Charles C. Little and James Brown, 1846), 729–730. Section 4 of the act prescribes the penalty.
38. Jones, *The Trial of Don Pedro León Luján*, 74–81, 88–89; "First Judicial Court," *Deseret News*, March 6, 1852, 4; John Greiner to Luke Lea, May 19, 1852, in *Official Correspondence of James S. Calhoun while Indian Agent at Santa Fe and Superintendent of Indian Affairs in New Mexico*, ed. Annie Heloise Abel (Washington, D.C.: Government Printing office, 1915), 536.
39. For a more thorough account of the trial see Jones, *The Trial of Don Pedro León Luján*, chapter 5.
40. Dan Vogel, ed., *The Wilford Woodruff Journals*, Typescript, 6 vols. (Salt Lake City: Benchmark Books, 2020), 2:473.
41. "Governor's Message," *Deseret* News (Salt Lake City, Utah), January 10, 1852, 18.
42. United States, 1850 Census, New Jersey.
43. Nathaniel R. Ricks, "A Peculiar Place for the Peculiar Institution: Slavery and Sovereignty in Early Territorial Utah" (Master's thesis, Brigham Young University, 2007), 101–103. John Brown from Mississippi brought an enslaved eleven-year-old girl named Betsy to Utah with him and his family in 1848. See Juli Huddleston, "Betsy Brown Fluellen," Century of Black Mormons, https://exhibits.lib.utah.edu/s/century-of-black-mormons/page/fluellen-betsy-brown.
44. Utah Territorial Legislature, Debate on Indian Slavery, possibly beginning January 23, 1852, CR 100 912, Church History Department Pitman Shorthand transcriptions, 2013–2021, Addresses and sermons, 1851–1874, Miscellaneous transcriptions, 1869, 1872, 1889, 1848, 1851–1854, 1859–1863, Utah Territorial Legislature, January–February 1852 CHL.
45. "Governor's Message," January 10, 1852, 18.
46. Stacey L. Smith, *Freedom's Frontier: California and the Struggle over Unfree Labor, Emancipation, and Reconstruction* (Chapel Hill: University of North Carolina Press, 2013), 135–136.
47. John G. Turner, *Brigham Young: Pioneer Prophet* (Cambridge, MA: Harvard University Press, 2012), 7–8, 14.
48. Newell G. Bringhurst, *Saints, Slaves and Blacks: The Changing Place of Black People within Mormonism*, 2nd ed. (Salt Lake City: Greg Kofford Books, 2018), 61n65.
49. "Governor's Message," January 10, 1852, 18.
50. An Act Concerning Masters and Apprentices, in *Acts, Resolutions, and Memorials, Passed by the First Annual, and Special Sessions of the Legislative Assembly of the Territory of Utah, Begun and Held at Great Salt Lake City, on the 22nd Day of September, A. D. 1851* (Salt Lake City: Brigham H. Young, Printer, 1852), 75–78.
51. "Governor's Message," January 10, 1852, 18.
52. Brigham Young, draft, January 5, 1852, Brigham Young Office Files, Governor's Messages to Territorial Legislature, 1851–1857, CR 1234 1, CHL.
53. "Governor's Message," January 10, 1852, 18.
54. Vogel, *Wilford Woodruff Journals*, 2:473.
55. Joseph Smith, Jr., *General Smith's Views of the Powers and Policy of the Government of the United States* (Nauvoo, IL: J. Taylor Printing, 1844), 7.
56. Davis, *Inhuman Bondage*, chapter 12, 310–311. It should be noted that the British program of compensated emancipation required emancipated slaves to continue to work for their masters for a further four years as apprentices.
57. Davis, *Inhuman Bondage*, chapter 13; Manisha Sinha, *The Slave's Cause: A History of Abolition* (New Haven, CT: Yale University Press, 2016), chapter 3.
58. It is not clear if Young ever considered Blackstone's position that even where slavery was not legal under the common law, a slave might still be required to provide service to his or her master as a servant.

59. "Governor's Message," January 10, 1852, 18. Almost seventy years before, the Connecticut clergyman Levi Hart had similarly argued that Black children who were freed under gradual emancipation statutes should be required to labor for a time in order to repay their masters "an equivalent for their education." Joanne Pope Melish, *Disowning Slavery: Gradual Emancipation and "Race" in New England, 1780–1860* (Ithaca, NY: Cornell University Press, 1989), 61.
60. "Governor's Message," January 10, 1852, 18.
61. "Governor's Message," January 10, 1852, 18.
62. "Governor's Message," January 10, 1852, 18.
63. Leonard J. Arrington, *Great Basin Kingdom: An Economic History of the Latter-day Saints, 1830–1900* (Urbana: University of Illinois Press, 2005), 139, 145, 312, 497.
64. Edmund S. Morgan, *American Slavery, American Freedom: The Ordeal of Colonial Virginia* (New York: W. W. Norton, 1975), 177–178.
65. Arrington, *Great Basin Kingdom*, 134–141, 355–356.
66. Horace Greeley, "Letter of Horace Greeley. Two Hours with Brigham Young," *New York Herald*, August 24, 1859, 2.
67. *Journals of the House of Representatives, Council, and Joint Sessions of the First Annual and Special Sessions of the Legislative Assembly of the Territory of Utah. Held at Great Salt Lake City, 1851 and 1852* (Great Salt Lake City, Utah: Brigham H. Young, printer, 1852), 85.
68. Brigham Young, testimony in U.S. v Pedro León case of libel, 46–47, UDARS.
69. Jones, *The Trial of Don Pedro León Luján*, 101–102; Kerns, *Sally in Three Worlds*, chapter 7.
70. Isaac Morley, testimony in U.S. v Pedro León case of libel, January 15, 1852, First District Court, Minute Book, 1851–1896, series 10035, reel 1, 47–48, UDARS.
71. Vogel, *Wilford Woodruff Journals*, 2:473.
72. George A. Smith, December 26, 27, 1850, Journal of George A. Smith President of the Iron County Mission, Commenced December 7th 1850, George A. Smith papers, MS 1322, box 2, folder 5, CHL.
73. Phillipe Santiago Archuleta, testimony in U.S. v Pedro León case of libel, January 16, 1852, First District Court Case Files, series 25011, reel 1, box 10, folder 12, 325–328, UDARS.
74. First District Court, Minute Book, 1851–1896, series 10035, reel 1, 52–53, UDARS.
75. *Journals of the House of Representatives, Council, and Joint Sessions*, 85.
76. Utah Territorial Legislature, Debate on Indian Slavery, possibly beginning January 23, 1852, CR 100 912, Church History Department Pitman Shorthand transcriptions, 2013–2021, Addresses and sermons, 1851–1874, Miscellaneous transcriptions, 1869, 1872, 1889, 1848, 1851–1854, 1859–1863, Utah Territorial Legislature, January–February 1852, CHL.
77. "First Judicial Court," *Deseret News*, March 6, 1852, 4.
78. An Act to Regulate Trade and Intercourse with the Indian Tribes, 729.
79. An Act to Regulate Trade and Intercourse with the Indian Tribes, 729–730.
80. Jones, *The Trial of Don Pedro León Luján*, 83; for a more thorough discussion of the complicated nature of the legal arguments regarding Indian country, see also 82–85.
81. *Statutes at Large and Treaties of the United States of America*, vol. 9, 31st Cong., 2nd Sess. (Boston, MA: Little, Brown, 1862), 587.
82. Jones, *The Trial of Don Pedro León Luján*, 84–85; "First Judicial Court," *Deseret News*, March 6, 1852, 4.
83. "First Judicial Court," *Deseret News*, March 6, 1852, 4.
84. John Greiner, Santa Fe, New Mexico, to Luke Lea, Washington D.C., May 19, 1852, in *Official Correspondence of James S. Calhoun*, 536–537; Jones, *The Trial of Don Pedro León Luján*, 90.
85. Jones, *The Trial of Don Pedro León Luján*, 90.

Chapter 5

1. Ned Blackhawk, *Violence over the Land: Indians and Empires in the Early American West* (Cambridge, MA: Harvard University Press, 2009), 70–80; James A. Brooks, *Captives and Cousins: Slavery, Kinship, and Community in the Southwest Borderlands* (Chapel Hill: University of North Carolina Press, 2002), 60–64, 71–72; Stacey L. Smith, *Freedom's Frontier: California and the Struggle over Unfree Labor, Emancipation, and Reconstruction* (Chapel Hill: University of North Carolina Press, 2013), 18–24; William S. Kiser, *Borderlands of Slavery: The Struggle over Captivity and Peonage in the American Southwest* (Philadelphia: University of Pennsylvania Press, 2017), chapter 3.
2. Smith, *Freedom's Frontier*, 18–24.

3. An Act for the Government and Protection of Indians, in *The Statutes of California Passed at the First Session of the Legislature* (San Jose: J. Winchester, State Printer, 1850), 409.
4. An Act for the Government and Protection of Indians, 408–410.
5. An Act to Provide for the Appointment and Prescribe the Duties of Guardians, in *The Statutes of California Passed at the First Session of the Legislature*, 268–273.
6. Smith, *Freedom's Frontier*, 109–140.
7. Smith, *Freedom's Frontier*, 122–123, 147–148.
8. Smith, *Freedom's Frontier*, 133–134, 139–140, 156–161.
9. An Act Amendatory of an Act entitled "An Act for the Government and Protection of Indians," passed April twenty-second, one thousand eight hundred and fifty (April 18, 1860), in *Statutes of California Passed at the Eleventh Session of the Legislature, 1860* (Sacramento: Charles T. Botts, State Printer, 1860), 196.
10. Smith, *Freedom's Frontier*, 184.
11. An Act for the Repeal of Section Three of an Act for the Protection and Government of Indians, passed May twenty-second, one thousand eight hundred and fifty, and Section One of an Act amendatory thereof, passed April eighteenth, one thousand eight hundred and sixty (April 27, 1863) in *Statutes of California Passed at the Fourteenth Session of the Legislature, 1863* (Sacramento: Benjamin P. Avery, State Printer, 1863), 743.
12. Smith, *Freedom's Frontier*, 183–191.
13. Brooks, *Captives and Cousins*, 299, 327–329.
14. Michael Steck to William P. Dole, January 13, 1864, in Kiser, *Borderlands of Slavery*, 1.
15. Law regulating contracts between masters and servants, July 24, 1851, in *Acts, Resolutions, and Memorials of the Legislative Assembly of the Territory of New Mexico, Passed at a Session Begun and Held June 2, A.D. 1851* (Santa Fe: James L. Collins & Co., Printers, 1852), 183–185.
16. It was not until several complaints were presented before the federal judiciary that the law appeared to have any effect at all. In January 1857, shortly before the U.S. Supreme Court decided *Dred Scott*, two such cases came before the Territorial Supreme Court. In both cases, the court ordered peons to be released from servitude based on various abuses. However, the court still upheld the basic legality of peonage as long as it was "formed by mutual contract." *Jaremillo v. Romero*, 1 N.M., 206 (1857). See Robert F. Casto, "Rescuing Catalina: Law, Storytelling, and Unearthing the Hidden History of Southwestern Slavery," *Berkeley La Raza Law Journal* 12 (2000): 123–135; Laura E. Gomez, "Off-White in an Age of White Supremacy: Mexican Elites and the Rights of Indians and Blacks in Nineteenth-Century New Mexico," *Chicana/o Latina/o Law Review* 25, no. 1 (2005): 9–59; William S. Kiser, "A 'Charming Name for a Species of Slavery': Political Debate on Debt Peonage in the Southwest, 1840s–1860s," *Western Historical Quarterly* 45 (Summer 2014): 179; Kiser, *Borderlands of Slavery*, 12–22.
17. Brooks, *Captives and Cousins*, 345–349; Kiser, *Borderlands of Slavery*, 12–22.
18. *Congressional Globe*, 39th Cong., 2nd Sess. (Washington, D.C.: F. and J. Rives, 1867), 240.
19. *Congressional Globe*, 39th Cong., 2nd Sess., 240.
20. *Congressional Globe*, 39th Cong., 2nd Sess., 240.
21. An Act to Abolish and Forever Prohibit the System of Peonage in the Territory of New Mexico and Other Parts of the United States, March 2, 1867, in *Statues at Large, Treaties, and Proclamations, of the United States of America from December, 1865, to March, 1867* (Boston: Little, Brown, 1868), 546; Aviam Soifer, "Federal Protection, Paternalism, and the Virtually Forgotten Prohibition of Voluntary Peonage," *Columbia Law Review* 112 (2012): 1607–1639.
22. Brooks, *Captives and Cousins*, 351–353; William Aloysius Keleher, *Turmoil in New Mexico, 1846–1868* (Santa Fe: Rydal Press, 1952), 471; Gomez, "Off-White in an Age of White Supremacy," 47–56.
23. *Journals of the House of Representatives, Council, and Joint Sessions of the First Annual and Special Sessions of the Legislative Assembly of the Territory of Utah. Held at Great Salt Lake City, 1851 and 1852* (Great Salt Lake City: Brigham H. Young, printer, 1852), 85.
24. Utah Territorial Legislature, Debate on Indian Slavery, possibly beginning January 23, 1852, CR 100 912, Church History Department Pitman Shorthand transcriptions, 2013–2021, Addresses and sermons, 1851–1874, Miscellaneous transcriptions, 1869, 1872, 1889, 1848, 1851–1854, 1859–1863, Utah Territorial Legislature, January–February 1852, CHL.
25. George A. Smith, December 26, 27, 1850, Journal of George A. Smith President of the Iron County Mission, Commenced December 7, 1850, George A. Smith Papers, MS 1322, box 2, folder 5, CHL; Sondra Jones, *The Trial of Don Pedro León Luján: The Attack against Indian*

Slavery and Mexican Traders in Utah (Salt Lake City: University of Utah Press, 2000), 41–52, 74, 99–119.
26. Michael Bennion, "Captivity, Adoption, Marriage and Identity: Native American Children in Mormon Homes, 1847–1900" (Master's thesis, University of Nevada-Las Vegas, 2012), 246.
27. Bennion, "Captivity, Adoption, Marriage and Identity," 246.
28. *Journals of the House of Representatives, Council, and Joint Sessions*, 85.
29. Utah Territorial Legislature, Debate on Indian Slavery.
30. Utah Territorial Legislature, Debate on Indian Slavery.
31. A Preamble and An Act for the Relief of Indian Slaves and Prisoners, in *Acts, Resolutions, and Memorials, Passed by the First Annual, and Special Sessions of the Legislative Assembly of the Territory of Utah, Begun and Held at Great Salt Lake City, on the 22nd Day of September, A. D. 1851* (Salt Lake City: Brigham H. Young, Printer, 1852), 91–94.
32. Utah Territorial Legislature, Debate on Indian Slavery; An Act for the Relief of Indian Slaves and Prisoners, 93–94.
33. An Act Concerning Masters and Apprentices, in *Acts, Resolutions, and Memorials*, 75–78; for examples dealing with vagrancy see *Acts, Resolutions, and Memorials*, 183, 191, 199.
34. "Governor's Message," *Deseret News*, January 10, 1852, 18.
35. A Preamble and An Act for the Relief of Indian Slaves and Prisoners, 91–94; Utah Territorial Legislature, Debate on Indian Slavery.
36. *Journals of the House of Representatives, Council, and Joint Sessions*, 89–90.
37. Utah Territorial Legislature, Debate on Indian Slavery.
38. Utah Territorial Legislature, Debate on Indian Slavery.
39. Watt recorded the name of this speaker as "Pratt," but the speech immediately follows Pratt and disagrees with Pratt. The sentiments expressed most closely reflect those articulated by George A. Smith in the rest of the debate.
40. Utah Territorial Legislature, Debate on Indian Slavery.
41. *Congressional Globe*, 31st Cong., 1st Sess. (Washington, D.C.: John C. Rives, 1850), 1135.
42. *Congressional Globe*, 31st Cong., 1st Sess., 1135–1136; 1141–1144.
43. *Congressional Globe*, 31st Cong., 1st Sess., 1135–1136; 1141–1144.
44. Utah Territorial Legislature, Debate on Indian Slavery.
45. Utah Territorial Legislature, Debate on Indian Slavery.
46. Utah Territorial Legislature, Debate on Indian Slavery.
47. Utah Territorial Legislature, Debate on Indian Slavery.
48. Utah Territorial Legislature, Debate on Indian Slavery.
49. Utah Territorial Legislature, Debate on Indian Slavery.
50. Utah Territorial Legislature, Debate on Indian Slavery.
51. An Act for the Relief of Indian Slaves and Prisoners, 93.
52. Utah Territorial Legislature, Debate on Indian Slavery.
53. Utah Territorial Legislature, Debate on Indian Slavery.
54. Utah Territorial Legislature, Debate on Indian Slavery. The lawmaker was likely George A. Smith although it is impossible to verify. The sentiments expressed match comments Smith makes elsewhere in the debate.
55. Utah Territorial Legislature, Debate on Indian Slavery.
56. Utah Territorial Legislature, Debate on Indian Slavery.
57. Willard Richards to Thomas Kane, January 29, 1852, Willard Richards Journals and Papers, 1821–1854, MS 1490, box 3, folder 12, CHL.
58. A Preamble and An Act for the Relief of Indian Slaves and Prisoners, 91, 93.
59. A Preamble and An Act for the Relief of Indian Slaves and Prisoners, 91–93.
60. A Preamble and An Act for the Relief of Indian Slaves and Prisoners, 93–94. On New Jersey's gradual emancipation law see Arthur Zilversmit, *The First Emancipation: The Abolition of Slavery in the North* (Chicago: University of Chicago Press, 1967), 220–222.
61. Daniel W. Jones, *Forty Years among the Indians: A True yet Thrilling Narrative of the Author's Experiences among the Natives* (Salt Lake City: Juvenile Instructor Office, 1890), 53; Sandra G. Jones, *Being and Becoming Ute: The Story of an American Indian People* (Salt Lake City: University of Utah Press, 2019), 95.
62. Jones, *Being and Becoming Ute*, chapters 5 and 6; Jones, *The Trial of Don Pedro León Luján*, chapters 6 and 7; Howard A Christy, "The Walker War: Defense and Conciliation as Strategy," *Utah Historical Quarterly* 47 (Fall 1979): 395–420; John R. Alley Jr., "Prelude to

Dispossession: The Fur Trade's Significance for the Northern Utes and Southern Paiutes," *Utah Historical Quarterly* 50 (Spring 1982): 104–123.

Chapter 6

1. Nathaniel R. Ricks, "A Peculiar Place for the Peculiar Institution: Slavery and Sovereignty in Early Territorial Utah" (Master's thesis, Brigham Young University, 2007).
2. Newell G. Bringhurst's discussion of the law has been the most accurate to date. Although he describes the law as providing "legal recognition to black slaveholding" in Utah, he adds that Brigham Young and other Latter-day Saints "looked upon Utah's institution of servile bondage as something like the practice of black indentured servitude that existed in Mormonism's former gathering place of Illinois." Newell G. Bringhurst, *Saints, Slaves, and Blacks: The Changing Place of Black People within Mormonism*, 2nd ed. (Salt Lake City: Greg Kofford Books, 2018), 70, 72.
3. Stacey L. Smith, *Freedom's Frontier: California and the Struggle over Unfree Labor, Emancipation, and Reconstruction* (Chapel Hill: University of North Carolina Press, 2013); Leonard L. Richards, *The California Gold Rush and the Coming of the Civil War* (New York: Vintage Books, 2008); Mark J. Stegmaier, "A Law That Would Make Caligula Blush?: New Mexico Territory's Unique Slave Code, 1859–1861," *New Mexico Historical Review* 87 (Spring 2012): 209–242.
4. J. Ross Browne, *Report of the Debates in the Convention of California on the Formation of the State Constitution, in September and October, 1849* (Washington, D.C.: Printed by J. T. Towers, 1850); Smith, *Freedom's Frontier*, 7.
5. Stegmaier, "A Law That Would Make Caligula Blush."
6. Christopher B. Rich, Jr., "The True Policy for Utah: Servitude, Slavery, and 'An Act in Relation to Service,'" *Utah Historical Quarterly* 80 (Winter 2012): 54–74. See also Bringhurst, *Saints, Slaves, and Blacks*, 70–74.
7. William P. MacKinnon, *At Sword's Point, Part 1: A Documentary History of the Utah War to 1858* (Norman, OK: Arthur H. Clark, 2008); William P. MacKinnon, *At Sword's Point, Part 2: A Documentary History of the Utah War, 1858–1859* (Norman, OK: Arthur H. Clark, 2016).
8. On the decade of division and eventual disunion, see David M. Potter and Don E. Fehrenbacher, *The Impending Crisis, 1848–1861* (New York: Harper & Row, 1976); and Eric Foner, *The Fiery Trial: Abraham Lincoln and American Slavery* (New York: W. W. Norton, 2010).
9. An Act to Secure Freedom to All Persons within the Territories of the United States," Bills and Resolutions, House of Representatives, 37th Cong., 2nd Sess., H.R. 374 (1862), available at: A Century of Lawmaking for a New Nation: U.S. Congressional Documents and Debates, 1774–1875, https://memory.loc.gov/cgi-bin/ampage?collId=llhb&fileName=037/llhb037.db&recNum=2143.
10. *Journals of the House of Representatives, Council, and Joint Sessions of the First Annual and Special Sessions of the Legislative Assembly of the Territory of Utah. Held at Great Salt Lake City, 1851 and 1852* (Great Salt Lake City: Brigham H. Young, Printer, 1852), 104–110; "Governor's Message," *Deseret News*, January 10, 1852, 18.
11. On New York's and New Jersey's gradual emancipation laws see Arthur Zilversmit, *The First Emancipation: The Abolition of Slavery in the North* (Chicago: University of Chicago Press, 1967), chapters 6–8; on Illinois see M. Scott Heerman, "In a State of Slavery: Black Servitude in Illinois, 1800–1830," *Early American Studies: An Interdisciplinary Journal* 14 (Winter 2016): 114–139.
12. Matthew J. Grow and Ronald W. Walker, *The Prophet and the Reformer: The Letters of Brigham Young and Thomas L. Kane* (New York: Oxford University Press, 2015), 68–69; Orson Hyde, "Slavery among the Mormons," *Frontier Guardian*, December 11, 1850, 2.
13. Smith, *Freedom's Frontier*, 7; Stegmaier, "A Law That Would Make Caligula Blush."
14. Smith, *Freedom's Frontier*, 7–14, 23, 100. During the California Constitutional Convention, there was even a concerted effort to bar all free African Americans and other minorities from entering the future state. Said one delegate, "I am opposed to the introduction into this country of negroes, peons of Mexico, or any class of that kind; I care not whether they be free or bond. It is a well established fact, and the history of every State in the Union clearly proves it, that negro labor, whether slave or free, when opposed to white labor, degrades it." Browne, *Report of the Debates in the Convention of California*, 143.
15. Smith, *Freedom's Frontier*, 8, 39–42; see also Richards, *The California Gold Rush*.
16. Smith, *Freedom's Frontier*, 64–66.
17. Constitution of California 1849, art. 1 sec. 18.
18. Smith, *Freedom's Frontier*, 57–63.

19. Smith, *Freedom's Frontier*, 232; Stacey L. Smith, "Pacific Bound: California's 1852 Fugitive Slave Law," *BlackPast*, January 6, 2014, https://www.blackpast.org/african-american-history/pacific-bound-california-s-1852-fugitive-slave-law/.
20. An Act Respecting Fugitives from Labor, and Slaves Brought to this State Prior to Her Admission into the Union, sec. 4, Act of April 15, 1852, in State of California, in *The Statutes of California Passed at the Third Session of the Legislature* (San Francisco: G. K. Fitch and Company and V. E. Geiger and Company, 1852), 67–69.
21. Soon after the legislature passed the Fugitive Slave Act, the California Supreme Court upheld its provisions and solidified slaveholders' temporary rights in the state. In a concurring opinion, one justice even went so far to argue that since California had no positive law for the emancipation of slaves, the provisions of the state constitution that prohibited slavery and involuntary servitude merely asserted "a principle" that by itself was "inert and inoperative." "Strike the present law from the statute book," the justice wrote, "and there is not a solitary slave, who was brought here as such, but will remain so in the absence of any other legislation." In the Matter of Carter Perkins and Robert Perkins, Supreme Court of California, 2 Cal. 424 (October 1852), 455–457.
22. Brian McGinty, *Archy Lee's Struggle for Freedom: The True Story of California Gold, the Nation's Tragic March toward Civil War, and a Young Black Man's Fight for Liberty* (Guilford, CT: Lyons Press, 2020).
23. James F. Brooks, *Captives and Cousins: Slavery, Kinship, and Community in the Southwest Borderlands* (Chapel Hill: University of North Carolina Press, 2002), 309.
24. Brooks, *Captives and Cousins*, 309–310; Stegmaier, "A Law That Would Make Caligula Blush," 210.
25. An addendum to the Constitution addressed to the people of New Mexico explained that "Slavery in New Mexico is naturally impracticable, and can never, in reality, exist here;—wherever it has existed it has proved a curse and a blight to the State upon which it has been inflicted,—a moral, social and political evil. The only manner in which this question now effects us is politically; and on grounds of this character, with its general evil tendencies, we have unanimously agreed to reject it—if forever." See *Reports of Committees of the House of Representatives for the First Session of the Fifty-Third Congress, 1893* (Washington, D.C.: Government Printing Office, 1893), 28, for a reprinting of New Mexico's proposed 1850 Constitution, including this addendum.
26. Similar laws were passed in a number of free states. In February 1853 the Illinois legislature passed a bluntly titled law called "An Act to Prevent the Immigration of Free Negroes into This state." The statute criminalized the introduction of any African slave into the state whether the slave was later emancipated or not. An exception was made for slaves merely "traveling through" the state. But if a free African American entered the state and did not depart within ten days, she could be fined $50 upon conviction by a justice of the peace. If she did not pay the fine, she would then be sold at public auction as a servant to whomever satisfied the judgment and court costs. The law indicated that this period of servitude would not be open-ended but provided no maximum length. And if the freeperson refused to leave Illinois after her punishment was over, the fines would be increased and the process repeated. For the full text of the law see David W. Lusk, *Politics and Politicians: A Succinct History of the Politics of Illinois from 1856 to 1884. With Anecdotes and Incidents, and Appendix from 1809 to 1856* (Springfield, IL: H. W. Rokker, 1884), 330–333. There is evidence that the law was enforced by Illinois courts, although perhaps selectively. Six months after the statute was passed, newspapers reported the following: "A colored man, after a confinement of six weeks in the county jail was, on the 20th, sold to Marcus G. Faulkner, of Grand Point, for the sum of $4.75, for one month. At the expiration of that time, unless he leaves the State, he is again to be arrested, and sold to the highest bidder, which may be for a month or a year, or a dozen years, or for life." "The Illinois Slave Law," *The National Era* (Washington, D.C.), August 4, 1853. The last statement was probably editorial hyperbole, but it did seem possible under the ambiguous terms of the law. Some states even went so far to include similar provisions in their constitutions. When Oregon Territory passed a state constitution in November 1857, it not only prohibited slavery, but it also prohibited free African Americans from thereafter settling in the state, owning real property, making contracts, or engaging in a lawsuit. *The Oregon Constitution and Proceedings and Debates of the Constitutional Convention of 1857*, ed. Charles Henry Carey (Salem, OR: State Printing Department, 1926). The Indiana Constitution of 1851 likewise declared that "No negro or mulatto shall come into or settle in the State." Indiana Constitution 1851, art. 13, "Negroes and Mulattoes," sec. 1, https://www.in.gov/history/about-indiana-history-and-trivia/explore-indiana-history-by-topic/indiana-docume

nts-leading-to-statehood/constitution-of-1851-as-originally-written/article-13-negroes-and-mulattoes/.
27. An Act Concerning Free Negroes, 29 January 1857 (repealed 1865), in *Revised Statutes and Laws of the Territory of New Mexico, in Force at the Close of the Session of the Legislative Assembly Ending February 2, 1865* (St. Louis, MO: R.P. Studley, 1865), 456–459.
28. Laura E. Gomez, "Off-White in an Age of White Supremacy: Mexican Elites and the Rights of Indians and Blacks in Nineteenth-Century New Mexico," *Chicana/o Latina/o Law Review* 25, no. 1 (2005): 40–42, https://doi.org/10.5070/C7251021154. A few days before the legislature acted on the slave code, it adopted a separate peonage law providing that runaway servants could be treated as fugitives from justice, limiting the ability of individuals to employ another's servant, and allowing masters to "correct" their servants without court supervision as long as such correction was "not inflicted in a cruel manner with clubs nor stripes." An Act Amendatory of the Law Relative to Contracts between Masters and Servants, January 26, 1859, in *Revised Statutes and Laws of the Territory of New Mexico*, 548–551.
29. Stegmaier, "A Law That Would Make Caligula Blush," 212.
30. Stegmaier, "A Law That Would Make Caligula Blush," 214, 226–232.
31. Stegmaier, "A Law That Would Make Caligula Blush," 226–232.
32. Stegmaier, "A Law That Would Make Caligula Blush," 219–225.
33. *Journals of the House of Representatives, Council, and Joint Sessions*, 85.
34. Previous commentary incorrectly presumed that secs. 2 and 3 of the act were conjunctive clauses; that is to say that an "and" should be read between the two sections. However, the legislative debates make it clear that these sections were intended to be read as disjunctive clauses; in other words that an "or" should be read between them. George A. Smith's comments on February 2, 1852, when he read the "Bill on Servitude" to the legislature, makes it evident that sec. 2 was aimed to regulate servitude for white immigrants. See George A. Smith, February 2, 1852, CR 100 912, Debate on Indian Slavery, possibly beginning January 23, 1852, Church History Department Pitman Shorthand transcriptions, 2013–2021, Addresses and sermons, 1851–1874, Miscellaneous transcriptions, 1869, 1872, 1889, 1848, 1851–1854, 1859–1863, Utah Territorial Legislature, January–February 1852, CHL. For an early draft of the bill see Territorial Legislative Records, 1851–1894, series 3150, reel 1, box 1, folder 55, 700–703, UDARS. For a copy of the bill that shows edits and corrections see Utah Territory Legislative Assembly Papers, 1851–1872, MS 2919, First Session, 1851–1852, Acts numbers 15–39, box 1, folder 3, CHL. For a draft of the bill that passed into law see Territorial Legislative Records, 1851–1894, series 3150, reel 1, box 1, folder 55, 704–706, UDARS. For the published version of the bill see *Acts, Resolutions, and Memorials, Passed by the First Annual, and Special Sessions of the Legislative Assembly of the Territory of Utah, Begun and Held at Great Salt Lake City, on the 22nd Day of September, A. D. 1851* (Salt Lake City: Brigham H. Young, Printer, 1852), 80–82.
35. Utah Territory Legislative Assembly Papers, MS 2919, CHL.
36. William Crosby to Brigham Young, c. March 12, 1851, Brigham Young Office Files, CR 1234 1, box 22, folder 6, CHL; Brigham Young to William Crosby, March 12, 1851, Brigham Young Office Files, CR 1234 1, box 22, folder 6, CHL.
37. Heerman, "In a State of Slavery"; Allison Mileo Gorsuch, "To Indent Oneself: Ownership, Contracts, and Consent in Antebellum Illinois," in *The Legal Understanding of Slavery: From the Historical to the Contemporary*, ed. Jean Allain, (New York: Oxford University Press, 2012), 135–151; Paul Finkelman, "Evading the Ordinance: The Persistence of Bondage in Indiana and Illinois," *Journal of the Early Republic* 9 (Spring 1989): 21–51.
38. Utah Territory Legislative Assembly Papers, MS 2919, CHL.
39. Frederick Douglass, *Narrative of the Life of Frederick Douglass, an American Slave* (New York: Dell, 1997), 33, 38. See also David W. Blight, *Frederick Douglass Prophet of Freedom* (New York: Simon & Schuster, 2018), 39. For examples of slave codes outlawing the education of free and enslaved Black people see Virginia's An Act to Amend the Act Concerning Slaves, Free Negroes and Mulattoes (April 7, 1831), in *Acts Passed at a General Assembly of the Commonwealth of Virginia* (Richmond, VA: Thomas Ritchie, 1831), 107–108, which made it illegal for a white person to teach free and enslaved "negroes or mulattoes to read or write." In Alabama, "any person or persons who shall attempt to teach any free person of color, or slave, to spell, read, or write" could be fined between $250 and $500. See "Slaves, and Free Persons of Color," in *A Digest of the Laws of the State of Alabama: Containing all the Statutes of a Public and General Nature, in Force at the Close of the Session of the General Assembly, in January 1833* (Philadelphia, PA: Alexander Towar, 1833), 397.

40. Utah Territory Legislative Assembly Papers, MS 2919, CHL.
41. Smith, February 2, 1852.
42. "An Ordinance Incorporating the Perpetual Emigrating Company," in *The State of Deseret*, ed. Dale L. Morgan (Logan: Utah State University Press, 1987), 152.
43. For an example of a PEF contract see "Perpetual Emigrating Fund Company," *Latter Day Saints' Millennial Star* (Manchester, UK), January 12, 1856, 26.
44. Scott Allen Carson, "Indentured Migration in America's Great Basin: An Observation in Strategic Behavior in Cooperative Exchanges," *Journal of Institutional and Theoretical Economics* 157, no. 4 (December 2001): 651–676.
45. For examples of the payment of PEF debt as a prerequisite to leaving Utah Territory, see Polly Aird, "'You Nasty Apostates Clear Out': Reasons for Disaffection in the Late 1850s," *Journal of Mormon History* 30 (Fall 2004): 143, 149–150.
46. Carson, "Indentured Migration in America's Great Basin," 654; "Perpetual Emigrating Fund Company," 26.
47. Leonard J. Arrington, *Great Basin Kingdom: An Economic History of the Latter-day Saints, 1830–1900* (Urbana and Chicago: University of Illinois Press, 2004), 102.
48. Robert J. Steinfeld, *The Invention of Free Labor: The Employment Relation in English and American Law and Culture, 1350–1870* (Chapel Hill: University of North Carolina Press, 1991), 172; Gordon S. Wood, *Empire of Liberty: A History of the Early Republic, 1789–1815* (New York: Oxford University Press, 2009), 345–348.
49. Utah Territory Legislative Assembly Papers, MS 2919, CHL.
50. Utah Territory Legislative Assembly Papers, MS 2919, CHL.
51. An Act Relative to German and Swiss Redemptioners, in *Laws Made and Passed by the General Assembly of the State of Maryland, at a Session Begun and Held at the City of Annapolis, on Monday the First Day of December, Eighteen Hundred and Seventeen*, vol. 636 (Annapolis: Jonas Green, 1818), 223; An Act for Regulating the Importation of German and Other Passengers, in *Laws of the Commonwealth of Pennsylvania from the Fourteenth Day of October One Thousand Seven Hundred*, vol. 7 (Philadelphia: John Bioren, 1822), 33.
52. William S. Kiser, *Borderlands of Slavery: The Struggle over Captivity and Peonage in the American Southwest* (Philadelphia: University of Pennsylvania Press), 109.
53. Hosea Stout, February 2, 1852, CR 100 912, Debate on Indian Slavery, possibly beginning January 23, 1852, Church History Department Pitman Shorthand transcriptions, 2013–2021, Addresses and sermons, 1851–1874, Miscellaneous transcriptions, 1869, 1872, 1889, 1848, 1851–1854, 1859–1863, Utah Territorial Legislature, January–February 1852, CHL.
54. An Act Concerning Masters and Apprentices, in *Acts, Resolutions, and Memorials*, 75–78.
55. Smith, February 2, 1852.
56. Utah Territory Legislative Assembly Papers, MS 2919, CHL.
57. During the Gold Rush period, a large number of immigrants arrived in California from Latin America and the Pacific Rim under various forms of contract labor and debt servitude. Some of the earliest Chinese laborers arrived in California under three-year indenture contracts. In the mid-nineteenth century, passage rates across the Pacific were still relatively high. Consequently, workers immigrating to California adopted the same strategy that Europeans had utilized for the previous 250 years; they obtained passage on credit that was secured by their future labor. However, local courts in California would not criminally enforce these agreements, and the legislature failed to pass a measure that would have authorized their specific performance. A large number of Chinese also arrived under the so-called credit ticket system that left them indebted to creditors in Asia with their property and even relatives held as collateral. Free-soil politicians strenuously objected to such arrangements, and during the 1850s they sponsored several "anti-coolie" bills aimed at protecting free labor against this kind of "contract slavery." David W. Galenson, "The Rise and Fall of Indentured Servitude in the Americas: An Economic Analysis," *The Journal of Economic History* 44 (March 1984): 15–24; Smith, *Freedom's Frontier*, 24–39, 80–108; Steinfeld, *The Invention of Free Labor*, 177–178.
58. A previous interpretation of the law incorrectly asserted that it explicitly required proof of consideration in order for these indentures to be legally binding. However, the statutory requirement for consideration applied to immigrant indentures under sec. 2 rather than to African indentures under sec. 3. Still, it is possible that a court might have read a requirement for consideration into any such arrangement before it determined the contract to be valid. Rich, "The True Policy for Utah," 68, 74.
59. Utah Territory Legislative Assembly Papers, MS 2919, CHL.

60. Utah Territory Legislative Assembly Papers, MS 2919, CHL.
61. St. George Tucker, *Blackstone's Commentaries: With Notes of Reference to the Constitution and Laws of the Federal Government of the United States and of the Commonwealth of Virginia*, 5 vols. (Philadelphia: William Young Birch and Abraham Small, 1803), 2:424.
62. Gorsuch, "To Indent Oneself," 135–151, 143; Finkelman, "Evading the Ordinance," 21–51.
63. Manisha Sinha, *The Slave's Cause: A History of Abolition* (New Haven, CT: Yale University Press, 2016), 84–85.
64. Brigham Young, before Territorial Legislature, January 23, 1852, CR 100 912, Church History Department Pitman Shorthand transcriptions, 2013–2021, Addresses and sermons, 1851–1874, Miscellaneous transcriptions, 1869, 1872, 1889, 1848, 1851–1854, 1859–1863, Utah Territorial Legislature, January–February 1852, CHL.
65. Young, January 23, 1852.
66. "Death of Sister Jones" and "Deaths," *Deseret News*, May 6, 1895, 1, 5; Ronald D. Dennis, "Dan Jones, Welshman," *Ensign*, April 1987.
67. Here Young signals his preference for contractual labor agreements. Young, January 23, 1852.
68. Young, January 23, 1852.
69. Young, January 23, 1852.
70. Mark A. Noll, "The Bible and Slavery," in *Religion and the American Civil War*, ed. Randall M. Miller, Harry S. Stout, and Charles Reagan Wilson (New York: Oxford University Press, 1998), 43–73; Larry E. Tise, *Proslavery: A History of the Defense of Slavery in America, 1701–1840* (Athens: University of Georgia Press, 1987), 278; W. Paul Reeve, *Religion of a Different Color: Race and the Mormon Struggle for Whiteness* (New York: Oxford University Press, 2015), 125.
71. Joseph Smith Jr., "For the Messenger and Advocate," *Latter Day Saints' Messenger and Advocate* (Kirtland, OH), April 1836.
72. Joseph Smith, *General Smith's Views of the Powers and Policy of the Government of the United States*, Nauvoo, IL, February 7, 1844, 3–4, 9, 11.
73. Young, January 23, 1852.
74. Brigham Young, "Intelligence, Etc.," October 9, 1859, *Journal of Discourses*, vol. 7 (London: Latter-day Saints' Book Depot, 1860), 290.
75. On the curse of Cain in the broader Christian tradition see David M. Goldenberg, *The Curse of Ham: Race and Slavery in Early Judaism, Christianity, and Islam* (Princeton, NJ: Princeton University Press, 2003), 178–182; and for an example of its use in 1829, the year before Joseph Smith founded the LDS faith, see David Walker, *Walker's Appeal, in Four Articles; Together with a Preamble, to the Coloured Citizens of the World, but in Particular, and Very Expressly, to Those of the United States of America, Written in Boston, State of Massachusetts, September 28, 1829* (Boston: David Walker, 1830), 68.
76. Young, January 23, 1852.
77. Goldenberg, *The Curse of Ham*, 1.
78. Young, January 23, 1852.
79. Zilversmit, *The First Emancipation*, chapters 6–8. For evidence of freedom suits and other ways Black people rejected such arguments about their ability to function in a free society see Sinha, *The Slave's Cause*, chapter 3.
80. A List of President Brigham Young's Family Residing in the 18th Ward, March 19, 1855, Brigham Young Office Files, CR 1234 1, Miscellaneous files, 1832–1878, Family information, c. 1853–1858, CHL; Brigham Young Financial Files, Ledgers, 1849–1859, CR 1234 1, box 91, folder 3, items 18, 20, 33, 65; box 93, folder 1, item 177–178, CHL; John G. Turner, *Brigham Young: Pioneer Prophet* (Cambridge, MA: Belknap Press of Harvard University Press, 2012), 218.
81. Young, January 23, 1852.
82. Brigham Young, September 5, 1866, Church History Department Pitman Shorthand transcriptions, 2013–2023, Addresses and sermons, 1851–1874, Brigham Young, 1851–1877, CHL.
83. Molly Oshatz, *Slavery and Sin: The Fight against Slavery and the Rise of Liberal Protestantism* (New York: Oxford University Press, 2012), 43–44.
84. *Journals of the House of Representatives, Council, and Joint Sessions*, 104–110; "Governor's Message," *Deseret News*, January 10, 1852, 18.
85. Oshatz, *Slavery and Sin*, 56–57.
86. Young, January 23, 1852.
87. For a complete assessment of nineteenth-century "Antislavery Moderation," see Oshatz, *Slavery and Sin*, chapter 2.

88. Young, January 23, 1852.
89. Young, January 23, 1852.
90. Young, January 23, 1852.
91. *Journals of the House of Representatives, Council, and Joint Sessions*, 85.
92. Territorial Legislative Records, 1851–1894, series 3150, reel 1, box 1, folder 55, 700–706, UDARS; *Journals of the House of Representatives, Council, and Joint Sessions*, 86–90.
93. Orson Pratt, before the Territorial Legislature on slavery, January 27, 1852, CR 100 912, Church History Department Pitman Shorthand transcriptions, 2013–2021, Addresses and sermons, 1851–1874, Miscellaneous transcriptions, 1869, 1872, 1889, 1848, 1851–1854, 1859–1863, Utah Territorial Legislature, January–February 1852, CHL.
94. Watt recorded *in*; the intent was *it*.
95. Pratt, January 27, 1852.
96. Orson Pratt, January 27, 1852.
97. Orson Pratt, January 27, 1852.
98. Orson Spencer, before the Territorial Legislature on slavery, January 27, 1852, CR 100 912, Church History Department Pitman Shorthand transcriptions, 2013–2021, Addresses and sermons, 1851–1874, Miscellaneous transcriptions, 1869, 1872, 1889, 1848, 1851–1854, 1859–1863, Utah Territorial Legislature, January–February 1852, CHL.
99. Spencer, January 27, 1852.
100. Spencer, January 27, 1852.
101. Spencer, January 27, 1852.
102. Ibram X. Kendi, *Stamped from the Beginning: The Definitive History of Racist Ideas in America* (New York: Nation Books, 2016), 68.
103. Jay H. Buckley, "'Good News' at the Cape of Good Hope: Early LDS Missionary Activities in South Africa," in *Go Ye into All the World: The Growth and Development of Mormon Missionary Work*, ed. Reid L. Nielson and Fred E. Woods (Provo, UT: Religious Studies Center, 2012), 471–502. For examples of converts of Black African descent from the 1853 mission to South Africa, see Elizabeth Egleston Giraud, "Johanna Dorthea Louisa Langeveld Provis," Century of Black Mormons, https://exhibits.lib.utah.edu/s/century-of-black-mormons/page/provis-johanna-dorothea-louisa-langeveld; W. Paul Reeve, "Raichel Hanable," Century of Black Mormons, https://exhibits.lib.utah.edu/s/century-of-black-mormons/page/hanable-raichel; and W. Paul Reeve, "Sarah Hariss," Century of Black Mormons, https://exhibits.lib.utah.edu/s/century-of-black-mormons/page/hariss-sarah.
104. Spencer, January 27, 1852.
105. Tonya Reiter, "Redd Slave Histories: Family, Race, and Sex in Pioneer Utah," *Utah Historical Quarterly* 85 (Spring 2017): 109–126.
106. Utah Territory Legislative Assembly Papers, MS 2919, CHL.
107. Brigham Young, before the Territorial Legislature on slavery, January 27, 1852, CR 100 912, Church History Department Pitman Shorthand transcriptions, 2013–2021, Addresses and sermons, 1851–1874, Miscellaneous transcriptions, 1869, 1872, 1889, 1848, 1851–1854, 1859–1863, Utah Territorial Legislature, January–February 1852, CHL. The record of the legislative debates only refers to "Young" making these comments. However, it is doubtful that this referred to Joseph Young (1797–1881), Brigham Young's older brother who later objected to sec. 4. Joseph was serving in the House of Representatives, elected from Salt Lake County, and would not have been present in the Council chamber where this address was made. As a result, the speaker had to be Brigham Young.
108. An Ordinance in Reference to Vagrants (February 10, 1851) in *Laws and Ordinances of the State of Deseret* (Salt Lake City: Shepard Book, 1919), 74; Joint Resolution Legalizing the Laws of the Provisional Government of the State of Deseret (October 4, 1851) in *Acts, Resolutions, and Memorials*, 205.
109. Young, January 23, 1852.
110. Young, January 27, 1852.
111. Young, January 23, 1852.
112. Rich, "The True Policy for Utah," 62–64, 69–71. A Hobson's choice means an illusion of choice, when an ostensibly free choice is offered but in reality there is little to no choice available. It may derive from Thomas Hobson (1545–1631) who ran a horse rental business in Cambridge, England. He reportedly did not allow his customers to choose among his horses but assigned them a horse nearest the stable door. Their choice was the horse assigned or no horse at all. It was thus Hobson's choice, not the customer's.

113. Consent at the outset of a labor relationship has traditionally been the dividing line between slavery and other forms of unfree labor. Until the early to mid-nineteenth century, indentured servitude was viewed as something inherently different than slavery because it was based on consent. But when slaves entered long-term indenture contracts, questions of consent became far murkier. For this reason, many Northern jurists saw such arrangements as "involuntary servitude" as opposed to "voluntary servitude." Steinfeld, *The Invention of Free Labor*, 98–187; Robet J. Steinfeld, *Coercion, Contract, and Free Labor in the Nineteenth Century* (New York: Cambridge University Press, 2001), 253–275; Nathan B. Oman, "Specific Performance and the Thirteenth Amendment," *Minnesota Law Review* 93, no. 6 (2009): 2020–2056; James Gray Pope, "Contract, Race, and Freedom of Labor in the Constitutional Law of 'Involuntary Servitude,'" *Yale Law Journal* 119, no. 7 (2010): 1474–1567.
114. Pheobe, a woman of color v. Jay, 1 Ill. 268 (Ill. 1828).
115. Steinfeld, *Coercion, Contract, and Free Labor in the Nineteenth Century*, 255–385; Nathan B. Oman, "Specific Performance and the Thirteenth Amendment," *Minnesota Law Review* 93 (2020): 2047–2048.
116. M. Scott Heerman, "In a State of Slavery: Black Servitude in Illinois, 1800–1830," *Early American Studies: An Interdisciplinary Journal* 14 (Winter 2016): 114–139, 126–127.
117. Young, January 27, 1852.
118. Brigham Young, before Territorial Legislature, January 29, 1852, CR 100 912, Church History Department Pitman Shorthand transcriptions, 2013–2021, Addresses and sermons, 1851–1874, Miscellaneous transcriptions, 1869, 1872, 1889, 1848, 1851–1854, 1859–1863, Utah Territorial Legislature, January–February 1852, CHL; Brigham Young, January 29, 1852, Historian's Office Reports and Speeches, 1845–1885, CR 100 317, box 1, folder 15, CHL.
119. Ronald W. Walker, "The Affairs of the 'Runaways': Utah's First Encounter with the Federal Officers, Part 1," *Journal of Mormon History* 39 (Fall 2013): 1–43; Ronald W. Walker and Matthew J. Grow, "The People Are 'Hogaffed or Humbugged': The 1851–52 National Reaction to Utah's 'Runaway' Officers, Part 2," *Journal of Mormon History* 40 (Winter 2014): 1–52.
120. *Journals of the House of Representatives, Council, and Joint Sessions*, 94–97.
121. By the end of the eighteenth century, most states had amended their laws to allow children to be apprenticed only until the ages of twenty-one for males and eighteen for females. Steinfeld, *The Invention of Free Labor,* 133n48.
122. George A. Smith, Hosea Stout, and Joseph Young, February 2, 1852, CR 100 912, Debate on Indian Slavery, possibly beginning January 23, 1852, Church History Department Pitman Shorthand transcriptions, 2013–2021, Addresses and sermons, 1851–1874, Miscellaneous transcriptions, 1869, 1872, 1889, 1848, 1851–1854, 1859–1863, Utah Territorial Legislature, January–February 1852, CHL.
123. Utah Territory Legislative Assembly Papers, MS 2919, CHL. This version of the bill appears to be a working draft on which lawmakers made corrections, but it offers no evidence as to when revisions were made, who made them, or why.
124. Sec. 4 of the Service Act now provided that "if any master or mistress shall have sexual or carnal intercourse with his or her servant or servants of the African race, he or she shall forfeit all claim to said servant or servants to the commonwealth." Sec. 8 continued, "Any person transferring a servant or servants contrary to the provisions of this Act, or taking one out of the Territory contrary to his, or her will . . . shall forfeit all claims to the services of such servant or servants, as provided in the fourth section of this act."
125. Brigham Young, before the Territorial Legislature on slavery, January 27, 1852.
126. In 1859, A. B. Miller brought suit against Thomas S. Williams concerning "two negro women." During the case, Seth M. Blair claimed that the "property" in question had been forfeited to the territory and that he would institute a suit for its recovery. It does not appear that he did so, however, and the two women were later included in a suit concerning Williams's estate. "Third Judicial District Court," *Deseret News*, August 24, 1859.
127. Utah Territory Legislative Assembly Papers, MS 2919, CHL. See also, Territorial Legislative Records, 1851–1894, series 3150, reel 1, box 1, folder 55, pages 704–706, UDARS.
128. Utah Territory Legislative Assembly Papers, MS 2919, CHL. *Acts, Resolutions, and Memorials,* 80-82.
129. Even under the original wording, it is possible to argue that this did not apply to the descendant of a slave who was born in Utah. Rather, it applied to a slave or the child of a slave who was brought to Utah from elsewhere pursuant to a mutual agreement. This interpretation is bolstered by the marginal note to the final statute that emphasized the movement of

a servant from one jurisdiction to another. For the original draft of sec. 3 see Utah Territory Legislative Assembly Papers, MS 2919, CHL, and for the law that passed see *Acts, Resolutions, and Memorials*, 81.
130. *Acts, Resolutions, and Memorials*, 81.
131. *Acts, Resolutions, and Memorials*, 80–82.
132. *Acts, Resolutions, and Memorials*, 80–82.
133. *Acts, Resolutions, and Memorials*, 80–82.
134. *Acts, Resolutions, and Memorials*, 80–82.
135. M. Scott Heerman, *The Alchemy of Slavery: Human Bondage and Emancipation in Illinois Country, 1730–1865* (Philadelphia: University of Pennsylvania Press, 2018), 89.
136. Alice Baumgarten, *South to Freedom: Runaway Slaves to Mexico and the Coming of the Civil War* (New York: Basic Books, 2021), 5, 58; Rich, "The True Policy for Utah," 55–60.
137. The most relevant court case concerning the Service Act was the preliminary hearing against Williams Camp for kidnapping his servant, Daniel, in 1856. This will be explored in chapter 8. But in 1875, the California Supreme Court ruled on the legality of a marriage contracted with an allegedly enslaved woman in Utah Territory during the 1850s. The court conceded that it was possible to legally hold someone as a slave in Utah Territory. However, it is not clear on what basis the court made this concession. One attorney made a passing reference to the requirements of the Service Act and stated that they had not been fulfilled. But the arguments to the court also referenced the *Dred Scott* decision, and the fact that the parties were merely "passing through" Utah. The court ultimately found that the woman had already been freed before she came to Utah or that the act of marriage freed her. Consequently, the court did not spend significant time interpreting Utah statute law. See Pearson v. Pearson, 51 Cal. 120 (Cal. 1875).
138. Thiriot, *Slavery in Zion*, 90–93, 95, 154–155.
139. Thiriot, *Slavery in Zion*, 18–25, 87–97; Schedule of Property of David Lewis, deceased, Utah Territory, Probate Court Records, Salt Lake County, Series 1621, Reel 1, Box 1, Folder 41, UDARS.
140. Schedule of Property of David Lewis.
141. Smith, *Freedom's Frontier*, 129–131; "Suit for Freedom," *Los Angeles Star*, February 2, 1856.
142. *Acts, Resolutions, and Memorials*, 80–82.
143. Another possible explanation lies in the political context of the legislative session. Before the legislature went into secret session on January 30, Brigham Young first read accounts of the runaway judges to the assembled body. By this time, it was clear that this situation might have dire consequences for the Latter-day Saints and their relative autonomy in Utah. A law permitting African Americans to be held in perpetual servitude expressly based on the curse of Canaan was likely to be noticed in Congress, which under the Utah organic act had the authority to veto any territorial legislation. This would have only added to the problems set in motion by the runaways. Thus, Young and other leaders may have concluded that it was wiser to delete this language from the service bill in order to avoid congressional attention. However, there is no evidence on record to support this supposition.
144. Pratt, January 27, 1852.
145. Young and Spencer, January 27, 1852; *Acts, Resolutions, and Memorials*, 81.
146. This marginal note was retained in the published version of the bill. See Utah Territory Legislative Assembly Papers, MS 2919, CHL, for the original version and *Acts, Resolutions, and Memorials*, 81, for the published version.
147. Duritha Lewis, Slave Registration, Utah Territory, Third District, Probate Court Records, series 373, reel 6, box 5, folder 11, UDARS; Affidavit of Diannah Camp in regard to Negro boy Shepherd, filed July 10, 1856, series 373, reel 5, box 4, folder 26, UDARS; Affidavit of Williams Camp in regard to Negro boy Shepard, filed July 10 1856, series 373, reel 5, box 4, folder 26, UDARS.
148. *Acts, Resolutions, and Memorials*, 80–82.
149. *Journals of the House of Representatives, Council, and Joint Sessions*, 122; Brigham Young, February 4, 1852, CR 100 912, Church History Department Pitman Shorthand transcriptions, 2013–2021, Addresses and sermons, 1851–1874, Miscellaneous transcriptions, 1869, 1872, 1889, 1848, 1851–1854, 1859–1863, Utah Territorial Legislature, January–February 1852, CHL; Brigham Young, February 4, 1852, Historian's Office reports of speeches, 1845–1885, CR 100 317, box 1, folder 16, CHL.
150. "Governor's Message," *Deseret News*, December 25, 1852, 116.

151. "Governor's Message," 116.
152. Smith, *Freedom's Frontier*; Kiser, *Borderlands of Slavery*.

Chapter 7

1. Hosea Stout, *On the Mormon Frontier: The Diary of Hosea Stout, 1844–1861*, ed. Juanita Brooks, 2 vols. (Salt Lake City: University of Utah Press and Utah State Historical Society, 1964), 2: 423.
2. Gordon S. Wood, *Empire of Liberty: A History of the Early Republic, 1789–1815* (New York: Oxford University Press, 2009).
3. Sean Wilentz, *The Rise of American Democracy: Jefferson to Lincoln* (New York: W. W. Norton, 2005), 425.
4. Alexander Keyssar, *The Right to Vote: The Contested History of Democracy in the United States* (New York: Basic Books, 2000), 54–60.
5. Jon Meacham, *American Lion: Andrew Jackson in the White House* (Random House: New York, 2008), 302–304; Daniel Walker Howe, *What Hath God Wrought: The Transformation of America, 1815–1848* (New York: Oxford University Press, 2007), 497–498; Wilentz, *The Rise of American Democracy*, 192–195, 327, 507–518, 598–599.
6. Joanne Pope Melish, *Disowning Slavery: Gradual Emancipation and "Race" in New England, 1780–1860* (Ithaca, NY: Cornell University Press, 1998), 97–100, 109–110, 122–137, 189–209; Howe, *What Hath God Wrought*, 260–266; Keyssar, *The Right to Vote*, 54–55.
7. Keyssar, *The Right to Vote*, 55.
8. Gerald Leonard, *The Invention of Party Politics: Federalism, Popular Sovereignty, and Constitutional Development in Jacksonian Illinois* (Chapel Hill: University of North Carolina Press, 2002).
9. Marvin S. Hill, *Quest For Refuge: The Mormon Flight from American Pluralism* (Salt Lake City: Signature Books, 1989).
10. Kenneth H. Winn, *Exiles in a Land of Liberty: Mormons in America, 1830–1846* (Chapel Hill: University of North Carolina Press, 1989).
11. See Richard L. Bushman, *Joseph Smith: Rough Stone Rolling* (New York: Alfred A. Knopf, 2005); Patrick Q. Mason, "God and the People: Theodemocracy in Nineteenth Century Mormonism," *Journal of Church and State* 53 (Summer 2011): 349–375; Mark Roscoe Ashurst-McGee, "Zion Rising: Joseph Smith's Early Social and Political Thought" (PhD diss., Arizona State University, 2008); Benjamin E. Park, *Kingdom of Nauvoo: The Rise and Fall of a Religious Empire on the American Frontier* (New York: Liveright, 2020).
12. Joseph Smith, Jr., et al., *Doctrine and Covenants of the Church of the Latter Day Saints* (Kirtland, OH: F. G. Williams, 1835), sec. 49 and 102. But see Bushman, *Joseph Smith*, 101–105, 265–269, 309, 353–354, 520–525. Bushman argues that while there were democratic aspects to Mormon institutions, they were not truly based on popular sovereignty.
13. Peter Crawley, "The Constitution of the State of Deseret," *BYU Studies* 29, no. 4 (1989): 7–22.
14. Dale L. Morgan, *The State of Deseret* (Logan: Utah State University Press, 1987).
15. Norma Ricketts, *Mormon Battalion: United States Army of the West, 1846–1848* (Logan: Utah State University Press, 1997).
16. "Ordinances of the High Council," in Morgan, *The State of Deseret*, 196.
17. *Constitution of the State of Deseret, with the Journal of the Convention Which Formed It, and the Proceedings of the Legislature Consequent Thereon* (Kanesville, IA: Orson Hyde, 1849), art. V, sec. 10.
18. An Act to Establish a Territorial Government for Utah, September 9, 1850, *Statutes at Large*, vol. 9, 31st Cong., 1st Sess. (Boston: Little, Brown, 1862), 454.
19. Brigham Young, February 4, 1852, CR 100 912, Church History Department Pitman Shorthand transcriptions, 2013–2021, Addresses and sermons, 1851–1874, Miscellaneous transcriptions, 1869, 1872, 1889, 1848, 1851–1854, 1859–1863, Utah Territorial Legislature, January–February 1852, CHL.
20. Watt wrote "legislative."
21. Young, February 4, 1852.
22. Young, February 4, 1852.
23. Brigham Young, February 5, 1852, CR 100 912, Church History Department Pitman Shorthand transcriptions, 2013–2021, Addresses and sermons, 1851–1874, Miscellaneous transcriptions, 1869, 1872, 1889, 1848, 1851–1854, 1859–1863, Utah Territorial Legislature, January-February 1852, CHL.

24. Young, February 5, 1852.
25. Dan Vogel, ed., *The Wilford Woodruff Journals*, Typescript, 6 vols. (Salt Lake City: Benchmark Books, 2020), 2:510-511.
26. Historians Office History of the Church, also known as "History of Brigham Young," January 5, 1852, 1-2, CR 100 102, reel 9, box 9, vol. 22, CHL. A margin note on page 1 reads, "This years [*sic*] history compiled and copied by Robt. S. Campbell and read to Geo. A. Smith."
27. Vogel, *Wilford Woodruff Journals*, 2:510-511.
28. Vogel, *Wilford Woodruff Journals*, 2:510.
29. Young, February 5, 1852.
30. Watt here recorded the word "one" twice.
31. Young, February 5, 1852.
32. This and the next two paragraphs are taken from W. Paul Reeve, *Religion of a Different Color: Race and the Mormon Struggle for Whiteness* (New York: Oxford University Press, 2015), 159-160. Young, February 5, 1852; Vogel, *Wilford Woodruff Journals*, 2:510-511.
33. A. Leon Higginbotham, Jr. and Barbara K. Kopytoff, "Racial Purity and Interracial Sex in the Law of Colonial and Antebellum Virginia," in *Interracialism: Black-White Intermarriage in American History, Literature, and Law*, ed. Werner Sollors (New York: Oxford University Press, 2000), 83-89; Ariela J. Gross, *What Blood Won't Tell: A History of Race on Trial in America* (Cambridge, MA: Harvard University Press, 2008), 43-44; John G. Mencke, *Mulattoes and Race Mixture: American Attitudes and Images, 1865-1918* (Ann Arbor, MI: UMI Research Press, 1979), 37-87.
34. Higginbotham and Kopytoff, "Racial Purity," 89-94; for a nineteenth-century discussion of the issue see Charles W. Chesnutt, "What Is a White Man?" *The Independent* 41, no. 2113 (May 30, 1889): 5-6, 693-694, in Sollors, *Interracialism*, 37-42. The assertion regarding Young's speeches is based on an electronic search of the five volumes in Richard S. Van Wagoner, *The Complete Discourses of Brigham Young*, 5 vols. (Salt Lake City: The Smith-Pettit Foundation, 2009) and an electronic search of Carruth transcriptions of Brigham Young speeches recorded by George Watt.
35. Extract from George F. Richards Record of Decisions by the Council of the First Presidency and the Twelve Apostles (no date given but the next decision in order is dated February 8, 1907) in George A. Smith Family Papers, MS 36, box 78, folder 7, Manuscripts Division, Special Collections, JWML.
36. For evidence of the continuing confusion over the Woodruff versus Watt version of Young's speeches to the legislature, see note 38 in the Introduction.
37. *Journals of the House of Representatives, Council, and Joint Sessions of the First Annual and Special Sessions of the Legislative Assembly of the Territory of Utah. Held at Great Salt Lake City, 1851 and 1852* (Great Salt Lake City: Brigham H. Young, Printer, 1852), 125-127.
38. Young, February 5, 1852.
39. Young, February 5, 1852.
40. *Dred Scott v. Sanford*, 60 U.S. 393 (1857).
41. Young, February 5, 1852.
42. Young, February 5, 1852.
43. Young, February 5, 1852.
44. Young, February 5, 1852.
45. Young, February 5, 1852.
46. David M. Goldenberg, *The Curse of Ham: Race and Slavery in Early Judaism, Christianity, and Islam* (Princeton, NJ: Princeton University Press, 2003), 178-182.
47. Young, February 5, 1852.
48. Brigham Young, "Intelligence, Etc.," October 9, 1859, *Journal of Discourses*, 26 vols. (London: Latter-day Saints' Book Depot, 1860), 7:290; Reeve, *Religion of a Different Color*, 154.
49. David Walker, *Walker's Appeal, in Four Articles; Together with a Preamble, to the Coloured Citizens of the World, but in Particular, and Very Expressly, to Those of the United States of America, Written in Boston, State of Massachusetts, September 28, 1829* (Boston: David Walker, 1830), 68.
50. Reeve, *Religion of a Different Color*, 155.
51. Young, February 5, 1852.
52. Young, February 5, 1852; Jonathan Stapley, *The Power of Godliness: Mormon Liturgy and Cosmology* (New York: Oxford University Press, 2018), 20-22.
53. Young, 5 February 1852.

54. "Church History," *Times and Seasons*, March 1, 1842.
55. Orson Pratt, "The Pre-Existence of Man," *The Seer* (Washington, D.C.), April 1853, 56.
56. For instance, see B. H. Roberts, "To the Youth of Israel," *The Contributor* 6, no. 8 (May 1885): 296–297.
57. Young, February 5, 1852.
58. Young, February 5, 1852.
59. Orson Pratt, March 22, 1856, before the 1856 Utah Constitutional Convention, Church History Department Pitman Shorthand transcriptions, 2013–2021, Addresses and sermons, 1851–1874, Utah Constitutional Convention, March 1856, CHL; Facsimile transcript, CR 100 912, CHL.
60. Young, February 5, 1852.
61. Young, February 5, 1852; for ways that other nineteenth-century religious thinkers dealt with Old and New Testament notions of slavery, see Jordan Watkins, *Slavery and Sacred Texts: The Bible, the Constitution, and Historical Consciousness in Antebellum America* (New York: Cambridge University Press, 2021), chapter 3.
62. Church Historian's Office, General Church Minutes, 1839–1877, CR 100 318, box 1, folder 52, March 26, 1847, CHL; Reeve, *Religion of a Different Color*, 128–135; W. Paul Reeve, *Let's Talk about Race and Priesthood* (Salt Lake City: Deseret Book, 2023), 66–67. On Q. Walker Lewis see Jordan T. Watkins, "Quack Walker Lewis," Century of Black Mormons, https://exhibits.lib.utah.edu/s/century-of-black-mormons/page/lewis-quack-walker.
63. General Church Minutes, CR 100 318, box 1, folder 59, December 3, 1847, 6–7, CHL. See Reeve, *Religion of a Different Color*, chapter 4; and Reeve, *Let's Talk about Race*, chapters 7–9 for a contextual understanding of these events.
64. Young, February 5, 1852.
65. Young, February 5, 1852.
66. *Journals of the House of Representatives, Council, and Joint Sessions*, 127–128. On the sometimes tense relationship between Pratt and Young see Gary James Bergera, *Conflict in the Quorum: Orson Pratt, Brigham Young, Joseph Smith* (Salt Lake City: Signature Books, 2002).
67. *Acts, Resolutions, and Memorials, Passed by the First Annual, and Special Sessions of the Legislative Assembly of the Territory of Utah, Begun and Held at Great Salt Lake City, on the 22nd Day of September, A. D. 1851* (Salt Lake City: Brigham H. Young, Printer, 1852), 107, 178, 193; *Journals of the House of Representatives, Council, and Joint Sessions*, 127–128; Stout, *On the Mormon Frontier*, 2:423; Reeve, *Let's Talk about Race*, 69.
68. Reeve, *Religion of a Different Color*, chapters 4–7.
69. Stout, *On the Mormon Frontier*, 2:424.
70. On the announcement of polygamy see David J. Whittaker, "The Bone in the Throat: Orson Pratt and the Public Announcement of Plural Marriage," *Western Historical Quarterly* 18 (July 1987): 293–314.

Chapter 8

1. James Thomas Wilson, "Reminiscences of James Thomas Wilson," *Saints by Sea: Latter-day Saint Immigration to America*, HBLL, https://saintsbysea.lib.byu.edu/mii/account/336.
2. United States, 1850 Census, Slave Schedule, Hickman County, Tennessee.
3. Wilson, "Reminiscences of James Thomas Wilson."
4. Wilson, "Reminiscences of James Thomas Wilson."
5. Wilson, "Reminiscences of James Thomas Wilson."
6. Wilson, "Reminiscences of James Thomas Wilson."
7. Church of Jesus Christ of Latter-day Saints, Record of Members Collection, Sugar House Ward, microfilm 26792, FHL.
8. Abraham O. Smoot, Bill of Sale of Lucinda to Thomas S. Williams, March 1, 1852, series 373, reel 5, box 4, folder 26, UDARS.
9. Margaret Thompson McMeans Smoot Sketch Book, Abraham Owen Smoot Family Papers (1836–1947), MSS 3843, box 3, folder 5, L. Tom Perry Special Collections, HBLL. We are indebted to Mindy Smoot Robbins for sharing these references.
10. United States, 1860 Census, Slave Schedule, Salt Lake County, Utah Territory.
11. Utah, Death Register, 1847–1966, Salt Lake County, 1862, series 21866, UDARS; Salt Lake County, Utah, Death Records, microfilm 7,579,295, FHL.
12. Bills and Resolutions, House of Representatives, 37th Cong., 2nd Sess., Bill 374, A Century of Lawmaking for a New Nation: U. S. Congressional Documents and Debates, 1774–1875, https://memory.loc.gov/cgi-bin/ampage?collId=llhb&fileName=037/llhb037.db&recNum=2143.

13. Julius Taylor, "Slavery in Utah," Broad Ax (Salt Lake City), March 25, 1899.
14. Abraham O. Smoot, Bill of Sale of Negro to Thomas S. Williams, March 1, 1852, series 373, reel 5, box 4, folder 26, 7, UDARS.
15. Amy Tanner Thiriot, Slavery in Zion: A Documentary and Genealogical History of Black Lives and Black Servitude in Utah Territory, 1847–1862 (Salt Lake City: University of Utah Press, 2022), 17, 19–20, 81–82.
16. Smith confirmed in his journal that the county court was in session on March 1, but he adjourned court until the next Monday because there was "little business to be done." Elias Smith, Journal, March 1, 1852, MS 1319, Elias Smith Journals, 1836–1888, CHL.
17. Abraham O. Smoot, Bill of Sale of Negro to Thomas S. Williams.
18. Abraham O. Smoot, Bill of Sale of Negro to Thomas S. Williams.
19. Abraham O. Smoot, Bill of Sale of Negro to Thomas S. Williams.
20. Thiriot, *Slavery in Zion*, 23, 27, 115–120, 137, 189–195, 343–351.
21. Brigham Young Office Files, Journal, June 9, 1856, CR 1234 1, box 72, folder 2, CHL; Thiriot, *Slavery in Zion,* 118–120.
22. United States v. Williams Camp et al. (1856), Salt Lake County Probate Court Case Files, series 373, box 4, folder 2, UDARS.
23. Brigham Young Office Files, Journal, June 16, 1856, CR 1234 1, box 72, folder 2, CHL.
24. United States v. Williams Camp et al.
25. Elias Smith, Journal, June 18, 1856; Thiriot, *Slavery in Zion*, 119.
26. "Notice," Deseret News, March 4, 1857, 12.
27. Thiriot, *Slavery in Zion*, 119.
28. Affidavit of Diannah Camp in regard to Negro boy Shepherd, filed July 10, 1856, series 373, reel 5, box 4, folder 26, UDARS; Affidavit of Williams Camp in regard to Negro boy Shepard, filed July 10, 1856, series 373, reel 5, box 4, folder 26, UDARS; Affidavit of William T. Dennis in regard to Negro boy Shepherd, filed July 10, 1856, series 373, reel 5, box 4, folder 26, UDARS; Affidavit of Williams Camp in regard to his Servant Daniel, filed July 10, 1856, reel 5, box 4, folder 26, UDARS.
29. Abraham O. Smoot, Bill of Sale of Negro to Thomas S. Williams.
30. Thiriot, *Slavery in Zion*, 89–90, 348–351.
31. Thomas S. Williams, Bill of Sale for Dan to William H. Hooper, August 17, 1859, Great Salt Lake County Recorder's Office, in Kate B. Carter, The Story of the Negro Pioneer (Salt Lake City: Daughters of Utah Pioneers, 1965), 43.
32. Thiriot, *Slavery in Zion*, 27, 117–120, 190–193, 343–348.
33. Hosea Stout, On the Mormon Frontier: The Diary of Hosea Stout, 1844–1861, ed. Juanita Brooks, 2 vols. (Salt Lake City: University of Utah Press and Utah State Historical Society, 1964), 2:597.
34. Utah Constitutional Convention Speeches, MS 2988, CHL; Minutes of Utah Constitution Convention, Council House, March 21–27, 1856, MS 2988, CHL.
35. Thiriot, *Slavery in Zion*, 89–90, 119.
36. Thiriot, *Slavery in Zion*, 27, 69–70, 90–97, 238–243; Schedule of Property of David Lewis, deceased, Utah Territory, Probate Court Records, Salt Lake County, series 1621, reel 1, box 1, folder 41, UDARS.
37. Duritha Lewis, Slave Registration, August 4, 1858, Utah Territory, Third District, Probate Court Records, series 373, reel 6, box 5, folder 11, UDARS.
38. Thiriot, *Slavery in Zion*, 70, 90–93, 240–243.
39. Brigham Young to Duritha Lewis, January 3, 1860, Brigham Young Office Files, CR 1234 1, reel 27, box 19, folder 1, CHL.
40. Horace Greeley, "Letter of Horace Greeley. Two Hours with Brigham Young," New York Herald, August 24, 1859, 2.
41. Brigham Young to Duritha Lewis, March 31, 1860, Brigham Young Office Files, CR 1234 1, reel 27, box 19, folder 5, CHL.
42. "Drowned," Deseret News, June 19, 1861, 8; Thiriot, *Slavery in Zion*, 69–70, 81, 91–92, 95–96, 238–239.
43. "The Missouri Compromise," Deseret News, June 24, 1857, 6.
44. Thomas S. Williams, Bill of Sale for Dan to William H. Hooper; Greeley, "Letter of Horace Greeley."
45. Thiriot, *Slavery in Zion*, 93.

46. Acts, Resolutions, and Memorials Passed at the Several Sessions of the Legislative Assembly of the Territory of Utah (Salt Lake City: Henry McEwan, Printer, 1866).
47. Schedule of Property of David Lewis.
48. An Act for the Relief of Indian Slaves and Prisoners, in *Acts, Resolutions, and Memorials, Passed by the First Annual, and Special Sessions of the Legislative Assembly of the Territory of Utah, Begun and Held at Great Salt Lake City, on the 22nd Day of September, A. D. 1851* (Salt Lake City: Brigham H. Young Printer, 1852), 93; see Michael Bennion, "Captivity, Adoption, Marriage and Identity: Native American Children in Mormon Homes, 1847–1900," (Master's Thesis: University of Nevada-Las Vegas, 2012), 246, for examples of the various ways Latter-day Saints acquired Indigenous children.
49. Brian Q. Cannon, "'To Buy Up the Lamanite Children as Fast as They Could': Indentured Servitude and Its Legacy in Mormon Society," Journal of Mormon History 44 (April 2018): 20–29.
50. Bennion, "Captivity, Adoption, Marriage and Identity," chapters 4 and 5.
51. An Act in Relation to Masters and Apprentices, in Acts, Resolutions, and Memorials, Passed by the First Annual, and Special Sessions, of the Legislative Assembly of the Territory of Utah, Begun and Held at Great Salt Lake City, on the 22nd day of September, A. D., 1851 (Great Salt Lake City: Brigham H. Young, Printer, 1852), 76.
52. Cannon, "'To Buy Up the Lamanite Children,'" 7.
53. Donald G. Godfrey and Rebecca S. Martineau-McCarty, eds. An Uncommon Common Pioneer: The Journals of James Henry Martineau, 1828–1918 (Provo, UT: Religious Studies Center, Brigham Young University, 2008), 17, 338.
54. Benjamin F. Johnson, My Life's Review: The Autobiography of Benjamin F. Johnson (Provo, UT: Grandin Book, 1997), 206.
55. For additional evidence of such exchanges see Cannon, "'To Buy Up the Lamanite Children,'" 13–14.
56. Brian Q. Cannon, "Adopted or Indentured, 1850–1870: Native Children in Mormon Households," in Nearly Everything Imaginable: the Everyday Life of Utah's Mormon Pioneers, ed. Ronald W. Walker and Doris R. Dant (Provo, UT: Brigham Young University Press, 1998); Sondra G. Jones, "'Redeeming the Indian': The Enslavement of Indian Children in New Mexico and Utah," Utah Historical Quarterly 67 (Summer 1999): 220–241.
57. Thomas Benson, Indenture of Sarah, October 1, 1853, Iron County, Utah; John Beal, Indenture of Samuel, February 1, 1859, Sanpete County, Utah, Utah Historical Records Survey, Inventory of the County Archives of Utah, no. 20, Sanpete County, Utah Historical Society, Salt Lake City, Utah.
58. Thomas Benson, Indenture of Sarah.
59. Thomas Benson, Indenture of Sarah.
60. Thomas Benson, Indenture of Sarah.
61. John Beal, Indenture of Samuel.
62. John Beal, Indenture of Samuel; On Arapeen see Sondra G. Jones, Being and Becoming Ute: The Story of an American Indian People (Salt Lake City: University of Utah Press, 2019), chapter 6.
63. John Beal, Indenture of Samuel.
64. John Beal, Indenture of Samuel.
65. United States, 1870 Census, Parowan, Iron County, Utah Territory; United States, 1880 Census, Apache County, Arizona Territory; Sarah Benson Harrup, FindAGrave.com, https://www.findagrave.com/memorial/161458745/sarah-harrop.
66. Virginia Kerns, Sally in Three Worlds: An Indian Captive in the House of Brigham Young (Salt Lake City: University of Utah Press, 2021), 42, 78, 242–243.
67. Brigham Young, testimony in U.S. v Pedro León case of libel, January 15, 1852, First District Court, Minute Book, 1851–1896, series 10035, reel 1, 46–47, UDARS.
68. A List of President Brigham Young's Family Residing in the 18th Ward, March 19, 1855, Brigham Young Office Files, CR 1234 1, box 170, folder 26, CHL; United States, 1870 Census, Ward 18, Salt Lake City, Salt Lake County, Utah Territory.
69. Kerns, Sally in Three Worlds, 91–95, 127, 144–146.
70. Kerns, Sally in Three Worlds, 42–43, 67, 146, 309n19.
71. Kerns, Sally in Three Worlds, chapter 10, 226–227.
72. Church of Jesus Christ of Latter-day Saints, Record of Members Collection, Salt Lake 18th Ward, CR 375 8, CHL; "Funeral of a Lamanite," Deseret News, December 18, 1878, 16; Kerns, Sally in Three Worlds, 216, 226–227, 324n25.

73. "Funeral of a Lamanite," 16.
74. Jacob Hamblin to Brigham Young, June 23, 1860, Brigham Young Office Files, box 27, folder 14, CHL.
75. Jacob Hamblin and James A. Little, Jacob Hamblin: A Narrative of His Personal Experience as a Frontiersman, Missionary to the Indians and Explorer, 2nd ed. (Salt Lake City: Deseret News, 1909), 35; Todd M. Compton, A Frontier Life: Jacob Hamblin, Explorer and Indian Missionary (Salt Lake City: University of Utah Press, 2013), 38.
76. Compton, *A Frontier Life*, 485–488.
77. Compton, *A Frontier Life*, 234. See also Ronald W. Walker, Richard E. Turley Jr., and Glen M. Leonard, Massacre at Mountain Meadows (New York: Oxford University Press, 2008), 151, 198, 207, 217; and Richard E. Turley Jr. and Barbara Jones Brown, Vengeance Is Mine: The Mountain Meadows Massacre and Its Aftermath (New York: Oxford University Press, 2023), 6, 60-61.
78. Compton, *A Frontier Life*, 114.
79. Compton, *A Frontier Life*, 169–170, 192.
80. Albert Hamblin to Brigham Young, February 6, 1861, Brigham Young Office Files, box 28, folder 7, CHL; Compton, *A Frontier Life*, 192.
81. Hamblin, *A Narrative of His Personal Experience*, 99; Compton, *A Frontier Life*, 225.
82. Hamblin, *A Narrative of His Personal Experience*, 106.
83. "Died [David Lewis]," Deseret News, September 26, 1855.
84. Journal of the Southern Indian Mission: Diary of Thomas D. Brown, ed. Juanita Brooks (Logan: Utah State University Press, 1972), 163; Jones, *Being and Becoming Ute*, 104.
85. *Journal of the Southern Indian Mission*, 111.
86. Thiriot, *Slavery in Zion*, 19–21, 27, 69–70, 84, 89–96, 118–123, 238–243, 348–351; Schedule of Property of David Lewis.

Chapter 9

1. Brent M. Rogers, *Unpopular Sovereignty: Mormons and the Federal Management of Early Utah Territory* (Lincoln: University of Nebraska Press, 2017), chapters 1 and 4.
2. Utah Constitutional Convention Speeches, MS 2988, CHL; Minutes of Utah Constitutional Convention, Council House, March 21–27, 1856, MS 2988, CHL.
3. On the 1849 Constitution Convention that was fabricated in order for delegations to get the statehood application to Washington, D.C. in time for Congress to consider it, see Peter Crawley, "The Constitution of the State of Deseret," *BYU Studies* 29, no. 4 (1989): 7–22; Minutes of Utah Constitutional Convention.
4. Constitution of the State of Deseret (working copies), 1856, MS 2988, CHL; Utah Constitutional Convention Speeches.
5. Constitution of the State of Deseret (working copies), 1856.
6. Utah Constitutional Convention Speeches.
7. Minutes of Utah Constitutional Convention.
8. *Council of Fifty, Minutes, March 1844–January 1846*, ed. Matthew J. Grow, Ronald K. Esplin, Mark Ashurst-McGee, Jeffrey D. Mahas, Matthew C. Godfrey, and Gerrit J. Dirkmaat (Salt Lake City: Church Historian's Press, September 2016), 117–118.
9. Utah Constitutional Convention Speeches.
10. Utah Constitutional Convention Speeches.
11. Utah Constitutional Convention Speeches.
12. Utah Constitutional Convention Speeches.
13. Minutes of Utah Constitutional Convention; Utah Constitutional Convention Speeches.
14. Minutes of Utah Constitutional Convention; Utah Constitutional Convention Speeches. The Pitman shorthand transcript implies that the amendment was introduced by Thomas S. Williams. However, the longhand minutes of the convention indicate that the amendment was introduced by Blair, and the name Williams is crossed out.
15. Utah Constitutional Convention Speeches.
16. Utah Constitutional Convention Speeches.
17. Minutes of Utah Constitutional Convention; Utah Constitutional Convention Speeches.
18. Minutes of Utah Constitutional Convention, emphasis added.
19. Utah Constitutional Convention Speeches.
20. Minutes of Utah Constitutional Convention.

21. Orson Pratt, March 22, 1856, before the 1856 Utah Constitutional Convention, Church History Department Pitman Shorthand transcriptions, 2013-2021, Addresses and sermons, 1851-1874, Utah Constitutional Convention, March 1856, CHL.
22. Orson Pratt, March 22, 1856.
23. Orson Pratt, March 22, 1856.
24. For ways that other nineteenth-century religious thinkers rejected biblical slavery as applicable to the nineteenth century, see Jordan Watkins, *Slavery and Sacred Texts: The Bible, the Constitution, and Historical Consciousness in Antebellum America* (New York: Cambridge University Press, 2021), 111-112, 125-128.
25. Smith's name was originally included in the "Nay" column but was crossed out and added to the end of the "Yea" column. See Minutes of Utah Constitutional Convention.
26. Minutes of Utah Constitutional Convention.
27. Minutes of Utah Constitutional Convention.
28. Minutes of Utah Constitutional Convention; Constitution of Deseret art. VII, sec. 2. There was debate about whether African Americans and Native Americans were citizens and could vote, but so far as the records show, the argument was inconclusive. See Utah Constitutional Convention Speeches.
29. Brigham Young, Salt Lake City, Utah, to Thomas L. Kane, Kane, Pennsylvania, October 26, 1869, Brigham Young Office Files, CR 1234 1, Letterbook 11, CHL.
30. Young to Kane, October 26, 1869.
31. Historian's Office General Minutes, 1839-1877, March 23, 1856, CR 100 318, CHL; we are indebted to Sylvia Ghosh for her transcription of the Bullock shorthand in these minutes.
32. Historian's Office General Minutes, 1839-1877, March 23, 1856.
33. Brigham Young to Thomas L. Kane, April 14, 1856, in Matthew J. Grow and Ronald W. Walker, eds., *The Prophet and the Reformer: The Letters of Brigham Young and Thomas L. Kane* (New York: Oxford University Press, 2015), 195-196.
34. Horace Greeley, "Letter of Horace Greeley. Two Hours with Brigham Young," *New York Herald*, August 24, 1859.
35. General Church Minutes, 1839-1877, DR 100 318, box 1, folder 53, April 25, 1847, CHL; W. Paul Reeve, *Religion of a Different Color: Race and the Mormon Struggle for Whiteness* (New York: Oxford University Press, 2015), 133, 145-148. Apostle John Taylor did suggest that the descendants of Ham were "apostate[s] of the holy priesthood" in 1845, but he does not refer to a priesthood curse. He instead supports enslavement based on a standard biblical interpretation of Genesis 9:25. "The descendants of Ham, besides a black skin which has ever been a curse that has followed an apostate of the holy priesthood, as well as a black heart, have been servants to both Shem and Japheth, and the abolitionists are trying to make void the curse of God, but it will require more power than man possesses to counteract the decrees of eternal wisdom." See John Taylor, "A Short Chapter on a Long Subject," *Times and Seasons* 6 no. 6 (April 1, 1845): 857.
36. For evidence of Gunnison's publication timeline and friendship with Carrington, see Brigham D. Madsen, "John W. Gunnison's Letters to His Mormon Friend, Albert Carrington," *Utah Historical Quarterly* 59 (Summer 1991): 264-267; and Reeve, *Religion of a Different Color*, 147.
37. John W. Gunnison, *The Mormons, or, Latter-day Saints, in the Valley of the Great Salt Lake* (Philadelphia: Lippincott, Grambo, 1852), 51, 143.
38. Christopher C. Jones, "'A very poor place for our doctrine': Religion and Race in the 1853 Mormon Mission to Jamaica," *Religion and American Culture: A Journal of Interpretation* 31 (Summer 2021): 262-295.
39. "To the Saints," *Deseret News*, April 3, 1852, 2; Orson Pratt, "The Pre-Existence of Man," *The Seer* (Washington, D.C.) April 1853; "Southern Women and Slavery," *St. Louis Luminary* (St. Louis, MO), March 24, 1855, 70; "African Discoveries," *Western Standard* (San Francisco), February 7, 1857, 2; "Remarks on J. R. Giddings's Letter," *The Mormon* (New York), September 12, 1857, 2.
40. "The Book of Abraham," *Times and Seasons*, March 1, 1842, 705.
41. This discussion of the Book of Abraham and its influence on the Latter-day Saint racial restrictions is taken from W. Paul Reeve, *Let's Talk about Race and Priesthood* (Salt Lake City: Deseret Book, 2023), chapter 8.
42. Terryl Givens with Brian M. Hauglid, *The Pearl of Greatest Price: Mormonism's Most Controversial Scripture* (New York: Oxford University Press, 2019), 131-137; Matthew L. Harris and Newell G. Bringhurst, *The Mormon Church and Blacks: A Documentary History* (Urbana: University of Illinois Press, 2015), 12-13.

43. Reeve, *Religion of a Different Color*, chapter 5, 205–208; Givens and Hauglid, *The Pearl of Greatest Price*, 1–22.
44. "To the Saints," 2.
45. "To the Saints," 2.
46. "To the Saints," 2.
47. "To the Saints," 2.
48. Givens and Hauglid, *The Pearl of Greatest Price*, 256–257.
49. Pratt, "The Pre-Existence of Man."
50. Pratt, "The Pre-Existence of Man."
51. Pratt, "The Pre-Existence of Man."
52. This is based on electronic key words searches of his known speeches and writings, including those in the *Journal of Discourses*. He speaks frequently of "curses" but never again in any know speech does he return to a priesthood curse.
53. Pratt, "The Pre-Existence of Man."
54. *Speech of Elder Orson Hyde Delivered Before the High Priests' Quorum, in Nauvoo, April 27th, 1845* (Liverpool: James and Woodburn, 1845), 30.
55. Dan Vogel, ed., *The Wilford Woodruff Journals*, Typescript, 6 vols. (Salt Lake City: Benchmark Books, 2020), December 25, 1869, 4:185.
56. "Race and the Priesthood," Gospel Topics Essays, ChurchofJesusChrist.org.
57. See Reeve, *Let's Talk about Race*, chapter 11, for further evidence of how the two competing explanations played out over time.
58. "Southern Women and Slavery," 70. For Able and Lewis, see Reeve, *Religion of a Different Color*, chapters 4, 5, and 7; and W. Paul Reeve, "Elijah Able," Century of Black Mormons, https://exhibits.lib.utah.edu/s/century-of-black-mormons/page/able-elijah; and Jordan T. Watkins, "Quack Walker Lewis," Century of Black Mormons, https://exhibits.lib.utah.edu/s/century-of-black-mormons/page/lewis-quack-walker.
59. David Livingstone, *Missionary Travels and Researches in South Africa* (London: John Murray, 1857).
60. "African Discoveries," 2.
61. George A. Smith Family Papers, MS 36, box 78, folder 7, Council Minutes, August 18, 1900, Manuscripts Division, Special Collections, JWML; Reeve, *Religion of a Different Color*, 205–208.
62. We are indebted to Brent Rogers for this insight into Taylor's travels in 1857. Taylor gave an address in Salt Lake City on August 9, 1857.
63. "Remarks on J. R. Giddings's Letter," 2.
64. "Remarks on J. R. Giddings's Letter," 2.
65. "Remarks on J. R. Giddings's Letter," 2.
66. Sean Wilentz, *No Property in Man: Slavery and Antislavery at the Nation's Founding* (Cambridge, MA: Harvard University Press, 2018), 45.
67. John G. Turner, *Brigham Young: Pioneer Prophet* (Cambridge, MA: Harvard University Press, 2012), 225.
68. Molly Oshatz, *Slavery and Sin: The Fight against Slavery and the Rise of Liberal Protestantism* (New York: Oxford University Press, 2012), chapter 2.
69. Brigham Young, 23 January 1852, Papers of George D. Watt, MS 4534, box 1, folder 3, 1, CHL.
70. Brigham Young, "The Persecutions of the Saints—Their Loyalty to the Constitution—The Mormon Battalion—The Laws of God Relative to the African Race," March 8, 1863, *Journal of Discourses*, 26 vols. (Liverpool: Latter-day Saints' Book Depot, 1865), 10:110–111.
71. Oshatz, *Slavery and Sin*, 56–57.
72. Young, "The Persecutions of the Saints," 110.
73. Manisha Sinha, *The Slave's Cause: A History of Abolition* (New Haven, CT: Yale University Press, 2016); David W. Blight, *Frederick Douglass Prophet of Freedom* (New York: Simon & Schuster, 2018).
74. Wilentz, *No Property in Man*, 31.
75. Alfreda Eva Bell, *Boadicea the Mormon Wife: Life Scenes in Utah* (New York and Buffalo: Arthur R. Orton, 1855), 54–55.
76. "Joseph Cooks Lectures," *The Congregationalist* (Boston), December 10, 1879.
77. Kirk H. Porter and Donald Bruce Johnson, eds., *National Party Platforms, 1840–1956* (Urbana: University of Illinois Press, 1956), 27.

78. For additional context on white slavery and the conflation of polygamy and slavery, see Reeve, *Religion of a Different Color*, 46–51, 161–170. For Latter-day Saint rhetoric against abolitionists in defense of slavery see Newell G. Bringhurst, *Saints, Slaves, and Blacks: The Changing Place of Black People within Mormonism*, 2nd ed. (Salt Lake City: Greg Kofford Books, 2018), 106–113.
79. C. C. Goen, *Broken Churches, Broken Nation: Denominational Schisms and the Coming of the American Civil War* (Macon, GA: Mercer University Press, 1985).
80. Bringhurst, *Saints, Slaves, and Blacks*, 104.
81. Goen, *Broken Churches, Broken Nation*, 83.
82. This number of Black converts by 1852 is based on the ongoing research at Century of Black Mormons, a digital history database designed to name and number all Black Latter-day Saints baptized into the faith between 1830 and 1930. See http://centuryofblackmormons.org.
83. "Governor's Message," *Deseret News*, January 10, 1852, 18.
84. An Act in Relation to Service, in *Acts, Resolutions, and Memorials, Passed by the First Annual, and Special Sessions of the Legislative Assembly of the Territory of Utah, Begun and Held at Great Salt Lake City, on the 22nd Day of September, A. D. 1851* (Salt Lake City: Brigham H. Young, Printer, 1852), 80–82.
85. Brigham Young, before the Territorial Legislature on Slavery, January 27, 1852, CR 100 912, Church History Department Pitman Shorthand transcriptions, 2013–2021, Addresses and sermons, 1851–1874, Miscellaneous transcriptions, 1869, 1872, 1889, 1848, 1851–1854, 1859–1863, Utah Territorial Legislature, January–February 1852, CHL.
86. "Governor's Message."
87. Brigham Young, January 23, 1852, CR 100 912, Church History Department Pitman Shorthand transcriptions, 2013–2021, Addresses and sermons, 1851–1874, Miscellaneous transcriptions, 1869, 1872, 1889, 1848, 1851–1854, 1859–1863, Utah Territorial Legislature, January–February 1852, CHL.
88. Brigham Young, February 5, 1852, CR 100 912, Church History Department Pitman Shorthand transcriptions, 2013–2021, Addresses and sermons, 1851–1874, Miscellaneous transcriptions, 1869, 1872, 1889, 1848, 1851–1854, 1859–1863, Utah Territorial Legislature, January–February 1852, CHL.
89. Presiding Bishopric, Minutes of Bishops' Meetings, 1851–1884, CR 4 2, CHL. We are indebted to Jonathan Stapley for bringing this reference to our attention.
90. Reeve, *Religion of a Different Color*, conclusion.
91. Brigham Young to Thomas L. Kane, April 14, 1856, in *The Prophet and the Reformer: The Letters of Brigham Young and Thomas L. Kane*, ed. Matthew J. Grow and Ronald W. Walker (New York: Oxford University Press, 2015), 193–197.
92. Greeley, "Letter of Horace Greeley," 2.
93. Utah Territorial Legislature, Debate on Indian Slavery, possibly beginning January 23, 1852, CR 100 912, Church History Department Pitman Shorthand transcriptions, 2013–2021, Addresses and sermons, 1851–1874, Miscellaneous transcriptions, 1869, 1872, 1889, 1848, 1851–1854, 1859–1863, Utah Territorial Legislature, January–February 1852, CHL.
94. 2 Nephi 26:33; Doctrine and Covenants 101:79, 38:16.
95. Pratt, "The Pre-Existence of Man," 56.
96. Orson Pratt, March 22, 1856.
97. Utah Territorial Legislature, Debate on Indian Slavery.
98. "First Judicial Court," *Deseret News*, March 6, 1852, 4.
99. Orson Pratt, before the Territorial Legislature on Slavery, January 27, 1852, CR 100 912, Church History Department Pitman Shorthand transcriptions, 2013–2021, Addresses and sermons, 1851–1874, Miscellaneous transcriptions, 1869, 1872, 1889, 1848, 1851–1854, 1859–1863, Utah Territorial Legislature, January–February 1852, CHL.
100. Pratt, January 27, 1852.
101. Brigham Young, "Gathering the Saints—Honoring the Priesthood, etc.," July 28, 1861, in *Journal of Discourses*, 9:143.
102. Bringhurst, *Saints, Slaves, and Blacks*, 111.
103. "Governor's Message," *Deseret News*, December 25, 1852, 116.
104. Young, February 5, 1852.
105. David J. Whittaker, "The Bone in the Throat: Orson Pratt and the Public Announcement of Plural Marriage," *Western Historical Quarterly* 18 (July 1987): 293–314.
106. Greeley, "Letter of Horace Greeley," 2.
107. Wilentz, *No Property in Man*, chapter 5.

Chapter 10

1. John M. Bernhisel, Washington, D.C., to Brigham Young, Salt Lake City, June 13, 1862, Brigham Young Office Files, CR 1234 1, reel 71, box 61, folder 6, CHL. For Bernhisel's role as a mediator between Brigham Young and lawmakers in Washington, D.C., see Bruce W. Worthen, *Mormon Envoy: The Diplomatic Legacy of Dr. John Milton Bernhisel* (Urbana: University of Illinois Press, 2023).
2. Kirk H. Porter and Donald Bruce Johnson, eds., *National Party Platforms, 1840–1956* (Urbana: University of Illinois Press, 1956), 27.
3. "From Washington," *Deseret News*, July 2, 1862, 4.
4. W. Caleb McDaniel, *Sweet Taste of Liberty: A True Story of Slavery and Restitution in America* (New York: Oxford University Press, 2019), 166–177.
5. McDaniel, *Sweet Taste of Liberty*, 190–193.
6. Julius Taylor, "Slavery in Utah," *Broad Ax* (Salt Lake City), March 25, 1899.
7. Tonya Reiter, "Redd Slave Histories: Family, Race, and Sex in Pioneer Utah," *Utah Historical Quarterly* 85 (Spring 2017): 112–116; Tonya Reiter and Kaitlyn Benoit, "Marinda Redd Bankhead," Century of Black Mormons, https://exhibits.lib.utah.edu/s/century-of-black-mormons/page/bankhead-marinda-redd.
8. Reiter, "Redd Slave Histories," 116–117; Spanish Fork Ward general minutes, 1851–1883, Spanish Fork Ward, LR 8611 11, CHL.
9. Taylor, "Slavery in Utah."
10. Reiter and Benoit, "Marinda Redd Bankhead."
11. Benjamin Kiser, "Green Flake," Century of Black Mormons, https://exhibits.lib.utah.edu/s/century-of-black-mormons/page/flake-green.
12. "The Pioneers of 1847," *Deseret Weekly News*, August 25, 1894, 2; Kiser, "Green Flake."
13. "The Opening Day of the Jubilee," *Salt Lake Tribune*, July 20, 1897, 1; Kiser, "Green Flake."
14. "Green Flake Passes Away," *Deseret Evening News*, October 22, 1903, 1; "Green Flake Is No More," *Salt Lake Tribune*, October 23, 1903; "Died," *Salt Lake Tribune*, October 23, 1903; "News of the State," *Ogden Standard*, October 23, 1903; "Died," *Salt Lake Herald*, October 23, 1903; Kiser, "Green Flake."
15. Julia Huddleston, "Betsy Brown Fluellen," Century of Black Mormons, https://exhibits.lib.utah.edu/s/century-of-black-mormons/page/fluellen-betsy-brown.
16. Huddleston, "Betsy Brown Fluellen."
17. An Act to Secure Freedom to All Persons within the Territories of the United States, 37th Cong., 2nd Sess., Chapter CXI (June 19, 1862).
18. *Acts, Resolutions, and Memorials Passed at the Several Sessions of the Legislative Assembly of the Territory of Utah* (Salt Lake City: Henry McEwan, Printer, 1866).
19. Richard Kitchen, "Mormon Indian Relationships in Deseret: Intermarriage and Indenture, 1847–1877" (PhD diss., Arizona State University, 2002); Michael Bennion, "Captivity, Adoption, Marriage and Identity: Native American Children in Mormon Homes, 1847–1900," (Master's thesis, University of Nevada–Las Vegas, 2012).
20. *The Compiled Laws of the Territory of Utah, Containing All the General Statutes Now in Force, to Which Is Prefixed the Declaration of Independence, Constitution of the United States, Organic Act of Utah, and Laws of Congress Especially Applicable to this Territory* (Salt Lake City: Deseret News Steam Printing, 1876).

Appendix 1

1. *Journals of the House of Representatives, Council, and Joint Sessions of the First Annual and Special Sessions of the Legislative Assembly of the Territory of Utah. Held at Great Salt Lake City, 1851 and 1852* (Great Salt Lake City: Brigham H. Young, Printer, 1852), 104–110; "Governor's Message," *Deseret News*, January 10, 1852, 18.
2. Watt was apparently not present when his election took place. The Council minutes state that following his election, a "messenger was dispatched for Mr. Watt, who, upon his arrival was duly qualified by the President." *Journals of the House of Representatives, Council, and Joint Sessions*, 19, 60. Regarding his election as reporter, Watt recorded:

The House of Representatives on the 5th of January 1852 in which house I was appointed as reporter. Present: W[illard] Richards, Heber C. Kimball, Father [John] Smith [chaplain of the Council], Orson Pratt, Bishop [Edward] Hunter, Daniel [H.] Wells, Orson Spencer, [Aaron] Johnson, [Lorin] Farr, Father [Isaac] Morley, [Charles R.] Dana, John S. Fullmer, George A. Smith, [Jedediah M.] Grant.

W. Richards inquired if [there is] anything on record on the form of government of the council?

Answer no.

I wish to say one word on that while the subject presents itself to me: the first point is that no motion [is] to be presented before this council except in writing. Unless any motion be presented in the writing, [then] the council was not ready to act upon [it]. It is one of [the] most important items [that] could be present[ed] to a body of this kind. Another thing I should wish that [myself] [and] that the council decide what to do about it: that if any bill shall pass the council or some different presentation [we should] not have more than [two] reading[s] on any one day before it passes the third reading. (Utah Territorial Legislature, January 5, 1852, CHL)

Watt received $90 compensation for thirty days of work as reporter and another $60 for twenty days of work doing "extra services in writing out reports."

Of the people Watt listed as present for his appointment, all were members of the legislative Council, not the House (although he was also elected reporter for the House), except John Smith who served as chaplain of the Council. See *Acts, Resolutions, and Memorials, Passed by the First Annual, and Special Sessions of the Legislative Assembly of the Territory of Utah, Begun and Held at Great Salt Lake City, on the 22nd Day of September, A. D. 1851* (Salt Lake City: Brigham H. Young, Printer, 1852), 102; and Utah State Archives staff, "Territory of Utah: Legislative Assembly Rosters, 1851–1894," UDARS, https://archives.utah.gov/research/guides/legislative-assembly.htm.

3. *Journals of the House of Representatives, Council, and Joint Sessions*, 85.
4. Brigham Young, before Territorial Legislature, January 23, 1852, CR 100 912, Church History Department Pitman Shorthand transcriptions, 2013–2021, Addresses and sermons, 1851–1874, Miscellaneous transcriptions, 1869, 1872, 1889, 1848, 1851–1854, 1859–1863, Utah Territorial Legislature, January–February 1852, CHL; Brigham Young Collection, CR 100 317, box 1, folder 14, CHL.
5. *Journals of the House of Representatives, Council, and Joint Sessions*, 85.
6. Utah Territorial Legislature, Debate on Indian Slavery, possibly beginning 23 January 1852, CR 100 912, Church History Department Pitman Shorthand transcriptions, 2013–2021, Addresses and sermons, 1851–1874, Miscellaneous transcriptions, 1869, 1872, 1889, 1848, 1851–1854, 1859–1863, Utah Territorial Legislature, January–February 1852, CHL.
7. *Journals of the House of Representatives, Council, and Joint Sessions*, 36.
8. *Journals of the House of Representatives, Council, and Joint Sessions*, 87.
9. *Journals of the House of Representatives, Council, and Joint Sessions*, 88.
10. *Journals of the House of Representatives, Council, and Joint Sessions*, 88–89.
11. *Journals of the House of Representatives, Council, and Joint Sessions*, 89.
12. *Journals of the House of Representatives, Council, and Joint Sessions*, 89.
13. Utah Territorial Legislature, Debate on Indian Slavery.
14. *Journals of the House of Representatives, Council, and Joint Sessions*, 89–90.
15. *Journals of the House of Representatives, Council, and Joint Sessions*, 90.
16. *Journals of the House of Representatives, Council, and Joint Sessions*, 90.
17. Orson Pratt, before the Territorial Legislature on slavery, January 27, 1852, CR 100 912, Church History Department Pitman Shorthand transcriptions, 2013–2021, Addresses and sermons, 1851–1874, Miscellaneous transcriptions, 1869, 1872, 1889, 1848, 1851–1854, 1859–1863, Utah Territorial Legislature, January–February 1852, CHL.
18. Orson Spencer before the Territorial Legislature on Slavery, January 27, 1852, CR 100 912, Church History Department Pitman Shorthand transcriptions, 2013–2021, Addresses and sermons, 1851–1874, Miscellaneous transcriptions, 1869, 1872, 1889, 1848, 1851–1854, 1859–1863, Utah Territorial Legislature, January–February 1852, CHL.
19. Brigham Young before the Territorial Legislature on Slavery, January 27, 1852, CR 100 912, Church History Department Pitman Shorthand transcriptions, 2013–2021, Addresses and sermons, 1851–1874, Miscellaneous transcriptions, 1869, 1872, 1889, 1848, 1851–1854, 1859–1863, Utah Territorial Legislature, January–February 1852, CHL.
20. *Journals of the House of Representatives, Council, and Joint Sessions*, 91.
21. Brigham Young before Territorial Legislature, January 29, 1852, CR 100 912, Church History Department Pitman Shorthand transcriptions, 2013–2021, Addresses and sermons, 1851–1874, Miscellaneous transcriptions, 1869, 1872, 1889, 1848, 1851–1854, 1859–1863, Utah Territorial Legislature, January–February 1852, CHL; Brigham Young Collection, CR 100 317, box 1, folder 15, CHL.

22. *Journals of the House of Representatives, Council, and Joint Sessions*, 94.
23. *Journals of the House of Representatives, Council, and Joint Sessions*, 95–96.
24. *Journals of the House of Representatives, Council, and Joint Sessions*, 96.
25. Hosea Stout, *On the Mormon Frontier: The Diary of Hosea Stout, 1844–1861*, ed. Juanite Brooks, 2 vols. (Salt Lake City: University of Utah Press and Utah State Historical Society, 1964), 2:420; *Journals of the House of Representatives, Council, and Joint Sessions*, 117. On the runaway federal officials see Ronald W. Walker, "The Affairs of the 'Runaways': Utah's First Encounter with the Federal Officers, Part 1," *Journal of Mormon History* 39 (Fall 2013): 1–43; Ronald W. Walker and Matthew J. Grow, "The People Are "Hogaffed or Humbugged": The 1851–52 National Reaction to Utah's 'Runaway' Officers, Part 2," *Journal of Mormon History* 40 (Winter 2014): 1–52; Bruce W. Worthen, "'Zachary Taylor Is Dead and in Hell and I am Glad of it!': The Political Intrigues of Almon Babbitt," *Utah Historical Quarterly* 84 (Spring 2015): 84–97.
26. Stout, *On the Mormon Frontier*, 2:421.
27. Stout, *On the Mormon Frontier*, 2:420.
28. Stout, *On the Mormon Frontier*, 2:421; *Journals of the House of Representatives, Council, and Joint Sessions*, 119.
29. *Acts, Resolutions, and Memorials*, 91–93.
30. Stout, *On the Mormon Frontier*, 2:422.
31. *Journals of the House of Representatives, Council, and Joint Sessions*, 122.
32. Brigham Young, February 4, 1852, CR 100 912, Church History Department Pitman Shorthand transcriptions, 2013–2021, Addresses and sermons, 1851–1874, Miscellaneous transcriptions, 1869, 1872, 1889, 1848, 1851–1854, 1859–1863, Utah Territorial Legislature, January–February 1852, CHL.
33. Heber C. Kimball, February 4, 1852, CR 100 912, Church History Department Pitman Shorthand transcriptions, 2013–2021, Addresses and sermons, 1851–1874, Miscellaneous transcriptions, 1869, 1872, 1889, 1848, 1851–1854, 1859–1863, Utah Territorial Legislature, January–February 1852, CHL.
34. Stout, *On the Mormon Frontier*, 2:423.
35. *Acts, Resolutions, and Memorials*, 82.
36. Brigham Young, February 5, 1852, CR 100 912, Church History Department Pitman Shorthand transcriptions, 2013–2021, Addresses and sermons, 1851–1874, Miscellaneous transcriptions, 1869, 1872, 1889, 1848, 1851–1854, 1859–1863, Utah Territorial Legislature, 1852 January–February, CHL.
37. Stout, *On the Mormon Frontier*, 2:423.
38. *Journals of the House of Representatives, Council, and Joint Sessions*, 127.
39. *Journals of the House of Representatives, Council, and Joint Sessions*, 128.
40. Stout, *On the Mormon Frontier*, 2:424; *Journals of the House of Representatives, Council, and Joint Sessions*, 131.
41. *Journals of the House of Representatives, Council, and Joint Sessions*, 133.
42. Stout, *On the Mormon Frontier*, 2:424; *Journals of the House of Representatives, Council, and Joint Sessions*, 141.
43. Stout, *On the Mormon Frontier*, 2:426.
44. *Journals of the House of Representatives, Council, and Joint Sessions*, 143.
45. Stout, *On the Mormon Frontier*, 2:427; *Journals of the House of Representatives, Council, and Joint Sessions*, 143–144.
46. *Journals of the House of Representatives, Council, and Joint Sessions*, 144.
47. Stout, *On the Mormon Frontier*, 2:428; *Journals of the House of Representatives, Council, and Joint Sessions*, 146–147. Only Stout records a repeal of the vote; the Joint Session minutes do not mention it. *Acts, Resolutions, and Memorials*, 94, lists the bill's final approval date as March 6, 1852, which is the date when Brigham Young would have signed it into law.
48. *Acts, Resolutions, and Memorials*, 94.
49. Stout, *On the Mormon Frontier*, 2:430.
50. *Acts, Resolutions, and Memorials*, 94.
51. Stout, *On the Mormon Frontier*, 2:431; *Journals of the House of Representatives, Council, and Joint Sessions*, 158.

Index

For the benefit of digital users, indexed terms that span two pages (e.g., 52–53) may, on occasion, appear on only one of those pages.

Tables and figures are indicated by an italic *t* and *f* following the page number.

Abel, 134, 166–69, 208–9, 211
Able, Elijah, 211–12
abolition (abolitionists)
   at 1852 convention, 136–37, 155–56, 161, 169, 170–71
   at 1856 convention, 200
   Act for the Gradual Abolition of Slavery, 34
   in antebellum America, 21
   anti-abolitionists, 44–45, 51
   and apprenticeship, 131
   and Brigham Young, 56–57, 77–81, 155–56, 184, 211–16, 221–23
   gradual, 33–35
   immediate, 7–8, 33
   and Latter-day Saints, 44–45, 49–52, 56–57, 200, 211–13
   and movements to end unfree labor, 22
   Peonage Abolition Act, 105
   Somerset, 65
   and Utah's positions on slavery before 1852, 65, 77–79
   See also emancipation; and *individual abolitionists by name*
Abraham, 142–44, 162
Act for the Government and Protection of Indians, 103
An Act for the Protection of the Rights of Indians, 82, 97–98, 106, 126
Act for the Relief of Indian Slaves and Prisoners (Indian Indenture Act *or* Bill)
   and apprenticeship, 16
   and child separation, 113–19
   and debates over slavery, 111–13
   early awareness of, 19
   historical implications of, 186–88, 189–97
   historical introduction to, 9–10, 102–5
   introduced to legislature, 105–10
   national contexts informing, 7–8, 82, 110–11
   original name, 82
   passage of Act, 117–18
   preamble approved, 117–18
   termination, 229–30
Act in Relation to Elections, 164
Act in Relation to Masters and Apprentices, 185–86, 187
An Act in Relation to Service (Service Act or Servant Code)
   Brigham Young insists on name change, 14–16, 138
   and children of enslaved, 152–54
   and contractual view of servitude, 93–94
   and gradual emancipation, 151–52
   historical introduction to, 7–8, 9–10, 120–26
   implications of, 173–97
   lasts a decade, 20
   and lifetime of bondage, 154–55
   moderate, 7–8
   not a slave code, 4, 14–17, 127–28, 164, 182, 185
   Orson Pratt's objections to, 139–42, 157
   Orson Spencer response to Pratt, 141–44
   passage of Act, 155
   and racial restriction justification, 133–37, 164
   and treatment of those in bondage, 127–33, 138
   twin focus of bill, 126–27, 147–51
   Young pleased with outcomes, 155–56
   Young response to Pratt, 144–46
An Act Regulating Elections, 9–10, 164
Act to Secure Freedom, 224, 228–29
agency, 41, 127, 135–36, 146–51, 168, 173, 188, 190, 209–11, 213, 217. *See also* servitude, voluntary
Alabama, 43–44, 45–46, 127–28
Alvord, John W., 50–51
American Anti-Slavery Society, 50
American Revolution, 3, 22, 24, 25, 26–27, 29–30, 32–33, 35, 41–42, 151, 158
Andrew, James O., 43–44

Anglo-American, 23, 31–32, 42, 93, 124, 131
Anti-Peonage Act (1867), 229
Apache, 83–84
Appleby, William I., 59–60, 180–81, 212–13
apprenticeship (apprentice)
  Act Concerning Masters and Apprentices, 185–86, 187
  Act in Relation to Masters and Apprentices, 185–86, 187
  and disorderly persons, 12–14, 27, 35, 41–42
  and English law, 27–29
  and involuntary servitude, 16, 26–27, 35, 108, 111, 118, 187–88
Arapeen, 119, 190–91
Archuleta, Philippe Santiago, 97
Auld, Hugh, 127–28

Babbit, Julia, 189
Babbitt, Almon W., 62, 64, 66–68, 71, 200–1, 202–3, 216
Bacon, Leonard, 136–37
Bankhead, Alex, 176–77, 225–26
Bankhead, George W., 75–77
Bankhead, John, 75–77, 80–81, 88–89, 91, 137
Bankhead, Marinda Redd. *See* Redd, Marinda
Baptiste, 2, 85, 95, 192, 193–94
Baptists, 6, 44, 45–46, 49–50, 51, 56, 57, 136, 216
Beal, John, 190–91
Benson, Ezra T., 199, 202–3
Benson, Richard, 189–90
Benton, Thomas Hart, 62, 110, 111, 124
Bernhisel, John M., 20, 62–63, 64, 66–68, 69–70, 71, 224
bishops, 19, 25, 27, 43–44, 54, 115–16, 128–29, 179, 180, 201–176, 218, 226
Black Code (New Mexico, 1857), 124, 125
Black Codes, 225
Blackstone, William, 32, 33–34, 38, 131, 154–55
Blair, Seth M., 94–95, 117–18, 199–203, 216, 221–22
Book of Abraham, 167, 207–8, 209–10, 212–13
Book of Mormon, 44–45, 158, 167, 191
Book of Moses, 167
Brooks, James, 67–68
Brown, James, 155
Brown, John, 19, 43, 45–46, 228
Brown, Thomas D., 197
Bullock, Thomas, 12, 89–90
Burns, Thomas, 61
Burton, John, 45
Burton, Robert T., 179

Calhoun, John C., 59, 62, 86, 101, 113

California
  "An Act Respecting Fugitives from Labor, and Slaves" 123
  and African American slavery, 3–4, 62–63, 69–70, 74–78, 122–24, 155–56
  and apprenticeship, 90, 108–9, 111, 118–19, 126
  and Deseret, 65–66
  free state, 3–4, 65, 68, 70, 120
  George Q. Cannon in, 212
  gold, 3–4, 61, 69–70
  and guardianship, 153
  Hispanic population, 42
  migration to, 1
  Monterey Convention, 66–67
  and Native American unfree labor, 1–2, 3–4, 42
  and Native slavery, 103–4, 108–9
  Native slave trading network, 85–86, 113–14
  San Bernardino party, 69–70, 74–78, 80–81, 127, 152–53, 155–56, 177, 181
  Sutter's Mill, 122
  testifying against whites by Blacks, 180
  and voluntary servitude, 73, 145–46
Call, Asa, 65, 70–71
Camp, Daniel (Negro Dan), 178–81, 185, 217
Camp, Diannah, 154–55, 178–79, 180–81
Camp, Williams, 154–55, 178–82, 183, 198–99
Canada, 67–68, 123
Cannon, George Q., 212–13
Cannon, Martha Hughes, 18
Caroline (Lewis), 152–53, 183–84, 185, 196–97
Carrington, Albert, 200, 206
Carruth, LaJean Purcell, 5–6, 10
Cass, Lewis, 59, 68
Charlotte, 43, 45–46, 178
Cheever, Henry A., 175
China (Chinese), 166
Church, Abraham, 173–74
Church, Haden Wells, 174–76
civil rights, 31–32, 35, 134–35, 182
Comanches, 83–84
Committee on Indian Affairs, 116–17
Compromise of 1850, 68, 76–77, 85–86, 88, 120
constitutions (constitutional)
  California, 66–67, 111, 120–23
  Deseret, 5–205
  Illinois, 40–41
  Indiana, 39
  of the Kingdom of God, 200
  Mexico, 58
  New Mexico, 124

INDEX 291

New York, 35–36
United States, 3, 24, 26, 54, 55–56, 65–69, 165, 201–4, 228
Utah, 198–99, 205–6, 209–10, 219, 221–22
Vermont, 215–16
contracts
and African Americans, 120–21, 123, 125–27, 138, 150–51
and immigration, 127–33, 138
indentured, 24–26, 28–29, 37–38, 40–42, 73, 93–94, 104–5, 123, 126–33, 138, 145–48, 154–55, 187–88
and marriage, 31–32
between masters and servants, 104–5, 145–51, 181–82
and Native Americans, 103, 110–11
and statutory servitude, 33–34
convict leasing, 14, 39, 61, 104, 145
Copeland, Reuben, 43, 45–46
Cora, 188–89
Council of Fifty, 55–57, 62
Cowdery, Oliver, 48–51
Crosby, Oscar, *See* Smith, Oscar
Crosby, William, 74–76
Curse of Cain, 60, 122, 134–35, 140–41, 145, 162–63, 164–71, 202–3, 208–9, 210–12, 213, 220, 222–23
Curse of Ham *or* Canaan, 51–52, 53, 60, 78–81, 93–94, 122, 131, 133–36, 140–42, 145, 148–50, 152–55, 162, 164, 169–70, 184, 207, 209, 210, 211–13, 219

Dana, Charles R., 111
debt
and apprenticeship, 42
debt servitude peonage, 12–14, 22–23, 27, 84–85, 93–94, 103–5, 110–11, 130
and immigration, 61, 128–33, 141
and indentured servitude, 27–30
and slavery, 147
Decker, Charles, 85, 192
Declaration of Belief Regarding Governments and Laws in General, 49–50
Democratic Party (Democrats), 158
Free-Soil, 104
Jacksonian, 157–58
Southern, 121
Dennis, William T., 144–45, 180–81
Deseret (state)
and Black suffrage, 203–4
Constitution, 64, 124, 156, 162
constitutional convention, 9, 177, 178–79, 200–1

and immigration, 128–29
Petition, 66, 71–72
and slavery, 62–64, 65–68, 124, 162, 198–99, 200–1, 203, 204–6
and statehood, 91, 122, 158–60, 198, 204–6
Douglass, Frederick, 127–28
Douglas, Stephen, 39–40, 59, 110–11, 121, 124–25, 185
Freeport Doctrine, 121, 124–25, 185

Eddy, Thomas, 21–22, 33, 41–42, 215
education
and African Americans, 32–33, 35, 52, 80, 91, 93, 127–28, 135, 169, 218, 219
in An Act Related to Service, 127–28, 135, 151, 217, 219
in An Act in Relation to Masters and Apprentices, 187, 219
and apprenticeship, 25–26, 90, 108, 109–10, 187
and Brigham Young, 80, 91, 93, 135, 169, 218
and immigrants, 127–28
and Indigenous peoples, 84, 90, 108, 111, 188, 191–92, 219
election (elected), 8, 18, 19, 157–72, 201–2
electorate, 9
See also An Act Regulating Elections
emancipation
in An Act in Relation to Service, 120–21, 151–54, 217–19
and Brigham Young, 80, 91–92, 122, 169, 215
celebrated, 76
compensation for, 123, 214
in Deseret, 203
Emancipation Proclamation, 228
in federal territories, 224
and George A. Smith, 109–10
gradual, 7–8, 15–16
and indenture law, 118–19
and Joseph Smith, 45, 52–53, 54–55, 71–72, 78–79, 92, 133–34, 135, 137, 145, 169–70, 213
and LDS Southerners, 221–23
in Missouri, 47–48
and New Mexico, 124–25
in northern states, 19, 21–22, 30–35, 36
in the Northwest (Midwest), 37, 39–42
and Quakers, 78–79
in the South, 73–74
as theft, 3
See also Garrison, William Lloyd
England, 21, 25, 27, 31–32, 56, 89, 128–30, 132, 138. *See also* Great Britain

INDEX

Europe (Europeans), 12–16, 18, 27–29, 31, 59, 83–84, 121, 127, 128, 130–33, 138–41, 147–48, 155, 156, 178, 181, 219–20, 222–23, 229
Euro-Americans, 1–2, 16, 18, 101, 103–4, 187–98

Farr, Lorin, 109–10, 111–16
Flake, Abraham, 226–27
Flake, Agnes, 75–76
Flake, Green, 1, 60–61, 74–77, 78–80, 91, 183–84, 222, 226–28
Flake, Lucinda, 226
Flake, Martha Ann Morris, 226–27
Fluellen, Betsy Brown, 228
France (French), 21–22, 37, 191–92
free womb laws, 15–16, 33, 152, 217
Freeman, Daniel, 76
free-soil, 6–7, 59, 62, 64, 65, 66–67, 78–79, 91, 104, 122–23, 137
Fugitive Slave Act, 72, 123. *See also Scott v. Sanford*

Garrison, William Lloyd, 33, 49, 78–79, 80
Giddings, Joshua R., 212–13
Goshute, 58–59, 113–14, 194–95
Grant, Jedediah M., 199
Great Britain (British), 21–22, 28, 33, 53, 56–57, 92, 141, 143, 173, 221
Greeley, Horace, 93–94, 184, 185, 205–6, 219
Greer, Shepard, 178, 180–81
Greiner, John, 101
Griffin, Joseph L., 45–46
guardianship, 16, 79, 93, 103–4, 109–10, 153, 187, 189–90
Gunnison, John W., 70–71, 206–7
guns, 2, 83, 114–15
Guy, Abby, 163

Hamblin, Albert, 195–97
Hamblin, Jacob, 194–97
Hamblin, Priscilla, 195
Harrop, Henry, 191–92
Hispanics, 42, 84–85, 103, 124–25
Hispanos, 104–5
Hodge, Charles, 133
Hooper, William H., 63–64, 178, 181, 202–3, 216, 221–22
horses, 87–88, 97, 188–89, 196–97
Hunter, Edward, 19, 115–16
Hurt, Garland, 199, 202–3
Hyde, Orson, 64–65, 66–67, 71–74, 80–81, 211

Illinois, 18–19, 37, 39–41, 48–49, 52, 73, 111–12, 120–21, 122, 124–25, 127, 131, 145–46, 150–51, 152. *See also* Nauvoo, IL

immigration, 12–15, 27–30, 37–39, 41–42, 59, 121, 123, 127–33, 138–41, 152, 156, 181, 219–20, 229. *See also* Perpetual Emigrating Fund (PEF)
indentured servitude
and An Act in Relation to Service, 120–21, 123, 127–31, 144–48, 152, 154, 217
in antebellum America, 22–24, 27–32, 35, 37–42
and apprenticeship, 90
Brigham Young and Native indenture, 108–9, 117–18, 121
contracts, 24–26, 28–29, 37, 38, 40–41, 73, 93–94, 104–5, 123, 126–33, 138, 145–48, 154–55, 187–88
and debt, 27–30
and emancipation, 118–19
for European immigrants, 12–14, 219–20
and involuntary servitude, 29
and judges, 38–39
labor distinction, 14, 22–23
Native American Indenture Act, 229–30
for Native Americans, 7–8, 106–14, 115–19, 141, 185–92, 219–20
and sexual exploitation, 144–45
and slavery, 73
in wake of US-Mexico War, 61, 79
See also Act for the Relief of Indian Slaves and Prisoners (Indian Indenture Act *or* Bill)
Indian Country, 98–100, 102, 107, 111–12, 115–18
Indian Indenture Act. *See* Act for the Relief of Indian Slaves and Prisoners (Indian Indenture Act *or* Bill)
Indian Territory, 111–12, 117–18
Indiana, 37–40, 120–21, 127, 131, 152
An Act Concerning Servants, 38–39
An Act Concerning the Introduction of Negroes and Mulattoes, 37–38
involuntary servitude
and apprenticeships, 16, 26–27, 35, 108, 111, 118, 187–88
and California Law, 122–23
and the Compromise of 1850, 42, 59
in Illinois, 40, 73
and indenture, 29
in Indiana, 39–40
and Native Americans, 102, 105, 108, 111, 118
and the Northwest Ordinance, 37
outlawed in territories, 6, 9–10, 20, 59, 73, 120–21, 156, 183, 185–86, 199, 216, 224–25, 228–30
and slavery, 33–34, 42, 120–21
types of, 24

and Utah, 70–71
for vagrancy, 25–26, 61, 90, 103–4, 108, 111–12, 113–14, 145, 146, 187, 222
voluntary, 24, 26–27, 40–42, 105, 135–36, 145–46, 150–51, 188, 191, 229
See also An Act in Relation to Service; servitude; slavery
Islam (Muslims), 79, 83–84, 134

Jackson, Alexander, 124–25
Jamaica, 207
James, Isaac, 79–80, 135–36
James, Jane Manning, 45, 79–80, 135–36
Japan, 166
Jay, John, 21–22, 35–36, 215
Jay, Peter, 35–36
Jefferson, Thomas, 3, 175
Jerry, 176, 183–85
Jews, 79, 134, 165
Johnson, Benjamin Franklin, 189
Johnson, Sarah Jane, 189
Jones, Dan, 56, 132
judges
  and Anglo-Mexican law, 42
  and apprentice law, 127
  and Black testifying, 180–83
  and indenture law, 38–39
  justices of the peace, 38–39, 103
  and Native slavery, 82, 103–4
  probate judge, 17, 108, 114, 118, 129–31, 148t–51, 154–55, 174–76, 177–83, 185, 188–89, 192
  runaway judges, 147
  and voluntary agreements, 146, 150–51
  See also individual judges by name

Kane, Thomas L., 6, 62–63, 64–65, 66–68, 71–72, 77–78, 88–89, 116–17, 203–4, 205, 211, 219, 223
Kanosh, 85, 194
Kanosh, Sally or Pidash (Kah-peputz) Young, 192–93f
Kansas Territory, 9, 173–74, 198, 223
Kansas-Nebraska Act, 198, 200–1
Kemo, 189
Kent, James, 26
Kentucky, 19, 33, 37, 54, 73, 130, 178, 184
Kimball, Heber C., 5, 19, 25
Kinney, John F., 199, 202–3
kinship, 16, 82–83, 84–85, 101, 105, 114–15, 186, 194–95

labor
  free labor, 12–14, 19, 23–25, 27, 41–42

indenture contracts, 24–26, 28–29, 37, 38, 40–41, 73, 93–94, 104–5, 123, 126–33, 138, 145–48, 154–55, 187–88
  negotiation, 145–46, 154
  sold to third parties, 38–39
  See also unfree labor
Lay, Hark, See Wales, Hark
Lay, William, 74–76
Lewis, David, 183, 186, 196–97
Lewis, Duritha, 154–55, 183–84, 185, 196–97
Lewis, Elizabeth, 132
Lewis, Enoch, 59–60, 134–35, 144–45
Lewis, Q. Walker, 59–60, 170–71, 211–12
Lincoln, Abraham, 39–40, 78–79, 92, 124–25, 224
Livingstone, David, 212
London Missionary Society, 212
Long, John V., 199
Lucinda (Lucy), 175–76, 177
Luján, Don Pedro León
  and 1852 Utah legislative session, 88–101, 102, 122, 140
  and free soil concerns, 7, 97–98, 220–21
  historical context to legal case, 82–85
  LDS context to legal case, 85–88
  and Native Americans in New Mexico, 113
  and Native Americans in Utah, 105–7, 115–18, 197
  and Seth Blair, 199
  and status of enslaved people, 74
  and Zerubbabel Snow's ruling, 97–101, 111–12, 117, 140, 149–50, 151

Mack, Solomon, 26
manumission
  21, 34–36, 39–40, 43, 145, 222
marriage (marry)
  and apprenticeship, 31–32
  and enslaved people, 31–32, 75
  and free African Americans, 47–48, 183, 226–28
  and indenture, 29
  and Native American marriages, 85, 186–87, 194
  and Native American slavery, 82
  See also race, interracial relationships; polygamy
Martineau, James Henry, 188–89
Mather, Cotton, 144
Matthews, Benjamin, 63
McKown, Francis, 63–64
Methodism (Methodists) 6, 43–44, 45–46, 49–50, 51, 56, 57, 136, 216

294 INDEX

Mexico (Mexicans)
   Alta California, 42, 58, 66, 159
   Anglo-Mexican law, 42
   Brigham Young on, 92–93, 166
   as buffer zone between Indigenous peoples, 1
   constitution, 58
   freed slaves in, 53
   free womb laws, 15–16, 33, 152, 217
   and Indigenous slave trade, 115, 119
   and LDS racial restriction, 166
   in Luján case, 96–97
   Mexican Cession, 3–4, 42, 59, 61–62, 65, 66–67, 68–69, 99–100, 102, 110, 120, 126, 156
   Mormons explore immigration to, 2, 55
   prohibitions on slavery, 70
   slave codes, 120
   US-Mexico War, 2–4, 42, 82, 159–60
Miller, George, 54–55
missions (missionaries)
   African-descended peoples prohibited from serving, 5
   to enslaved peoples, 45–46, 48, 52
   of enslavers, 43, 46, 48, 52, 54
   and Indigenous peoples, 101, 115–16, 186, 195–97
   in Jamaica, 207
   London Missionary Society, 212
   slavery damaging to proselytizing, 141, 143
   See individual missionaries by name
Missouri
   enslaved baptisms in, 45
   Hawn's Mill Massacre, 183
   Jackson County, 46–49, 59, 62, 71, 78
   Missouri Compromise, 59, 61–62, 198
   Mormon expulsion from, 52–53, 62, 112
Morley, Isaac, 88, 95–97
Mormon Battalion, 159
Mosheim, 188–89

natural rights, 90–91, 199–201, 217–18
Nauvoo, IL, 2, 39, 41–42, 45, 55, 59–60, 77–78, 127, 183, 207
Navaho/Navajo, 2, 83–84, 85–86
Nauvoo Legion, 25
New England, 32–33, 158, 159–60
New Mexico
   Act to Provide for the Protection of Property in Slaves, 125
   Black Code (New Mexico, 1857), 124, 125
   constitution, 124
   emancipation in, 124–25
   Indigenous slave trade, 1–3, 7–8, 58–59, 82, 83–88, 89, 100–1, 103, 105–6, 114–15, 118–19

and interracial relationships, 42
peonage in, 110–11, 124–26, 130, 156, 229
and popular sovereignty, 68–69
rescate, 84, 99, 104, 105–6, 108–13, 118–19
slave code, 120, 121–23, 124–26, 156, 185
southern sympathizers in, 9, 223
and statehood, 61–62
unfree labor in, 3–4, 83–84, 108–9, 124–25
New York
   Act for the Gradual Abolition of Slavery, 34
   Act Relative to Slaves and Servants, 34
   and African American suffrage, 35
   constitution, 35–36
   enslaved people in, 32–33, 67–68, 110
   and gradual emancipation, 19, 31, 34–35, 37, 122, 151–52, 219
   and *The Mormon*, 207, 212–13
   and *The Seer*, 209–10
   New York Manumission Society, 21, 35–36
   servitude in antebellum New York, 30–31
Northwest Ordinance of 1787, 37, 39–41, 120–21, 201

Old Spanish Trail, 58, 85–86, 103
Oregon, 1, 9, 212

Pacific Islanders, 166
Pahvant, 85, 192, 194
Paiute. *See* Southern Paiute
Partridge, Edward, 25
paternalism
   and apprenticeship, 25–26, 27, 90, 93–94, 108, 187–88
   and Brigham Young, 79–80, 90, 93–94, 122, 169, 171, 184, 218
   and the LDS racial restriction, 122, 135–36, 169, 171, 218
   and Native Americans, 101, 108, 113–15, 118, 186, 191, 220
   and peonage, 85
Pawnee, 84
Pennington, James W. C., 31–32
peonage
   Anti-Peonage Act (1867), 229
   debt peonage, 14, 85, 103, 111, 130
   in New Mexico, 110–11, 124–26, 156, 229
Peonage Abolition Act, 105
Perpetual Emigrating Fund (PEF), 61, 128–30
Peter ("Black Pete"), 45
Phelps, William Wines, 46–49
Piede (Pah Ed), 189–91, 196–97
Pitman, Isaac, 10–12
Pitman shorthand, 4–6, 10–12, 13f, 162–63, 199

Polk, James K., 58, 61–62, 65
polygamy, 18–19, 172, 179, 186–87, 188–89, 192, 194–95, 198, 216, 223, 224
popular sovereignty, 59, 68–69, 77, 88, 110, 124, 158–59, 198, 200–1
Pratt, Orson
　and 1856 convention, 199–203
　and African American slavery, 138–45, 147, 150, 154, 155, 169, 198–202, 220–21
　and African American voting, 157–58, 203, 204, 218
　Brigham Young responds to, 160–61, 164
　and justification of racial curses, 168, 209–14
　on Legislative Council, 19
　and Native Americans, 8, 10, 15–16, 102, 109–10, 111–13, 116–18, 126, 138, 219–21
　rejects African slavery, 141, 169–70, 221
　response to Brigham Young, 5, 8, 15–16, 169, 171–72
Pratt, Parley P., 206, 208
Pratt, Thomas, 110
Presbyterianism (Presbyterians), 6, 44, 46, 49–50, 56, 57, 133, 216
priesthood
　and citizenship rights, 133, 162, 165–67, 204, 218–19
　LDS racial restriction and, 4–5, 45–46, 57, 133–35, 157–58, 164, 165–66, 167, 204, 211–12, 218–19, 222–23
　ordination of Black Mormons, 46, 57, 59–60, 166, 211–12
　See also racial restriction
Protestantism (Protestants), 44–45, 56, 133, 136–37, 167, 214–15

Quakers, 21–22, 49–50, 78–79, 179

race
　and Blackness, 208–9, 212–13
　and blood, 53, 55–56, 60, 162–64, 165, 207, 208–9
　environmental explanations for, 35, 52, 80
　interracial relationships, 47–51, 53, 59–60, 104, 106, 134–35, 144–45, 170–71, 186–87, 188–89, 191–92, 194–95, 211–12, 213, 222–23, 226
　one drop rule, 162–64
　and whiteness, 211
　See also Curse of Cain; Curse of Ham or Canaan; racial restriction
racial restriction
　at 1852 convention, 8, 10, 12–14

　and An Act in Relation to Service, 14–15, 133–37, 164
　Black men to eventually receive priesthood, Genesis, mark, 135, 167, 168–69
　and Brigham Young, 8, 59–61, 79–80, 132–37, 140–41, 144–46, 157–58, 161–72, 202, 208–11, 218, 220
　and language of servitude, 12, 79, 122, 131, 133–50, 152, 206, 211–12, 220
　in newspapers, 211–13
　ordination of Black Mormons, 46, 57, 59–60, 166, 211–12
　paternalism of, 122, 135–36, 169, 171, 218
　racial "mark," 134, 140–41, 166–67, 209, 211
　specific anti-Blackness of, 166
　temple implications, 20
　war in heaven used as justification for, 168
　See also Curse of Cain; Curse of Ham or Canaan; temple
Rande, 63
Redd, Elizabeth Hancock, 144–45
Redd, John Hardison, 144–45, 225–26
Redd, Marinda, 5, 144–45, 225–26
Reese, Enoch, 201
Relief Society, 194, 226
religious freedom, 1, 44–45
Republican Party (Republicans), 104, 176, 199, 216, 224
Reynolds, John, 39–40
Rice, William, 188–89
Richards, Willard, 19, 62, 64–65, 70–71, 98–99, 116–18, 162, 208–9, 211–12
Rigdon, Sidney, 55
Rockwood, Albert P., 160–61
Rocky Mountains, 2–3, 39
Roman Catholicism (Catholic), 19, 49–50, 89, 104, 114–15
Rose, 76–77, 79–80

Salt Lake City
　City Council, 17–19
　High Council (church), 60–61, 63, 158–60
Samuel, 190–92
San Bernardino, California, 69–70, 74–75, 76–78, 80–81, 127, 152–53, 177, 181
Sarah, 189–92, 195
Scott, Dred. See Scott v. Sanford
Scott v. Sanford, 68–69, 121, 124–25, 156, 165, 185–86, 205–6, 228–29
servitude
　and African Americans, 12–14, 16, 98–99, 122, 179, 185–86, 196–97
　in antebellum America, 21–42

servitude (*cont.*)
    and Blackstone, 33–34
    for immigrants from Europe, 12–14, 41–42, 126–27, 128–32, 139–40, 219–20
    and kinship, 83
    and LDS racial restriction, 12, 79, 122, 131, 133–50, 152, 206, 211–12, 220
    as middle ground in slavery debate, 7–8, 14–15, 79, 92–94, 102–3, 155–56, 219
    and Native Americans, 12–14, 16, 82, 89, 98–99, 104–11, 113–14, 115–19, 122, 186, 199
    notes on terminology, 15–16
    as punishment, 12–14
    See also An Act in Relation to Service; indentured servitude; peonage
Seward, William H., 110–11
sex, 144–45, 211–12, 217, 222–23
Shephard, 178–79
Shoshone, 1, 194–95, 196
slave codes
    federal, 121
    in Mexico, 120
    in New Mexico, 122, 124–26, 156, 185
    in Southern states, 127–28, 225
    in Utah, 127–28
slavery
    de jure, 24, 40, 131
    as divine institution, 219
    enslaved converts to Mormonism, 5, 144
    heritable condition, 15–16, 31–32, 33–34, 38, 95, 105, 109–10, 130–31, 145–51, 152–55, 187–88
    as metaphor, 138
    as Native diplomacy, 82
    neutrality towards, 6, 62, 64–65, 66–67, 71–72, 77, 198–99, 200–1, 204–5, 217–18, 223
    separation of families, 75–77, 113–14
    slave patrol, 16, 178–79
    small number of enslaved African Americans in Utah, 6, 70, 124, 181
    terminology in book, 15–16
    trafficking, 8, 58–59, 82, 85–86, 95, 101, 102, 105–7, 113, 116–17, 186, 197
slavery (African)
    baptisms of enslaved people, 45
    and Brigham Young, 88–94, 122, 126, 132–37, 144–50
    in California, 3–4, 62–63, 69–70, 74–78, 122–24, 155–56
    and Joseph Smith, 49–57, 62, 71–72
    and marriage, 31–32, 75
    and Orson Pratt, 138–45, 147, 150, 154, 155, 198–202, 220–21
    and servitude, 12–14, 16, 98–99, 122, 179, 185–86, 196–97
    small number of enslaved African Americans in Utah, 6, 70, 124, 181
    and US territories, 6, 9–10, 20, 174, 176, 183–86, 199, 218–19, 221, 224–25, 228–30
    See also laws related to African slavery by name; individual enslaved people by name
slavery (Indigenous)
    and California, 85–86, 103–4, 108–9, 113–14
    and marriage, 82
    in New Mexico, 1–3, 7–8, 58–59, 82, 83–88, 89, 100–1, 103, 105–6, 114–15, 118–19
    prisoners of war, 28, 82, 103–4, 106–8, 111, 186, 188, 196–97
    See also laws related to Native slavery by name; individual enslaved people by name
Smith, Elias, 175–76, 177–78, 179–81, 183
Smith, George A.
    at 1856 constitutional convention, 199, 219
    and African slavery, 111, 131–32, 181–82, 201–5
    and An Act in Relation to Service, 147
    on City Council, 19
    and immigration, 128–31
    and Indigenous servitude, 106–7, 109–10, 138, 141–42
    and Luján case, 88, 94–97
Smith, Joseph
    and abolition, 46–51, 200, 201–2
    Black men ordained during lifetime, 166
    and emancipation, 52, 71–72, 78–79, 92, 169–70, 213, 221
    New York childhood, 30–31, 34–35
    and racial curses, 59–61, 133–34, 168, 169–70, 207, 209
    and slavery, 49–57, 62, 71–72
    universalism, 44–45, 53–54, 143–44
Smith, Oscar, 1, 60–61
Smith, Robert, 63
Smoot, Abraham O., 173, 174, 175–76, 177, 184
Smoot, Margaret Thompson McMeans, 175–76, 177
Snow, Erastus, 2, 56, 211–12
Snow, Lorenzo R., 202–3
Snow, Zerubbabel, 7, 15–16, 91, 94–95, 97–101, 107, 109, 111–12, 117–18, 140, 149–50, 151, 199, 220–21
social welfare, 82, 108, 118, 187–88
Southern Paiute, 58–59, 82, 89, 113–14, 194–96, 197
Spain (Spanish), 1–2, 7, 14, 58–59, 83–84, 85–86, 94–95. *See also* Old Spanish Trail

Spencer, Orson, 5, 10, 94, 106, 115–16, 126–27, 129, 130–32, 138, 141–44, 145, 147–48
Stansbury, Howard, 206
Stiles, George P., 200, 202–3
Stout, Hosea, 61, 117–18, 130, 147, 157, 172, 179, 181
Stout, Louisa, 178, 179
suffrage
    Black, 8, 35–36, 134–36, 157–58, 161, 164–66, 171–72, 203–4, 210–11, 218–19, 220
    women, 18, 60, 79–80, 160, 164

Tampian (Lewis), 152–53, 183–85, 196–97
Taney, Roger B., 68–69, 165, 185
Taylor, John, 2, 25, 212–13
Taylor, Zachary, 65, 124
temples, 4–5, 20, 57, 164, 172, 191–92, 194
Texas, 54–55, 73, 94–95, 178–80, 182, 199, 225
theodemocracy, 158
Thurber, Albert King, 226
Tom, 173–76
Tompkins, Daniel D., 34
Trade and Intercourse Act (1834), 87–88, 89, 94–95, 99–100, 111–12, 116–18
Turner, Nat, 48

unfree labor, 3–4
    and the 1852 convention, 12–14
    in the 1856 convention, 219
    in An Act in Relation to Service, 128–29, 156
    in antebellum America, 22–25, 28, 40, 41–42
    and Brigham Young, 79, 90, 93
    in California, 103
    divisions of, 14–15, 24
    in New Mexico, 83–84, 108–9, 124–25
    and Orson Pratt, 109–10, 141, 214, 219–21
    as "the other slavery," 17
    in Reconstruction, 222
    in US Congress, 111
    and Utah before 1852, 61, 82, 118
universalism (LDS), 46, 133
University of Deseret, 5, 17
US Census, 6, 30–31, 32–33, 69–70, 88, 176, 191–92, 215–16
US Congress
    and African slavery, 122–23, 124–26
    and An Act in Relation to Service, 120, 121
    and Brigham Young, 221
    and Deseret territory, 57, 58–59, 64, 66–69, 71–72
    and Joseph Smith's presidential platform, 53, 92
    and Mexican cession, 42, 61–63, 65, 99–100
    and Native labor, 117–18, 119
    and the Northwest Ordinance, 37, 40
    outlaws slavery in territories, 6, 9–10, 20, 174, 176, 183–86, 199, 218–19, 221, 224–25, 228–30
    and peonage, 105, 110–13
    and the twin relics of barbarism, 216
    and Utah statehood, 198–99, 200–1, 204–6
    and Utah territory, 158–59
    and voting, 160
    See legislation by name
US Constitution, 3, 26, 54, 55–56, 68, 165, 202
    Thirteenth Amendment, 24, 40, 105, 228, 229
US House of Representatives, 67–68, 89, 224
US South (southern)
    and African American suffrage, 35–36
    in California, 3–4, 122, 123, 223
    Confederacy, 9, 125–26, 223
    converts to Mormonism from, 5, 46, 48, 52–53, 56–57, 71, 130–31, 136–37, 140, 173, 176–77, 179, 181, 214, 216–18, 221–22
    Democrats, 121
    and emancipation, 3
    and the expansion of slavery, 42, 59
    fire-eaters, 215
    and gradual emancipation, 22, 33, 73–74
    Joseph Smith and, 50–55
    and Methodism, 43–44, 216
    and national slave code, 124–25
    and notes on terms, 14–15
    and one-drop policy, 163
    and slavery in Utah, 59, 63, 71, 75
    in Utah or Deseret legislature, 7–9, 19, 88–89, 147, 154–55, 156, 198–99, 214, 222
    and Utah statehood, 62–63, 67–68, 200–122, 204–6
    Utahns try to distinguish labor from southern slavery, 141–43
US Supreme Court, 24, 61–62, 68–69, 121, 165. See also Scott v. Sanford
US-Mexico War, 2–4, 42, 82, 159
Utah
    as free state (if accepted to Union), 45, 151–52, 184–85, 205–6, 219, 223
    Council House, 17–18f, 89, 199
    House of Representatives, 18–19, 89, 164
    Legislative Council, 18–19, 89, 94, 98–99, 106, 109, 116–18, 126, 132, 133, 138–41, 145, 157, 162, 164, 171
    Probate Register of Servants, 178, 180–81, 183, 184–85
    secret session of legislature (January 30), 147

Utah Organic Act, 112–13, 160
Utah War, 17
Utes (tribe), and the slave trade, 1–2, 8, 16, 58–59, 82, 85–86, 89, 91, 95–97, 101, 103, 105–6, 107, 111–15, 118–19, 186, 188–89, 192–94, 196–97

Venus, 144–45
Violet, 76–77, 79–80
Viret, 189
voluntary servitude. *See* servitude, voluntary

Wákara, 85–86, 196–97
Wales, 56, 128, 132
Wales, Hark, 1, 60–61, 74–77, 183–84
Walker, David, 167
Walker, Isaac, 110
Walker War, 8, 119
War of 1812, 25
wards, 16, 32–33, 118, 190, 195
Watt, George D., 5, 10–13*f*, 97–98, 106–7, 116–17, 132, 155, 161–63
Wells, Daniel H., 17, 106, 109–10, 111–12, 114–15, 116–17, 202–3
West, Ira, 61
Whigs, 157, 158
Wight, Lyman, 54–55
Williams, Mary Ann, 179
Williams, Thomas S., 175–76, 177, 179, 180–82, 183, 185, 196–97, 200–1, 202–3, 204–5, 216, 221–22
Wilmot, David, 59
Wilmot Proviso, 59, 61–62, 64–66
Wilson, James, 65–66
Wilson, James Thomas, 173
Wood, Henrietta, 225
Woodruff, Wilford, 19, 61–63, 70–71, 161–64
Woolley, Edwin D., 27, 160–61, 179–80, 182–83
Woolley, Franklin, 181

Yearsley, David D., 55
Young, Brigham
  and abolition, 56–57, 77–81, 155–56, 184, 211–16, 221–23
  and African American slavery, 88–94, 122, 126, 132–37, 144–50
  and Albert, 195–96
  and anti-Black racial restrictions, 8, 132–37, 140–41, 144–46, 161–67, 202, 208–11, 218, 220
  benevolent paternalism, 79–80
  and Black slavery in Utah after 1852, 178–79, 182–86, 196–97, 204–7
  and contractual servitude, 154–55
  desire to escape federal authority, 57, 69–71
  and early Black Mormons, 59–61
  early years, 24–25, 27, 30–31, 34–35, 36, 41–42
  and enslaved families, 127
  February 5 speech, 4–5, 10, 12, 161
  and free soil, 6–7
  governor of Utah, 4, 15–16, 45, 77–78, 85–87*f*, 89, 90–91, 95, 100, 121, 144–45, 155, 171, 199, 221
  and immigration, 12–14, 128–29, 132–33, 138
  and interracial marriage, 170–71, 222–23
  January 5, 1852 speech, 4–5, 12, 17, 88, 89, 102, 108–9, 122, 126, 132, 133, 138, 161–62, 217–18
  January 23, 1852 speech, 10, 12, 13*f*, 88, 97–99, 134–38, 145
  and Luján's trial, 82, 88, 94–97, 102
  moderate approach to "servitude," 75–76, 126, 136–37, 156, 214–18
  and Native indenture, 108–9, 117–18, 121
  and Native slavery, 8, 85–87, 88–97, 105–6, 192–94
  paternalism, 79–80, 90, 93–94, 122, 169, 171, 184, 218
  republicanism, 135–36, 166, 169
  and servitude, 7–8, 14–16, 32, 100–1, 155–56, 214–15
  slavery in pre-1852 Utah, 63–67, 71–73, 74–77
  superintendent of Indian Affairs, 85–86
  and territories, 58, 62
  and voting, 157–58, 160–61, 166–67, 171–72, 203–4, 218–19
Young, Clara (Clarissa) *or* Caroline Decker, 192–94
Young, John, 25
Young, Joseph, 147
Young, Samuel, 36

Zion, 1, 2, 46–47, 49–50, 60–61, 132, 222–23